PUBLICATIONS OF THE DEPARTMENT OF
ROMANCE LANGUAGES
UNIVERSITY OF NORTH CAROLINA

General Editor: ALDO SCAGLIONE

Editorial Board: JUAN BAUTISTA AVALLE-ARCE, PABLO GIL CASADO, FRED M. CLARK, GEORGE BERNARD DANIEL, JANET W. DÍAZ, ALVA V. EBERSOLE, AUGUSTIN MAISSEN, EDWARD D. MONTGOMERY, FREDERICK W. VOGLE

NORTH CAROLINA STUDIES IN THE
ROMANCE LANGUAGES AND LITERATURES

ESSAYS; TEXTS, TEXTUAL STUDIES AND TRANSLATIONS; SYMPOSIA

Founder: URBAN TIGNER HOLMES

Editor: JUAN BAUTISTA AVALLE-ARCE
Associate Editor: FREDERICK W. VOGLER

Other publications of the Department: *Estudios de Hispanófila, Hispanófila, Romance Notes, Studia Raeto-Romanica*

*Distributed by:*

INTERNATIONAL SCHOLARLY BOOK SERVICE, INC.
P. O. BOX 4347
Portland, Oregon   97208
U. S. A.

NORTH CAROLINA STUDIES IN THE
ROMANCE LANGUAGES AND LITERATURES

Number 137

JARDÍN DE NOBLES DONZELLAS,
FRAY MARTÍN DE CÓRDOBA:
A CRITICAL EDITION AND STUDY

# JARDÍN DE NOBLES DONZELLAS, FRAY MARTÍN DE CÓRDOBA:
## A CRITICAL EDITION AND STUDY

BY

HARRIET GOLDBERG

CHAPEL HILL
NORTH CAROLINA STUDIES IN THE ROMANCE
LANGUAGES AND LITERATURES
U.N.C. DEPARTMENT OF ROMANCE LANGUAGES
1974

Library of Congress Cataloging in Publication Data
Martín de Córdoba, d. ca. 1476.
    Jardín de nobles doncellas.

    (North Carolina Studies in the
Romance Languages and Literatures, no. 137)
    Published in 1500 under title: Jardin de las nobles donzellas.
    Includes bibliographical references.
    1. Woman. I. Goldberg, Harriet, ed.
II. Title. III. Series: North Carolina.
University. Studies in the Romance Languages and
Literatures, no. 137.
    HQ1201.M25 1974        301.41'2        73-17431
    ISBN: 978-0-8078-9137-7

DEPÓSITO LEGAL: 317 - 1974

ARTES GRÁFICAS SOLER, S. A. — JÁVEA, 28 — VALENCIA (8) — 1974

## ACKNOWLEDGEMENTS

It is with deep gratitude that I express my thanks to Samuel G. Armistead, Arnold G. Reichenberger, and Paul M. Lloyd of the University of Pennsylvania for their encouragement and help in the preparation of this edition.

Particular thanks are due to the Hispanic Society of America for their kind permission to publish their unique copy of the 1500 edition of the Jardín de nobles donzellas. The staffs of the Van Pelt Library of the University of Pennsylvania, the Falvey Library of Villanova University, and the Mc Cabe Library of Swarthmore College were ever-helpful.

I would also like to acknowledge the invaluable suggestions and emendations made by J.B. Avalle-Arce of the University of North Carolina, many of which saved me from falling into the error of prolixity, and even more, into errors of fact.

It goes without saying that this work could not have been completed without the active cooperation and tolerant forebearance of my husband, Jim and my children, Laura, Joan, Richard, and Robert.

# TABLE OF CONTENTS

|  | Page |
|---|---|
| ACKNOWLEDGEMENTS | 7 |
| INTRODUCTION | 11 |

PART I: BACKGROUND OF FRAY MARTÍN AND HIS WORKS

| I. | The author and his readership | 17 |
|---|---|---|
| II. | Works | 52 |
| III. | Sources and allusions | 71 |
| IV. | Structure, language and style | 89 |
| V. | The inter-relationship of "Advice to Princes" and the feminism/anti-feminism controversy in the *Jardín de nobles donzellas* | 95 |

PART II: JARDÍN DE NOBLES DONZELLAS ... 127

*Primera Parte* ... 133
    Capítulo Primero ... 143
    Capítulo .ij. ... 150
    Capítulo Tercero ... 158
    Capítulo Quarto ... 165
    Capítulo Quinto ... 170
    Capítulo Sesto ... 174
    Capítulo Séptimo ... 178
    Capítulo Octavo ... 182
    Capítulo .IX. ... 187

*Segunda parte deste tractado* ... 191
    Capítulo Primero ... 193
    Capítulo Segundo ... 198
    Capítulo Tercio ... 203
    Capítulo Quarto ... 208

|  |  |
|---|---|
| Capítulo Quinto | 213 |
| Capítulo Sesto | 217 |
| Capítulo Séptimo | 221 |
| Capítulo Octauo | 225 |
| Capítulo .IX. | 231 |
| Capítulo .X. | 235 |
| *La tercera parte deste libro* | 239 |
| [Capítulo Primero] | 241 |
| Capítulo Segundo | 245 |
| Capítulo Tercio | 250 |
| Capítulo .iiij. | 255 |
| Capítulo Quinto | 260 |
| Capítulo vj. | 265 |
| Capítulo .vij. | 269 |
| Capítulo viij. | 275 |
| Capítulo .ix. | 279 |
| Capítulo .x. | 283 |
| BIBLIOGRAPHY | 289 |
| INDEX OF PROPER NAMES | 298 |
| SUBJECT INDEX | 305 |

INTRODUCTION

The *Jardín de nobles donzellas* enjoyed two early printings — one in 1500 by Juan de Burgos in Valladolid and another in 1542 in Medina del Campo "a costa de Juan de Espinosa, mercader de libros." The present edition is based on the earlier printing. The copy is at present in the Library of the Hispanic Society of America in New York. It is, as far as I can ascertain, unique. A microfilm copy of the 1500 edition, kindly made available to me by the Hispanic Society and a microfilm copy of the 1542 edition obtained from the British Museum have been compared for textual variations. Another copy of the 1542, Medina del Campo ed. is in the Biblioteca Nacional of Madrid.

Three modern editions have been consulted, none of which have been prepared in keeping with modern norms. In 1953, P. Felix García prepared an edition with Prologue for the *Colección Joyas Bibliográficas* commemorating Isabel's birth (April 22, 1451), under the literary direction of Justo García Morales, with typography designed by Rafael Gómez Menor. Is has been called "edición fotográfica," which it is not. Rather it is a diplomatic edition. Three years later, P. García repeated much of the material of the Prologue in the preparation of a modernized version in 1956 for the *Biblioteca de Autores Cristianos*. Fernando Rubio Álvarez (whose valued edition of the *Compendio de la fortuna* of Fray Martín de Córdoba appeared in 1958) published the *Jardín* in the *BAE* 171 (Madrid, 1964) basing his work on the previous efforts of P. García and the 1542 ed. in the Biblioteca Nacional of Madrid.

P. García relied solely on the 1542 ed. in Madrid and referred to the rumour that there was "una edición suelta en el

British Museum." [1] He did not consult the 1500 ed. in New York. P. Rubio also explained his use of the 1542 ed. because of its accessibility and his conclusion that the geographical proximity of Valladolid and Medina del Campo ensured that the later printing would be a faithful copy of the earlier one. [2]

The present edition is based on the 1500 ed., a decision based on simple priority, which is supported by F. Bowers' observation: "No variant in a later edition in the simple transmission of a text can possibly have any authority (even if it corrects an error in the primary text), since no fresh authority has intruded." [3] This is particularly true in the case of the *Jardín* since both printings took place after the death of Fray Martín in 1476. In addition, reliance can be placed on Conrad Haebler's evaluation of Juan de Burgos (the printer of the 1500 ed.) as a craftsman. Haebler praises him for "neatness of type and quality of paper [which] vie with the best productions of the period...." [4] F. J. Norton gives a brief description of Juan de Burgos' activities: "In 1489 a second press was set up in Burgos. Its owner, Juan de Burgos, was presumably of local extraction, but his initial material like Fadrique's has the appearance of deriving from the Rhine valley. By 1499 he had printed some twenty books — *Baladro del sabio Merlín con sus profecías*, 1498, the strikingly illustrated *Doze trabajos de Ércules* of Enrique de Villena, 1499, and the only recorded edition of Martín de Córdoba. It is known that he moved his activities to Valladolid and that he was succeeded by his son." [5]

My own observation is that the 1542 ed. which is described as having been produced "a costa de Juan de Espinosa, mer-

---

[1] Félix García, ed., *Jardín de nobles donzellas* by Martín de Córdoba (Madrid, 1953), p. xxxi, n. 52.

[2] Fernando Rubio Álvarez, ed., *Jardín de nobles donzellas* by Martín de Córdoba *BAE* 171 (Madrid, 1964), p. xxxiii.

[3] Fredson Bowers, "Textual Criticism," in *The Aims and Methods of Scholarship on Modern Languages and Literature*, ed. James Thorpe (New York: MLA, 1963), p. 30.

[4] Konrad Haebler, *The Early Printers of Spain and Portugal* (London, March 1896 for 1897), p. 67.

[5] Frederic J. Norton, *Printing in Spain 1501-1520* (Cambridge, 1966), p. 62. Norton mentions a forth-coming book by Luisa Cuesta Gutiérrez and Justo García Morales which will deal with printing in Burgos (p. 4, n. 1).

cader de libros" contains more compositorial errors than the 1500 ed. These errors have not been noted in this edition when they take the form of *esriatura* for *es criatura* or similar errors in the setting of the type. The discrepancies between the two eds. have been noted in the footnotes when the meaning of the passage is substantially changed.

A few general observations can be made about the two editions. Both reproduce scribal calligraphy, employing the two *r*'s, the two *s*'s, the *n* frequently indicated by a *tilde*, the abbreviated *de*, the abbreviated *per*, *pro* and *por* prefixes, the abbreviated *que* and *qui*, and the lower case ampersand. There, is, however, more attention to end punctuation in the 1542 ed. and what is more striking, the later printer uses the modern comma instead of the lateral slash employed by Juan de Burgos. Both eds. have decorated initial letters at the beginning of each chapter. Those in the 1500 ed. tend to be abstract or to suggest flowers and foliage, while many of those in the 1542 ed. represent either the human form or animal figures. This difference does not seem to represent greater artistry on the part of the second printer, rather a difference in artistic taste or style. The 1500 ed. has frequent underscorings and marginal notations some of which take the form of the index (the drawing of the pointing hand). As is the case with other people's emphatic markings of books, there is no discernible pattern to the markings and they will be noted only when they seem to be relevant.

There is no way of knowing how closely the manuscript of the author and the first edition resembled each other in terms of abbreviations, spelling and punctuation. We do not know whether the abbreviations were Fray Martín's or whether they represent the printer's justification of the lines. For this reason all abbreviations will be written out. The *tilde* presents a special problem. Undoubtedly it was at one time used to indicate any nasal sound, either *n* or *m*. In the text the confusion arises most frequently in *siempre* and *hombre*. These words appear as frequently spelled out with the *n* as with the *m*. It will be assumed that the *tilde* stood for the *n*. No attempt will be made to correct the spelling variations in the text of the 1500. In gross cases such as the substitution of *varón* for *valor*, the difference will appear in the footnotes; the presumably correct reading will be shown in square brackets in the text. Other consistent spelling variations such as *muger* for *mujer*, *agora* for *ahora* and *quanto* for *cuanto* will be reproduced without comment. The uncontrasted *b/v/u*, *c/z*, *j/i/y* and initial *f/h* will be retained without comment. The unvoiced *s* is given as *ss* in the 1500 ed. (particularly in the recurring expression *es assaber*). Variant spellings of the same word often appear, even in the same sentence: *flechible/flexible*.

The irregularity of capitalization in both eds. has been modernized. Modern accents have been added as well. In neither edition is the end punctuation absolutely clear. The instances in which this edition differs from the end punctuation suggested by P. García in his modernization will be noted.

The 1500 edition sets off most quotations with a period or by capitalizing the first word and in a few instances by the use of a *calderón* mark. For uniformity, all quotations will be set off by a dash. The modern ampersand will be substituted for the lower case ampersand used generally in both eds. Natural word separation will be introduced in those cases where the running together of words appears to have resulted from the exigencies of the printer. Other natural arrangements, on the other hand, such as *ala, dela, delas, delos* and *enel* will be retained; a modern separation would violate the integrity of the text. The adverbial ending *mente* will be separated when it is clearly separated in the text. Paragraphing is a product of the present editor's judgment. Both editions print the *tabla* at the beginning of the book. For purposes of clarity, the various chapters will be headed by these descriptions.

# PART I

# BACKGROUND OF FRAY MARTÍN AND HIS WORKS

I

THE AUTHOR AND HIS READERSHIP

A study of a work belonging to the didactico-moral tradition must include an assessment of the rôle of the author and his works in his own time, since the avowed purpose of didactic literature is to instruct, to delight and to persuade. Keeping this purpose in mind, the extent and identity of the readership must be assessed as far as possible in order to determine whether the work did indeed fulfill its purpose. This task is peculiarly important in the case of Fray Martín de Córdoba, O.S.A., only four of whose works have come to light thus far. Of the four, two are of singular importance in that they are dedicated to persons of great eminence in the history of Spain: D. Álvaro de Luna and Isabel de Castilla. Some of the questions to be asked within the framework of an inquiry into the influence of such didactic works as the *Jardín de nobles donzellas* and the *Compendio de la fortuna* are: Is it correct to take these dedications to the mighty at face value, as do some modern Augustinian scholars, and therefore to assume that the books did in fact instruct and delight the people to whom they were dedicated? Is the survival of these works a sign of their own impact on society, or are the dedications a sign of reflected popular interest in D. Álvaro and in Isabel? The *Jardín*, which is dedicated to Isabel has the added distinction of having been among the books to be printed in Spain a scant half century after the development of moveable type. The *Jardín* had a second printing in 1542. Faced with our limited information as to the criteria of the early printers and without a truly complete catalogue of early printing, what deductions can be made about the work and the author on the basis of the selection of the *Jardín* for two such early editions?

In this section, I will examine contemporary Augustinian records together with secular historical chronicles of the period in the hope that Fray Martín's relative importance in his own time can be established. First, considering the historical evidence, an attempt will be made to isolate and evaluate the documented facts of Fray Martín's life and works. For this purpose, the later bibliographies by Andreas Schott and Nicolás Antonio together with Augustinian records will serve to show the persistence of Fray Martín's fame. There is little value in seeking data in sources later than Nicolás Antonio, since later bibliographies, with the exception of Gregorio Santiago Vela, consistently repeat information from earlier sources.[1]

To start with the bare documented facts of his life, the only indication that we have of Fray Martín's date and place of birth is found in a history of the convent at Salamanca, written by Tomás de Herrera and published in 1652. It was Herrera's contention that Salamanca had always been a teaching convent. He cites in Latin the authorizations for study he found in the records and then he translates them into Spanish. Unfortunately for our scholarly purposes, he does not describe the documents themselves, although it may be assumed that he was working from the actual conventual records. Pertinent to this study is the authorization made by the Father General, Agustín Romano, August 4, 1420: "Concessimus Fr. Martino Alphonsi, Lectori Provinciae Castellae, filio Conventus Cordubensis, quod possit legere Sententias in nostro Conventu Salmantino, cum illis gratiis et exemptionibus, quibus Bacchalarii formati gaudere solent, dummodo tamen Provincialis dictae Provinciae et Magistri ipsius sint de hoc

---

[1] An example of this confused bibliographical information is found in Rafael Ramírez de Arellano's *Ensayo de un catálogo biográfico de escritores de la provincia y diócesis de Córdoba*, 2 vols. (Madrid, 1921). A Fr. Alonso de Córdoba is listed as a Nominalist who taught in Salamanca in 1474 and died in 1504 with a list of the works of Fray Martín. The entry ends with the observation that this author was non-existent and has been confused with Fray Martín (I, 159). Under Fray Martín, the same works are listed with the brief summary of the facts of Fray Martín's life found in Nicolás Antonio and Andreas Schott (I, 165-6).

contenti."[2] Very possibly the inclusion of the Latin text of the records here and the later citation of a bull written by Pope Nicholas V in 1451 in the Latin and then in translation suggests that Herrera was indeed working with authentic documents. From the information that Fray Martín was admitted as a "Lector" in 1420, a guess can be made as to his birth date which can be placed at the end of the fourteenth century or the beginning of the fifteenth century. His identification as "filio Conventus Cordubensis" together with the evidence of his name can establish his birth place as Córdoba. Further confirmation of his birth date can be found in the date of his death of 1476, so that he might be assumed to have lived about seventy six years. There is a mention of a Martín Alfonso Major in 1403 as a "clérigo cordobés, bachiller en decretos, estudiante de gramática en Salamanca" in a collection of papal bulls,[3] which might suggest an earlier birth date. However, Vicente Beltrán de Heredia, the compiler of the collection makes mention of the arrival of our Fray Martín de Córdoba to Salamanca in 1420.[4]

Aníbal Sánchez Fraile cites an eighteenth-century history of the convent at Salamanca by Manuel Vidal to the effect that in 1424 Fray Martín de Córdoba was granted the post of "Lector" in the Convent of Zaragoza.[5]

In the Salamancan convent and also in other religious communities in Spain at this time, there was apparently a great deal of dissension which Herrera attributes to "la relaxación que se introduxo en las Religiones con la ocasión de la peste general, que tanto afligió la Europa."[6] This difficulty took the form of

---

[2] Tomás de Herrera, *Historia del convento de San Agustín de Salamanca* (Madrid, 1652), p. 54.
[3] Vicente Beltrán de Heredia, *Bulario de la Universidad de Salamanca (1219-1549)*, 3 vols. (Salamanca, 1967), I, 581. The entry reads: "Item Martino Alfonsi Majori, cler. Corduben., baccalar. in decretis, de benef. eccl, Hispalen."
[4] Beltrán de Heredia, I, 80.
[5] The reference is to Manuel Vidal, *Historia del observantíssimo convento de San Agustín de Salamanca* (Salamanca, 1751), quoted by Aníbal Sánchez Fraile, *Un tratado del siglo XV sobre la predestinación, en castellano debido al V. P. Fray Martín Alfonso de Córdoba* (Salamanca, 1956), p. xxv.
[6] Herrera, p. 89.

the abandonment of the "observances" and a conflict between those who felt the primary function of the convent was to be a place of holy spiritual retreat and those who thought its main function was as a teaching institution which reached out into the community of the laity. Herrera mentions a reform movement started by Fr. Antonio de Córdoba in 1430 in the Salmantine convent which returned the convent to its rôle as a spiritual retreat as opposed to a seat of learning. [7] The implication is that, in the face of such a widespread and inexplicable disaster as the pestilence, there was a falling away from the Faith and from the careful observance of the ritual. William T. Walsh sees another, more practical problem resulting from the plague, the effects of which had long-lasting effects. He observes: "The Church in Isabel's time had not yet recovered from the terrible blow. It [the plague] had almost annihilated her priesthood; and even to fill partially the places of the dead, she had been compelled to lower her standards, accepting men ignorant of Latin." [8] The introduction into the religious orders of devout but unscholarly men after such a period of social and moral chaos as had been caused by the plague, doubtless created the perfect breeding ground for the subsequent quarrels between the *observantes* and the *claustrales* which were a consequence at Salamanca of Fray Antonio's reforms.

Therefore, it comes as no surprise that Fray Martín (an opponent of Fray Antonio de Córdoba), was permitted, or better yet, ordered to study at the University of Toulouse in 1431. [9] Later developments in his life prove him to have been firmly allied with the cause of the faction in favor of teaching in the community. Two stays in France, one in 1431 and the other in 1461 must be assumed on the basis of Herrera's confirmation of the early one and the later appointment as "conventual de Tolosa" by P. General Boechio in 1461 which is also corroborated by Fray Martín's comment that he had written his *Comentarios*

---

[7] Herrera, p. 90.

[8] William Thomas Walsh, *Isabella of Spain: The Last Crusader* (New York, 1930), p. 73.

[9] Herrera reports that Fray Martín was made a "bachiller" by the Father General of the Order, Geraldo de Arímino, and was given permission to study at Toulouse (where he "octuvo y regentó Cátedra"), p. 54.

*y cuestiones sobre las epístolas de San Pablo* in Toulouse. (See n. 13). Fray Martín must have been in France earlier than 1453. He writes in the *Compendio* about his return from France. "Onde a mi mismo conteció en una graue enfermedad que oue quando venía de Francia." [10] (He also tells the story of Jani, the poor shoemaker and the rich man as though it were a story he had heard in France: "Aquí viene un enxemplo que me dixeron que auía acontecido en París en nuestros tiempos.") [11] The dating of the *Compendio* must be before 1453 because of its dedication to D. Álvaro de Luna who was decapitated in 1453.

About the second trip to France, both Fernando Rubio Álvarez and Aníbal Sánchez Fraile mention his appointment as "conventual de Tolosa" in 1461 [12] and Fray Martín is said to have mentioned it in a work which is now lost, decribed by Ambrosio de Morales in the *Viage*, a book compiled at the behest of Felipe II, in which the contents of the libraries of Spain were listed. The reference is to a Ms. identified as *Comentarios sobre las epístolas de San Pablo* which is described by Morales as beginning: "y dice al principio como lo escribió leyendo en Tolosa el

---

[10] Martín de Córdoba, *Compendio de la fortuna*, ed. Fernando Rubio Álvarez (Madrid, 1958), p. 32.

[11] *Compendio*, p. 125. La Fontaine later used the story as "Le savetier et le financier." Stith Thompson classifies related stories under the motifs J 1085. *Money does not always bring* happiness; J 1085.1. *The happy friar becomes unhappier as he receives... more money. Gets rid of money and is happy as before* (Aarne-Thompson Type 754). The story appears in T.F. Crane's *Exempla of Jacques Vitry* (London, 1890) and in the *Scala Coeli*. There is a reference in John Esten Keller's index of folk motifs in medieval Spanish *exempla: King sees poor man far happier than himself.* The closest version is the "Cock" of Lucian in that the protagonist is a shoemaker as he is in the *Compendio* and later in La Fontaine. It is tempting to trace the story to a French source and to accept at face value what Fray Martín says of it. It is perhaps significant that a Frenchman, La Fontaine, subsequently made use of the story but the fact remains that Lucian can be considered a common source. See Lucianus Samosatensis, *The Works of Lucian of Samosata*, trans. H.W. and F.C. Fowler (Oxford, 1905), III, 105-126. Lucian's version contains the sophisticated dialogue and sybaritic detail for which he is famous. Fray Martín tells the story in a more straight forward manner that suggests a folkloric origin. Of the two references to France in the *Compendio*, the first, in n. 10, seems to be the only one that can be used as internal evidence of the author's trip to France.

[12] Fernando Rubio Álvarez, ed. *Compendio de la fortuna* by Martín de Córdoba (Madrid, 1958), p. xxxiii; Aníbal Sánchez Fraile, p. xxvii.

año MCCCCLXI." [13] Once again, the Church sources seem to be confirmed by Fray Martín himself.

Neither Andreas Schott ("Primum in Gallia Tholosonus, deinde Salmanticense in Hispania Gymnasia [sic] summa auditorum frequentia annis plurimis rexit & gobernauit") [14] nor Nicolás Antonio ("Cum Galliae Tolosam, & apud nos Salmanticam professor theologus nobilitasset...") [15] mention two separate stays, but they both acknowledge Fray Martín's having spent time in Toulouse. One might seek another conflict within the convent during the years adjacent to 1461 on which the surmise can be based that being sent to Toulouse was a sort of honorable exile inflicted twice on Fray Martín, once following the first reform program of Fray Antonio de Córdoba in 1430, and next following a renewal of the conflict which came about after the bull of Nicholas V in 1451.

Clearly the two opposing factions had not resolved their differences judging from the text of the papal bull of Nicholas V dated September 28, 1451 in Rome. Herrera does not translate this document in full; he summarizes the principal points because he says it is so long and wordy. The bull is addressed to the Reverend Father General and begins: "Concessisse Observantibus Conuentum Salamantinum, ut illum reducerent ad vitam regularem; & instituisse in Suum Vicarium M. Martinum de Corduba, eo pacto ut studium non amoueretur; quoniam manifeste cognoscebamus destructionem illius studij esse fomentum & nutrimentum ignorantiae in tota illa Provincia...." [16] The Pope goes

---

[13] Ambrosio de Morales, *Viage de Ambrosio de Morales por orden del Rey D. Phelipe II. A los Reynos de León y Galicia y Principado de Asturias*, ed. Enrique Flórez (Madrid: Antonio Marín, 1765), p. 9.

[14] Andreas Schott, *Hispaniae Bibliotheca seu de Academiis ac Bibliothecis*... (Frankfort, 1608), p. 267.

[15] Nicolás Antonio, *Bibliotheca Hispana Vetus*... (Madrid, 1788), II, 307.

[16] Herrera says: "Es tan larga y prolija esta Bula, que me a parecido no traduzirla en Romance, sino referir en suma a los puntos principales." There is a discrepancy between the date September 28, 1451 (p. 34) and the "II Maij, 1453 which Santiago Vela cites ("Notas de interés," *Archivo Histórico Hispano-Agustiniano*, 20 [1923], pp. 52-65: 63). Beltrán de Heredia reproduces two bulls dated September 28, 1451 pertaining to the convent at Salamanca, neither of which contains any mention of Fray Martín (III, 56, 57) and another bull of July 19, 1453 which deals with the restoration

on to explain that at some earlier date the Observants had ousted Fray Martín and the other teachers at a time when there were many monks in the convent but that now there were few and those who remained were ignorant, all of which did not redound to the honor of God, the Order, nor to the edification of the people. If the date of 1430 given above for the beginning of the reforms instituted by Fray Antonio and the date of 1431 given for the first stay in Toulouse are considered in the light of Pope Nicholas' mention (in the bull of 1451) of an ouster of Fray Martín from the convent, it might be conjectured that Fray Martín was sent to France to study because he was no longer permitted to teach in Salamanca. Herrera continues to give the high points of the bull writing that Pope Nicholas: "Quéxasse luego de que los Observantes no le obedecían; y añade, que no se espanta, porque lo mismo solía hazer, *antiquis eorum Vicarius*, el antiguo Vicario." [17] Herrera explains that the reference is to Fray Juan de Alarcón who after receiving a bull from Eugenio IV did nothing more than "confirmar las gracias que les auía dado el P. General." Herrera also reports pressure from Juan II in a letter "del Seveníssimo Rey de Castilla en que nos exhorta que proueamos de otra manera a aquel Conuento; y vistas también cartas de todos los Maestros y Padres de aquella Prouincia, para que socorramos a un tan grande Conuento que va a caerse. Dize que les mande que hechen dél a los Observantes y que les reduzgan al antiguo estado de estudio." [18] There are no figures given for the fall in population of the convent, but the concern of the Pope, the King and the Provincial officials confirms that the dispute had indeed affected the community.

Aníbal Sánchez Fraile quotes Father Manuel Vidal who wrote in 1751 that the *Observantes* sent their Prior to Rome in 1454 and there, "negoció quanto podía desear" so that the General wrote from Avignon: "qui in eo Conventu Salmanticensi Deo

---

of studies at the Convent "suprimidos desde que entraron en él los reformadores" (III, 68). This last bull mentions a request from Juan II for the return of studies and also refers to the return as a remedy for the spread of ignorance.

[17] Herrera, p. 35.
[18] Herrera, p. 36.

serviunt, ibidem permanerent." [19] It is Sánchez Fraile's opinion that, at this point, Fray Martín as the Vicar of the teaching brothers must have left Salamanca, and must have gone to Valladolid with his staff. On the other hand, Fernando Rubio Álvarez surmises that a compromise was reached between the two groups after 1454 resulting in "un plantel de sabios y santos." [20]

Up to this point in the reconstruction of Fray Martín's life, reliance on the testimony of Tomás de Herrera has established Fray Martín's arrival at Salamanca as "Lector" in 1420, the reforms of Fray Antonio which began in 1430, and Fray Martín's subsequent departure for Toulouse and his having been made Vicar in 1451. We are also confronted with the reports of the subsequent negotiations of those who wanted the convent to abandon its teaching functions in 1454, and the evidence that Fray Martín was once again in Toulouse in 1461. There remains the problem of determining if and when Fray Martín held a chair at the University of Salamanca. Germane to this problem, Gregorio Santiago Vela made a most valuable find in the form of a handwritten marginal notation in a Venice Ms. dated 1513. At the end of the Ms. was written: "Hic liber est ad usum f. didaci de montanches; pertinet ad conventum XPtifere Virginis del pilar nuncupate de opido de Arenis." [21] This notation identifies the

---

[19] Aníbal Sánchez Fraile, p. xxvii. This change of heart is described by Herrera: "29 Decembris, 1454. — Revoca [el P. General] lo que había ordenado del Convento de Salamanca, y manda a Fernando de Paredes, Vicario de la Observancia, *qui in eo Conventu Deo serviunt, ibidem permanerent*. Concédele gracias. *Hortamur te caeterosque Patres Conventus Salmantini, ut omnem diligentiam adhibeant ut ibi sint illius Provinciae juvenes, qui literis aptis dignoscuntur. Item quod in Conventu possint tenere aliquem regularem, vel saecularem, qui legat fratribus.*" (p. 248).

[20] Aníbal Sánchez Fraile, p. xxvii. Fernando Rubio Álvarez, p. xxxii. The basis for Rubio Álvarez' opinion might be the ambiguous nature of the order cited in n. 9 above. It should be made clear that this controversy between those devoted to learning and instruction and those who advocated a contemplative life was not peculiar to the Augustinians. See Beltrán de Heredia (I, 142-150). Mosén Diego de Valera writes of a similar dispute among the Franciscans, resolved in part by Enrique IV who, according to Valera, built a new monastery for the Observants "y [Enrique] le dio muy ricos ornamentos y todas las cosas necesarias al culto divino." (*Memorial de diversas hazañas*, BAE 70: *Crónicas de los reyes de Castilla desde Alfonso el Sabio hasta los Reyes Católicos*, III [Madrid, 1953], 47-48).

[21] "Notas de interés," p. 53.

owner of the Ms. as a monk who made use of the book after 1513, which in itself does not serve to date this note nor the other inscriptions in the Ms. However, Santiago Vela finds mention in the *Centurias* of Jerónimo Román of a Juan de Montanches, author of a *Crónica Agustiniana* in 1517. Santiago Vela supposes a confusion of first names similar to what happened to Jerónimo Roman who is alternately referred to as Juan. It is therefore his opinion that Juan de Montanches and Diego de Montanches are the same chronicler of Augustinian material. The pertinence of this identification and the dating of 1517 is that in the same Ms. there are other marginal notations written in the same hand which are a series of praises of Augustinian authors, among whom is Fray Martín de Córdoba. Montanches writes: "Martinus de Corduba ordinis heremitarum doctor tan excellentissimus quod meruit appellari secundus Augustinus: fecit multa opera tam in philosophia quam in theologia. Super Genesis de opere sex dierum. Super epistolas pauli: Super Apocalipsin [sic]. Super multos libros Aristotelis. Fecit etiam in vulgari aliquos tractatus; praecipue ad reginam nostram dominam Isabelam: ut est ille intitulatus Jardin de nobles donzellas. Et ille de virginitate ad sanctimoniales et alia multa quae adhuc in lucem non prodierunt. Hic fuit cathedraticus in scholis Salmanticae." [22] This is the most nearly contemporary mention we have of Fray Martín and his works, and what is important to us here, his position at the University of Salamanca. The problem is, then, to try to establish when Fray Martín taught at Salamanca. Santiago Vela quotes the modern historian Esperabé Arteaga's *Historia de la Universidad de Salamanca* which identifies Pedro Martínez de Osma as the holder of a chair in *Filosofía Moral* from 1457 to 1480. Esperabé Arteaga, relying on Manuel Vidal who in 1751 had made a search of the Salamancan records without finding Fray Martín's name, conjectures that Fray Martín "a su regreso de Tolosa donde se había graduado de Doctor, incorporó el grado en la Universidad Salmantina, dándosele entonces una cátedra." [23] The period of his first stay at Toulouse has already been

---

[22] "Notas de interés," p. 54.
[23] "Notas de interés," p. 61. Aníbal Sánchez reports what appears to be an answer to his own inquiry to Toulouse: "Hechas las pertinentes

tentatively established between the first trip to Toulouse in 1431 and the publication of the *Compendio* in 1453 where Fray Martín refers to his return from France. We have Herrera's testimony that he was Vicar of the Convent at Salamanca in 1451. There is evidence that Álvaro de Salamanca held a chair in theology from 1411 to 1422 and that Juan Alfonso de Segovia succeeded him until 1431 when he went to Rome. However, as Beltrán de Heredia points out these chairs were often held in titular fashion with others acting as substitutes. [24] There is also the problem of deciding to which of the three levels Fray Martín was entitled — *cátedra de biblia, cátedra de vísperas* or *cátedra de prima*. Apparently his doctorate from Toulouse made him eligible for the highest rank. We also know that Pedro Martínez de Osma and Pedro de Caloca "litigaba por la prima de teología" in 1463. [25] We do not have enough facts to date Fray Martín's having been a "catedrático" since as Beltrán de Heredia points out, university records at the time were used for administrative purposes only and were not preserved. [26] As far as a terminal date is concerned, Padre Antolínez (1554-1626), in a speech, lauded Fray Martín's loyalty to Salamanca stating that he refused other posts remaining in the service of the University forever. [27] There is no way of knowing whether Padre Antolínez exaggerated his praise of Fray Martín's loyalty or whether the chair was held in absentia. One might conjecture several periods during which Fray Martín could have taught at the University of Salamanca; the first being upon his return from Toulouse and before the restoration of studies at the convent and the second after 1454 when he was expelled again. From 1464 to 1480 we have a rather complete record in the *Extractos de los libros de claustros de la Universidad de Salamanca; Siglo XV (1464-1481)* edited by F. Marcos (Salamanca, 1964) without a mention of Fray Martín.

---

investigaciones, lamento tener que comunicarle que no poseemos ningún registro de graduados, ni libros de Claustro alguno de la época en que el P. Córdoba debía tener su cátedra en Tolosa" (n. 10, p. xxvi).

[24] Beltrán de Heredia, I, 162-163.
[25] Beltrán de Heredia, I, 155.
[26] Beltrán de Heredia, I, 155.
[27] "Notas de interés," p. 62.

It is of interest to note here that by 1454, Fray Martín had already written the *Compendio de la fortuna* in which the author identified himself as "maestro en Teología, fraire de Sant Agustín;"[28] by this time D. Álvaro de Luna had been beheaded; Juan II had died; his widow Isabel of Portugal had retreated to Arévalo with her two children, Isabel and Alfonso, and Juan's son by his first marriage to María de Aragón, Enrique IV had succeded to the throne.

Of his earlier academic career, Herrera writes that the Father General appointed him "Lector en el Conuento de Zaragoça, y con ello quedasse por Lector Conuentual del Conuento de Salamanca." In 1431 he was made a "Bachiller en Teología" and was graduated from the University of Toulouse. In 1453 on May 11, he was the Vicar General of the Salamancan Convent. On the 15th of April, 1461 he was made Conventual of the Convent at Toulouse. Herrera gives the following chronology: "y el año de 1465. a dos de Junio, y el de 1468. a primero de Enero, y el de 1471. a tres de Mayo, y el de 1473. a 27. de Julio fue señalado por Presidente en primer lugar del Capítulo de la Prouincia de Hispaña." In 1469 apparently Fray Antonio was the Provincial for the second time and he and Fray Martín had a dispute which Fray Martín appealed to the General of the Order. On June 9, 1469 the Father General appointed Maestro Fr. Alonso de San Martín of the Convent of Burgos to adjudicate the dispute and Herrera tells us: "y salió el M. Fray Martín libre de la causa."[29] Could this disagreement have had its roots in the difference of opinion between Fray Martín and Fray Antonio in 1430 when Fray Antonio first advocated the return to a spiritual life as opposed to the more active pedagogical life? Just a year before, in 1468, the young Alfonso had died and Isabel had been named heir to the throne. Presumably, Fray Martín had already written the *Jardín* which he dedicated to the young princess after the death of her brother.

In 1470 he was appointed Vicar General of the Convent of

---

[28] *Compendio*, p. 3. Cf. his designation of himself in the *Prohemio* of the *Jardín* as "el su humilde seruidor Fray Martín de Córdoua, de la Orden de Sant Agustín, Maestro de Sancta Theología," (p. 135).

[29] Herrera, p. 54.

Valladolid and on June 7, 1476, he was promoted to the governance of the convent.[30] In the *Prólogo* of the *Tractado de la predestinación,* Fray Martín identifies himself as "el muy deuoto padre Fray Martín, de la Orden Agustina de Valladolid, Dotor en Artes, Maestro en Santa Theología."[31] It is Aníbal Sánchez Fraile's opinion that although Fray Martín was undoubtedly the author of the introduction to the *Tractado,* there are signs of its having been edited by another person.[32] Nevertheless, we can acknowledge the evidence of Fray Martín's presence in Valladolid until he died in 1476. Tomás de Herrera writes: "En tiempo deste noueno Priorato del Vener. P. Iuan de Salamanca murió en Valladolid el doctíssimo M. Fr. Martín Alfonso de Córdoua...." The date of 1476 is given in the heading. Another confirmation of Fray Martín's presence in Valladolid is the mention in the speech by Padre Antolínez (1554-1626) that: "Hállanse cosas escritas de su mano en la librería del Monasterio de N.P. San Agustín el Real de Valladolid."[33]

What emerges from this rather sketchy biographical material up to this point is the portrait of a scholarly, erudite priest who valued the active side of the priesthood rather than the contemplative. Andreas Schott praised Fray Martín's oratorical talents, "Concionibus ad populum habendis ita excelluit ut quocunque vellet, facile auditorum animos impelleret."[34] More rhetor than philosopher, aware of himself as a teacher, even to the extent of engaging in an extensive battle to maintain the Convent of Salamanca as a teaching institution,[35] Fray Martín apparently filled a need in his world and served the Church well.

---

[30] Herrera, 54.
[31] *Tractado,* p. 3.
[32] Sánchez Fraile, p. cxxxi.
[33] "Notas de interés," 52. See *infra* nn. 1, 3, 4 to the section *Works* for a description of the early holdings of Fray Martín's works at Valladolid.
[34] Andreas Schott, p. 267.
[35] Cf. n. 21 to *Capítulo primero, primera parte* for an indication of Fray Martín's self-image as a teacher. He takes a common exegetical observation about the Old Adam and the New Adam and turns it into a didactic act on the part of God. Also see n. 2 to *Capítulo séptimo, primera parte* where Fray Martín refers to Nature as God's pupil, although the usual reference is to God's vicar.

What follows is an attempt to evaluate other biographical references to Fray Martín, particularly those of an inspirational, exemplary nature. Just as Fray Martín made use of saints' lives and episodes from antiquity, authors such as Alonso de Orozco, Jerónimo Román and in our century Félix García have elaborated upon the episodes in Fray Martín's life for didactic purposes. To emphasize his humility, he has been portrayed as an adviser to the royal family, persistently avoiding the worldly honors which were offered to him. (See nn. 38-42). Admittedly the documented facts about his life are few. Before evaluating his rôle at court, and the generally idealized portrait of Fray Martín, we must mention the confusion of identity with a later Augustinian, Fray Alonso de Córdoba (d. 1540) perhaps caused initially by Tomás de Herrera's reference to him as Martín Alfonso de Córdoba. (See n. 1 to this chapter).

This kind of confusion of identities emphasizes the need for extreme caution in the recreation of the life of a literary personage who did not achieve great fame. Proceeding with caution, hopefully, certain aspects of Fray Martín's life as reported by the scholars of the Church and the secular chroniclers will be examined in order to achieve the aim of assessing Fray Martín's impact on his own time and his influence at court, apart from his literary activities and his teaching duties at the University and the Convent.

In addition to the problem of confused identity, it is necessary to separate facts from inspirational material when working with biographical material about Church figures. Many authors seem to be determined to write exemplary lives of famous personages to guide the reader into the path of righteousness and piety. [36] It is my opinion that much of what has been written about Fray Martín de Córdoba falls into this category. [37]

---

[36] Nor is this failing limited to Church figures. Consider the case of Prescott who wanted to write a flattering biography of Isabel and yet in spite of this desire was embarrassed by the laudatory tone of many sources. He had to admit that it was not easy to write a dispassionate biography of such a personage as Isabel. William H. Prescott, *History of the Reign of Ferdinand and Isabella*, 3 vols. (Philadelphia, 1883), I, 206-7.

[37] Guidance as to the value of early sources can be sought in the careful, scholarly work of P. Gregorio Santiago Vela who offers valuable comments

In the course of assessing Fray Martín's influence at court, which will be dealt with before any attempt is made to assess his influence on the thought of his time, Santiago Vela's cautious characterization of Alonso de Orozco's *Crónica* can serve as a reminder that from time to time references to Fray Martín's influence at court might merely be directed to the task of idealizing a member of the Order, rather than the simple preservation of the facts.

There are two main aspects of the stories that describe Fray Martín as a counselor of the mighty. First, there are references to important posts at court which he rejected in favor of his monastic work and secondly, several allusions to his personal influence on D. Álvaro de Luna, to whom he dedicated the *Compendio*, and on Isabel for whom he wrote the *Jardín*.

Of the first group of references, appearing both in the *Crónica* and in the *Centurias* (and, incidentally, not in Tomás de Herrera), is the idealized portrait of Fray Martín's resistance to the importuning of Juan II and Enrique IV that he accept high posts in the court or in the Church hierarchy. Alonso de Orozco argues that: "como fuese rogado del rey don Enrique para que anduviese con él en la corte, le suplicó que no se lo mandase porque no era él más de su monasterio y su celda." [38] Jerónimo Román de Hi-

---

concerning the accuracy of early sources. He says, for instance, of the *Crónica del glorioso padre y doctor de la Iglesia S. Agustín y de los santos y beatos y de los doctores de su Orden*... (Sevilla, 1551), by the Beato Alonso de Orozco: "Como éste no propusiera componer un trabajo rigurosamente biográfico sino un libro espiritual que sirviera de edificación a los jóvenes religiosos, no se debe confiar... en la *Crónica*." While he praises the much later work of Manuel Vidal, *Agustinos de Salamanca: Historia del observantíssimo Convento de San Agustín N.P. de dicha ciudad* (Salamanca, 1751), he doubts the scholarly value of the *Chrónica de la Orden de los Ermitaños del Glorioso Padre Sancto Agustín: Dividida en doce Centurias* (Salamanca, 1569) by Jerónimo Román de Higuera, a work most commonly referred to as the *Centurias*, where the wide scope of twelve hundred years permits the author to offer only "resumen, compendio o extracto de hechos." Santiago Vela recommends Tomás de Herrera's *Historia del Convento de San Agustín de Salamanca* (Madrid, 1652) (*Ensayo de una biblioteca iberoamericana de la Orden de San Agustín*, 8 vols. [Madrid, 1913-1931], I [1913], x).

[38] Herrera, p. 55. Herrera points out that Alonso de Orozco did not mention the bishopric of Badajoz although Joseph Pamphilo and Antonio Possevini did.

guera reports repeated requests from Juan II that Fray Martín serve him, with the response: "que no se hizo fraile ni dexó el mundo para volver a el." [39] There is also a mention in the *Centurias* of the offer by Enrique that Fray Martín take the post of Bishop of Badajoz, which was also refused, because, "ni con su predicación ni consejo pudo sosegar a los Grandes del Reino entre los cuales había grandes disensiones en aquel tiempo." [40] Padre Antolínez refers to this refusal alluding to "aquel insigne varón Fr. Martín de Córdoba, a quien el Rey Don Enrique dio el Obispado de Badajoz, aunque no lo aceptó, quedándose siempre en servicio de esta Escuela," [41] Joseph Pamphilo in 1581, states: "Quo tempore cum episcopatu Pacensi cohonestaretur humilitate oblatam renuit dignitatem." [42] The picture is one of a devout, humble man who scorns worldly honors, preferring to remain apart from the wicked court; who even rejects ecclesiastical honors in favor of his teaching, writing and the simple life. P. Antolínez even credits Fray Martín with loyalty to the University of Salamanca though there is ample documentation that he did indeed leave Salamanca to go to Valladolid.

Although it is difficult to draw conclusions from negative evidence, it must be noted that Fray Martín's name does not appear in the *Crónica de Juan II*, Enríquez del Castillo's *Crónica del Rey Don Enrique el Quarto*, nor in the *Décadas* of Alonso de Palencia. One would not expect to find these specific rejections in a royal chronicle; what is significant is that Fray Martín's name does not appear in these works in which lists of those present at specific events are commonplace. This is true also of the *Memorial de diversas hazañas* of Mosén Diego de Valera and the subsequent chronicles of the reign of Ferdinand and Isabel such as the *Crónica de los señores Reyes Católicos Don Fernando y Doña Isabel de Castilla y de Aragón* by Hernando del Pulgar; nor is he mentioned in the *Crónica de D. Álvaro de Luna*,

---

[39] Félix García, ed. *Jardín de nobles donzellas* (Madrid, 1956), p. 28.
[40] Herrera, p. 55. García, p. 28.
[41] Santiago Vela, "Notas de interés," p. 62.
[42] Joseph Pamphilo, *Chronica Ordinis fratrum eremitarum Sancti Augustini* (Romae: ex typographiae Georgii Ferrarii, 1581), p. 87.

*Condestable de los reynos de Castilla y de León*,[43] a work particularly crammed with catalogues and rosters of important personages. Although one would not expect to find a record of a royal entreaty that had been refused, in a chronicle, one might expect to find at least some mention of the recipient of such an important appointment.

Such offers and noble refusals are picked up by later bibliographers. Andreas Schott quotes Pamphilo exactly. Nicolás Antonio, in discussing Fray Martín's devotion to sacred tasks, writes: "ut nec Pacensis Ecclesiae infulis, nec praecipuo quodam apud eos loco dignitatis & caritatis iisdem duobus Regibus olim invitatus, animi propositum quod sibi fecerat, in paupertate, longeque a saecularibus manendi, usquam mutaverit."[44] It is a reasonable assumption that Schott and Nicolás Antonio were merely relating what they had found in 16th-century ecclesiastical sources as Jerónimo Román, Alonso de Orozco, and, of course, Joseph Pamphilo. They are not adding new information or corroboration to the stories. This becomes particularly clear when the word for word similarity between Pamphilo and Schott is recognized. In the absence of any secular documentation of the royal entreaties, a certain skepticism must be maintained in regard to Fray Martín's importance at the court, if the proof of that importance is his supposed rejection of royal pleas for his services. It must be borne in mind that humility and rejection of worldly honor were certainly traits that were to be inculcated in the "jóvenes religiosos" whom Santiago Vela considered to be the audience for the *Crónica* of Alonso de Orozco.

A corollary of Fray Martín's resistance to the royal entreaties is his biographers' view of him as a powerful influence at court and particularly in the household of Isabel of Portugal during the childhood of her illustrious daughter. The resolution of the

---

[43] This chronicle was in the past attributed to Juan de Mena (with hostile interpolations by Diego de Valera) (Josef Miguel de Flores, ed. *Crónica de D. Álvaro de Luna* [Madrid, 1784], p. xxvi) and, more recently, to Gonzalo Chacón by Juan Mata de Carriazo in his edition.

[44] Nicolás Antonio, II, 307. Francisco Méndez gives the date of 1462 for the offer of the bishopric without citing a source. His biographical material is sketchy in other respects. See Francisco Méndez, *Tipografía española* (Madrid, 1861), p. 122.

question of whether or not Fray Martín played a significant rôle in the life of Isabel, or of D. Álvaro, is of importance to a study of the *Jardín*. The dedication to Isabel (a peculiarly timely one) was written just at the moment when it was clear she would inherit the throne of Spain. Its timeliness parallels the dedication of the *Compendio* to D. Álvaro de Luna at a moment shortly before the *Condestable* was to learn, at first hand, the variability and transitory nature of fortune. Fernando Rubio Álvarez bases his opinion that Fray Martín "disfrutó de gran ascendiente en la corte de Castilla" [45] on a textual examination of these dedications, supporting his conjecture with the testimony of Jerónimo Román and Alonso de Orozco. We have already noted that Santiago Vela casts some doubt on the historical accuracy of Jerónimo Román's *Centurias* because of its vast scope, and on the accuracy of Alonso de Orozco's *Crónica* because of its inspirational intent. It is pertinent to note that Tomás de Herrera does not repeat the same material about Fray Martín's influential position, giving rather a spare report of his works and his various clerical and teaching appointments. If it is assumed that Jerónimo Román and Alonso de Orozco were relying on the dedications to the *Jardín* and the *Compendio* when they wrote of Fray Martín's importance at court, then it is not valid to use their observations as corroboration of these same dedications, as does Fernando Rubio Álvarez. Since the dedications to the *Jardín* and the *Compendio* seem to be central to the resolution of the question of Fray Martín's influence at court, the purpose of dedicating a book to a prominent personage must be examined. The sort of dedication made by Horace to Maecenas (which has come to represent dedications based upon a clear exchange of favors or patronage) is the one that comes most readily to mind. However, there is no question that many books were dedicated to prominent persons merely for the purpose of calling attention to the work itself without there having been any real relationship between the author and the famous person. Such works might be thought of in modern terms as "open letters" published in a newspaper for the purpose of espousing a certain point of view and directed

---

[45] Rubio Álvarez, ed. *Jardín* BAE 171, p. xxxvii.

to a prominent person solely to arouse the interest of the general readership. Within the framework of this last type of dedications, occasionally one finds some specific personal detail designed to add verisimilitude.

According to Ernst Curtius: "Innumerable medieval authors assert that they write by command. Histories of literature accept this as gospel truth. Yet it is usually a mere *topos*."[46] Whether or not one believes that Curtius tends to see *topoi* at every turn, it seems reasonable to accept the general notion that often dedications cannot be taken literally as an indication of a personal relationship between the author and the object of the dedication. In the case of the *Jardín*, Fray Martín frequently states a general moral rule and then observes that if the rule holds true for ordinary women, then certainly it is much more valid when applied to princesses, queens, or noble ladies. At the very least, this is an indication that he had in mind a dual audience.

The bizarre aptness of the dedication of the *Compendio de la fortuna* (one might almost characterize it as grisly), a work whose announced purpose was "declarar que cosa es buena fortuna,"[47] to a man who had been for many years the most powerful and fortunate man in Spain and who was shortly to die on a public scaffold, can only lead the reader to consider the book as an exemplary or cautionary tale on the subject of the vagaries of power and fortune. The choice of D. Álvaro de Luna as the person to whom the work was dedicated might, therefore, be regarded as an antonomastic device, particularly in the light of what is known of contemporary attitudes toward him.[48] In other

---

[46] Ernst Robert Curtius, *European Literature and the Latin Middle Ages*, trans. Willard R. Trask (1953; rpt. New York: Harper Torchbooks, 1963), p. 85.

[47] *Compendio*, p. 5.

[48] Perhaps the most peculiar and the most engaging story of the influence of the *Condestable* is the one reported by Fernán Pérez de Guzmán who writes of Juan II: "seyendo él moço bien conplisionado e teniendo a la reyna su muger moça e fermosa, si el Condestable ge lo contradixiese non iría a dormir a su cámara della nin curaua de otras mugeres, aunque naturalmente era inclinado a ella." (*Generaciones y semblanzas*, ed. J. Domínguez Bordona [Madrid: Clásicos Castellanos, 1924], p. 126). Obviously any royal advisor who is said to be able to dominate a king to this extent in the popular mind must have been thought of as a frighteningly powerful force in the kingdom.

words, the *Compendio* appears to be a sermon on the subject of excessive power and the changeable nature of fortune, based upon current events and written at a sizeable social distance from the principal figure to whom it is dedicated. In this sense, the dedication serves as the text upon which the sermon will be based or, again, as the *exemplum* on the basis of which a general statement can be made. (See *infra* "Works" for Jerónimo Román's recognition of the ironic quality of the dedication). From such a perspective there is no reason to assume a personal relationship between Fray Martín and D. Álvaro de Luna. But again, conclusions based on negative evidence are difficult to prove. Yet in such a laudatory work as the *Crónica de D. Álvaro* in which the comings and goings of D. Álvaro de Luna and his entourage are described in great detail, some mention of Fray Martín might, as we have said, be expected if he had had any sort of personal relationship with D. Álvaro de Luna at all. For example, Juan de Mena is mentioned as a chronicler,[49] as are the young Prince Enrique's tutors, among whom was Pero Manuel de Lando. These men were not powerful political figures any more than was Ruy Díaz de Mendoza "mayordomo mayor," who was ordered to maintain a constant guard over Prince Enrique.[50] It cannot be said therefore, that only political partisans and important men of affairs were named and that the chroniclers did not mention authors or men of little influence.

Chronology is an additional problem, since it is, as we have seen, relatively certain that Fray Martín spent some years after 1431 in France, studying and teaching. We do not know when he returned but he must have been back at the Convent at Salamanca for some time before Pope Nicholas named him Vicar in 1451. From 1451 to 1453, Fray Martín may be assumed to have been rather fully occupied by his struggle with the Observants who in 1454 once again won a skirmish against him. It can also be assumed that Fray Martín must have had teaching duties at the University of Salamanca before 1453 even without evidence of his having held a chair. During this period he would have

---

[49] *Crónica de D. Álvaro de Luna*, p. 259.
[50] *Crónica de D. Álvaro de Luna*, p. 129.

been occupied with his writing and his teaching at the Convent and the University which would have left him little time to serve at the court in the entourage of D. Álvaro de Luna.[51] For these negative reasons I conclude that the dedication to D. Álvaro de Luna probably belongs to the "open letter" type, directed to prominent persons whose lives in themselves serve to highlight the topic of the didactic work in question, and that it does not represent a serious, literal dedication to an employer and personal friend. One might compare Fray Martín's dedication to the *Condestable* with the more candid and direct tone adopted by Camões in 1572 when he addressed himself to his king saying: "Mas eu que falo, humilde, baxo e rudo/ de vos não conhecido nem sonhado" (Canto X, 154)[52] in the hope that his king would make himself worthy of praise.

The dedication of the *Jardín de nobles donzellas* to the Infanta Isabel can be examined in the same way — seeking confirmation of the relationship between Fray Martín and Isabel outside of Augustinian records to verify any personal connection between the young princess and the author. Fernando Rubio Álvarez sees a real sign of friendship between Fray Martín and Isabel's younger brother, Alfonso, in a passage in the *Prohemio*.[53] The text of the *Prohemio* suggests that the *Jardín* was written

---

[51] It must be admitted that Beltrán de Heredia's documentation of activities at the University of Salamanca suggests that at times, even the holders of chairs were absent for long periods.

[52] Luis de Camões, *Os Lusíadas* (Lisbon; Porto Editora, n.d.), p. 337. Camões assumes the posture of affected modesty and asserts that not only was the king not his acquaintance, the royal person would never even dream of his existence. Nevertheless, he gives him some rather harsh critical advice.

[53] Fernando Rubio Álvarez uses the *Prohemio* and the dedication of the *Compendio* as evidence of Fray Martín's importance at court. He writes: "Disfrutó de gran ascendiente en la corte de Castilla, como ya se ha visto por los testimonios del beato Orozco y del Padre Román los cuales él mismo corrobora con la dedicatoria de su obra *Jardín de nobles doncellas* a la reina doña Isabel, en la que además, pone de manifiesto la amistad que le unía a su hermano don Alfonso, de la que se muestra en cierto modo orgulloso. Otro testimonio de tal ascendiente es la dedicatoria del *Compendio de la fortuna* al privado de Juan II, don Álvaro de Luna" (p. xxxvii). If, as is possible, Alonso de Orozco and Jerónimo Román used the dedications as the basis for their assessments of Fray Martín's importance, their statements cannot be used for corroboration.

shortly after the death of Alfonso (the son of Juan II and Isabel of Portugal).[54] Fray Martín consoles Isabel for the loss of her brother reminding her that he too is bereaved since he loved the young prince as well. A problem arises when we try to explain Fray Martín's allusion to "el rey don Alfonso, vuestro hermano" (p. 141). According to Ramón Menéndez Pidal, by 1467 Spain was a kingdom with two kings — Enrique and Alfonso.[55] Clearly the partisans of Alfonso would call him their king after the events at Ávila (See n. 18 to the Prohemio). Both sides claimed victory after the battle of Olmedo and it is pointed out that Alfonso (not yet fourteen) had led his troops in battle while Enrique had not been present.[56] In spite of all the partisan rhetoric, Enrique was still the king — a fact which Isabel recognized when she refused the throne when it was offered to her.[57] The second problem is related to Fray Martín's use of the expression "la grand deuoción que él en mí tenía por su dulce y real clemencia" (p. 141). It is true that Alfonso had gained the reputation for clemency as a result of the story of the demands of the envoys from Toledo.[58] It must be remembered that the story comes from Palencia, an

---

[54] See n. 20 to the *Prohemio* for a brief description of the events that led up to his having been named heir to the throne, instead of Enrique's daughter, Juana.

[55] Ramón Menéndez Pidal, *La España de los Reyes Católicos (1474-1516)*, Vol. XVII of *Historia de España*, ed. Ramón Menéndez Pidal (Madrid, 1969), xlv.

[56] Ramón Menéndez Pidal, p. xlvii.

[57] Ramón Menéndez Pidal sees the refusal as a sign of her desire to preserve the peace (p. liv). The language that Mosén Diego de Valera reports suggests a respect or even reverence for the established order since Isabel declared: "que nunca pluguiese a Dios que viviendo su hermano el Rey Don Enrique, ella toma la gobernación ni título de Reyna de Castilla; y lo que entendía de facer sería que trabajaría con su hermano quanto a ella posible fuese porque tuviese otra forma en la gobernación destos Reynos..." (*Memorial de diversas hazañas*, Mosén Diego de Valera, BAE 70, [*Crónica de los reyes de Castilla*] [Madrid, 1953], p. 46).

[58] Palencia, a supporter of Alfonso reported that envoys from Toledo came to Alfonso asking that he sanction the expulsion of the *conversos* and the confiscation of their goods. They threatened to throw their support to Enrique if he did not agree. Alfonso answered: "Rebélense en buena hora, que yo no sancionaré iniquidades; bastante es que las tolere, por lo revuelto de los tiempos en que estamos" (Ramón Menéndez Pidal, XVII, xlix—1).

adherent of Alfonso.⁵⁹ Alfonso died at the age of fourteen and a half on July 5, 1468, after having spent his first nine years in retirement with Isabel of Portugal in Arévalo until he was called to the court with his sister Isabel in 1462 on the occasion of the birth of Juana, the daughter of Enrique and Juana of Portugal. From the age of nine until the time of his death, the unfortunate young prince was either in the custody of the Marqués de Villena or, after 1463, in the care of the newly made Conde de Ledesma, Beltrán de la Cueva.⁶⁰ The poor child spent at least five years in the hands of the partisans of Enrique who were the enemies of his own supporters, and Alfonso therefore could not be considered to have had the opportunity to have fulfilled the rôle of king assigned to him by Fray Martín. Can the expression, "grand deuoción que él en mí tenía" be construed to mean that Alfonso enjoyed the devotion and support of Fray Martín? Both Aníbal Sánchez Fraile and Rubio Álvarez suggest that the prince was the one who was devoted.⁶¹ It seems more likely that Fray Martín would ally himself to the cause of Alfonso when one considers Enrique's reputation as a heretic. Called "el Impotente," Enrique was regarded as a threat to the faith. He associated with "moros, rústicos y criminales" and even more ominously it is said of him that "los olores gratos le repugnaban y prefería el de los cascos de caballo o del cuero quemado."⁶² This strange olfactory comment seems to imply that Enrique was suspected of witchcraft. What is even worse is that Enrique IV had been accused by the *grandes, prelados y caballeros* of having ordered a priest to preach that "el huracán de Sevilla, castigo divino por la pública depravación, según las gentes, era puro efecto de leyes naturales."⁶³

---

⁵⁹ Ramón Menéndez Pidal admits that Palencia's authority has been questioned as to objectivity, however it is his opinion that in spite of some excesses that might be considered malicious, Palencia is to be relied upon for accurate observation of events (XVII, xv).

⁶⁰ Tarsicio de Azcona, *Isabel la Católica* (Madrid, 1964), p. 78.

⁶¹ Admittedly Sánchez Fraile makes this observation on the basis of what Fray Martín says in the *Prohemio* (p. xxvii) just as Rubio Álvarez had. See n. 53 *supra*.

⁶² Antonio Paz y Melia, *El cronista Alonso de Palencia* (Madrid, 1914), p. lxii.

⁶³ Paz y Melia, p. lxiv.

In contrast to this dangerously unorthodox king,[64] the malleable young prince promised a return to othodoxy. It was hoped that Alfonso would take a stand against the *conversos* who had flourished under Enrique, and, in fact, in 1467 Alfonso wrote that he desired "que ni oficio ni beneficio [los conversos] goce ni le sea dado, porque a otros generalmente fallaron que judaizaban en muchas y diversas maneras."[65] All of this seems to indicate that the clergy would have been deeply involved in Alfonso's claim to the throne and that his cause had inspired their devotion. It is my conclusion, therefore that without further evidence to the contrary that the dedication of the *Prohemio* to the *Jardín* reveals Fray Martín's adherence to the cause of Alfonso and later that of Isabel and not the personal relationship suggested by the language of the *Prohemio*.

To cast further doubt on Alfonso's devotion to Fray Martín, the negative evidence of the chronicles must be taken into account. The names of Alfonso's tutors, as well as others whe were responsible for the direction of the young prince's education are mentioned in many of the chronicles. The *Crónica de D. Álvaro de Luna*, after the description of the *Condestable*'s death in 1453 provides an account of those involved with him. Gonçalo Chacón, *Comendador de Montiel*, whose wife belonged to the household of Isabel of Portugal, is named as the person in charge of the education of Isabel and Alfonso, not Fray Martín.[66] The testament of Juan II in 1454 reveals the uneasiness of the king in regard to his wife's stability when he prescribes: "un régimen de tutoría y administración, presidido por la reina madre pero siempre de acuerdo y con consejo de Lope de Barrientos[67] y de

---

[64] In addition to being called "el Impotente" and being accused of giving undue preferment to the Jews and Muslims at court, Enrique was also accused of being a practicing homosexual. The nobles wrote in the *Representación:* "Llega el Monarca en su afeminación a ir de madrugada a casa de su nuevo favorito Pacheco a distraerle en su enfermedad cantando acompañado de la cítara" (Paz y Melia, p. lxiv). Ramón Menéndez Pidal mentions a relationship with Miguel Lucas de Iranzo and with Beltrán de la Cueva (XVII, xxix).

[65] Tarsicio de Azcona, p. 383.

[66] *Crónica de D. Álvaro de Luna*, p. 250.

[67] The appearance of Fray Lope de Barrientos in a position of authority over the education of the young *infantes* is interesting in the light of what

González de Illescas, y con lo tocante al infante, también de Juan de Padilla." [68] Isabel of Portugal's instability appears in various accounts. Even a modern biographer such as William T. Walsh, determined to idealize her illustrious daughter describes her post-partum depression, although he attributes it to poisons administered during her confinement and delivery. [69] Paz y Melia refers to the "grave dolencia e irremediable tristeza" that she experienced after the birth of Isabel and names D. Álvaro de Luna as the probable poisoner. He goes on to observe that the death of Juan II finally caused Isabel of Portugal to retreat to her chambers in "triste silencio, próximo a degenerar en locura." [70] Closest to the period is Hernán del Pulgar's statement, in 1482, that after the death of Juan II, the queen mother had fallen into an illness from which she could not recover. [71] The record thus yields a picture of a mother suffering from a serious depression. Such a situation does not match the observations of P. Félix García, who evokes: "La celosa y religiosa Isabel de Portugal, que tanto se desveló por la educación cristiana y civil de sus hijos ... vio en el austero agustino ... la verdad y las normas de la vida cristiana.... Ella le conoció y trató y en él buscó apoyo y fortaleza en las horas de amargura y ausencia cuando

---

Aníbal Sánchez Fraile says concerning his relationship to Fray Martín. They appear to have been rivals if not adversaries. In Sánchez Fraile's opinion, Fray Lope de Barrientos wrote his *Tratado de Caso e Fortuna, del Dormir y de la Adivinanza* at the request of Juan II and that Fray Martín wrote the *Tratado de la predestinación* at the request of Enrique IV. Sánchez Fraile assumes a relationship between the two authors and also points out, among other issues they disagreed on the dangers of the influence of the Jews. Fray Martín feared their influence, while Fray Lope defended them in his "Contra algunos cizañadores de la nación de los convertidos del pueblo de Israel" (pp. xlviii—xlix). If the two men were indeed rivals and Fray Lope was named by Juan II in his will as one of the people in charge of the education of the young royal children, then the absence of Fray Martín's name from the list is explicable. It should be noted that Fray Lope's name appears in twelve separate entries in Beltrán de Heredia's *Bulario* (III, 543).

[68] Tarsicio de Azcona, p. 16.
[69] Walsh, p. 2.
[70] Paz y Melia, p. 419.
[71] Hernán del Pulgar, *Crónica de los señores Reyes Católicos Don Fernando y Doña Isabel de Castilla y de Aragón escrita por su cronista Hernando del Pulgar* in BAE 70 (Madrid, 1953), p. 229.

se hubo de recluir en Arévalo para atender al negocio de su salvación y el cuidado de sus hijos, formados en la buena sobriedad y el silencio." [72] P. García offers no evidence in support of the close relationship between Isabel of Portugal and Fray Martín — "el austero agustino" — other than the contents of the *Prohemio*. It is doubtful that this depressed, withdrawn woman would have been able to select a tutor for Alfonso and Isabel. Considering the enmity between Lope de Barrientos and Fray Martín, [73] it is unlikely that Fray Lope acting in accordance with the will of Juan II would have countenanced the entry of Fray Martín into the household of Isabel and her offspring. The royal children were in Arévalo with their mother from 1454 to 1462. Admittedly during this period there is no clear evidence as to Fray Martín's activities until 1461 when he was named "Conventual" in Toulouse. We can only speculate that during this time he either held the chair of *Filosofía Moral* at Salamanca (until 1457), or that he and his fellow teachers had already gone to Valladolid, or, again that in 1461 he had gone to Toulouse. But we know nothing for certain. However, it seems very doubtful that the unstable, widowed queen made the sort of arrangement for the protection of her daughter, Isabel, that Félix García suggests when he writes that Isabel of Portugal: "encomendó a Fray Martín de Córdoba que escribiese un doctrinal o directorio de avisos y cautelas, que sirviera de guía y de lección ascética a la Infanta Isabel...." [74]

In 1462 the two young people were called to court where according to Enríquez del Castillo, "serían mejor criados." [75] At court, Alfonso's tutor was to be "Diego de Ribera, caballero de limpia sangre e crianza de mucha virtud." Isabel was entrusted to Queen Juana de Portugal, shortly before the birth of the "hija de la reina," Juana de Castilla, [76] who, incidentally, was not

---

[72] Félix García, ed. *Jardín de nobles donzellas* (Madrid, 1956), pp. 31-2.
[73] See n. 67 *supra*.
[74] García, p. 32.
[75] *Crónica del Rey D. Enrique el Quarto de e:te nombre, por su capellán y cronista Diego Enríquez del Castillo*, ed. Josef Miguel de Flores (Madrid, 1787), p. 59.
[76] Enríquez del Castillo, p. 59.

called *La Beltraneja* in the chronicles until well into the reign of Ferdinand and Isabel. The designation "hija de la reina" was apparently pointed enough to question her paternity, without naming her putative father.

By 1464, the nobles were protesting in the *Representación* that Beltrán de la Cueva, Conde de Ledesma had Isabel and Alfonso in his power ("los quales él agora tiene presos"). [77] It is to be remembered that before April, 1463, they were said to have been in the power of Juan Pacheco, the Marqués de Villena. [78] In another document which is dated 1464 without day or month, the Conde de Ledesma is accused of having "procurado otras cosas por interés suyo en desordenamiento del dicho Infante don Alonso; por manera que si así pasasen estas cosas, todos los dichos reynos irían en final destruición." [79] At this time, Isabel was thirteen and Alfonso, nine. In the encounter between the two factions at Cigales and Cabezón, Enrique's enemies demanded that he hand over the Infante Alfonso to the Marqués de Villena and that he acknowledge the young prince as his heir. [80] It seems that during this period the children were alternately in the power of the Conde de Ledesma (Beltrán de la Cueva) and the Marqués de Villena, but there is no evidence that either of these two courtiers had any known connection with Fray Martín, whose name does not appear in the narrations of any of the struggle to gain custody of the two young people. The demand that Alfonso be handed over to the Marqués de Villena was apparently complied with, although Isabel was left once again with Queen Juana.

Another strong influence on the young heirs to the throne seems to have been Alfonso de Carrillo, Archbishop of Toledo and uncle of the Marqués de Villena. Diego de Valera describes the meeting with Isabel and Enrique IV at Toros de Guisando: "E como se acercasen los unos de los otros, el Arzobispo que traía a la Princesa, dejó la rienda, e la Princesa se llegó al Rey

---

[77] Paz y Melia, pp. 65-6.
[78] See n. 60 *supra*.
[79] Paz y Melia, p. 69. Is the suggestion here that the young prince was being enticed into homosexual practices?
[80] Enríquez del Castillo, p. 115.

por le besar la mano, el qual no se la quiso dar por mucho quella lo porfió; y en todo esto el Arzobispo ningún acatamiento ni reverencia fizo al Rey ni habló a ninguna otra persona, e la Princesa se llegó a él, y muy quedo le dijo que besase la mano al Rey, el le ficiese el acatamiento que debía; a lo qual el Arzobispo de Toledo respondió que ninguna cosa él faría fasta que el Rey la declarase por legítima heredera e sucesora destos Reynos." The quiet drama of this scene ended with Enrique's capitulation. He named Isabel his successor. [81] Clearly, Alfonso de Carrillo played an important part in Isabel's life. So strong was his advocacy of her cause that the supporters of Juana, *La Beltraneja* burned Carrillo in effigy chanting the following: "Esta es Simancas/ Don Opas traydor/ Esta es Simancas/ que no Peñaflor." [82] Here Carrillo is identified with the traitorous D. Opas, brother of the Conde Julián. It was Alfonso de Carrillo who approached Isabel with the proposition that she seize the crown after the death of Alfonso. Her reply is reported by Mosén Diego de Valera: "que nunca pluguiese a Dios que viviendo su hermano el Rey Don Enrique, ella toma la gobernación destos Reynos..." [83] Isabel's refusal of the offer on the grounds that Enrique was still the king puts Fray Martín's designation of Alfonso as king in perspective. There is, however, no mention of Fray Martín in connection with the offer made by Alfonso de Carrillo. Later, it was Carrillo who was one of the drafters of the *Capitulaciones* signed on the occasion of the marriage of Ferdinand and Isabel. Thus it is seen that a series of prominent nobles and clergy were closely identified with Alfonso and Isabel during their formative years and that nowhere, except in the records of the Augustinian Order, does Fray Martín appear in close connection with the members of the royal family and with the court. It is my suspicion that the subsequent allusions to this relationship are based on the questionable testimony of the dedications of the *Jardín* to Isabel and of the *Compendio* to D. Álvaro de Luna.

Keeping in mind the dedication of the *Jardín* — suggestive of a certain degree of intimacy which this study has tended to place

---

[81] *Memorial de diversas hazañas*, pp. 47-8.
[82] Enríquez del Castillo, p. 138.
[83] *Memorial de diversas hazañas*, p. 46.

in doubt — yet another negative fact may be added. The *Jardín* does not appear in the extant catalogues of the two hundred and fifty volumes that make up the two libraries of Isabel. We have a catalogue of her library in the Alcázar of Segovia, compiled by Rodrigo de Tordesillas in 1503, and another catalogue prepared by her chamberlain, Sancho de Paredes, of a collection whose location is not specified. [84]

It is pertinent to this study to attempt an analysis of Isabel's library with the end in view of determining if there is any significance in the absence of Fray Martín's works from the collection. We may ask: were these really Isabel's books or was this a state library? Is there a suggestion that Isabel had other books which she kept for her personal use in some other place? Are there any titles which might conceivably be Fray Martín's although his name is not associated with them? How does the collection compare with the library of the Marqués de Santillana in terms of erudition and of breadth of interest?

It is the opinion of one modern historian that the library of two hundred and fifty volumes and manuscripts in Spanish, Portuguese, French, Italian and Latin represented a personal collection which the Queen had selected and had used herself. [85] The personal nature of the library seems to be verified by the inclusion of such domestic items as "Cinco cartapacios borrados de cuando al Príncipe se mostraba latín; dos libros de dibujar de box" and "un libro sin ojas que es un barril, e que se dice Breviario sobre la sed." [86] There are also several books with blank pages. The impression is of a personal library.

Among the books in Segovia, there are two which might possibly be identified as Fray Martín's: "Otro libro de marca mayor, escripto en pargamino de mano en latín, ques el Apocalipsis" [87] and "Otro libro que dice que está la fortuna" [88] and there exists the possibility that some of the books in the library that are identified as the works of Aristotle may be Fray Martín's. Diego

---

[84] Both catalogues are reproduced by Manuel Ballesteros Gaibrois, *Isabel de Castilla: Reina Católica de España* (Madrid, 1964), pp. 205-27.
[85] Ballesteros, p. 150.
[86] Ballesteros, p. 221.
[87] Ballesteros, p. 205.
[88] Ballesteros, p. 220.

de Montanches says that Fray Martín wrote "Super multos libros Aristotelis" (See n. 22). The early bibliographers list a work of Fray Martín's on the subject of the Apocalypse and of course the *Compendio* deals with the nature of fortune. The descriptions in the catalogue are too vague to definitely identify these works. Other authors are identified quite clearly so that the very least that can be said is that Fray Martín was not well known to the cataloguers, if these were indeed his works.

There are three works in the collection dealing explicitly with women as does the *Jardín:* "Otro libro de pliego entero de mano en papel de romance, que se dice el tercero tratado del libro de las mugeres que hizo el maestro Jiménez de la Orden de los predicadores." [89] This is apparently Francesch Eiximenis' *Libro de les dones.* Also mentioned are "Otro libro de pliego entero en papel de mano en romance que se dice el ARCIPRESTE DE TALAVERA, con unas tablas de papel que habla de las mugeres," and "Otro libro de pargamino de mano que es de las VIRTUOSAS E CLARAS MUGERES, que hizo el maestro Don Álvaro de Luna." [90]

The collection shows a breadth of interests ranging from psalters, missals and other devotional works through the *Siete Partidas,* the *General Estoria,* the *Crónica general,* a history of Spain written in Portuguese (which might be the *Crónica of 1344* or that of *1404),* many legal works, *fueros, ordenamientos, privilegios,* some correspondence and five or six *regimientos de príncipes.* Of these last, there is one which is described in terms of its costliness ("el libro dos mil y quinientos maravedís") followed by a reference to a "regimiento trobado por Juan Rodríguez de Villalobos." [91] Another called *Oficios de los nobles* might be the *Nobiliario* of Fernán Mexía or the *Espejo de verdadera nobleza* of Mosén Diego de Valera. Yet another is the *Caída de los príncipes* of Boccaccio. The Church Fathers, St. Jerome, St. Thomas, St. Isidore, St. Augustin and St. Gregory are well represented. Portions of the Bible (in part in *romance*) and the

---

[89] Ballesteros, p. 209.
[90] Ballesteros, pp. 217-18.
[91] Ballesteros, p. 224.

expected exegetical materials are in the collection as well as a number of hagiographical works.

Isabel's library also contained the works of classical authors, sometimes in Latin and sometimes in translation: Enrique de Villena's translation of the *Aeneid*, the works of Seneca, Livy, Pliny, Xenophon, Aristotle, Terence, Plutarch, Quintus Curtius, Cicero, several versions of the life of Alexander (none specifically identified as the *Libro de Alexandre*), and several narrations of the events at Troy, one of which is a *Crónica troyana*.

A number of didactic works are to be found: The *Trabajos de Hércoles* (not attributed here to Enrique de Villena), *Flores de filosofía*, *Bocados de oro*, *Isopete*, *Calila e Dimna*, *El Conde Lucanor* and Boethius' *Consolación*. Also represented are works on hunting, music, warfare, medicine, astrology and the rules of the various religious Orders; Nebrija's grammar and vocabulary, as well as another by Alonso de Palencia; several Latin grammars are also listed.

The novels include those of Boccaccio and his "Frometa" *(Fiammetta)*. There are also Arthurian works, not identified as to author, dealing with the Grail, Joseph of Arimathea, Merlin and Lancelot. The poetry includes the *Coplas de Juan de Mena, Coplas de Alonso Álvarez de Villasandino, Miraglos de Nuestra Señora* (not identified as to author), a *Tratado de Alonso de Baena*, several French *cancioneros,* and "Otro libro que se dice el ARCIPRESTE DE HITA, en papel e de mano de cuarto de pliego en romance, que son las coplas del Arcipreste de Hita." [92]

A number of dedications to Isabel are mentioned in the catalogue, including Nebrija's grammar; but the *Jardín*, a work dedicated to her most specifically, is conspicuously absent from the list. It might be assumed that the *Jardín* was a bedside book as were her prayer books, which is admittedly a limitation on any use of the contents of Isabel's library as evidence that she did not particularly value the works of Fray Martín. If this were the case, one might reasonably expect to find some mention of his other works in the list of books in her two libraries.

---

[92] Ballesteros, p. 216.

To sum up: while again recognizing the scholarly peril involved in basing a hypothesis on negative evidence, it still seems fair to assume that the dedications to Isabel and to D. Álvaro merely represent a literary device. It should be reiterated that the only positive evidence of a personal relationship between Fray Martín and D. Álvaro de Luna and Isabel is the author's own identification of himself as D. Álvaro de Luna's "deuoto e capellán" (possibly a formulaic reference to Fray Martín's religious status), and the consolatory advice given to Isabel on the death of Alfonso, the reference to the young prince and the phrase: "la grand deuoción que él en mí tenía."

The dedications themselves can be examined in the light of what is known about the various *topoi* which appear in similar dedications, and the posture which an author of a didactic work dedicated to an eminent person may be thought to assume. Once again, the dual purpose of such works must be recognized. They are intended to convince the eminent person and to convince the general reader of a given position. One of the most effective postures which an author of a didactic or persuasive work can assume is that of "affected modesty." Fray Martín characterizes himself in the *Compendio* as an "hombre que fue dado a letras" but quickly says that it is his intention to serve with his efforts the "ingenio celestial" [93] of D. Álvaro de Luna. Clearly this is an expression of what Curtius describes as affected modesty. [94] Within this framework, can be recognized the pose of the humble person who shares the general humility of the reader, daring to offer his thoughts to someone recognized by the reader and the author as a brilliant thinker, or a powerful person, or both, and consequently the author shares a common experience with the reader. The content of a didactic work is really directed to the general reader. As Hafter puts it: "Moralist treatises, even though planned for the leaders of society, have as their point of departure the perennial human problems." [95] Among the different manners of addressing a prominent person, there are

---
[93] *Compendio*, p. 3.
[94] Curtius, pp. 83-5.
[95] Monroe Hafter, *Gracián and Perfection* (Cambridge, Massachusetts, 1966), pp. 2-3.

several sub-divisions: that of Camões who disclaims any personal relationship but still dares to offer advice, that of Fray Martín who in the *Jardín* suggests an affectionate intimacy and offers advice and another form, described by Alice Adèle Hentsch, in which the advice offered has less importance because the author's intention is not so much to advise the eminent person as it is to flatter him. [96]

While the kinds of dedication under discussion can be found in works other than *regimientos de príncipes*, both the *Compendio* and the *Jardín* fall into the group of works which offer advice to the powerful, although the advice also addresses itself to "perennial human problems." In a sense, historians also can be thought of as authors of *regimientos de príncipes*, offering advice to the powerful. The tendency to write the history of a period in the hope of influencing a ruler or of influencing the thinking of his subjects is described by R.B. Tate who says that Sánchez de Arévalo described "the aspects of Enrique's character in response to a composite ideal of the Castilian monarch based on his interpretation of the historical past which he hopes Enrique will try to emulate." [97] Apparently this was not a question of supine, servile flattery but the conviction that the King would live up to his description or the people would demand that he do so. The parallel can be seen between Sánchez de Arévalo's dedication of the *Vergel de Príncipes* in 1455 to Enrique IV in which he predicted that Enrique would not only reconquer Granada but would cross the straits and capture the African province, [98] and Fray Martín's advice to Isabel that she be merciful to her own people and daring against the enemy and that she continue the reconquest of the peninsula, begun by her ancestors (See n. 18 to the *Prohemio*).

The author of a didactic work addressed to an eminent personage can be assumed, therefore, to have adopted one or another

---

[96] Alice Adèle Hentsch, *De la littérature didactique du Moyen Age s'addressant specialment aux femmes* (Halle, 1903), p. 6.

[97] R. B. Tate, "An Apology for Monarchy: A Study of an Unpublished 15th-Century Castilian Historical Pamphlet," *RPh* XV (1961-1962), 111-123: p. 120.

[98] Ramón Menéndez Pidal, XVII, xii.

of the postures described above. Certainly he can be writing to a personage with whom he has the intimacy he claims; he can be writing as did Camões from an acknowledged distance; or he can be pretending to an unreal intimacy to make his suggestions more persuasive and interesting to the reader; or, again, in the course of writing a chronicle he can address himself to specific issues without any overt mention of a relationship. In the light of these various attitudes, the author of a didactico-moral work can be seen to have two parallel motives: a sincere desire to instruct and to improve the performance of a ruler (with or without the right to address him directly) and, at the same time, a more general motive to express himself about "perennial human problems," using what might be described as an open-letter technique in the hope that the dedication will stimulate his readers' interest in his views on political, moral or theological questions.

This is not to say, however, that the dedication to a prominent person is simply an attention-getter — the author is also acknowledging that he is a humble person barely able to form a coherent sentence who stands in awe of the brilliance of the eminent person — e.g. the "ingenio celestial" of D. Álvaro de Luna. In the *Prohemio* to the *Jardín,* a later work than the *Compendio,* Fray Martín has dropped this part of the pose of affected modesty. In the *Compendio,* the reader is invited to join with the humble author in recognizing basic home truths about the changeable nature of fortune; in the *Jardín* he is invited to participate in the warm, intimate relationship of an elderly priest and the lovely princess of the realm. Either way, the reader is flattered, because he is taking part in the affairs of the mighty and therefore both dedications can be included in the large general classification of *captatio benevolentiae.*

In the *Jardín,* Fray Martín manipulates the reader in still another way. He addresses Isabel: "Algunos, Señora, menos entendidos ... pero yo, como abaxo diré, soy de contraria opinión" (p. 136). Thus he creates a bond between Isabel and himself by indirectly assuming that she shares his opinion and not that of the less perceptive with whom neither of them agrees. What reader could resist the temptation to join the elite group of those who agree with Fray Martín and Isabel? (In this case the opinion is that women are fit to rule). In the *Tratado,* he describes the people who "non tienen otro estudio syno el dinero y non curan del tesoro de la fe." [99] Then he asserts: "Pues yo en este triste tiempo, faré por el contrario." The two approaches are not exactly similar, but, in each case, Fray Martín established his superiority over others, and the reader is put in the position of choosing to agree with the author if he does not want to ally himself with the wrong sort of people. On the basis of the similarity between the two literary devices, it would be wrong to assume that in the *Jardín* Fray Martín was, in truth, referring to a known opinion held by the princess, although the passage certainly makes the *Prohemio* sound more personal.

In the dedication to the *Compendio,* Fray Martín indulges in affected modesty referring to his "subdorosos trabajos" as opposed to the "celestial ingenio" of D. Álvaro de Luna and, in the *Jardín* he calls his book "vna breue escriptura." There is no reason to think that these expressions are anything more than rhetorical formulas. It is worthy of note that in his *Tratado,* a work less popular in tone than the *Compendio* and the *Jardín,* Fray Martín writes in the hope that he will save those who have fallen into error through ignorance. In this case, he refers to his work as "esta breve obra en cantidat; mas en calidat muy alta & grand." [100] All three introductory statements have in common, in varying degrees, the signs of an author who is sure of his own intellectual powers, although this self confidence is somewhat disguised in the *Compendio* and in the *Jardín.*

From this brief analysis of the dedications to the *Compendio* and the *Jardín,* it can be seen that there are reasons to consider them as part of the rhetorical tradition, rather than as personal documents, even though the most convincing arguments against their personal nature are negative ones. In the case of the *Compendio,* we must suppose that Fray Martín chose D. Álvaro de Luna — a man whose fortunes had soared, but whose good fortune and power was clearly destined to cause his inevitable fall — as a sort of eponymous figure. In the *Jardín,* the *Prohemio* clearly shows

---

[99] *Tratado,* p. 6.
[100] *Tratado,* p. 3.

Fray Martín's advocacy of Isabel's cause. He directly criticizes Enrique's negligence in not having pursued the reconquest of Granada. He refers to Solinus in order to praise a system of selection of a ruler based on his wisdom and strength. The personal touches in the *Prohemio* are subordinated to the political commentary which he offers. However, by 1468, considering all the dissension faced by Enrique IV and the turbulent nature of his reign, Fray Martín would have been allying himself with an already successful cause and therefore flogging a dead horse.

There remains the unanswered question of the contemporary importance attained by the *Jardín*, an importance sufficient to warrant its having enjoyed two early printings. The first printing in 1500 can be thought of as a reflection of contemporary interest in Isabel; the second printing in 1542 might have been in preparation for a commemoration of her birth in 1451. The dedication to Isabel of a work in praise of women, in which it is shown that their good qualities are particularly applicable to the task of ruling, would seem to be a most logical dedication. The suggestion of a personal relationship could only have stimulated the interest of the reader and have ensured an audience for the author's opinions.

It is, therefore, my conclusion that there is scant evidence that Fray Martín de Córdoba played the influential rôle in the court that is suggested by Alonso de Orozco, Jerónimo Román and subsequent Augustinian scholars. All the same, I believe that his books did indeed influence the thought of his contemporaries to the degree that they were read. The two printings of the *Jardín* at a time when many worthy works did not achieve publication suggests a certain popularity for this singularly timely work.

II

WORKS

A bibliography of the works attributed to Fray Martín de Córdoba and clearly established as his can be constructed from various sources. I have used the bibliography of Santiago Vela [1] as a starting point, adding whenever possible the corroboration available in earlier sources more nearly contemporary to Fray Martín. I have tentatively accepted the testimony of such sources in attempting to establish the titles of works which have not as yet been found. I have also accepted the internal evidence found in the explicit of the *Ars praedicandi* [2] as well as the conclusion of Aníbal Sánchez Fraile that the "Fray Martín, de la Orden Agustina de Valladolid, Dotor en Artes, Maestro en Santa Theología, grandísimo letrado & predicador & de buena & honesta vida" [3] of the introduction to the *Tratado* is our Fray Martín de Córdoba.

Concerning the physical fate of Fray Martín's manuscripts, Alonso de Orozco (1500-1591) observes: "Sus valiosos escritos quedaron en el convento de Valladolid, y viéndose los religiosos en un tiempo muy necesitados los empeñaron a los PP Benedictinos de la misma ciudad." [4] P. Antolínez (1554-1626) states: "Hállanse cosas escritas de su mano en la librería del Monasterio de San

---

[1] Gregorio Santiago Vela, *Ensayo de una biblioteca*, II, 90. See also n. 37 to "The Author and His Readership."

[2] Fernando Rubio Álvarez, "*Ars praedicandi* de Fray Martín de Córdoba," *La Ciudad de Dios*, CLXXII (1959), 329-348.

[3] *Tratado*, p. 3.

[4] *Herrera*, p. 55. All references to the list of Fray Martín's works reported by Alonso de Orozco are to be found here.

Agustín el Real de Valladolid."[5] Jerónimo Román also testifies that the Benedictines had a copy of Fray Martín's *De próspera y adversa fortuna*.[6] Later Ambrosio de Morales in his mission to seek out in 1572 by order of Felipe II, "Libros, ms. de las Cathedrales y Monasterios," describes in detail a handwritten copy of *Sobre las Epístolas de San Pablo*,[7] which he found in Valladolid. Ambrosio de Morales is very explicit about his investigations, describing the physical details of the collection he examined. For example of Valladolid, he says: "Hay dos librerías, que por los sitios llaman alta y baja; en la baja hay más libros de mano: y aunque algunos parecen raros son de autores no muy de estimar. Así no porné sino los que parece la tienen."[8] Enrique Flórez, the eighteenth-century editor of Ambrosio de Morales, explains the fact that *De próspera y adversa fortuna* was not mentioned by Morales in the *Viage*: "Este, o no perseveraba en el 1572 o no le conoció Morales. Mantiénese el primero."[9] Morales showed his familiarity with Fray Martín in his description of the *Epístolas* so we must assume that he had either overlooked it or the Ms. had already disappeared from the library. Jerónimo Román, writing in 1581 says that the Benedictines of Valladolid had a copy of *De próspera y adversa fortuna* but his information does not appear to have been at first hand.[10] The present location of other books and manuscripts will be included in their descriptions whenever possible.

Although there is an expected fluidity of title which harks back to medieval manuscript practice,[11] reasonable identification

---

[5] Santiago Vela, "Notas de interés," p. 62.
[6] Herrera, p. 55. All references to Jerónimo Roman's comments are to be found here.
[7] Enrique Flórez, ed. *Viage de Ambrosio de Morales*, p. 9.
[8] Enrique Flórez, ed. *Viage de Ambrosio de Morales*, p. 9, n. 1.
[9] Enrique Flórez, *Viage de Ambrosio de Morales*, p. 9, n. 1.
[10] Jerónimo Román begins his sentence with the expression "Dízese" which sounds as if he were reporting what he had heard and not seen himself.
[11] H. J. Chaytor describes the *incunabula* in this respect: "A very cursory examination of early *incunabula* will show that the printer did his best to reproduce the text in manuscript form; there will be no title nor title page, the scribe's abbreviations will be reproduced, his proportion of text to margin observed and so on." (*From Script to Print: An Introduction to Medieval Vernacular Literature* [New York, 1967], p. 137).

of Fray Martín's books is possible through the comparison of the various references, using as a convenient starting point and standard, the titles used by Santiago Vela.

1. *Exameron, sive operibus sex dierum* is referred to by Diego de Montanches as "Super Genesis de opere sex dierum;" [12] Alonso de Orozco says Fray Martín "Sobre el Génesis hizo un libro que se dize Exameron; quiere dezir de las obras de los seis días, que Dios obró." Antonio Possevini, a Jesuit whose *Apparatus sacer* was published in 1603 and 1606 in Venice calls the work *In tria prima Geneseos capita*, [13] and Joseph Pamphilo, whose *Chronica* was published in 1581, designated the same work as *Expositio in tria prima capita Geneseos*. [14] Although this work of Fray Martín's has as yet not come to light, it is my opinion that it must have contained the same three-part organization of the events of Creation that appears in *Capítulo cuatro, primera parte* of the *Jardín* (see n. 1 to I, iv). Later bibliographies also mention this work: Andreas Schott calls it *Expositio in tria prima capita Geneseos* [15] while Nicolás Antonio writes: "Latina haec Scilicet: *Hexaemeron, sive in Genesis priora capita de opere sex dierum.*" [16]

2. *Comentarios sobre el Apocalipsis de San Juan:* Diego de Montanches states that Fray Martín wrote "Super Apocalipsin" [sic]. Alonso de Orozco also affirms that he "declaró el Apocalipsi, libro bien dificultoso de entender" but it is not altogether clear whether the *beato* Alonso de Orozco is commenting on the difficulties of Revelations or on Fray Martín's erudition. Joseph Pamphilo calls the same book *Expositio in Apocalipsim beati Ioanis;* Possevini gives the title as *in Apocalipsim D. Joannis.* Although the topic is a common one in exegetical literature, it

---

[12] Santiago Vela, "Notas de interés," p. 54. All subsequent references to Diego de Montanches are to be found here.

[13] Antonio Possevini, *Apparatus sacer ad Scriptores veteris & noui Testamenti* ... (Venetiis: Apud Societatem Venetam, 1606) II, 402. All subsequent references to Possevini are to p. 402.

[14] Joseph Pamphilo, *Cronica Ordinis fratrum eremitarum Sancti Augustini* (Romae: ex typographiae Georgii Ferrarii, 1581), p. 87. Subsequent references to Pamphilo are to p. 87.

[15] Andreas Schott, p. 267. Subsequent references are to p. 267.

[16] Nicolás Antonio, II, 307. References to Nicolás Antonio are to be found on p. 307 unless otherwise stated.

should be noted that there is a volume listed in the catalogue of Isabel's library dealing with this subject. The author is not identified. Later bibliographers also mention this work: Schott lists *Expositionem in Apocalipsim B. Ioannis* and Nicolás Antonio calls it *Apocalypsis explanatio*.

3. *Comentarios y Cuestiones sobre las Epístolas de San Pablo* is referred to by Montanches as *Super epistolas pauli;* Alonso de Orozco says: "Sobre las Epístolas de San Pablo excriuió Comentarios y questiones" and Pamphilo changes the title to *Comentaria in omnes D. Pauli epistolas*. Antonio Possevini prefers *In omnes D. Pauli Epistolas*. Andreas Schott gives the title as *Comentaria in omnes diui Pauli* and Nicolás Antonio calls it *In divi Pauli epistolas commentaria & quaestiones*. Nicolás Antonio calls attention to the description in Ambrosio de Morales' *Viage* as follows: "Quod saltem opus apud laudatos sodales S. Benedicti Pincianos asservari ad Philippum II Regem Ambrosius Morales retulit, in *Itinerario* suo, quod cum inscriptione *Del santo viage* confecit, servaturque manu exaratum." Although an extant copy of this work has not been found to date, we do have a description of the copy in the lower library of the Convent at Valladolid made by Ambrosio de Morales during his 1572 survey at the behest of Felipe II: "Un libro antiguo de mano en papel grueso: es sobre las Epístolas de S. Pablo, e escribiólo el M. Fray Martín de Córdoba de la Orden de San Agustín, y dice al principio como lo escribió leyendo en Tolosa en año MCCCCLXI. Por Autor Español es preciado." [17] Morales may have added the comment on Fray Martín's value as a writer to distinguish him from the other authors of the books stored in the lower library, of whom, as we have seen, he had written: "En la baja hay más libros de mano: y aunque algunos parecen raros son de autores no muy de estimar." The corroborative detail of Fray Martín's having written the book in 1461 in Toulouse firmly establishes the existence of this now lost work.

4. *Lógica y Filosofía* is listed by Santiago Vela as the title of a work by Fray Martín. The closest analogous reference is in Diego de Montanches' list: "Fecit multa opera tam in philosophia

---

[17] Enrique Flórez, *Viage de Ambrosio Morales*, p. 9.

quam in theologia" — but this is quite inconclusive for the purpose of specific identification. Alonso de Orozco states that Fray Martín "escribió lógica y filosofía y fue muchos años catedrático en Salamanca y en Tolosa de Francia," which also is too vague to be taken as the title of a specific work. Neither Joseph Pamphilo, Antonio Possevini, nor Andreas Schott mention any such work. However, Nicolás Antonio has an entry 663: *Logicam & Philosophiam*. It is worth noting that before listing the titles of the works of Fray Martín, at the end of paragraph 659, Nicolás Antonio writes "Latina haec scilicet" and then lists the *Hexameron, In divi Pauli epistolas*..., *Apocalypsis*, and *Logica & Philosophia*. In the same manner, at the end of paragraph 663, he writes "Vulgaris quoque linguae haec," which introduces the titles of two works of Fray Martín in *romance*. This does not establish clearly Nicolás Antonio's familiarity with *Logica & Philosophia* although it might be assumed that he was familiar with some such work in Latin. Santiago Vela does not explain why he chooses to list the title in Spanish since it might have been written in Latin. In spite of the shadowy evidence concerning the existence of *Logica & Philosophia*, it would be rash to make a categorical denial of its existence in the light of Fulgencio Riesco Bravo's discovery of Fray Martín's *Tratado de la predestinación* in 1917 (a work which, incidentally, is not mentioned in the early bibliographies). See *infra* section 9.

5. *Alabanza de la virginidad, para religiosas* is included by Montanches in a list of works "in vulgari" as "Et ille de virginitate ad sanctimoniales." Alonso de Orozco calls it "Otros [que] hizo de alabança de la virginidad para religiosas." Pamphilo calls the book *De laude virginitatis ad puellas religiosas*," while Possevini's title is *De laude Virginitatis, puellis religiosis dicatus*. Schott's title is *De laude Virginitatis Religiosis velatisque Virginibus dedicatum*. Nicolás Antonio gives the title in *romance: Alabanzas de la virginidad*. He describes the book as follows: "Ad Virgines Deo sacras. Quae quidem ei Alphonsus de Horosco, vir sanctitate & doctrina clarissimus, adtribuit opera." José Simón Díaz lists an anonymous work: "*Vergel de virginidad con el Edificio spiritual de la caridad. Y los mysterios de la ángeles. Con treze seruicios que haze el Angel custodio*. Compuesto por un religioso de

los menores de la prouincia de Santiago. (Burgos; Juan de la Junta, 1539). Ded. a la emperatriz Isabel." [18] There is not enough evidence to assume that this is Fray Martín's work although an examination of the work, copies of which are in the Biblioteca Nacional and in San Lorenzo del Escorial might afford us some insight into the content of the lost *Alabanza*.

6. *Compendio de la fortuna* is not mentioned by Diego de Montanches, nor by Joseph Pamphilo in his *Chronica*, nor by Schott, Possevini and Alonso de Orozco. However, Nicolás Antonio notes that Pamphilo mentions the *Compendio* in a work which I have not been able to locate, entitled *De Scriptoribus Augustinianis*. Jerónimo Román de Higuera wrote: "Escriuió muchos libros, que no quedan impressos. Quedaron en Valladolid, y empeñaronlos los Frayles de aquella Casa a los Monjes Benitos. Dízese que tienen allí vno, *De próspera & aduersa fortuna*, dirigido al gran Condestable don Álvaro de Luna; aunque le aprouechó poco este libro para conocer sus mudanças." It is not clear whether Jerónimo Román was simply lamenting D. Álvaro de Luna's incapacity to take advantage of the advice offered to him or whether he was recognizing the paradoxical nature of the dedication as a literary device. Nicolás Antonio gives the following description of the 16th-century references: "*De próspera y adversa fortuna* Alvaro a Luna Comestabili, fato quodam, qui exemplum exstitit utriusque mirabile, nuncupatum. Auctores de his habuimus Iosephum Pamphilum *De Scriptoribus Augustinianis*, Hieron, Romanum, & Alphonsum de Horosco, in historiis huiusmet Ordinis, & Tomam de Herrera in ea quam scripsit *Augustinianae domus Salmantinae*."

In his modern edition of the *Compendio*, Fernando Rubio Álvarez used two codices: Ms. 66 of the Biblioteca Provincial de Toledo and Ms. 15 of the Biblioteca de Menéndez y Pelayo in Santander. It is the Toledo Ms. which Francisco Méndez (1725-1803) mentions and locates in the "villa de Arenas en la librería

---

[18] José Simón Díaz, *Impresos del XVI: Religión* (Madrid, 1964), p. 13. Simón Díaz seems to be relying on Bartolomé José Gallardo's *Ensayo de una bibiloteca española de libros raros y curiosos*, 4 vols. (Madrid, 1866), I, 1227, N. 1267. Gallardo says that the work was dedicated to Isabel, the wife of Carlos V, which clearly marks it as unrelated to Fray Martín.

del Serenísimo Señor Infante Don Luis de Borbón...." [19] Gallardo describes the same Ms., printing the Table of Contents and assorted passages. [20] Rubio Álvarez disagrees with Gallardo and Méndez that this might be an autograph manuscript, basing his opinion on the fact that: "la letra es de un copista profesional, y el rasgueo en dibujos de las letras de las líneas primeras y últimas de cada plana lo confirman." He also finds a number of easily recognizable errors that the author would have corrected before presenting the work to an eminent personage. [21] The Santander Ms. is incomplete, lacking the dedication, and, although the pages are numbered consecutively, there are several lacunae. There is no evidence to identify this Ms. of the *Compendio* as the one that appears in the "*Inventario* de libros que fueron entregados para su custodio a los diputados del Monasterio de San Lorenzo el Real por Hernando Bribiesca, guarda-joyas de Su Majestad, el 30 de Abril de 1576." [22] This volume, is assumed to have been destroyed in the fire of 1671 at the Escorial. There is also no explanation beyond the speculations of Enrique Flórez for the absence of the *Compendio* from the list made by Ambrosio de Morales in his *Viage*. There is, however, no problem of attribution in connection with this work and, as has been seen, Fray Martín makes several personal references in the *Compendio*.

7. *De mística et Vera Theología* is listed by Santiago Vela but by no one else. The reference depends on an edition of *Canonis misse interpretatio* published in 1499, in which Méndez (1725-1803) sees the participation of two authors. The first, writing in 1412, is identified as "maestro Pedro, maestro en artes y teología (sin decir la patria);" the second, "el adicionador principal" wrote in Salamanca. [23] It is the second author who quotes "el célebre Fray Martín de Córdoba del mismo instituto" and who mentions a book by Fray Martín entitled *De Mística et vera Theología*. Obviously the absence of any other reference to this work does not preclude the possibility of its future discovery. The

---

[19] *Compendio*, pp. xlvii-xlix.
[20] Gallardo, *Ensayo de una biblioteca*, II, 569 .
[21] *Compendio*, p. lxix.
[22] *Compendio*, pp. l-li.
[23] Méndez, *Tipografía española*, p. 123.

probability of its existence seems to be even greater than *Logica & Philosophia,* since the Salamanca "adicionador" of the *Canonis misse interpretatio* refers to it by name in 1499, barely twenty three years after the death of Fray Martín.

8. *Libro de diversas historias* is quoted in the *Nobiliario* of Hernán Mexía: "Maestro Martjn de Córdoua enel libro llamado de diuersas istorias dize que marqués en latín dize marchió...."[24] The quotation sounds authentic if one judges from the various bits of etymological information that Fray Martín scatters through the *Jardín de nobles donzellas.* Curiously enough, Nicolás Antonio, refers to this quotation but does not include the title in his brief biography of Fray Martín. He mentions the *Libro* in a section devoted to 15th-century writers of uncertain date: "Martinus de Corduba, magistri ornatus titulo, scripsit librum Diversarum historiarum quem laudat Ferdinandus Mexia in suo *Nobiliario* lib. I, cap. 76."[25] In the Vatican Ms. St. Bar B B of the *Nobiliario,* I can find no other mention of Fray Martín. Is "quem laudat" too strong an expression to describe the brief mention cited above? Another question to be answered is the exclusion of the *Libro de diversas historias* from Nicolás Antonio's principal list of Fray Martín's works and its inclusion in a separate section. One possible explanation might simply be that Nicolás Antonio was more certain of the identity of the works in the principal list. His allusion to the *Libro* in a separate section might be his way of expressing scholarly caution. If the reference is indeed to our Fray Martín, this would be the earliest reference to him as a literary figure, since the *Nobiliario* is best known in the 1492 edition of Sevilla. The work is thought to have been written between 1477 and 1485. The title, *Libro de diversas historias* might suggest that the book was a compilation of *exempla.* In spite of what might be considered a show of doubt on the part of Nicolás Antonio as to the identity of the author of the *Libro,* the date of the *Nobiliario,* the title "Maestro Martjn de Córdoba," and the familiar ring of the explanation "dize que

---

[24] Hernán Mexía, *Libro intitulado nobiliario perfecta/mente copylado y ordenado por el/ on/rrado cauallero Ferranto Mexía veynte quatro de Jahen &c.,* Biblioteca apostólica vaticana. St. Bar B B, IV 32, Cap. lxxvj.

[25] Nicolás Antonio, II, 272.

marqués en latín dize marchió" are fairly convincing evidence that Hernán Mexía was referring to our Fray Martín.

9. *Tratado de la predestinación* is not mentioned by Santiago Vela in his *Ensayo de una biblioteca...* although he does discuss this work in "Notas de interés," an article published after Fulgencio Riesco Bravo printed an unedited version of the *Tratado* in the *Basílica Teresiana* in 1917. In his 1923 article in *Archivos históricos,* Santiago Vela gives the title as *Tractado de la Predestinación enel que se desuanecen los errores de muchos que por inorancia pecan e viuen mal por no entender lo que significa la diuinal predestinación.* [26] This work is not mentioned in any of the contemporary sources. Aníbal Sánchez Fraile, the editor of an excellent modern edition printed in 1956, bases his attribution of the *Tratado* to Fray Martín on the author's identification of himself as "el muy deuoto padre Fray Martín, de la Orden Agustina de Valladolid, Dotor en Artes, Maestro en Santa Theología." [27] Sánchez Fraile identifies the writing of the manuscript as late fifteenth or early sixteenth century and sees textual similarities between the *Tratado,* the *Jardín* and the *Compendio.* [28] These textual parallels are not solely stylistic, but include doctrinal similarities as well, and, perhaps most importantly, the manner of reasoning from "tesis-antitesis de la protasis para concluir en la apódosis." [29] Even without contemporary references, the modern attribution seems justified. We know that Fray Martín was in the convent at Valladolid from 1470 to 1476, although there is some doubt whether he went there in 1454 (which is Sánchez Fraile's opinion). The *Tratado* can thus be dated between 1470 and 1476 in Valladolid.

10. The *Ars praedicandi* is not mentioned by contemporary sources, nor by Santiago Vela. It was found by Fernando Rubio Álvarez in Ms. 2 of the collection of theological Mss. in the Cathedral of Pamplona, a volume of 268 folios written by differents hands. [30] The *Ars praedicandi* is in 15th-century hand

---

[26] Santiago Vela, "Notas de interés," p. 57.
[27] *Tratado,* p. 3.
[28] *Tratado,* p. xvii.
[29] *Tratado,* pp. xx-xxiii.
[30] *Ars praedicandi,* pp. 329-48.

writing. Rubio Álvarez published an unannotated edition in *La Ciudad de Dios,* CLXXII (1959), 329-348, where it occupies eighteen pages. Ms. 2 contains a variety of other materials, mostly of a theological nature. The *explicit* reads: "Ars praedicandi edita a reuerendo in sacra pagina magistro Martino Cordubensi Deo eiusque Genetrici Marie eiusque gracias. Amen." [31] The *Ars praedicandi* is included in the hand-list of Harry Caplan among the "Tracts in manuscripts of which the *Initia* have not been obtained" [32] and in the extensive study of the genre by Th.-M. Charland. [33] It is also mentioned in the catalogue of manuscripts in the Cathedral of Pamplona.

Before presenting bibliographical material concerning the *Jardín de nobles donzellas,* which perforce must occupy considerably more space than that devoted to the other works, brief mention should be made of some other possible works of Fray Martín. Up to this point, his authorship has been established either by contemporary references to works which have not as yet been found in the libraries and archives of Spain, or by modern finds of manuscripts like the *Tratado* (found in 1917) and the *Ars praedicandi* (first mentioned by H. Caplan in 1934; two years later by Charland, and finally published in 1959 by Rubio Álvarez), in which the paleographic dating and the declaration of the author himself serve to identify Fray Martín. In this regard, it should be pointed out that, although numerous scholars made reference to the *Compendio,* it was not until 1916 that Santiago Vela discovered a Ms. in the Biblioteca Nacional. Fernando Rubio Álvarez did not undertake his edition until 1938 when he found a manuscript (presumably the same one which Santiago Vela had seen earlier in the Biblioteca Nacional) in the Biblioteca Provincial de Toledo. He did not publish the edition until 1958. The *Jardín,* on the other hand, enjoyed two early printings in 1500 and 1542.

Still undiscovered are the *Alabanza de la virginidad,* the *Hexameron,* the *Comentario sobre las epístolas de San Pablo,*

---

[31] *Ars praedicandi,* p. 348.

[32] Harry Caplan, *Medieval artes praedicandi: A Hand-List* (Ithaca, 1934), No. 192.

[33] Th.-M. Charland, *Artes Praedicandi: Contributions à l'Histoire de la Rhétorique au Moyen Age* (Ottawa-Paris, 1936), p. 70.

the *Apocalypsis,* the *Libro de diversas historias, De mística et vera Theología, Logica* & *Philosophia.* A brief glance through Pamphilo or Possevini indicates that a great many clerics wrote praises of virginity, commentaries on the first three books of Genesis, on St. Paul's Epistles and on the Apocalypse of John. In the same manner that diligent, modern scholars such as Fulgencio Riesco Bravo, Fernando Rubio Álvarez and Gregorio Santiago Vela have found other works of Fray Martín, it is to be hoped that these yet undiscovered treatises will one day be found in the mass of still unedited theological Mss. in Spain.

Still unresolved is the question of the reference by Diego de Montanches in 1517 to "Super multos libros Aristotelis." Even a cursory examination of the *Jardín* shows that Fray Martín was quite familiar with Aristotle's *Ethics, Politics, Rhetoric,* and *Generation of Animals.* All these works are to be found in Isabel's library and the temptation is to think that one of the references in the catalogue might be to an Aristotelian work of Fray Martín. There is no way of knowing what Montanches' expression *multa opera* really covered,[34] nor do we know the fate of the works pawned by the Augustinians of Valladolid to the Benedictines of the same city.

The *Libro de diversas historias* presents a different problem, since this appears to be the title of a secular work or of a collection of *exempla* intended to aid the clergy in the preparation of sermons. The only clue we have to its existence is the use Hernán Mexía made of the work to define the word 'marqués.' The perplexing fact that Nicolás Antonio put the *Libro* in a list of books about whose authors little is known, instead of including it in the bibliography of Fray Martín's other works only adds to our difficulties. The *Libro,* as a collection of *exempla* would certainly be consistent with Fray Martín's interest in teaching and in his preparation of an *Ars praedicandi.* In the history of

---

[34] Possevini gives the bibliography of a Martinus Corbenus, Tolosanus who lived in 1330. He ends the entry with "... scripsisset in Aristotelem" (p. 402). It may be coincidental but this may be an indication that any erudite author was credited with having written either translations or commentaries on Aristotle. In both cases, the bibliographers first referred to specific titles and then added the general information that the author had written about Aristotle.

collections of Spanish *exempla* such as the *Disciplina Clericalis, Sendebar, Calila e Dimna,* the *A.B.C de Sánchez Vercial;* the *Libro de diversas historias* would represent an important milestone, if it were indeed a collection of *exempla.*

Gallardo offers two enigmatic entries under the name of Martín de Córdoba. One, listed under "Fray Martín de Córdoba," is obviously a reference to our author. Gallardo credits him with *De próspera y adversa fortuna,* reproducing the Table of Contents and selected quotations from what is apparently the Toledo Ms. [85] The second entry without the designation of *Fray* reads: "Martín de Córdova No. 1898 *Córdoba castigada con piedades en el contagio que padeció los años de 49 y 50* (Málaga, 1651)."

Palau y Dulcet lists the *Jardín* as No. 61878 adding: "El único ejemplar conocido figuró en la Biblioteca de Cánovas del Castillo. Después pasó a manos de Vindel y luego a las de L. Rosenthal quien lo anunció por 15.000 marcos. Existe otra edición impresa en Medina del Campo. Ha figurado en varias Bibliotecas. 480 ptas., Murillo 1878." [86] It would seem that the *Córdoba castigada* (mentioned by Gallardo and by Palau y Dulcet) and two other works from the 17th century represent the more secular production of a later Martín de Córdoba and not delayed publications of our Fray Martín. It would be convenient to include the *Libro de diversas historias* in this grouping, but unfortunately, the reference in the *Nobiliario* (1477-85) makes this scholarly tidiness impossible.

There is one more area of confusion to which we have already alluded briefly. See n. 1 to *The Author and His Readership.* Admittedly, the name is not uncommon; surviving documents are sparse, and there is evidence that the combination Martín Alfonso was a common one (for instance, in the Alcaudete family of Córdoba). [87] There is no evidence that our Fray Martín belonged to this family and only the circumstance that Fray Martín and Fray Alfonso were both Augustinians who had taught at Salamanca and had studied in France warrants the subsequent

---

[85] Gallardo, II, 569-72.
[86] A. Palau y Dulcet, *Manual del librero hispanoamericano,* 7 vols. (Barcelona, 1951), IV, 101.
[87] Herrera, p. 54.

confusion of identity. One hypothesis can be offered concerning the scarcity of biographical and bibliographical material about Fray Martín. In a period of transition between manuscripts and printed books, it is reasonable to expect that some hand written materials would have been discarded in the flush of excitement over the advent of printing. Among these discarded manuscripts, there might have been a number of references to Fray Martín. Consider, for example, the hand written notations in the Venetian Ms. made by Diego de Montanches. Logically it can be assumed that much earlier works in manuscript form might have been retained, but copies of the literary production of a man living at the time of the establishment of local presses might have been discarded because of the assumption that these writings would soon be printed, as was the *Jardín* in 1500.

Another possible explanation for his relative obscurity is that Fray Martín had little or no impact on his own times. However, the attention paid him by early bibliographers would seem to belie this idea. He had undoubtedly achieved a certain fame within the Church and at the University of Salamanca, judging from his inclusion in the works of the Jesuits, Andreas Schott and Antonio Possevini, and, of course, in the Augustinian records of Jerónimo Román, Alonso de Orozco, P. Antolínez and Tomás de Herrera. It is to be hoped that more will be learned about him in still undiscovered documents and in possible future discoveries of his other works.

11. *Jardín de nobles donzellas:* There are many references to the *Jardín,* starting with Diego de Montanches, who says that Fray Martín "fecit etiam in vulgari aliquos tractatus: praecipue ad reginam nostram dominam Isabelam: ut est intitulatus Jardín de nobles donzellas." Alonso de Orozco states: "También hizo un libro que intituló a la reina doña Isabel. Este fue en romance; llámase *Vergel de nobles donçellas*." P. Manuel Vidal calls the work *Huerto de nobles donçellas* and Possevini calls it *Hortus nobilium Virginum Isabellae Reginae,* a designation that Andreas Schott repeats exactly. Nicolás Antonio expands: "*Vergel de nobles doncellas*. Ad Elisabetham tunc Infantem, Henrici IV, sororem, nondum, ut credimus, regno inauguratam. Editum fuit anno MDXLII in 4º." showing that Nicolás Antonio was aware

of the 1542 ed. and not of the 1500 by Juan de Burgos of Valladolid.

It is appropriate here to interject a few words about the title and its variants. Instead of regarding the image, *garden = collection*, as a *topos* in Western literature in the manner of Ernst Robert Curtius, it is perhaps more felicitous to include it in the category of universal metaphors, such as time and the river, described by Jorge Luis Borges.[38] Certainly in the *Roman de la Rose* of Jean de Meung and G. de Lorris, in the 13th century, the garden allegory is a real one; in other words, the metaphor is extended throughout the work. In *Los milagros de Nuestra Señora* of Gonzalo Berceo, the metaphor is extended somewhat until he flatly explains that "las quatro fuentes claras que del prado manavan / Los quatro evangelios esso significavan."[39] From then on the metaphor is discarded — a literary step, which may represent an intermediate point between a work like the *Roman de la Rose* or the *Razón de amor*, in which the symbolism is maintained throughout the whole work, and books like the *Jardín* in which all that seems to remain is the use of the image in the title. The garden as a Christian symbol had various meanings. It is well to keep in mind the observation of Alfred Jacob who points out: "Symbols, like words, have fluid and multiple meanings, and recognition of them is not an equivocation, rather all meanings are necessary if medieval thinking is not to remain an enigma."[40] The Virgin is called *hortus conclusus* (based on Song of Solomon 4:12: "My sister, my bride is a garden close-locked").[41] In addition to the Virgin as garden, Jacob describes the garden or *locus amoenus* as the symbol of the Christian Church.[42] It is apparent that the garden image was a flexible one, in frequent use.

---

[38] Jorge Luis Borges, "The Metaphor," a lecture delivered at the University of Pennsylvania, February, 16, 1968.
[39] Gonzalo de Berceo, *Milagros de Nuestra Señora*, ed. Antonio G. Solalinde (Madrid: Clásicos castellanos, 1964), p. 6.
[40] Alfred Jacob, "The *Razón de amor* as Christian Symbolism," *HR*, XX (1952), 282-301.
[41] See n. 21 to *Capítulo tercero, primera parte*.
[42] Jacob, p. 290.

The idea of structuring a sermon or a book around an image reflects what might be thought of as the world view of the earlier Middle Ages when as Arthur O. Lovejoy says, the universe was "essentially picturable; the perspectives which it presented, however great, were not wholly baffling to the imagination." [43] In like manner, sermons were constructed so that, according to Th.-M. Charland "le thème en est la racine, le prothème le tronc, les parties de la division principal les grosses branches...," [44] and the development of the sermon was considered to be the leaves. In the *Ars praedicandi*, Fray Martín uses the horticultural images of ants and bees, and cedars and grass. [45] As is the case with persisting literary devices, their freshness begins to disappear. As Huizinga observes about fifteenth-century writing: "The symbolizing habit maintained itself, adding ever new figures that were like petrified flowers." [46]

Unlike the sustained imagery used by the author of the *Razón de amor*, the *Vergel de oración, monte de contemplación* of the *beato* Alonso de Orozco describes the Bridegroom who "cada día desciende al vergel de su Iglesia a coger azucenas y flores que son los cristianos que en la flor de su juventud mueren." [47] However, the imagery is not sustained throughout the work, although Alonso de Orozco does refer to the garden elsewhere by quoting Scripture: "Erat ibi hortus, in quem introivit Jesus, et discipuli ejus...." [48] An example of a use of the garden image only in the title of a work is found in the anonymous 14th-century Portuguese didactic work, *Orto do Esposo*. The editor, Bertil Maler, observes: "O título *Orto do Esposo* revela a dupla intenção do autor. Sabe-se que a palavra *hortus* e sinónimos empregava-se muito amiúde como título de compilações de diferentes clases.... E Esposo indica claramente o cunho religioso e

---

[43] Arthur O. Lovejoy, *The Great Chain of Being* (New York, 1965), p. 101.
[44] Charland, p. 113.
[45] *Ars praedicandi*, p. 330.
[46] Jan Huizinga, *The Waning of the Middle Ages* (1949; rpt. New York: Doubleday Anchor, 1954), p. 207.
[47] Alonso de Orozco, *Vergel de Oración, monte de contemplación*, ed. Fr. Tomás (Salamanca, 1895), p. 31.
[48] Alonso de Orozco, p. 17.

místico que o autor qui dar a obra enteira." [49] The garden image in the *Orto* is limited to the title as it is in the *Jardín*, but here it is the use of the word "Esposo" which is the sign of the religious nature of the work. Garden had already become secularized so that it meant only compilation, as is the case in the *Jardín*, where it might be considered to be an atrophied form of what was once a living allegorical tradition. [50] Fray Martín unself-consciously does not feel any compulsion to maintain the metaphor any more than did Esteban de Nájera in his *Cancionero llamado vergel de amores* [51] or Pero Mexía in his *Silva de varia lección*, [52] and Sánchez de Arévalo in the *Vergel de príncipes*. The allegorical garden of the *Roman de la Rose* or the *Razón de amor*, also used for a didactic purpose, had thus evolved into the merely vestigial use of the word as a synonym for an anthology of a collection in later centuries.

As to the selection of the *Jardín* for so early a printed edition, there are two factors to be considered. The first is that in 1500 there would have been considerable interest in the youthful character formation of the Queen. The second factor has to do more with the content of the *Jardín* than with its dedication. Although Cervantes' discussion of the early printing industry dealt with a later period, his observations are applicable here. Don Quijote described the plight of a printer "que cuando se vea cargado de dos mil cuerpos de libros, vea tan molido su cuerpo, que se espante, y más si el libro es un poco avieso y no nada picante." [53] A discussion of the superiority of women, or at least of their superior qualities, directed to the Queen might be classified as *picante* and not in the least *avieso*. The language is not difficult; the images are often popular and derived from

---

[49] Bertil Maler, ed. *Orto do Esposo: Texto inédito do fim do século XIV ou começo do XV*, 3 vols. (Stockholm, 1964), III, 22.

[50] The persistence of the use of the garden image in the title of collections is apparent when one considers the *Child's Garden of Verses* by Robert Louis Stevenson written in the 19th century.

[51] Esteban de Nájera, *Cancionero llamado vergel de amores*, ed. Antonio Rodríguez Moñino (Valencia, 1950).

[52] Pero Mexía, *Silva de varia lección* (Madrid, 1933).

[53] Miguel de Cervantes, *El ingenioso hidalgo Don Quijote de la Mancha*, ed. A. Herrero Miguel, 2 vols (Barcelona: Editorial Ramón Sopena, 1961), II, 567-568.

folklore and, in large part, it deals with the male-female relationship in a relaxed human fashion, avoiding vituperation and overly abstruse moralizing.

The *Jardín de nobles donzellas* is mentioned as early as 1517 by Diego de Montanches, but the first bibliographical reference that is clearly identifiable as an allusion to a printed edition is that of Nicolás Antonio: "Editum fuit anno MDXLII. in 4º," apparently referring to the Medina del Campo ed. of Juan de Espinosa. Ambrosio de Morales does not mention finding a copy in Valladolid nor does Francisco Méndez mention the *Jardín* in his *Tipografía española*. The first mention of the whereabouts of the 1500 ed. is that it appeared in the library of Cánovas del Castillo (1828-97). [54] Where Cánovas obtained his copy is not known. Haebler, writing in 1917, described the surprise of bibliophiles upon finding, in a sale catalogue of Ludwig Rosenthal of Munich, a hitherto unknown early edition of the *Jardín de nobles donzellas*. He describes it as follows: "*Jardín de nobles donzellas* — Valladolid, por Juan de Burgos, 1500 11 de noviembre — 4º — 64 hjs. no fols. — sign.:A⁸-H⁸ — a línea tirada — 28 líneas en cada plana — letra gótica de dos tamaños, Portada xilográfica." Haebler points out that the copy is well preserved and has a date, and that the details of the printing are in keeping with the other productions of Juan de Burgos. He did not doubt the authenticity of the 1500 edition, although he was shocked at the price of 15,000 German marks and therefore assumed that it must have been purchased by someone in America. He confirmed that Pedro Vindel had been the previous owner and cited the *Bibliografía gráfica* of Pedro Vindel (Madrid, 1910) in which the "*título xilográfico*" was reproduced (pp. 69-70). [55] In response to my inquiry, Miss Martha M. de Narváez, Assistant Curator of the Hispanic Society, kindly informed me that: "Miss [C.L.] Penney's information is that the *Jardín de nobles donzellas* by Martín de Córdoba was received in this Library on 14 December 1908, from Ludwig Rosenthal, possibly from his *Cata-*

---

[54] Palau y Dulcet, p. 101.
[55] Conrado Haebler, *Bibliografía ibérica del siglo XV, 2.ª parte* (La Haya, 1917), p. 49.

*logue 105* (Munich, ca. 1907)." [56] It would appear that the Hispanic Society was the American buyer about whom Haebler speculated.

There are two known copies of the 1542 edition, the provenance of which I have not been able to learn. One is at the Biblioteca Nacional, Madrid, R 9.717 [57] and the other, listed in Proctor, [58] and in Henry Thomas, [59] is in the British Museum. See the Introduction *supra* for a description of the modern editions. Aníbal Sánchez Fraile, writing in 1956, refers to a proposed edition by P. Miguel de la Pinta Llorente of the 1542 edition (Biblioteca Nacional R 9.717) to be published under the auspices of the Consejo Superior de Investigaciones Científicas. [60] To date this edition has not appeared.

The purpose of the present edition is to supplement the editions of Felix García and Fernando Rubio Álvarez through

---

[56] Letter dated February, 7, 1970.

[57] Félix García refers to R 9. 717 as "el ejemplar único existente en la Biblioteca Nacional" (p. xxi).

[58] Félix García writes: "Hay una referencia suelta de que existe otro ejemplar del *Jardín de las nobles donçellas* en el British Museum" (p. xxxi, n. 52). It is listed in Robert Proctor, *An Index to the Early Printed Books in the British Museum from the Invention of Printing to the year 1500 with Notes of those in the Bodleian Library* (London, 1960), No. 9598. The present study has been prepared using microfilms of this copy and the 1500 ed. from the Hispanic Society of New York.

[59] Henry Thomas, *Short-Title Catalogue of Spanish and Spanish-American Books Printed before 1601 in the British Museum* (London, 1966), p. 57. The ed. is also listed in the *British Museum General Catalogue*, Vol. 153, col. 840. The listing reads: "Martín de Córdova. *Jardín de las nobles donzellas* G. L. A costa de Iuan de Espinosa (Medina del Campo, 1542. 4º) C. 63. g. 34." There is a curious reluctance on the part of P. García to verify the British Museum copy (it appears in three different catalogues of the British Museum collection). He also does not consider of any importance the unique character of the 1500 edition at the Hispanic Society. He quotes Santiago Vela's description of the 1500 ed.: "Un volumen en octavo mayor que consta de sesenta y cuatro páginas sin foliar, signaturas A-H de ocho hs. cada una, veintinueve líneas por columna, letra gótica, iniciales, filigrana la mano y estrella. Portada xilográfica dividida en cuatro líneas. A la vuelta de la portada comienza la tabla que termina con el colofón siguiente: ..." (*Jardín de nobles donzellas* [Madrid: Clásicos Agustinos, 1956], pp. 45-46, n. 49). P. García then reproduces the colophon. P. García may be relying on P. Rubio Álvarez' judgment that the two editions did not differ greatly (*Prosistas castellanos del siglo XV, BAE 171*, p. xxxii).

[60] *Tratado,* p. ix.

the use of the 1500 edition which to date has remained unedited and at the same time to explain the various sources upon which Fray Martín relied. A discussion of the work's language, metaphors, symbolism, and references, both classical and theological, will hopefully afford some insight into the nature of 15th-century religious didactic prose. Of particular interest is the breadth of Fray Martín's interests and his inclusion of so much folkloric material intermingled with scholarly allusions. An identification of the sources of as many of these references as is possible should result in a double benefit. On an individual level, a portrait of the furnishings of the mind of a 15th-century Augustinian scholar should emerge. On the other hand, assuming that we are correct in conjecturing that the *Jardín* (although addressed to a princess) was really a didactic work directed to the general reader, then a study of its sources should also provide a fairly good picture of contemporary 15th-century thought.

III

SOURCES AND ALLUSIONS

An examination of the sources upon which the author of a didactic work draws to support his arguments or clarify his thoughts should reveal the common background of the author and his audience — or what Américo Castro calls the *morada vital*.[1] Equally important is the application of the source material. Has the author drawn a new moral from the tale that differs from the usual interpretation? If he has, two levels of awareness on the part of the reader must be assumed: first, he was aware of the original or common application of the quotation or *exemplum* and second, he had sufficient sophistication to discard the original sense and to accept the variant application as a clear and apropriate one.[2] Without this assumption of a common fund of references, each allusion and quotation would have to be explained anew in every work. That theological and scholarly speculations found their way into the common mass of popular assumptions by way of sermons is apparent. J. Huizinga describes a reciprocal situation in which folk wisdom and

---

[1] Américo Castro, *La realidad histórica de España* (México, 1954), p. 7.

[2] Although there are many examples of these slightly skewed application of texts, one from the *Jardín* will suffice as an illustration. In *Capítulo tercio, segunda parte*, Fray Martín quotes Mark 13: 42-3 telling the story of the poor widow and her mite. The story in Mark is used to praise the unusual generosity of a poor person, recognizing that her charitable contribution is of greater value than the unthinking largesse of a wealthy person. Fray Martín takes the story and uses it to demonstrate woman's particular generosity, although in the original context her femininity was not important.

theology influence each other: "The mental habits and forms characteristic of the high speculation of the Middle Ages nearly all reappear in the domain of everyday life." [3] Thus Fray Martín uses St. Anselm's elevated discussion of the relationship of the Holy Spirit, The Father, and the Son to comment on Eve's having proceeded from Adam (p. 147). In addition, it is safe to say, that the virtues Fray Martín praises — modesty, chastity, wifely duties, clemency, justice and liberality — must have been the desirable norms of folk wisdom, as well as virtues advocated in erudite theological speculations. Fray Martín made use of these sources as well as scriptural, classical, legendary and folkloric sources.

In many cases we may assume popular familiarity with allusions and quotations which would seem foreign to the modern reader, although others have persisted to the present time: Midas is still the symbol of unreasoning greed; Penelope, the faithful wife; Samson, the giant betrayed by a woman; Nero, the cruel and capricious ruler. These are examples of antonomasia still common in popular usage. Others such as Sardanapalus and Mithridates have lost their currency as common images.

In addition to these antonomastic figures, there are quotations from authorities whose very names evoke a response on the part of the reader. Is is a fair assumption that the 15th-century reader would have had a preconceived notion of what to expect of Ovid, Horace, Aristotle, Seneca, Plato and Pythagoras. It would be a difficult task to prove that the general reader was familiar with each specific quotation but it seems reasonable to suppose that many of the classical authorities had a stereotyped identity in the popular mind. A brief glance at the list of philosophers in the *Bocados de oro*, for example, reveals that the 15th-century reader must have been accustomed to encountering references to the wisdom of the ancient philosophers without any initial explanatory introduction of the sage. In the *Bocados*, the list includes: Hippocrates, Pythagoras, Diogenes, Socrates, Plato, Aristotle and Ptolemy, [4] among those who are well known today. The anon-

---

[3] Huizinga, pp. 225-26.
[4] Hermann Knust, *Mittheilungen aus dem Eskurial* (Tübingen, 1879), pp. 685-86.

ymous author provides the credentials of those not as well known: "Longinem fue negro, e nasció en tierra d'Ethiopia, e apriso el saber en tierra de Sem, e finó en tierra de Philebeus." [5] *Medargis* is identified physically instead of intellectually: "Medargis fue de [baça] color, e havía grandes orejas e chicos ojos y delgado cuerpo, e era de mucho callar e dulce lengua e de vagarosa fable, e havía buenos dientes, e tenía todavía en su mano una vara, e havía en somo della una figura de la luna." [6] The point is that an authority who was identifiable in any manner carried some weight. Fray Martín identifies his authorities and seems to select relatively well known ones. He occasionally refers to the Philosopher, or to the Wise one, and just once he cites an unidentified "doctor." The first two epithets are usually reserved for Aristotle and for Solomon, although Beryl Smalley finds instances of Seneca's having been called the Philosopher. [7] William of Auvergne, Bishop of Paris, a relatively obscure authority, is cited once and Fray Martín goes to great lengths to explain the quotation. One conclusion is that the more casual references, without mention of the specific work, might have represented the familiar and the well known. But when Fray Martín took the trouble to mention the book and chapter of a specific work (as for example, certain chapters in *The City of God* or specific letters of St. Jerome) he was accomplishing two things: first, he was reassuring the reader of the authenticity of all the quotations and second, he was clarifying what he may have considered to be an obscure point. As in the *Bocados de oro*, an allusion to Aristotle in the company of lesser authorities, for example, may have served to establish the authority of less renowned philosophers and of the author himself. Also to be taken into account is the observation of E. R. Curtius: "Medieval reverence for the *auctores* went so far that every source was held to be good. The historical and critical sense were both lacking." [8] My intention here is not to ascribe this sort of naivete to Fray Martín,

---

[5] Knust, p. 324.
[6] Knust, p. 342.
[7] Beryl Smalley, *The Study of the Bible in the Middle Ages* (Oxford, 1952), p. xi.
[8] Curtius, p. 52.

but to describe a frame of mind which undoubtedly persisted to some extent in 15th-century Spain.

It stands to reason that the intent of an author of doctrinal works is to instruct, to persuade the reader or to reinforce existing ethical norms. He would, therefore select his allusions and references with an eye to what his readers could recognize or at least accept. The hermetic, baroque prose of a Gracián stems from a later period and undoubtedly was directed to a different audience. In the *Jardín*, the allusions — classical and otherwise — are intended as clarifications first and as adornments second. The 15th-century author Mosén Diego de Valera, in contrast to Fray Martín whose assumption it was that his readers would not be puzzled by his literary allusions, felt it necessary to supply explanatory material in the form of footnotes to his *Tratado en defensa de virtuossas mugeres,* even to the extent of identifying Biblical heroines. [9]

In a discussion of the sources and allusions in the *Jardín de nobles donzellas,* it will be convenient to divide them into biblical, classical and patristic references, and allusions to folk wisdom. In the case of the Bible, the Wisdom books (Ecclesiastes, Ecclesiasticus, Proverbs) and the Apostles are the most frequent sources. Among the ancient writers, Aristotle prevails, although Seneca is quoted frequently as well. Among the Church Fathers, St. Augustin and St. Jerome are the most often cited. As will be seen, an exact designation of the source of folkloric material is often impossible.

One might characterize the Bible as Fray Martín's primary source. He uses Biblical matter on the two levels described by Paul Beichner: the *sensus litteralis* and the *sensus spiritualis*. [10] In the first category are the heroines, such as Judith, Esther, and victims such as Samson, David, and Solomon whose lives serve as examples to the reader. In the same sense are such originators of the arts as Noema, Jubal and Tubal Cain. In the New

---

[9] Mosén Diego de Valera, *Tratado en defensa de virtuossas mugeres* in *Epístolas y otros tratados enbiadas en diversos tiempos e a diversas personas,* ed. José Antonio de Balenchana (Madrid: Sociedad de Bibliófilos Españoles, 1878), pp. 143-66.

[10] Paul F. Beichner, "The Allegorical Interpretation of Medieval Literature," *PMLA,* 82 (1967), pp. 33-38.

Testament, Mary Magdalene and the Virgin also serve as exemplary figures as does the widow and her mite. In the spiritual sense, Fray Martín allegorizes Creation, and the creation of Eve; he often compares Adam and the second Adam, Jesus Christ, relying on Corinthians 15:45-47. He also makes use of the parable of the sower, the fish and the loaves and the five foolish virgins, applying their moral lessons to the topic at hand. Not only was the source extremely familiar to his readers, it is apparent that Fray Martín's application of the material was equally familiar. For example, the 15th-century reader would not only know the parable of the sower, he would recognize its application to a description of the three grades of chastity. [11] This recognition of the familiar is comforting to the reader and even flattering in the sense that he shares the wisdom of the scholarly priest.

The Wisdom literature is used in the same way by Fray Martín as are quotations from Aristotle, Seneca, Cicero or any other author. These quotations serve either as texts upon which he elaborates or as corroborative statements to support an argument based on some other text or idea. It is difficult, at times, for the modern reader to accept the seemingly inappropriate applications of specific texts. This inability on our part does not establish Fray Martín's faulty understanding of Scripture. Beryl Smalley notes that even a Latin concordance to the Vulgate might prove an inadequate tool for the translator of a medieval Latin text, because the author "may be alluding to a patristic or scholastic comment on the verses he is quoting, as clear to the author and his reader as it is unintelligible to the translator." [12] Once again, the modern scholar encounters the lack of common references, assuredly shared by the author and his reader. An example of this confusion is the perplexing citation from Ecclesiasticus: "Mejor es la maldad del varón, que el bien hecho de la mujer." [13] Fray Martín cites Proverbs: "No des vino ala muger...." Modern Biblical scholarship suggests a very different reading for the passage. [14] Both of

---

[11] See n. 1 to *Capítulo vij, tercera parte*.
[12] Smalley, p. xi.
[13] See p. 282 and n. 15 to *Capítulo ix, tercera parte*.
[14] See p. 277 and n. 10 to *Capítulo viij, tercera parte* for a discussion of Proverbs 31: 3-5.

these texts had already found their way into the misogynistic tradition, achieving the requisite familiarity in the mind of the reader. There was no need to re-examine the source to seek a consistent meaning with the rest of the Biblical passage; the citations were established anti-feminist aphorisms.

Certain formulaic catalogues appear in the *Jardín:* the list of heroic women in the Bible or the great men brought low by the treachery of a woman or by the sin of lust. Huizinga offers the following explanation of the origin of these and other catalogues: "If it is desirable to make someone pardon an offence, all the Biblical cases of pardon are enumerated to him." [15] In this fashion, the Bible served Fray Martín and his contemporaries as an ethical encyclopedia from which the reinforcements of any argument could be drawn. The emphasis is usually not on the authority of the Bible in this exemplary usage, except in those few instances where Fray Martín cites Moses as the author of the Pentateuch or when Fray Martín recounts events from the Gospels, citing the Apostles.

The Church Fathers' writings are relied on to furnish commentary and doctrine but they are also employed as encyclopedias. A clear example of this in the *Jardín* is Fray Martín's evident use of St. Augustin's *City of God* as a source of the contents of Varro's *Antiquities* [16] and his apparent reliance on St. Jerome and St. Ambrose for his stories of noble widows of antiquity. [17] St. Isidore's *Etymologies* is drawn upon not only as an etymological dictionary but also as a source of assorted in-

---

[15] Huizinga, p. 227.

[16] See nn. 3, 12 to *Capítulo primero, tercera parte.*

[17] See *Capítulo quinto, tercera parte* for the traditional tales about noble widows from St. Jerome and St. Ambrose. The bulk of the material about widows in St. Jerome can be found in the letters to Furia, Salvina, Ageruchia, and in Bk. I of *Against Jovinianus* in *Principal Works of St. Jerome,* trans. W. H. Fremantle with G. Lewis and W. G. Martley in *A Select Library of Nicene and Post Nicene Fathers of the Christian Church* 2nd Series (New York, 1893), pp. 102-9, 163-68, 230-38, 358-386. St. Ambrose's *Concerning Widows* appears in *Some of the Principal Works of St. Ambrose,* trans. H. de Romestin, E. de Romestin in *A Select Library of Nicene and Post Nicene Fathers of the Christian Church,* 2nd Series (1955 rpt.: Wm. B. Eerdmans Publishing Company, Grand Rapids, Michigan, 1893), pp. 391-407.

formation on the natural sciences, [18] although in some instances, the source of such information may have been an early bestiary such as the *Physiologus*.

As to commentary, one finds in the *Jardín* several passages in which Fray Martín summarizes St. Augustin's development of an idea, even to the extent of using the same examples to prove the point. [19] He draws heavily on the whole body of St. Augustin's works, not limiting himself to the major works. Even beyond the specific quotations, Augustinian influence is strong. At times, Fray Martín closely echoes an observation of St. Augustin's without indicating his source. This should not be considered to be a case of scholarly inattention, rather it is an indication of how deeply imbued Fray Martín was, as a result of his reading, with the viewpoint and ideas of St. Augustin. He was, after all, a member of the Augustinian Order. To a lesser extent, the same phenomenon occurs with St. Jerome. Although St. Isidore is not mentioned in the *Jardín*, there are two clear instances of this kind of repetition — in the etymology of *mulier* and, more strikingly in the enunciation of the names of Solomon. [20]

Various other patristic sources are specifically identified by Fray Martín: St. Anselm is referred to for the explanation of the

---

[18] Fray Martín's description of *papaver* might well have come from St. Isidore (*Etimologías*, trans. Luis Cortés y Góngora [Madrid: Biblioteca de Autores Cristianos, 1951], p. 51), as might the comments about the unicorn (pp. 292-93). Fray Martín uses St. Isidore's etymology of *mulier* (p. 153 of the *Jardín*). It is found in Bk. XI, p. 277 of the *Etimologías*. Obviously, it is impossible to say with certainty that the above information was derived directly from St. Isidore. It may have been a normal part of the information known to every well educated cleric of the 15th century. Vergil mentions the sedative properties of poppy seeds in the *Aeneid* IV, 486. See n. 20 *infra*.

[19] A most striking example of an instance where Fray Martín followed St. Augustin's reasoning, making use of the same examples is the description of the carnality of the Jews and their consequent unworthiness to hear about the angels from Moses in *Capítulo v, primera parte* of the *Jardín*, echoing the *City of God*, 3 vols. trans. Grace Monaghan and Gerald Walsh, in *Fathers of the Church* (New York, 1952), II, p. 200 (Bk. XI, Ch. ix).

[20] See p. 281 of the *Jardín*, n. 13 to *Capítulo ix, tercera parte*. A. G. Solalinde mentions a similar reticence on the part of Alfonso el Sabio: "... incluye abundantes noticias de este género, tomándolas de San Isidoro, a quien no se nombra" (Alfonso el Sabio, *General Estoria, Primera parte*, ed. Antonio G. Solalinde [Madrid, 1930], p. xvi).

relationship of the Father, The Son, and the Holy Spirit; [21] one of St. Gregory's dialogues is used in the condemnation of blasphemy. [22] Limited use is made of St. Bernard's commentary on the Song of Songs. [23] St. Ambrose is not only the source of anecdotal material in praise of virginity and chaste widowhood, but is used doctrinally as well. Fray Martín also quotes the *Chronicon* of St. Methodius which is no longer extant, so that no judgment can be made about his use of the material. [24] He may have been referring to some unidentified work of the pseudo-Methodius.

In the same way that we recognized the penetration of Augustinian ideas, not identified by Fray Martín, we must also proceed with caution when asserting that there is no apparent use of other Church Fathers, such as St. Thomas of Aquinas, St. Justin, St. Basil and St. Eusebius. There is no way of knowing to what extent Fray Martín might have been influenced by his reading of these patristic sources or to what extent these authors influenced the collective consciousness. What can be stated confidently is that his major dependence was upon St. Augustin, St. Jerome and St. Ambrose.

As an introduction to the topic of classical sources, some thought might be given to the observation of R. B. Tate who quotes Sánchez de Arévalo — who also wrote in the 15th-century — to the effect that "he intends to use non-Spanish sources (e.g. classical) lest readers doubt the accuracy of his statements." Tate goes on to note that Sánchez de Arévalo reworked the *Libellus* in order to quote Strabo rather than St. Justin. [25] The implication is that the 15th-century historian recognized a popular disinclination to be satisfied with the authority of the Fathers of the Church and a renewed interest in classical authority. In contrast

---

[21] See St. Anselm, *De Processione Spiritus Sancti* in *Opera Omnia*, 2 vols. ed. Franciscus Salesius Schmitt (Edinburgh, 1946), p. 203 and *Capítulo primero, primera parte*, n. 22.

[22] See p. 219 of the *Jardín* and n. 13 to *Capítulo vi, segunda parte*.

[23] See p. 281 of the *Jardín* and n. 14 to *Capítulo ix, tercera parte*.

[24] See n. 17 to *Capítulo sesto, primera parte* for a discussion of the problems that arise when trying to isolate a quotation from a work which is presumably lost. Apparently Alfonso el Sabio had access to Methodious only at second hand according to A. G. Solalinde (pp. xvi-xvii and n. 1).

[25] R. B. Tate, p. 114.

to this presumed desire on the part of Sánchez de Arévalo to derive greater authority from classical sources rather than patristic ones, Fray Martín makes no such statement. In fact, many of his classical references are indirect and stem from patristic sources, as was the case of the quotations from Varro which he takes from St. Augustin. Other classical references may have been commonplaces (or may be derived from secondary sources). Such is the case of a quotation from Terence: "When Ceres fails and Liber, Venus droops" which St. Jerome quotes (Letter LIV, p. 105). Although Fray Martín says he is quoting Terence (see p. 277), it is not possible to say with any certainty that he was not deriving the quotation second-hand from St. Jerome or that the quotations had not become a commonplace in sermons dealing with the sin of gluttony and its relationship to lust. The other Terentian quotation from the *Lady of Andros* is more difficult to pinpoint (see p. 211) since it is simply a recommendation of moderation. St. Augustin does cite the same play in the *City of God*, a work which is replete with classical references from specific authors and Roman mythology and legends. Arnold G. Reichenberger points out that Terence was not widely known as a dramatist but was commonly quoted as a philosopher.[26] Fray Martín shows an awareness of the plays referring to "la primera comedia" (p. 211). St. Jerome often quotes classical authors, as we have noted, and also draws upon Roman tales of virtue and vice for his examples, many of which were drawn upon by Fray Martín. A third possible source for these classical *exempla* are such contemporary works as D. Álvaro de Luna's *Libro de las claras mugeres* or Mosén Diego de Valera's *Tratado en defensa de virtuossas mugeres*. Here too, the possibility exists that these materials had become a part of the common fund of lore concerning the Romans and Greeks and an exact source may not be easily identifiable.

In the case of Valerius Maximus, there is no doubt that Fray Martín had access to his *Memorable Deeds*, since, at times, the *Jardín* offers an exact translation of Valerius' Latin.[27] Seneca

---

[26] Arnold G. Reichenberger, "Boscan and the Classics," *Comparative Literature*, III (Spring, 1951), 97-118.

[27] An example of such a direct translation is the story of Mithridates and Hypsicratea (p. 135), from Valerius Maximus, *Factorum et Dictorum*

presents a mixed problem. The quotation from Hercules Furens is extensive and literal,[28] yet many of the maxims attributed to Seneca by Fray Martín might stem from one of the various collections of aphorisms common in the Middle Ages which were attributed to Seneca. Fernando Rubio Álvarez calls Fray Martín a "senequista" on two counts, citing a similarity between the two in respect to the manner in which they confronted similar problems in their respective lives (a conclusion which differs from my own about Fray Martín's life), and, of course, a thorough knowledge of Seneca's work and an adherence to the principles of its moral doctrine.[29] Rubio Álvarez recognizes one instance in the *Compendio* where Fray Martín relied on St. Augustin's erroneous observation and not on Seneca: "Los estóicos creen que la salud del alma consiste en no sentir dolor, (*Sermones*, 348,3)."[30] How many more of Fray Martín's quotations from Seneca are also second hand is not easily determined by virtue of their not having been incorrect. The Senecan point of view found in the collections of aphorisms reflects the sentiments in Seneca's letters to Lucilius. Quite probably Fray Martín was familiar with Seneca, but he may have relied either on memory or on aphoristic hand-books when quoting him. To add to the confusion, in one instance Fray Martín cites Livy, but seems to be continuing the thread of a passage from Seneca.[31] On another occasion, Fray Martín quotes Seneca about women, vanity, cosmetics and inner beauty, when the reference seems to be Ovidian.[32] The conclusion is that Seneca had been awarded the generalized status of a popular sage, with a recognizable point of view. It is therefore

---

*Memorabilium Libri Novem cum Iulii Paridis et Ianvarii Nepotiani Epitomis*, ed. Carolus Kempf (Leipzig, 1888), pp. 199-200.

[28] See p. 216 of the *Jardín* and n. 9 to *Capítulo quinto, segunda parte*.

[29] Fernando Rubio Álvarez, "Presencia de Séneca en los prosistas agustinos del siglo XV," *La Ciudad de Dios*, CLXXX (1967), 552-569.

[30] Fernando Rubio Álvarez, "Presencia de Seneca," p. 563. Karl Alfred Blüher points out that Fray Martín does not rely on Seneca for his definition of Divine Providence in the *Compendio de la fortuna*, except indirectly through St. Agustin and Boethius (*Seneca in Spanien Untersuchungen zur Geschichte der Seneca-Rezeption in Spanien vom 13 bis 17 Jahrhundert* [München, 1969], p. 163). See also n. 6 to the *Prohemio*.

[31] See p. 202 of the *Jardín* and n. 9 to *Capítulo segundo, segunda parte* for the conjecture that Fray Martín is continuing to quote *De la clemencia*.

[32] See p. 279 of the *Jardín* and n. 4 to *Capítulo ix, tercera parte*.

reasonable to conclude that one would find a certain carelessness in quoting Seneca (see n. 6 to the *Prohemio*).

To some degree, Aristotle had achieved the same mythical status by the 15th century. The pseudo-Aristotle's advice to Alexander and the collections of aphorisms attributed to Aristotle in such works as *Bocados de oro* and the *Libro de los philósophos* are examples of the habit of attributing a wide variety of moral observations to Aristotle that did not necessarily come from his works. Clearly, he had achieved folk status in such tales as the *Lai d'Aristote,* which is reflected in his inclusion in the medieval catalogues of men betrayed by women ("femme chevaucha Aristote"). [33] In spite of this mythical status, Fray Martín relied directly on the *Politics, Rhetoric, Ethics* and the *Generation of Animals,* and several of the minor works. One might expect an awareness of Aristotelian works themselves in Spain as a result of the long coexistence with the Arab world. Certainly the Arab historian, Ibn Khaldûn (1332-1406) drew many of his ideas about political organization from Aristotle, albeit through the works of Avicenna. [34] It is not my assumption that Fray Martín read Greek; evidences of Latin and Spanish translations abound in the book lists of Queen Isabel and in the library of the Marqués de Santillana. Furthermore, the testimony of Diego de Montanches that Fray Martín had written many books about Aristotle must be taken into account. In the *Jardín,* he summarizes a passage from the *Politics* on the acquisition of wealth. [35] He relies heavily on Aristotle to define the relationship of the ruler and the ruled [36] and he draws frequently on the *Generation of Animals* for a

---

[33] See n. 18 to *Capítulo ij, primera parte* for this inclusion of Aristotle in the list of men betrayed by women.

[34] N. J. Dawood remarks that Ibn Khaldûn's ideas about human political organization stem from Avicenna's rendering of Aristotle's *Politics* (p. x). In fact, Ibn Khaldûn paraphrases the famous remark that "Man is 'political' by nature" in the first paragraph of his discussion of human organization (Ibn Khaldûn, *The Muqaddimah: An Introduction to History,* trans. Franz Rosenthal, ed. and abridged, N. J. Dawood [Princeton, New Jersey, 1967], p. 45).

[35] See pp. 222 of the *Jardín* and n. 3 to *Capítulo séptimo, segunda parte.*

[36] See the *Prohemio,* p. 138 and n. 13.

discussion of heredity and the generation of women. [37] There are only two instances where Fray Martín seems to err in his citation of Aristotle: the comment from the *Rhetorica ad Alexander*, which seems rather, to echo the *Poridat de las poridades* of the pseudo-Aristotle (p. 229) and the observation about woman's inconstancy (p. 250) which had become a commonplace in the misogynistic tradition. [38] Because of the importance of Aristotle in the intellectual life of the 15th century, it is sometimes difficult to ascertain the first-hand nature of some of Fray Martín's citations. The most striking examples of this difficulty arise from his use of the *Generation of Animals* and from *Problems*. The observations about natural phenomena, in connection with human reproduction, climate, heredity, and even speech may have long since passed into the general fund of information. It is true that Aristotle cites the authority of shepherds for some of his observations and that Fray Martín seems to be quoting him fairly directly, but the thought persists that these could be universal observations made by shepherds anywhere. [39] Once again, in our search for sources, it must be mentioned that what really matters is the establishment of a community of information between the author and his reader in the study of a didactic work. Just once Fray Martín attributes to another author (in this case, Valerius Maximus), a maxim that appears to have stemmed from Aristotle. [40] On the whole, his use of Aristotle was careful and this surely supports the idea that Fray Martín did indeed comment on some Aristotelian works in a lost book which may come to light in the future.

Fray Martín quotes Ovid only once directly (p. 286) to counsel discretion and the avoidance of the occasion of sin, using the image of great conflagrations from small embers, an obvious Christianization of Ovid. He may also have used the *Ovide*

---

[37] See pp. 184-86 of the *Jardín* and n. 1 to *Capítulo ix, primera parte*.

[38] See p. 229 of the *Jardín* and n. 23 *Capítulo octauo, segunda parte* for the suggestion that Fray Martín may be relying on the *Poridat de las poridades*. See p. 250 of the *Jardín* and n. 1 to *Capítulo tercio, tercera parte* for the comparison with a line from the *Aeneid*.

[39] See p. 187 and n. 1 to *Capítulo ix, primera parte*.

[40] See p. 156 of the *Jardín* and n. 26 to *Capítulo ij, primera parte*.

*moralisé* for the story of Arachne.[41] Horace is cited to the effect that marrying for money can only bring sorrow and that bad beginnings lead to bad ends (p. 281).[42] This identification is not absolutely clear and this may have been another instance of a vague attribution based solely upon a familiarity with Horatian attitudes. Plato is mentioned once in connection with the designation of kings as demi-gods but it is quite likely that this reference is derived from another source.[43]

The legendary material from the Greek and Roman periods is particularly hard to trace. In many instances, the origin is quite clear: anecdotes from Valerius Maximus, Quintus Curtius and the contemporary sources of D. Álvaro de Luna and Diego de Valera. In others, I suspect that the stories in question may have reached the status of folktales by the 15th century. One example is the reference to Penelope's weaving as a device to maintain her fidelity. Fray Martín does not refer to Homer; D. Álvaro de Luna credits Ovid's *Heroides* as his source.[44] Although the library of the Marqués de Santillana contained several *Iliads* and we are aware of Juan de Mena's translation, there are no contemporary allusions to the *Odyssey*. The story of Penelope is mentioned by Vergil in the *Aeneid*. Although Fray Martín would not have needed Enrique de Villena's translation, the existence of the translation and its presence in Isabel's library supports the idea that Vergil may have been the source of the tale. Nevertheless, we cannot say with any certainty that the story of Penelope was not so common that Fray Martín would not have needed a special source for it. St. Jerome and St. Augustin had also mentioned her and Alfonso el Sabio had told her story at a much earlier date.

---

[41] See p. 286 of the *Jardín* and n. 11 to *Capítulo x, tercera parte;* and p. 243 n. 8 to *Capítulo i, tercera parte*. Solalinde recommends a study of the *General Estoria* for evidence of which of the ancient writers were well known in the period before the Renaissance. He writes: "Ovidio es entre todos ellos, el más traducido y comentado; sus *Metamorfosis* son parangonadas con la Biblia, y como a la Biblia, se les busca el sentido oculto que puedan tener, ayudándose de glosadores medievales" (p. xiv).

[42] See p. 281 and n. 12 to *Capítulo ix, tercera parte*.

[43] See p. 211 of the *Jardín* and n. 5, *Capítulo sesto, segunda parte*.

[44] See p. 267 and n. 6 to *Capítulo vi, tercera parte*.

In the case of Dido as the symbol of noble, chaste widowhood, clearly, Fray Martín is not relying on Vergil. The version he tells is that of St. Jerome and of other medieval sources.[45] The story of how Athens was named, obviously a less familiar tale, is a direct quotation of Augustin's rendering of Varro.

The historical figures, Portia, Lucretia, Sardanapulus, Mithridates, Hasdrubal's wife, and Cornelia derive either from Valerius Maximus, St. Jerome, D. Álvaro de Luna or Diego de Valera. Portia appears in Plutarch as do Caesar Augustus, Mark Antony and Brutus. Fray Martín does not mention Plutarch at all, although Plutarch's works figure in the library of the Marqués de Santillana and therefore were available at the time. Judging from Fray Martín's sparseness of detail in relating these stories, it seems probable that they were common tales at the time. It is curious that, in these cases, there is none of the ambiguity of moralization that is at times found in the interpretation of the lessons based on Scriptural episodes: for example, the pro-feminist overtones of the widow and her mite. This fact is understandable if it is remembered that these classical tales probably circulated in the oral tradition, precisely because of their serviceability as exemplars of specific moral lessons. It was not a particularly fruitful activity to attempt the exegetical analysis of an old tale, nor would such a vain project have been proper since this activity was reserved for the examination of Scripture. In folk tradition and also in scholarly tradition, Penelope was the symbol of wifely fidelity; Cornelia, the proud mother who disdained wordly wealth; Sardanapalus, the effeminate, dissolute ruler. They and the other historical figures had lost their individuality and had become folk paradigms.

The identification of purely folkloric sources in the *Jardín* is difficult for several reasons. The first is that the culture of 15th century Spain represented an amalgam of Arabic, Jewish and Christian traditions. The second is that Fray Martín is known to have spent more than a few years in France, where he might have been exposed to those bits of folklore common to France. A third difficulty is inherent in the very nature of folklore and its trans-

---

[45] See p. 261 and n. 7 to *Capítulo v, tercera parte*.

mission. Unless a people have lived in isolation for a very long time to impede the borrowing and mixture of beliefs, there is no way of ascertaining the origin of a particular belief.

In the field of exegesis, there are striking parallels in Ginzberg's *Legends of the Jews* and in Fray Martín's version of some of the stories of Creation, an example of which is the tale of God's choice of Adam's rib for the creation of Eve, an obviously popular tale which lent itself to serious commentary. Even as late as the 19th century, we find the same playful explanation in an amusing song sung at weddings in the United States.[46] Sermons were doubtlessly more palatable when they contained this sort of popular exegesis, or folk references. It is probable that Fray Martín included folk wisdom and old saws quite intentionally in the *Jardín*. In this category fall his observation that women, being more modest than men, come to the surface after drowning, face down, and the statement, used to demonstrate the innate power and strength of men, that colostrum is more viscous if a pregnant woman is carrying a male child. These homely saws must have served as a bond between the scholarly priest and professor of moral theology and his reader. These last two bits of folk wisdom are not to be found in Stith Thompson's *Index* nor in the *Handwörterbuch des deutschen Aberglaubens* by E. Hoffman-Krayer and H. Bächtold-Staubli (10 vols. [Berlin-Leipzig,—Berlin, 1942]). They do appear in reverse form in Trachtenberg's *Jewish Magic and Superstition,* although no reasonable conjecture can be made about their source since Trachtenberg is of the opinion

---

[46] See p. 148 of the *Jardín*. Cf. Louis Ginzberg, *The Legends of the Jews*, 6 vols. (Philadelphia, 1909-1925), I, 66. Louis Réau traces this explanation to St. Thomas Aquinas and later to the *Speculum Humanae Salvationis* (*Iconographie de l'Art Chrétien*, Vol. II, *Iconographie de la Bible*, I, *Ancien Testament* [Paris, 1956], p. 73). Theodore Reik reports the following wedding song, performed in the United States on May 3, 1866. The song is said to have been a favorite of Abraham Lincoln's "This woman was not taken/ From Adam's feet we see,/ So he must not abuse her,/ The meaning seems to be./ This woman was not taken/ From Adam's head we know/ To show she must not rule him/ 'Tis evidently so./ This woman she was taken/ From under Adam's arm,/ So she must be protected/ From injury and harm." (*The Creation of Woman: A Psychoanalytic Inquiry into the Myth of Eve* [New York, 1960], p. 50). The obvious conclusion is that there was, indeed a common fund of European folklore and that this particular *jeu d'esprit* had had a universal appeal, as well as a long life.

that they are a part of the common European tradition.[47] Since the three peoples who lived together for so long on the Iberian peninsula shared so many aspects of Scripture and classical tradition, I have not found it possible to isolate strictly Arab references with the possible exception of Fray Martín's comment about women rulers.[48] He calls holders of the opinion that women should not rule "menos entendidos." Considering the deprecatory tone of Fray Martín's other reference to the Moors, this might be a reference to Moslem attitudes toward women.

To trace and identify specifically French traditions in the *Jardín* is a task beyond the scope of this study. However, it is worth mentioning the possible French origin of the story of "le savetier et le financier" in the *Compendio*, as an indication that Fray Martín's stays in Toulouse are, perhaps, reflected in his writings. He makes no direct reference to France in the *Jardín* and his only mention of an extra-peninsular event is the reference to Joanna I of Naples and her dissolute life.[49] Otherwise the *Jardín* is a most Spanish work in which the few recent historical allusions seem exclusively to pertain to problems of the nation and of the Trastámaras.

On the whole, the impression gained from a reading of the *Jardín* is of an author and of a reading public whose background was limited to those stimuli that had penetrated the Peninsula, with of course, the particular overlay of the Augustinian tradition, flavored with the thoughts of the Church Fathers, the lives of the saints and other ecclesiastical references. As a scholar, Fray Martín judiciously applies his erudition in the quotations from Aristotle, never citing him where the ideas would contravene popularly held notions. Even the seemingly daring approach to pro-feminism is actually a continuation of a literary trend which at the time had attained even greater prevalence and popularity

---

[47] See p. 190 and p. 194 in the *Jardín*. Cf. *Jewish Magic and Superstition* (New York, 1939), pp. 188-89. See also Samuel Clemens, *The Adventures of Huckleberry Finn* (New York: Harper Brothers, n.d.), p. 17 for the appearance of the superstition that drowned men float face down and women face up, in Mississippi River folklore in the 19th century.

[48] See p. 136 of the *Prohemio* and n. 3.

[49] See p. 285 and n. 9 to *Capítulo x, tercera parte*.

than anti-feminism. According to Jacob Ornstein,[50] there was a great preponderance of pro-feminist works in late medieval literature in Spain.

In answer to the basic questions posed by Stephen Nichols in his essay on criticism: "Does the work reflect the intellectual preoccupations of its time? Or, on the contrary, does it seek to escape time? Does its view of man complement or run counter to the views of the moment?",[51] the answer must be that in the *Jardín*, Fray Martín de Córdoba closely reflected the intellectual preoccupations of his time and did not oppose them in any way. This study has not uncovered any indication that might support the contention of Félix García that Fray Martín was the "Savonarola" of Spain.[52] He was not crying out against monstruous abuses of the ethical code, rather he was counseling adherence to already accepted norms, such as modesty, chastity, devotion, piety, clemency, and justice. However, it seems clear that by 1468 the general public was disenchanted with the uncertainty and divisions that had been so prevalent during the reigns of Juan II and Enrique IV, so that Fray Martín was simply expressing prevailing sentiments when he counseled Isabel to rule well with justice and clemency. The *Jardín* has been characterized by Fernando Rubio Álvarez as a political document whose specific purpose was to support Isabel's claim to the throne.[53] There is no doubt that Fray Martín supported Isabel's claim to the throne and opposed Enrique IV, but by 1468 her succession was assured. Enrique IV had already acknowledged Isabel's young brother as his heir at Cigales and Cabezón and it is unlikely that he would have been able to prevent Isabel's succession by his subsequent reversal of his disavowal of the claim of his daughter, Juana. The pro-feminist aspects of the *Jardín* might have held some special significance, if Enrique had had male issue; but at this point in

---

[50] Jacob Ornstein, "La misoginia y el profeminismo en la literatura castellana," *RFH*, III (1941), 218-32.
[51] Stephen G. Nichols, Jr., "Ethical Criticism and Medieval Literature: Le roman de Tristan," in *Medieval Secular Literature: Four Essays*, ed. William Matthews (Berkeley, 1965), p. 69.
[52] Félix García, ed. *Jardín de nobles donzellas* (Madrid, 1956), p. 29.
[53] Fernando Rubio Álvarez, ed. *Prosistas castellanos del siglo XV*, BAE 171 (Madrid, 1964), p. xxx.

history, the succession to the throne could only have been claimed legitimately by one of the two young princesses, so that the desirability of a female ruler was not a significant political argument. Either way, Castile would have had a female ruler. The conclusion is inescapable: the *Jardín* could not have had any measurable partisan political influence, nor was it running in any way counter to the views of the moment. Any allusions that seem to have the ring of timely references must have been well within the aforementioned fund of ideas and attitudes shared by the author and the reader.[54] It can be repeated, therefore, that Fray Martín prepared the *Jardín de nobles donzellas* with the intention of reflecting current opinions and awarenesses, making use of Biblical, classical, and legendary sources to reinforce these opinions. This is, perhaps, a definition of a truly successful didactic author who supports his readers in their prejudices and attitudes and, at the same time, guides them in the paths of righteousness as he sees them. Such a conclusion would hold at least a partial answer to one of the questions posed at the beginning of this study concerning the reason for the two early printings of this particular work.

---

[54] See Juan García de Castrogeriz, *Glosa castellana al "Regimiento de Príncipes de Egidio Romano,* ed. Juan Beneyto Pérez, 3 vols. (Madrid, 1947) II, 9-120 for sentiments similar to Fray Martín's expressed similarly even to the extent of using much of the same classical material. Although not printed until 1494 in Sevilla, the *Glosa* was dedicated to the *infante* Pedro before he succeded to the throne in 1350. See also n. 8 p. 100.

## IV

## STRUCTURE, LANGUAGE AND STYLE

In his *Ars praedicandi,* Fray Martín defines a sermon as follows: "Sermo est oratio informatiua ex ore predicatoris emissa, ut instruat fideles quid credere, quid agere, quid cauere, quid timere, quid sperare debeant." [1] He adds the warning from Seneca: "Sermo tuus non sit inanis, sed aut suadeat, aut moneat, aut consoletur, aut precipiat." [2] The *Jardín,* although not a sermon, follows these precepts. There is no doubt that he is instructing the faithful as to what to believe, what to do, what to beware of and fear, and what to hope for. What is more, he has certainly set out to avoid the dullness of which Seneca speaks, not so much through brilliance of language as through the wide range of his allusions and references. If creativity can be defined to some extent as the ability to make unexpected connections between seemingly unrelated ideas, then the *Jardín* is the product of a creative, fertile mind. Unfortunately the same praise cannot be extended to the language and style of the *Jardín* which often lacks variety, undoubtedly because of an overwhelming desire to achieve clarity and simplicity. This desire for clarity accounts for the rigid structure of the book, which, although satisfying in the sense that the reader knows what is coming next and what has come before, tends to impose a certain ponderous quality upon it as a whole. As has been stated in the section dealing with

---

[1] Fernando Rubio Álvarez, "*Ars praedicandi* de Fray Martín de Córdoba," *La Ciudad de Dios,* 172 (1959), p. 330.

[2] *Ars praedicandi,* p. 331.

the author himself, Fray Martín appears to have been at least as interested in reaching a general readership as in instructing the young princess Isabel. This might explain his emphasis on clarity at the expense of elegance.

The *Jardín* is clearly divided into three parts: who and what women are; how they should comport themselves; and lastly proofs from history which support these earlier observations. Within the text itself, Fray Martín uses the same tripartite division continually. He may introduce an idea with such a statement as: "La honra de Dios está en tres cosas: la primera en El solo adorar; la segunda en no blasfemar; la tercera enlas fiestas bien guardar" (p. 217). Women have three admirable qualities (pp. 193-207) and three less than admirable qualities (pp. 208-12); the noble lady must have three virtues in respect to her subjects (pp. 235-38). The noble lady must order life in such a way that she must control her heart (desire for worldly goods and honors), her mouth (immoderate speech and blasphemy) and her hands (evil or inappropriate actions) (pp. 231-234). This last triple admonition seems to be an echo of the advice given by "el Rey de Menton" to his son in *El Caballero Zifar*.[3] Cicero recommends four divisions but he includes the introduction in his scheme listing: "introduction ... while the second division, narrative, and the third, proof, are the parts that procure belief in what is said,"[4] adding an epilogue at the end of the speech. Curtius quotes Servius on the subject of the *Aeneid:* "In tres partes dividunt poetae carmen suum: proponunt, invocant, narrant."[5] This is not to say that the triple division was necessarily a conscious response to a manual of rhetoric; the pattern had long since become a common one. There is also no need to indulge in mystical speculations as to the significance of the number three in the Middle Ages; rather the pattern may be traced back to Scriptural style.

---

[3] *El libro del caballero Zifar,* ed. Charles Philip Wagner (Ann Arbor, Michigan, 1929), pp. 302-303.

[4] Cicero, *De partitione Oratoria* in *De Oratore,* trans. H. Rackham, 3 vols. (Cambridge, Massachusetts: Loeb Classical Library, 1960), II, 333.

[5] Curtius, p. 501.

In the first part of the *Jardín,* Fray Martín, drawing upon a number of patristic commentaries on Genesis, creates an elaborate allegorical description of woman, based on the manner of her creation, the place of her creation, and her relationship to man in regard to the purpose of her creation (another triple division). Although the modern reader may be tempted to assume a condescending attitude toward such arguments about the significance of the rib as the part of Adam's body from which Eve was formed, the value of allegory as a persuasive tool is undeniable. Italo Siciliano sees the use of allegory as a manifestation of an innate human tendency to "concevoir par la fantaisie, à croire par le mythe, à s'exprimer par la figure." [6] He refers to this medieval phenomenon as an epidemic. [7] Huizinga explains the relationship between symbolism and allegory, defining symbolism as "a sort of short-circuit of thought" and points out that "instead of looking for the relation between two things... thought makes a leap and discovers their relations, not in a connection of causes or effects, but in a connection of signification or finality." [8] He further distinguishes between symbolism which "expresses a mysterious connection between two ideas" and allegory which "gives a visible form to the conception of such a connection." [9] Certainly Fray Martín's allegory accomplished this leap of thought and undoubtedly amused his readers as well.

In the second part of the *Jardín,* allegory is abandoned and Fray Martín undertakes a description of the qualities, good and bad, of women. In this section, he uses similes, references to antiquity, and Biblical sources to assert that women are naturally modest, compassionate and "obsequiosa" ('devout'). It is in this section, with its graver tone, that Fray Martín repeatedly instructs Isabel directly on the subject of justice, liberality, affability, and chastity. He follows a consistent pattern in the second part. First he describes in general terms a particular attribute of women. If the quality is a good one, he observes that, although it is

---

[6] Italo Siciliano, *François Villon et les Thèmes Poétiques du Moyen Age* (Paris, 1933), p. 161.
[7] Siciliano, p. 162.
[8] Huizinga, p. 202.
[9] Huizinga, p. 205.

important for all women to be virtuous in this manner, it is particularly important for noble ladies, princesses and queens to be so. If the quality is a bad one, then all women should avoid this quality but queens, princesses and noble ladies should make a special effort to avoid falling into this error. He is not suggesting, however, that the queen must serve as an example to her subjects as much as he is recommending that she be better because of her increased responsibility.

In the beginning of the third part, Fray Martín recapitulates what he has written in the first two parts and introduces examples from history, classical tradition, and patristic sources to support his previous arguments. These examples constitute the kind of amplification described by Aristotle, even to the extent of being somewhat exaggerated.[10] Surely, Fray Martín is not recommending that Isabel imitate Judith's blood-thirsty act when he offers the Biblical heroine as an example of a strong woman; nor is he proposing that Isabel immolate herself, if widowed, rather than remarry in the style of the "judíos." Rather, in the tradition of the praises of famous women, such as those of Boccaccio and D. Álvaro de Luna, he is using these women as examples of strength or of chaste widowhood. The authority of Solomon and "doctores diversos" is brought in to uphold these observations. The final chapter might be considered an epilogue in the rhetorical sense, since Fray Martín reviews the qualities he has enunciated and also mentions some of the outstanding women of whom he has written before. However, this chapter is not set apart formally as one might expect an epilogue to be.

On the other hand, the *Prohemio* lives up to the rules for *exordia* as outlined by Aristotle.[11] The author offers his credentials, identifying himself as an intimate of the young princess and of her brother. He displays affected modesty by calling his book a "breue escriptura." He sets up imaginary opponents, the

---

[10] Aristotle, *The "Art" of Rhetoric*, trans. John Henry Freese (London: Loeb Classical Library, 1939), p. 264, note d. Freese comments: "Amplification is to be understood as the exaggeration of both great and small things. It is most suited to epideictic oratory, in which there is no doubt as to the facts; so that it is only necessary to accentuate their importance or non-importance."

[11] Aristotle, *The "Art" of Rhetoric*, pp. 427-437 (1414 b 24 — 1416 a 1).

"menos entendidos," who do not share his opinion that women are fit to rule, and, of course, he announces what he will endeavor to prove in the body of the *Jardín*.

The most conspicuous aspect of the structure of the *Jardín* is its unity, particularly when contrasted with other didactic prose of the same period. The *Arcipreste de Talavera*, for example, has three clearly defined sections which do not necessarily relate to each other. The *Doze trabajos de Hércoles* of Enrique de Villena relies on the linear structure of the *trabajos* themselves. The *Libro de las claras e virtuossas mugeres* is divided historically into the three divisions of women of the Bible, women of Greek and Roman history, and Christian martyrs. The unified structure of the *Jardín*, with its recapitulations represents an attempt at a more sophisticated rhetorical arrangement of the material which is certainly an aid to the reader, in the same way that the language and the style are designed to clarify the sequence of thought.

The peculiarities of language that are most obvious are clearly intended to add constant clarification, if not literary elegance. Fray Martín uses *donde* as a signal that he is going to give an explanatory example in the same way that he uses *unde* in the Latin of the *Ars praedicandi*. He also signals a forthcoming explanation with *es assaber* and *así que* or *quando pues. Ca* and *que* (for *porque*) also indicate that he will explain further. Lists of ideas in groups of three are frequently introduced: "De manera que toda criatura debe temer a Dios por tres cosas." This statement is followed by a three-part listing of the reasons. Several times, Fray Martín sets up a rhetorical question and follows it with *A esto digo*. A preponderance of the sentences are coordinate, harking back, perhaps, to Biblical style, particularly when Fray Martín is relating an anecdote. The more complex sentences usually include *aun que, quanto ... tanto, por quanto,* and *como si*. He does on occasion make use of the hypothetical *si* type of sentence. Other connectives are *así que, pues que, después que, desque,* and *aquí es*. He takes pains to explain neologisms such as *coenos*, adding a *que quiere dezir*, although it apparently was not necessary to explain most of the classical allusions.

The overall impression created by the language, style and structure of the *Jardín* is that of a work designed to be immediately comprehensible to a wide readership, prepared by a man with a strong sense of order. Although clarity of style has been emphasized, the intention is not to suggest that Fray Martín was condescending to his readers. An author who was assuming a superior attitude toward his readers would doubtlessly have limited the number of classical allusions in his book and would have included more explanations of his references.

His readership unquestionably shared a wealth of common references with the author. Strangely enough, one of the stories that Fray Martín felt called upon to expand in detail is that of Midas which today would not have needed expansion. The inclusion of the details of the Midas story may be viewed as an indication that his readers were not familiar with the tale. His explanation is not a sign of condescension as much as it is a sign of the particular status of the tale. Another bit of evidence that Fray Martín and his readers shared common references is the fact that while Fray Martín might have legitimately made use of Aristotle's advice about the use of fables: "Fables are suitable for public speaking, and they have this advantage that, while it is difficult to find similar things that have really happened in the past, it is easier to invent fables," [12] our author did not choose to invent his own fables to illustrate his ideas. The absence of fables in the *Jardín* gives us an idea of the breadth of experience of his readers, or of, at least, his confidence in their education. We may have stumbled upon another answer here to one of the questions proposed earlier, as to why this book had two early printings in 1500 and in 1542. It may well be that the clarity of style coupled with the richness of allusions made the *Jardín* a book that was at once easy to read and at the same time sufficiently stimulating to recommend it to the reading public of the 16th century.

---

[12] Aristotle, *The "Art" of Rhetoric*, p. 277 (1394 a 5-7).

V

THE INTER-RELATIONSHIP OF "ADVICE TO PRINCES"
AND THE FEMINISM/ANTI-FEMINISM CONTROVERSY IN
THE *JARDÍN DE NOBLES DONZELLAS*

The *Jardín de nobles donzellas* is frequently alluded to in lists of pro-feminist works of the 15th century. María del Pilar Oñate devotes several pages to Fray Martín's treatise in *El feminismo en la literatura española;* Jacob Ornstein mentions it along with the lost *Alabanza de la virginidad* and Barbara Matulka also cites it in her monograph on the *Repetición de amores*.[1] Before the 15th century, many peninsular didactic works, translated from Arab sources included anti-feminist elements of two types — jocular tales and bitter invective. The part of the *Disciplina Clericalis* by Petrus Alphonsi (born Moisés Sefardí in Aragón, 1062) that most fascinates the young man is the series of *exempla*

---

[1] Taking Jacob Ornstein's chapter on the feminist debate in his edition of Luis de Lucena's *Repetición de amores* ([Chapel Hill, 1954], pp. 12-32) as a good summary, it is obvious that pro-feminist works predominated in the 15th century. Ornstein denies the Hispanic nature of works translated from oriental sources such as the *Libro de los engaños y assayamientos de las mugeres* and the *Disciplina Clericalis* (p. 14). It is possible to quarrel with this assertion on two counts. First, Petrus Alphonsi was a Spaniard, writing in part, at least for Spanish clerics who would have been expected to read his work in Latin. Secondly, the translations of Arabic works turned them into national works, if only because these particular books were chosen for translation. The stories, compiled by Clemente Sánchez Vercial in *El libro de los ejemplos a.b.c.* (ed. John Esten Keller [Chapel Hill, 1961]) are not 15th-century inventions. Consider the tale of Rosinalda and Cacavo (p. 192) as an example of woman's treachery and lasciviousness, punished most horribly. The story had played a part in peninsular folklore for centuries.

dealing with the wickedness and astuteness of women. In the *Poridat de las poridades* (translated into Latin by Johannes Hispalensis during the period 1135-1153), Alexander is advised: "non queredes fornicio seguýr..." to preserve his health and to avoid putting himself in the power of women.² Socrates, in the *Libro de los buenos proverbios* (early 13th century), likens traffic with women to eating "carne mortezina;" Diogenes, upon seeing the burned corpse of a woman hanging from a tree remarks: "Oxalá llevasen todos los árboles tal fructo."³ From the same period, the *Bocados de oro* tells of a sage who, in response to his pupil's question as to whether their mothers were exempt from the general opprobrium, answers that all women are alike in their evil and like the prickly date palm do produce good fruits in spite of themselves.⁴ The *Libro de los engaños y assayamientos de las mugeres* (translated in 1253 by order of Fadrique, brother of Alfonso el Sabio) contains some marvelous examples of misogyny in a semi-serious vein. In the 15th century Sánchez Vercial compiled *exempla,* many of which continue the same jocular tradition, although one dealing with Rosinalda and el rey Cacavo is as bitter as the comments from the *Libro de los buenos proverbios.*⁵

The debate as a literary game appears to have started in the court of Juan II; Ornstein, for instance, reports that Juan II's first wife, María of Aragón issued an appeal for an answer to the *Arcipreste de Talavera,* a book, clearly in the semi-serious tradition. Ornstein does not see any of the pro-feminist works of the period, of which he lists sixteen, as a direct response; rather the *Maldezir de mugeres* of Pere Toroellas in 1440 is thought to have been the stimulus of a flood of defenses of women.⁶ At the end of the century Luis de Lucena wrote his *Repetición de*

---

² *Poridat de las poridades,* ed. Lloyd Kasten (Madrid, 1967), p. 66.
³ Knust, p. 24.
⁴ Knust, p. 192.
⁵ To recognize the two strains in anti-feminist literature, one need only contrast "el enxemplo del quarto privado o del bañador e de su muger" from *El libro de los engaños...* (ed. John Esten Keller [Chapel Hill, 1959], pp. 27-28) a humorous treatment of woman's lustful behavior with the story of Rosinalda.
⁶ Ornstein, p. 14.

*amores,* a counter-attack notable for its completeness. At about the same time, two novels, *Grisel y Mirabella* by Juan de Flores (1480) and Diego de San Pedro's *Cárcel de amor* (1492) appeared as the culmination of the pro-feminist argument. The prevailing tone of all the prose and poetry cited by Ornstein is a consciously literary one; the catalogues of famous women echo Boccaccio's *De claris mulieribus;* classical references abound. It would be rash to formulate any opinion about misogyny or pro-feminism as a national trait based on this body of literature.

The *Jardín de nobles donzellas* appears in the list, but it differs from such undiluted praises as that of Diego de Valera and D. Álvaro de Luna in that its primary purpose is not to defend and praise women. An analysis of the *Jardín* reveals that Fray Martín used pro-feminist material to fulfill his promise in the *Prohemio* that he would draw upon his knowledge of "las causas naturales & morales" and of history to prove that women are fit to rule. In the course of supporting his thesis, Fray Martín attributes to women moral superiority in a series of traits, all of which apply to the qualifications for governing well: e.g., women are naturally compassionate and will be especially well-equipped to show clemency to their subjects; women are naturally generous and therefore will be liberal rulers. In this sense, the *Jardín* may be considered to be a quasi-political document whose pro-feminism seems to be directed to the reader as a sort of affirmation of Isabel's claim to the throne and, in the tradition of advising princes, a commentary on the relationship of the ruler and the governed put in the framework of a purportedly personal document addressed to the sixteen year old princess (see *The Author*). Repeatedly throughout the *Jardín,* Fray Martín makes general observations about clemency, love of God, compassion, modesty, and chastity; and ends with the more specific remark that, if these virtues are important in ordinary women, then how much more important are they in the case of a woman destined to reign. In spite of the secondary nature of the theme of pro-feminism, the topic of misogyny must be examined in our study of the *Jardín,* if only to recognize the charges against women which Fray Martín chooses to refute. It should be made clear that Fray Martín's promise to explain why women are well suited to govern is not made and then discarded; he follows the plan he announces closely, describing the nature of women and their good qualities, warning of the pitfalls they must avoid and adducing examples of noble women to support his thesis.

Having observed the intertwining of the two principal themes: pro-feminism and "advice to princes," a third might now be mentioned in passing. There is a long history of letters and advice to maidens, outlined in a comprehensive and scholarly fashion by Alice Adèle Hentsch in her 1903 dissertation. Perhaps the best known examples of this genre are St. Jerome's letters to his disciples, Eustochium, Marcella and Blaesilla. Since the counsel offered is usually concerned with piety, chastity, temperance and good works, these advices can be considered to be a part of the pro-feminist tradition which also deals with the same virtues. In addition, since a large number of these works are addressed to princesses or noble ladies, they can be thought of as advice to the eminent. For this reason the *Jardín* will not be considered in the light of this tradition; rather an attempt will be made to see how the work fits into the two principal thematic categories showing at the same time their relationship.

Since it is my opinion that one must take Fray Martín at his word in regard to the purpose of the *Jardín,* the book must first be examined as a part of the literary tradition of advising princes and second as a pro-feminist work. Within the Judeo-Christian tradition, the practice of publicly reminding a ruler of his responsibilities can be traced back to two books of the Bible which were accepted quite early as canonical by the Catholic Church, although considered apochryphal by the Jews and the Protestants: The Wisdom of Solomon and Ecclesiasticus. These two books can be characterized as advices to princes in which the prince himself is not specified, although at the time of their composition the recipients of the advice might have been apparent. There is another type of political advice offered to a specific ruler and designed to resolve very real current questions which are easily identifiable. Such is the case with Cicero's *Philippics,* which was truly directed to Anthony, although it is equally clear that Cicero's intention was to sway the populace as well. What is common to these two examples is that, although they are addressed to a ruler, there is little doubt that the authors intended at the same time to influence a wider readership. An author who writes out of an ostensible concern for the welfare of a particular ruler can often make quite pointed criticisms with impunity while hiding behind his apparent desire to help the troubled monarch.

In Spanish literature the *Poridat de las poridades* is an example of another manner of advising a prince. Translated from the Arabic in the 12th century into Latin, the *Poridat* appeared in a Hebrew version by Judah al-Harizi at the beginning of the 13th century and in the same century was translated into Spanish. In the *Poridat* Alexander is given the secrets of good government by Aristotle. Could each of the translations have been intended to advise a contemporary ruler as the Arabic *Sirr al-asrār* must have been intended to advise a ruler whose identity we do not know? Similarly, Fray Martín's advice to Isabel about the need for justice and liberality could have been a criticism of the inequities of Enrique IV's reign. A third approach to the problem of advising rulers is perhaps best exemplified for Peninsular literature in *Os Lusíadas,* where Camões addresses his remarks to a ruler who in his remote majesty is neither aware of the poet nor even interested in his humbly offered advice (see n. 52 to *The Author*). Having established his own unimportance, Camões is then free to be quite harsh in his criticism of the government of Portugal. In fact, just as the *Jardín* is a pro-feminist work whose primary purpose is to offer political commentary, it might be thought that *Os Lusíadas* is a Renaissance epic whose celebration of the past glories of the Portuguese takes second place to a plea for a renewal of that glory.

Initially, Aristotle's *Politics, Ethics* and *Rhetoric* can be thought of as the root source of medieval political thought as reflected in "advices to princes." Much of this material was available through Arab sources and other secondary sources until according to Helen Sears: "William of Moerbeke made a fairly accurate Latin translation of the *Politics,* probably used by Thomas Aquinas in preparing his *De regimine principum,* and followed soon after by similar translations of other works...." [7] Born twenty years after Thomas Aquinas, Egidio Colonna (1247-1316), wrote a singularly influential *De regimine principum* (ca. 1284) upon which many subsequent authors relied, including Don Juan Manuel [8] and Pero López de Ayala, [9] both of whom cited him directly. Colonna's work was translated into French in 1296 and later into Spanish in 1345 by "frey Johan García de Castro Xeres," to instruct "el muy noble infante don Pedro, fijo primero heredero del muy alto e muy noble don Alfonso; rey de Castilla, de Toledo, de León, etc." [10] Castrogeriz' translation was printed in Sevilla in 1494. Fray Martín does not cite Egidio Colonna directly, referring back to Aristotle instead, although many of his sentiments are either echoes of Egidio de Colonna's or simply signs that these ideas had become commonplaces in discussions of good government. [11]

Other Spanish *regimientos de príncipes* participate in the Aristotelian tradition: the *Flores de filosofía,* written during the reign of Fernando el Santo; a chapter in *El libro del caballero Zifar* — "Castigos del rey de Mentón," which derives from the *Flores de filosofía; The Libro de los castigos e documentos* (attributed to Sancho IV) [12] and Don Juan Manuel's *Libro de los*

---

[7] Helen L. Sears, "The *Rimado de Palaçio* and the "De Regimine Principum" Tradition of the Middle Ages," *HR* XX (January, 1952), 1-27. See also Allan H. Gilbert, *Machiavelli's "Prince" and Its Forerunners: The Prince as a Typical Book de Regimine Principum* (Durham, 1938), pp. 238-245 for an extensive bibliography of "advices to princes" in the European tradition.

[8] José María Castro y Calvo, *El arte de gobernar en las obras de Don Juan Manuel* (Barcelona, 1945), p. 158. Castro y Calvo summarizes coincidences between the *De regimine* of Egidio Colonna and the works of Don Juan Manuel pointing out that although Egidio is cited, the influence is "meramente formal" (p. 208) and that the correspondences were due to the community of culture shared by the authors (213). See n. 54, p. 88.

[9] Sears, p. 1.

[10] Castro y Calvo, p. 208.

[11] For example, Egidio uses the image of the state as a physical body (Gilbert, p. 67) as does Fray Martín (p. 138). Egidio uses the story of Sardanapalus, "Aristotle's account through Justin" (Gilbert, p. 153). Fray Martín's version has echoes of Aristotle (p. 224 and n. 8).

[12] Castro y Calvo points out that this work also could be derived from the Arabic tradition: "de un catecismo políticomoral, tal como el *Solwan,* del siciliano Aben Zafer, y el *Collar de Perlas,* de Muza II, rey de Tremecén" (p. 65).

*estados* and the *Libro infinido*. The *Libro de los ejemplos del conde Lucanor o libro de Patronio* is in a sense a manual from which rulers might profit following more the tradition of oriental apologues than the expository tradition derived from Aristotle. The structure of the *Disciplina Clericalis* and the *Castigos y documentos* comes to mind.

The *Rimado de Palacio*, harking back to the *Siete partidas*, the *Poridat de las poridades*, Egidio de Colonna's *De regimine principum* and a common body of didactic prose designed to advise princes, is part of a literary trend prevalent in the Hispanic tradition to put these admonitions into verse. Such a practice can also be seen in parts of Juan de Mena's *Coronación*, Gómez Manrique's *Regimiento de príncipes* and, although different in tone in the *Coplas de Mingo Revulgo*, the *Coplas del Provincial* and *¡Ay panadera!*. Within the group of poetic advices, the *Laberinto de fortuna* of Juan de Mena is a highly political document, defending D. Álvaro de Luna and counseling Juan II as follows: "Fazed verdadera la grand Providencia, / mi guiadora en aqueste camino, / la qual vos ministra por mando divino, / fuerça, corage, valor e prudencia, / porque la vuestra real eçelencia / aya de moros pujante vitoria, / e de los vuestros assí dulçe gloria, / que todos vos fagan, señor, reverencia" (copla 297).[13] As is the case in *Os Lusíadas*, the *Laberinto* is not only a general statement concerning the nature of fortune and providence, and a celebration of national glory, it is also a political treatise. In both works, past glories are evoked to encourage the reigning monarch to do his best to emulate the triumphs of his predecessors (cf. the *Prohemio* of the *Jardín*). The Marqués de Santillana (1398-1458) also makes a political statement in his *Doctrinal de privados* which also could be considered as a warning against the kind of domination of a ruler represented by the excessive influence exerted by D. Álvaro de Luna. It can also be seen that in Spain the precedents for using a literary form to offer warnings and advice to rulers was a fairly common practice, especially in the period from the 13th century through the 15th

---

[13] Juan de Mena, *El laberinto de fortuna o las trescientas*, ed. José Manuel Blecua (Madrid: Clásicos Castellanos, 1960), p. 149.

century. The specific literary genre varied according to the talent and ability of the author. What was constant was a desire to reform or correct the ruler or to prevent the repetition of past errors and at the same time to address the general reading public.

In connection with the *Jardín* as an "Advice to princes" brief mention of an extra-peninsular author, Giraldus Cambrensis (1146?-1220) is useful in order to suggest the existence of a general European tradition without in any way trying to establish direct influence. Giraldus has a chapter entitled "De tyrannorum obitu et fine cruento," [14] and he advises the following virtues: "moderamen, mansuetudo, pudicitia, patientia, temperantia, clementia, munificentia audacia et animositas, religio ac devotio." [15]

With the same intention of showing how much a part of the general tradition, the *Jardín* was, Mosén Diego de Valera's *Espejo de verdadera nobleza,* directed to Juan II in 1441 can be compared with Fray Martín's advice to his daughter, Isabel. [16] An examination of the dedication of the *Espejo* reveals certain common postures, found also in the dedication of the *Jardín* to Isabel and in the dedication of the *Compendio* to D. Álvaro de Luna. [17] Valera explains that he is writing to avoid falling into the sin of "occio," which he believes to be the cause of all sin. He characterizes himself as a humble man whose audacity in offering advice to an eminent person is caused by his own personal weakness and not by the glaring errors of the eminent person. He writes not to change men's minds but to save his own soul. He has learned much in the court of Juan and in other royal courts

---

[14] Gilbert, p. 67.

[15] Gilbert, p. 78. Cf. the list of Franciscus Patricius Senensis in *De regno et regis institutione* (Paris, 1531): "magnificentia, misericordia, castitas, fortitudo, constantia, amicitia, religio, humanitas, facilitas, fides" (Gilbert, 78). Both lists contain all the qualities which Fray Martín praises in women and in women rulers, and each quality has a part in the anti-feminist tradition in the negative sense.

[16] Mosén Diego de Valera, *Espejo de verdadera nobleza* in *Epístolas enbiadas,* pp. 171-3.

[17] Cf. the dedication by Petrus Bizarrus of his *De optimo principe* to Queen Elizabeth of England; she doesn't need the advice; "rather for other kings and princes, a kind of form and idea..." is represented by Elizabeth (Gilbert, p. 17).

and wants to share his wisdom with "los que menos de mý leyeron." He explains in a footnote that this remark is not presumptuous because he would not dare to suggest that "sabios e letrados" could possibly benefit from his remarks. Fray Martín also discusses his own special qualifications in the *Jardín:* his knowledge of moral and natural causes and his familiarity with the chronicles of the past (p. 136). He refers to those "menos entendidos" who do not agree with him because they have obviously read less than he has (p. 136). Fray Martín presents his credentials in the same way as Valera and even refers to the same potential audience of less well-informed readers.

Continuing to maintain his affectedly modest posture, Valera describes his search for someone to whom he might dedicate his "pequeñuela obra" in the hope that he might find someone whose nobility and wisdom qualified him for the task of pointing out the errors in the *Espejo.* In the *Compendio,* Fray Martín seeks the same supposed aid from D. Álvaro de Luna, "si algo fue escripto non deuidamente que vuestra penetrable sotileza lo podrá enmendar." [18]

The *Prohemio* to the *Jardín* differs from both the *Compendio* and the *Espejo* in that Fray Martín directs his "breue escriptura" to Isabel whose wisdom and lively understanding qualify her to profit from the work. She is not however invited to correct any errors. Apparently, even when writing a formulaic dedication to a royal personage, some recognition of the realities had to be maintained. A scholar of advanced years, at least in his sixties, who enjoyed a certain eminence in scholarly circles, would not seek the corrections of a sixteen year old princess.

Further comparison of the *Espejo* and the *Jardín* reveals several other similarities. Both works condemn tyranny by using the same examples from antiquity: Sardanapalus and Nero, both of whom were brought low by their own people because of their cruelty and their vices. The principal criticism is not against absolute power as much as it is a declaration that vice and monarchy do not mix. Both authors rely heavily on Valerius Maximus for their examples. Both emphasize the importance

---

[18] Martín de Córdoba, *Compendio de la fortuna,* ed. Fernando Rubio Álvarez (Madrid, 1958), p. 3.

of the ruler's accepting full responsibility for the affairs of state and not delegating too much authority. Valera defines nobility by explaining that there may be degrees or grades of nobility, but the king must be considered to possess the highest degree even over his legitimately born brother. [19] In a succeeding chapter, Valera points out that nobility can only come from the ruler so that, even when nobility is lost through the commission of evil acts, it can be restored only by the ruler. One wonders whether Valera is urging Juan II to play a more active part in his government and if he is specifically criticizing his relinquishing of power to D. Álvaro de Luna. In a letter written to Juan II in the same year, Valera quotes Seneca to describe the paternal nature of the king's rôle. Fray Martín also makes use of Seneca to describe the queen as mother of her people (p. 201). In the same vein, Fray Martín devotes *Capítulo ij* and *v* of the second part of the *Jardín* to a discussion of the nature of power and its responsibilities. Since neither her father, Juan II, nor her half-brother, Enrique IV shouldered their responsibilities with any show of strength, it might be thought that Fray Martín was warning her to avoid their errors in having permitted such men as D. Álvaro de Luna, the Marqués de Villena, and Beltrán de la Cueva to rule in their stead. Just as Valera had advised her father to assume the greater responsibility, [20] Fray Martín clearly advocates strength on the part of the queen. (Compare *Capítulo segundo, tercera parte,* pp. 250-54).

---

[19] After pointing out the Scriptural precedents for the ennobling of humble people by their rulers (Saul by Samuel; Joseph by the Pharaoh), Mosén Diego de Valera identifies three degrees of nobility: "noble, más noble e mucho más noble; para lo qual es de saber que el Rey tiene en su rreyno el soberano grado de la nobleza, en tanto que avn su hermano legítimo no es tan noble commo él" (*Espejo,* p. 201).

[20] *Espejo,* p. 202. In the notes to a letter to Juan II in 1441, José Antonio de Balenchana asserts that Valera's admonition to Juan II that he remember his royal status "dejando toda parcialidad e afición" is a reference to D. Álvaro de Luna's excessive influence upon him. Balenchana contends that it was this letter that signaled the beginning of the enmity between Valera and D. Álvaro de Luna, although he concedes that other authorities believe that their mutual hostility had existed before (*Epístolas enbiadas,* p. 98). In the aforementioned letter, Valera is concerned with a reinforcement of royal authority. He writes: "Traed a memoria, que soýs Rey, mirad bien quál es vuestro oficio" (p. 4). Valera uses the same image of the king

Fray Martín describes the three facets of a queen's power as follows: She is the merciful mother of her subjects, the shield or protector of her people, and their advocate in much the same way that the Virgin is man's advocate in the celestial realm (p. 201). Is he possibly cautioning Isabel against permitting her people to be subject to the domination of a foreign prince? Isabel married Fernando in 1469, a year after the composition of the *Jardín*. This union probably caused less fear of foreign domination than a French connection with the Duc de Guyenne or an English one with the Duke of Gloucester. Nevertheless the idea of Aragonese domination might have caused some uneasiness in the court of Castile.

In the *Prohemio*, Fray Martín is more specific in his criticism of weakness in a monarch. He advises Isabel to follow the example of her ancestors and continue the job of recapturing Granada from the Moors, whose continued control of that territory is the result of the negligence of the "modernos príncipes" (p. 140). That this was a recurring topic in works offering advice to Castilian princes is evidenced by the same advice offered to her father by Juan de Mena (see *supra*, n. 13). After a period of weakness shown by the last two monarchs and the expected dissension among the nobles, Fray Martín's plea for a strong, active monarchy is certainly a reflection of the specific problems suffered in Spain toward the end of the 15th century. Similarly Fray Martín's emphatic reminder to Isabel that unjust rulers suffer cruel punishments (p. 215) can be viewed as a reference to Enrique IV's alleged injustices. It is also apparent that, in the interest of unity, it was urgent to justify feminine rule, since there was no available male heir to the throne after the death of Alfonso.

It is clear also that Fray Martín's advocacy did not necessarily imply that he was Isabel's champion. The dedication of the *Jardín* indicates his partisanship, but it is important to

---

as father of his people: "Remiembre, pues, assimesmo Vuestra Merced que entre los otros magníficos títulos por qué los reyes soýs nombrados, soýs llamados padres de la tierra: esto porque conozcaýs el poder a vos dado, e de aquel sepaýs bien vsar, pareciendo a los buenos padres, los quales a sus hijos amados a vezes castigan con palabra, a vezes con açote, e muy atarde contece matarlos; saluo constreñido por estrema necessidad" (p. 5).

remember that in 1468 the only other possible heir to the throne was also a woman, Juana de Castilla, the daughter of Enrique IV and Juana de Portugal. Either way, Castile was destined to have a reigning queen and it seems that Fray Martín made his choice on the basis of national unity, because of the general support of Isabel and the general disapproval of Juana. One might venture a guess that Juana was tainted by her mother's reputation and that, as a result, Isabel's notable moral superiority made her a more likely candidate, even apart from the political intrigues of the period. What remains is an obvious necessity to justify the worthiness of a woman to rule Spain.

With an awareness of Fray Martín's intention to advocate a woman ruler for Spain, his description of the moral superiority of women (pp. 193-207) and his subsequent admonitions to Isabel fall into an orderly pattern. The creation of woman which is described in the first part of the book stresses her nobility, even pointing out that she was created in Paradise, while man was created outside of Eden (pp. 158-60). [21] The praise of her modesty (pp. 194-97), her compassionate nature (pp. 198-202), and her piety (pp. 203-07) is applied first to the individual woman and then to these qualities in a ruler. The particular faults which are to be found in women, such as intemperance, loquacity and inconstancy (p. 209), are elaborated upon with the clear intention to warn Isabel to avoid errors. In this context, the admonitions themselves serve as reminders that Isabel, the potential ruler, will be capable of overcoming these feminine flaws. In the second part of the *Jardín* and in the third, examples from antiquity, the Church Fathers, and the lives of the saints are adduced to support woman's natural superiority. In the course of this study, an attempt will be made to relate the two themes of pro-feminism and "advice to princes" and, whenever possible, to identify the topical references to the political scene in Spain in the last half of the 15th century.

---

[21] Ornstein cites an example of this type of reasoning: "mulier prefertur viro scilicet: Materia: Quia Adam factus de limo terre, Eva de costa Ade. Loco: Quia Adam factus extra Paradisum, Eva in Paradiso. Quia mulier concepit Deum, quod homo non potuit" (p. 13).

Thus, in the manner of other "advice to princes", Isabel is warned about the errors of her predecessors. She is encouraged because her femininity gives her special attributes which will make her an excellent ruler, and her course of action has been proclaimed: reconquer Granada and rule with strength and compassion.

She is warned that with power comes extra responsibility. She must love and fear God and learn about the administration of justice from God. In *Capítulo v, segunda parte*, Seneca's *Hercules Furens* and the Wisdom of Solomon are cited to remind the princess that earthly rulers must face God's anger if they have been unjust (pp. 215-16). Her punishment will be greater than that of a private person if she errs, because of her greater power. In *Capítulo tercio, segunda parte* (pp. 203-07), Fray Martín discusses woman's natural piety, an apparent answer made to the charge against women of "intractability to God's express commands" [22] which persisted and later appeared in stereotyped condemnations of women according to Ruth Kelso. The pattern is clear: woman is a devout creature who loves and fears God; a ruler has a special obligation to love and fear God; therefore a woman ruler will be especially devout and God-fearing, in spite of what has been said about the weaknesses of other women.

One of the accusations made against Enrique IV was that he was not devout. He surrounded himself with "infieles, cristianos por nombre, muy sospechosos en la fe, en especial que creen e dicen e afirman que otro mundo no aya si non nascer e morir como bestias." [23] There are reports of contests in blasphemy incited by Beltrán de la Cueva as a courtly pastime. [24] Thus the admonition that Isabel be a devout ruler also had topical significance. Furthermore, in *Capítulo sesto, segunda parte* (pp. 221-224) she is specifically warned about the dangers of blasphemy.

---

[22] Ruth Kelso, *Doctrine for the Lady of the Renaissance* (Urbana, Illinois, 1956), p. 12.

[23] Antonio Paz y Melia, *El cronista Alonso de Palencia* (Madrid, 1922), p. lxix, n. 1.

[24] Ramón Menéndez Pidal quotes Palencia, I, 397 in his introduction to the *Historia de España*, XVII to refer to these contests in blasphemy (p. xxxiv).

Here Fray Martín might have been making an oblique reference to the blasphemous nature of her half-brother, the king.

In *Capítulo séptimo, segunda parte* (pp. 221-24), the future queen is counseled to avoid indulgence in carnal pleasure, excessive displays of pomp and wealth, and dissolute living. In misogynistic literature woman is constantly referred to as sexually insatiable,[25] greedy,[26] and gluttonous.[27] Fray Martín warns her against these sins and in addition praises her natural modesty (pp. 194-97). In *Capítulo iiij, tercera parte* (pp. 255-59), he offers a praise of many chaste virgins in history, thus reminding both the reader and Isabel of woman's great potential for asceticism, virtue, and sexual restraint, in spite of anti-feminist characterizations. Here too, the topical nature of the material must be considered. One of the recurring accusations made against the court of Enrique IV was of licentiousness, particularly directed against his queen, Juana de Portugal.[28] The young princess, who had been placed in the care of Juana when she came to the court at the age of twelve, is thus counseled against practicing what she might have observed there.

In *Capítulo x, segunda parte* (pp. 235-58) Fray Martín returns to the subject of justice for the purpose of showing how it prevents discord in a realm. Fray Martín sees justice as being divided into two parts: commutative and distributive. Distributive justice has to do with the awarding of honors and privileges, while commutative is concerned with the settling of disputes. In misogynistic literature, woman is pictured as a sower of

---

[25] Luis de Lucena calls her "bestia insaciable" in the *Repetición de amores* (ed. Jacob Ornstein [Chapel Hill, 1954], p. 83), echoing the passage in the *Historia de Segundo* (Knust, p. 503) in which she is called a "bestia que nunca se farta."

[26] Ruth Kelso includes greed in her list (p. 12), a fault that is somewhat related to woman's sexual insatiability and intemperance.

[27] Drunkenness and gluttony also appear in Ruth Kelso's list (p. 12). Fray Martín cites what must have been a standard part of misogynistic lore in the distortion of Proverbs 31: 3-5 (see p. 277 for "no des vino ala muger...").

[28] See Ramón Menéndez Pidal (lviii). Palencia also reports a rumor that at birth an attempt was made to break Juana de Castilla's nose to increase her resemblance to her father, Enrique to reinforce her legitimacy (Paz y Melia, p. lxi).

discord.[29] In the *Jardín,* Fray Martín makes it quite clear that the queen must act as the shield, the advocate and the compassionate mother of her people (p. 199). She is particularly well-suited for the rôle because women are naturally generous and compassionate. Once again, these observations can be seen from a topical perspective. Another accusation leveled at Enrique IV and at his father, Juan II, as well, was that they gave posts of power and honor to unworthy people, a certain cause of discord.[30] Fray Martín might be alluding to the discord caused by the domination of Juan II by D. Álvaro de Luna and later by the Marqués de Villena, who also controlled Enrique IV as did Beltrán de la Cueva, the putative lover of the queen and father of Juana la Beltraneja. In any case, the two reigns were plagued by continuous dissension, culminating in the mock dethronement of Enrique IV at Ávila (see n. 18 to the *Prohemio*). In a country in which the monarchy was to become one of the principal themes of the finest period of the national theater,[31] there must have been a truly strong feeling of revulsion toward the previous

---

[29] See *Capítulo II, segunda parte* of the *Arcipreste de Talavera o corbacho,* ed. Joaquín González Muela (Madrid: Clásicos Castalia, 1970).

Alfonso Martínez de Toledo writes that she is "murmurante e detractadora" (p. 129), that she is a hypocrite ("cara con dos fazes", p. 146) and that she is a liar "jurando e perjurando" (p. 162). She is described in the *Historia de Segundo* as "cuydado que non fuye, guerra que non queda, peligro del omne que non ha en sí mesura" (Knust. p. 503). The whole burden of the *Libro de los engaños y assayamientos* is the wicked attempt of the king's favorite wife to dislodge his son, the prince, from his affection. She stirs up the whole court with her efforts to have the prince executed, but is ultimately defeated by the king's *privados* who restore harmony to the realm.

[30] Tarsicio de Azcona reports the charge made against Enrique IV that he gave "los cargos públicos y de gobierno a personas bajas, sin mérito e indignas, extorsionando al pueblo con sus impuestos" (*Isabel la Católica* [Madrid, 1964], p. 80).

[31] See Arnold G. Reichenberger, "The Uniqueness of the Comedia," *HR,* XXVII (1959), 303-16. Dr. Reichenberger describes the Spanish people as the true protagonists of the *comedia.* He writes: "From king to peasant, each person exists primarily as a member of his community, to whom are assigned definite duties. A king has to act as a king — to dispense justice; the nobleman, as a nobleman — to be a faithful vassal, or a reliable friend, or a passionate lover; the peasant as a peasant — to be proud, independent, and at the same time loyal to the king" (p. 305). This harmonious interdependence is hardly reflected in the episode at Ávila.

strife and a longing for the kind of just, benevolent rule that would lead to a unified and peaceful kingdom. It is apparent that the recommendation that the queen be liberal, affable, and just with her subjects (pp. 238-41) is directed at the problems of the realm. It goes without saying that the purpose of the advice is twofold: Isabel must be convinced of the right course, but even more importantly her subjects must be persuaded that her reign would lead to harmony and unity.

In the third part of the *Jardín*, Fray Martín follows the standard rhetorical practice of supporting his earlier statements with proofs, mainly from antiquity, Scripture, and the lives of the saints. In *Capítulo primero, tercera parte* (pp. 241-44), the princess is encouraged to love learning. A disdain for learning is not a standard part of previous misogynistic literature, so that we can assume that this counsel belongs more to the area of advice to princes, although it is not specifically enumerated in the various lists of recommended qualities of princes. In a large segment of anti-feminist writing, the woman is described as a wily, shrewd and astute person whose talents are employed in the deception of her husband or of others.[32] It was not customary to describe her as stupid, although her reading was to be limited to "reading lives of chaste virgins and renowned ladies who lived virtuously but not the lives of Aspasia, Cleopatra, Semiramis...."[33] Fray Martín uses the story from Varro about the vengeance of Neptune at the time of the founding of Athens (pp. 243-44) to explain why women had been excluded from the councils of government and from learning. He adds: "Pero entiéndese delas particulares mugeres & no delas claras, como son princesas & reynas, alas quales no es vedado estudiar en sabiduría como Sancta Catalina que hera hija de rey & hera instruýda en todas las artes liberales" (p. 244). Juan II was reputed to have interested himself in

---

[32] See nn. 60 and 61 *infra* for examples of her astuteness at deceiving her husband. Another kind of astuteness is attributed to women in the legend of Dido, who used the ruse of the coffers filled with sand, which also appears in the *Disciplina Clericalis* (ed. Ángel González Palencia [1948], p. 133) as the clever device of a woman. Cf. *Cantar de Mio Cid* vi. ff. One can add to the cult of the clever woman, *La doncella Teodora* whose wit and cleverness confounded the king and his wise men (Knust, p. 507).

[33] Ruth Kelso, p. 43.

intellectual pursuits; [34] his son, Enrique IV is neither praised nor blamed for his intellectual activities. [35] The admonition to value learning may have been directed to Isabel as a recommendation that she imitate her father. Since Fray Martín, himself, had benefited as a result of royal intervention in the controversy between the *Observantes* and the *Claustrales* in the Convent of Salamanca (see n. 16 to *The Author*); the author, a partisan of learning and scholarship might have been introducing a personal point of view in this advocacy of a love of learning, as well as echoing a commonplace. He does not recommend a liberal course of study for Isabel. She is merely told that she "debe catar algunas horas del día en que estudie y oya tales cosas que sean propias al regimiento del reino" (p. 244).

Fray Martín begins his plea that Isabel be a strong queen (pp. 245-49) with the observation that women are naturally weak and timorous, but, once aroused and able to conquer their fears, they are capable of prodigious feats which even giants would not dare to undertake. A cautionary note is sounded to the effect that this same release of forces, which results from the reversal of a natural tendency, can at times be misused in the case of woman's natural modesty and chastity. This caution leads into a praise of the strength of Semiramis, about whom maidens ordinarily were not even supposed to read (see *supra* n. 33). Fray Martín even credits Semiramis with the subjugation of India, a part of the legend which is disputed (see n. 6 to *Capítulo segundo, tercera parte*). Weakness and timorousness do not play a large part in the previous criticisms of women, so that it can be

---

[34] William H. Prescott mentions that Juan II had "a lively relish for intellectual enjoyment. He was fond of books, wrote and spoke Latin with facility, composed verses and condescended occasionally to correct those of his loving subjects" (*History of the Reign of Ferdinand and Isabella the Catholic,* 3 vols. [Philadelphia, 1883], I, 113). Hernán Pérez de Guzmán wrote of Juan: "Sabía fablar [e] entender latín, leýa muy bien, plazíanle muchos libros e istorias, oýa muy de grado los dezires rimados e conocía los vicios dellos" (*Generaciones y semblanzas,* ed. J. Domínguez Bordona [Madrid: Clásicos Castellanos, 1924], p. 124).

[35] According to Ramón Menéndez Pidal, Sánchez de Arévalo characterized Enrique as "magnífico, liberal, manso, humilde despreciador de los regios vestidos y de las comodidades de los baños, comparable en sus virtudes a Alejandro, a Publícola, a Adriano, a Antonino Pío" (p. xv).

concluded that this admonition is directly related to the counsel of princes. In a world where women normally owed obedience to their husbands, an exception would have to be made for Isabel, if Castile were to be protected from foreign domination. A reading of the *Capitulaciones del matrimonio entre la Princesa Doña Isabel y Don Fernando Rei de Sicilia* serves to confirm the concern felt by Isabel's advisers that she play an equal rôle in their joint reign. [36]

It is pertinent to note that five years after their marriage, when Enrique IV died (December 12, 1474), Isabel was crowned on the very next day, while Fernando was at the court of Aragón with his father, Juan II of Aragón. The hasty coronation is explained by Ballesteros Gaibrois as a measure to forestall any moves on the part of the partisans of Enrique's daughter, Juana, whose claim to the throne was admittedly weak. Enrique had named Isabel as his successor at Toros de Guisando on the 19th of September, 1468, thus repudiating his daughter. However, Enríquez del Castillo notes that later, having failed to arrange a marriage between Isabel and Alfonso V of Portugal, Enrique "determinó de tornar sobre la hija, e ayudarla para que subcediese ella y no la hermana." [37] Juana was subsequently married to Alfonso V and therefore had supporters in Portugal and also

---

[36] Ballesteros Gaibrois reproduces the *Capitulaciones* in the appendix of his life of Isabel (pp. 228-234). After promising to honor Enrique IV and to preserve the peace between Isabel and her brother, to honor the Archbishops of Toledo and Sevilla and other partisans of Isabel, Fernando swears that he will make no appointments without Isabel's consent. He will not make any royal decisions independent of her. What is more, he agrees that "por qualquier injuria que dicho señor Rey nuestro padre hobiese, o qualquier de los suyos, rescibido en otros tiempos en essos dichos Reynos, e assimesmo otro qualquier enojo o odio que aquel dicho Señor Rey nuestro padre e nos o otro qualquier de los suyos hobiese contra qualquier persona dessos dichos Reynos, no faremos por ellos alguna innovación contra estos tales: mas que por seruicio de Dios e por temptación de la dicha sereníssima princessa perdonamos a todos" (p. 231). Apparently a real transfer of loyalty was required of Fernando. On the other hand, Luis Suárez Fernández points out that the Archbishop of Toledo, Alfonso Carrillo, found it necessary to concede that Isabel owed obedience to her husband, in order to avoid humiliating Fernando, by requiring him to kiss Isabel's hand as a sign of submission. See *Los Trastámaras de Castilla y Aragón en el siglo XV*, in *Historia de España*, ed. Ramón Menéndez Pidal, XV (Madrid, 1964), 296.

[37] Enríquez del Castillo, p. 233.

in Spain among those who favored union with Portugal. At the last, however, Enrique died, without reiterating his selection of Isabel as his successor or his acknowledgment of Juana as his daughter and heir. In view of the weakness of Juana's claim, at least some of the haste evidenced in Isabel's immediate coronation might be ascribed to a desire on the part of her advisers that she be crowned first without Fernando. Isabel certainly showed herself to be a woman of great strength, not only in her political life, but in the way she strove to put a good face on her marital life, disposing of the fruits of Fernando's extra-marital activities, thereby assuring that above all the honor of the royal household be maintained publicly and also ensuring the succession to the throne of those children who were born legitimately to Isabel and Fernando. [38]

---

[38] Ballesteros Gaibrois notes that Isabel did not resent Fernando's liaison with Aldonza Iborra de Alamán previous to their marriage. In fact, the son of this union, Alfonso was made Archbishop of Zaragoza in 1478, when he was only ten years old. A daughter born of this same liaison married Bernardino Fernández de Velasco. After Isabel and Fernando's marriage, Isabel took a sterner view of this sort of activity on Fernando's part. The daughters produced from later relationships are said to have entered a convent at Madrigal at the instance of the Queen. Ballesteros Gaibrois goes on to quote Hernando del Pulgar who wrote that Isabel "amaba mucho a su marido, e celábalo fuera de toda medida." Ballesteros suggests it was not so much a question of intense love. Rather, she was deeply concerned about "las formas exteriores también guardadas y que nadie nunca, ni siquiera pudiera ser objeto de una hablilla o una murmuración" (pp. 101-102).

The records show Isabel's determined resistance to a number of marriages proposed by Enrique. She rejected Alfonso V of Portugal because her marriage had to be approved by the nobles of the realm. She also rejected a match with Charles, Duc de Guyenne, and the story is told of her night long prayer to God that He either kill her or D. Pedro Girón, the brother of the Marqués de Villena, who was actually on his way to marry her. This union would have effectively destroyed her claim to the throne. Mosén Diego de Valera reports that: "de súpito de la mano de Dios fue ferido de esquinencia de tal manera que dentro de tres días fue muerto" (*Memorial de diversas hazañas*, in BAE 70 [Madrid, 1953], p. 39). Girón is said to have died with imprecations on his lips cursing the fate that had permitted him to have come so near to such an illustrious union only to strike him down before fulfilling his destiny. This is the same Pedro Girón who is said to have attempted to force himself upon Isabel's poor, mad mother. Isabel certainly had reason to pray for his death. The story is presented by Valera and Enríquez del Castillo for the purpose of condemning his presumption or, as Enríquez del Castillo puts it, "la cobdicia desordenada que es la raíz de todos los malos..." (p. 208). Possibly, the

It is not possible to determine with any degree of certainty whether Fray Martín was counseling strength to an ordinary young woman who would later develop great personal strength or whether he was reinforcing an already evident tendency in the young princess. My guess is that the sort of strength she went on to display was not derived from inspirational reading matter and that she had already had the potential for great personal power. If the premise is accepted that Fray Martín's advice was not particularly necessary to Isabel, it might be assumed that the curious praise of Semiramis and Judith in *Capítulo segundo, tercera parte* was designed to reassure the general readership that they could have confidence in the reign of a woman who would not exactly follow the accepted idealized norms attached to the man/woman relationship and would not allow herself to be dominated by her consort.

Thus, after an examination of the *Jardín* as a politically oriented book, a pattern emerges. The faults customarily attributed to women are mentioned, then disputed by attributing their contrasting virtues to women. These virtues coincide with the traditional lists of virtues mentioned in the various "advices to princes." Reasoning from the general to the particular, Fray Martín applies his observations to Isabel and to her situation. The tone of the book, however, is still general. Fray Martín's only reference to Juan II is in the *titulillo*: "... del clementíssimo & de resplandeciente memoria el Rey Don Juan, postrimero deste nombre." Alfonso is mentioned as the young heir to the throne, whose death is to be lamented. The names of Enrique, his queen Juana and his daughter do not appear, nor do any of the powerful nobles and clergy. Nevertheless, the impression persists that Fray Martín was not writing in a moral ethical vacuum and that he intended his book to be read with the names of the prominent and powerful in mind. Having seen the inter-relationship between the task of advising Isabel and the theme of pro-feminism as it applies to all maidens and then to a ruler, there remains the necessity to examine the misogynistic tradition against which Fray Martín was reacting in the *Jardín*.

---

story of her prayers entered the "Isabel legend" to show her early strength and the power of her prayers.

In spite of our conclusion that the *Jardín* is only secondarily a pro-feminist work, it is obvious that Fray Martín had occasion to answer many of the lingering anti-feminist attitudes that persisted in the literature of the day. Ruth Kelso lists woman's less attractive qualities as follows: "licentiousness, instability, disloyalty, intractability to God's express commands, drunkenness and gluttony, pride, vanity, avarice, greed, seditiousness, quarrelsomeness, talkativeness." [39] Fernando de Rojas lists the following: "Sus disimulaciones, su lengua, su engaño, su oluido, su desamor, su ingratitud, su inconstancia, su testimoniar, su negar, su reboluer, su presunción, su vanagloria, su abatimiento, su locura, su desdén, su soberuia, su subjeción, su parlería, su golosina, su luxuria e suziedad, su miedo, su atreuimiento, sus hechizerías, sus embayamientos, sus escarnios, su deslenguamientos, su desvergüenza, su alcahuetería." [40] Alfonso Martínez de Toledo, the *Arcipreste de Talavera* says that women are avaricious; they are gossips who cause trouble for others; they are covetous; envious, inconstant, two-faced, disobedient; over-proud, untruthful; subject to excessive drinking, talkative, meddlers and undiscriminating in their choices of men. [41] Fray Martín chooses to emphasize that women are capable of prodigies of chastity and virtue; they are naturally merciful; especially devout and exceedingly generous. He specifically mentions the allegations that they are intemperate, talkative and therefore deceitful and that they are inconstant. In connection with their intemperance, he makes reference to the misogynistic admonition: "No des vino a la muger" and, of course, adds his own suggestion that they are weak and timorous which might be related to Fernando de Rojas' "su miedo." Fray Martín's insistence on woman's generosity might be considered to be a response to the Arcipreste de Talavera's suggestion implicit in the episode of the missing egg. [42]

---

[39] Ruth Kelso, p. 12. Miss Kelso considers that chastity was the most important virtue in women. She explains that in a society "where estates and titles were in question, the legitimacy of heirs easily assumed paramount importance" (p. 25).

[40] Fernando de Rojas, *La Celestina*, 2 vols. ed. Julio Cejador y Frauca (Madrid: Clásicos Castellanos, 1966), I, 49.

[41] Alfonso Martínez de Toledo, pp. 121-175.

[42] Alfonso Martínez de Toledo, pp. 124-127.

Miss Kelso does not include stinginess in her list, although elsewhere Fernando de Rojas does. Stinginess is certainly related to avarice and greed, the opposite of generosity. Some comment should be made about the seriousness of anti-feminist attitudes in the 15th century in Spain with the aim of separating the serious, visceral reactions from the serio-comic reactions deriving from a common fund of European folklore, and ultimately from oriental sources.

It is not difficult to recognize that Fray Martín's praise of woman's natural modesty and chastity is a direct response to the vast body of material that describes her as a sexually insatiable creature, incapable of restraint, and a snare of the devil's creation designed to entrap otherwise chaste men. Fray Martín makes two references to this dangerous trait in women which he views as a potential fault not an actual one. He explains that because God wants us to be good, He gives us certain natural restraints. Modesty or *vergüença* is woman's natural restraint. However, in her youth, when she lacks the reasoning powers of adulthood, this restraint might not function. He writes: "Las mugeres, pues moças, por dos cabos son flacas & caen, porque son mugeres & porque son moças. Pues si alos moços por falta de su hedad, con necessaria vergüença para refrenar los apetitos puerilles, mucho más es necessaria alas mugeres moças que si vergüença no las refrena del mal & las promoue al bien, yrán como bestia desenfrenada & como cauallo sin espuelas en todo mal & huyrán toda virtud" (p. 195). In an explanation of the theory of opposites, he writes: "Deximos que la muger natural mente es vergonçosa, pero si por alguna ocasión pierde la vergüença, natural mente no ay cosa más desuergonçada" (p. 245). Clearly, within women is to be found a strong natural impulse toward unrestrained sexuality, controllable only by the God-given restraints of maturity and modesty.

In connection with this view of woman as a lascivious creature, controlled by the somewhat shaky restraints of reason derived from maturity and modesty, there are several aspects to be considered. First, in a book with a demonstrable political orientation such as the *Jardín*, it is evident that the author was concerned with Juana of Portugal's sexual misbehavior, if only because of the problems of succession that it might have caused. It was important to stress woman's natural capacity for virtue and chastity which Fray Martín did (pp. 194-97) and later supported with evidence from the past (pp. 260-88), if only to restore public confidence in the monarchy. Secondly, it appears that Fray Martín was recognizing a popular attitude reflected in a long tradition of folk humor and in the more serious misogynistic tradition.

The roots of what can be called serious misogyny are varied. In the *Gilgamesh Epic,* Ishtar invites Gilgamesh to be her husband, promising him great treasures; he responds with a vituperative list of her damaging properties, ending anti-climactically with her lack of fidelity or constancy.[43] In the Greek legends, Pandora and her box represent the danger of consorting with women, according to H. R. Hays.[44] In Genesis, Eve is the cause of the expulsion from Paradise. Fray Martín relies on St. Augustin to establish the pure nature of the sexual act in Eden before the Fall (p. 182) and focuses the guilt on the devil, rather than on Eve to explain the expulsion. He denies woman's inherent guilt, supporting his contention with the evidence of her exemplary behavior in Eden, before the Fall and attributing all the guilt to Satan. He further contends that anything of which Eve was capable in Eden, other women can accomplish with the help of their aforementioned virtues: natural modesty and mature reason (p. 155). Norman Penzer describes the trajectory of the image of the poison damsel from India, moving westward. In these stories, the sweat glands of the damsel give off a contact poison sufficient to kill. In many of these tales, the emanation has been produced artificially by small doses of poison given to maidens since infancy and in others the danger is inherent in the woman.[45]

---

[43] Alexander Heidel, *The Gilgamesh Epic and Old Testament Parallels* (1946 rpt. Chicago: Phoenix, 1971), p. 50. See also A. M. Killen, "La Légende de Lilith," *Revue de la Litterature Comparée,* XII (1932), 279. Lilith, the embodiment of seductive reminine evil was apparently linked to Astarte, or Ishtar.

[44] H. R. Hays. *The Dangerous Sex: The Myth of Feminine Evil* (London, 1966), p. 86.

[45] Norman Penzer, *Poison-Damsels and other essays in Folklore and Anthropology* (London, 1952).

This particular story turns up in the Hispanic literary tradition in the *Poridat de las poridades*. The pseudo-Aristotle boasts of his astuteness in having warned Alexander that he not accept the present of a damsel from an Indian monarch: "Et uenga uos emiente del presente que uos enuió el rey de India, et enbió uos en el una muy fremosa manceba que fue criada a ueganbre fasta ques torno de natura de las bíuoras, et sy non fuesse por mí que lo entendí en su uista et de miedo que auíe de los sabios desa tierra pudiera uos matar; et después fue prouado que mataua con su sudor a quantos se llegaua." [46] The penetration of stories that convey a primitive dread of women as the cause of unrestrained sexuality is recognizable in the misogynistic references to her as a "bestia desenfrenada & como cauallo sin espuelas en todo mal."

In a less serious vein, anti-feminism became very early a part of folk humor, much of which was directed toward woman as a temptress in the service of the devil and as a wily astute creature whose principal aim was the deception of her husband. Within the framework of the view of woman as the initiator of all illicit sexuality, one finds her accused of provoking sin in the hearts of those ascetic clerics who had devoted themselves to a life of chastity. Stith Thompson classifies the stories of the ascetic hermit who resists the temptation of a woman under T 330-360 and John Esten Keller includes more than twenty-five variants in his motif-index of Spanish *exempla*. [47] The story of the crafty wife, skilled in cuckolding her husband, even convincing him that he has not been betrayed is classified by Stith Thompson as K 1510-1544 and nineteen examples appear in Keller's classification of the Spanish *exempla*. Many of these undeniably humorous *exempla* were undoubtedly used to enliven sermons which dealt with chastity and fidelity to the occasional dismay of the authorities because of their salacious content. María Rosa Lida de Malkiel mentions these abuses and points out that they were condemned as late

---

[46] Pseudo-Aristóteles, *Poridat de las poridades*, ed. Lloyd Kasten (Madrid, 1957), p. 41.

[47] See Stith Thompson, *Motif-Index of Folklore Literature*, 6 vols. (Bloomington, Indiana, 1955-1958) and John Esten Keller, *Motif-Index of Medieval Spanish Exempla* (Knoxville, Tennessee, 1949).

as 1624 at the Council of Bordeaux.[48] Their use was justified by the precedent of "l'exemplum introduit par le Sauveur lui même dans les enseignments du christianisme" according to Welter.[49] In the 15th century, they appeared in the *Arcipreste de Talavera* and of course in the collection of Clemente Sánchez Vercial. This jocular anti-feminism in Spain is reflected in the semi-serious courtly debate described by Jacob Ornstein in 15th-century Spain. Its trajectory from Oriental sources beginning with the *Disciplina Clericalis* and the *Libro de los engaños* in peninsular literature is easily seen.

Fray Martín responds to the allegation that women are a snare of the devil's invention for the purpose of leading men astray (p. 154) by pointing out that women are capable of great virtue and even greater sacrifices in order to preserve their virtue. Woman, as the instigator of the sexual act in the manner of Eve, has played a major rôle in that part of misogynistic literature that was dedicated to the promotion of clerical celibacy. It is of interest that clerical celibacy was first officially enjoined at the Council of Elvira in Spain in A.D. 305 when it was declared that the clergy should "maintain entire abstinence from their wives under pain of forfeiting their positions ... no ecclesiastic should permit any woman to dwell with him except a daughter or a sister."[50] Originally these regulations seem to have been concerned more with the cleric's ability to devote himself wholeheartedly to his duties, than as a condemnation of sexual behavior. For instance, St. Jerome cites Matthew 6:24 and Galatians 5:17 to point out that man cannot serve both the flesh and the spirit at the same time.[51] Justinian wrote even more practically in A.D. 528, counseling clerical celibacy to enable the cleric to "avoid converting to the use of the prelate's

---

[48] María Rosa Lida de Malkiel, "Tres notas sobre don Juan Manuel," *RPh*, IV (1950-51), 155. John Esten Keller mentions two other condemnations — at Sens in 1528 and at Milan in 1565 ("*El libro de los ejemplos por a.b.c.,*" *Hispania*, XL (1957), 179-186: 185).

[49] J.-Th. Welter, *L'Exemplum dans la Littérature Réligieuse et Didactique du Moyen Age* (Paris, 1927), p. 33.

[50] Henry Charles Lea, *The History of Sacerdotal Celibacy in the Christian Church* (New York, 1957), p. 30.

[51] St. Jerome, *The Principal Works*, Letter XLVIII, 20, p. 78.

family, the wealth of the Church." [52] St. Bonaventure, writing in the 13th century, is even more explicit about the practical reasons for advocating celibacy: "Since they already seize the goods of the Church for the benefit of distant relatives, what would they do if they had legitimate children of their own?" [53] Yet the Church was in the anomalous position of recognizing that marriage was the first sacrament, having been celebrated in Eden before the Fall. Fray Martín gives the reason for Eve's creation in Paradise as God's desire to honor matrimony. He remarks: "Los otros fueron instituýdos en estado de pecado; el matrimonio en estado de ynocencia" (p. 161). At the same time, Fray Martín disapproves of sexual pleasure recommending that the conjugal act "se hiziera con horden dela razón, no saliendo los límites de justicia & honestad, ... no mirando ala delectación, mas mirando ala sancta generación" (p. 185). Even this procreation was to have its limit when "el número delos escogidos que auían de ser conpañeros delos ángeles, que son vírgines" (p. 185) was reached (see Revelation 14:1). One would have thought that ecclesiastical marriages would have been more apt to produce the elect. The early basis for clerical celibacy seems thus to have been the practical one of freeing the priests from family allegiances, which would have made them less effective in their pastoral duties, rather than a general condemnation of sexuality which led early theologians to the brink of Manicheism and the heresy of Tatian, [54] to which Fray Martín refers (p. 270).

To avoid falling into the error of the dualistic view of good and evil professed by the Manicheans or the error of Tatian who said all marriages were sinful (p. 269), a scale of relative sinfulness was proposed: virginity, chaste widowhood, and chaste marriage, all three of which place the onus on women. Fray Martín, relying heavily on St. Jerome, writes of these three levels (pp. 255-74), establishing woman's great potential for virtue and clearing her of the charge of temptress or deceiver. Difficulties arise in the task of condemning lustful behavior while avoiding the afore-

---

[52] Lea, p. 65.
[53] Lea, p. 339.
[54] See n. 6 to *Capítulo vij, tercera parte* for St. Jerome's comments on Tatian.

mentioned heresies. Thus we find the commonplace that woman is the tool of the devil. Fray Martín writes: "Sathanás auía de hazer armadijo conla muger para engañar al varón." Adam's curved rib is like a hunter's bow (p. 154). He quotes St. Ambrose: "Que la muger es apta armadura para tomar las ánimas" (p. 154). The evil is transferred to woman who is put to use by the devil to serve as the temptress; marriage is not inherently evil in this mixture of misogyny and theological explanation. What is more, woman is helped by God to avoid serving the devil (p. 195), but, at times, she does not avail herself of this aid. Thus woman, the "continua tentación" [55] of 15th-century anti-feminism, causes sinful behavior. In spite of our awareness of the difficulty of translating humor across either regional or time barriers, it is not rash to agree with John Esten Keller as to the comic qualities in many of the anti-feminist *exempla*.[56] If we accept Henri Bergson's definition of the risible as a combination of the inversion of normal values, exaggeration, and the unawareness of the comic figure,[57] then the picture of the hermit steadfastly resisting the temptations of the flesh in the person of a woman is humorous to the person who does not share his convictions. The drama critic Walter Kerr in defining comedy, writes: "When a man can't help what his body is doing to him, he has begun to be a clown."[58] He also observes: "Sex must always be funny, because no man is free to be or not to be sexual. A man may choose to be celibate ... but he cannot choose to be sexless."[59] Having seen that many of the *exempla* dealing with woman as temptress are a part of the folk humor tradition of peninsular literature, intended to delight the hearer of a sermon while instructing him, we can consider

---

[55] Luis de Lucena, p. 85.

[56] Of the *Libro de los engaños*, he wrote: "Humor lay in the very claim to didacticism; the humor was perhaps the very genius of this particular inversion...." John Esten Keller, *Alfonso X el Sabio* (New York: Twayne, 1967), p. 54. J. P. S. Tatlock discusses the humorous nature of the *Disciplina Clericalis* ("Medieval Laughter," Speculum XXI [1946], 289-294: 290).

[57] Henri Bergson, *Le Rire: Essai sur la significance du comique* (Paris, 1938), p. 90; p. 126.

[58] Walter Kerr, *Tragedy and Comedy* (New York, 1967), p. 154.

[59] Walter Kerr, p. 161. Parallels of many of the *exempla* can be found in a modern study of sexual humor. See Gerson Legman, *Rationale of the Dirty Joke: An Analysis of Sexual Humor* (New York, 1968).

the *exempla* dealing with woman as the artful deceiver of her husband as a part of the same tradition. The common factor in all these stories is the complaisance of the cuckold in contrast to the wiliness of his mate. The explicit complaisance in the story told by the *quarto privado* in the *Libro de los engaños* concerning the *bañador*, his wife and the uninitiated prince, [60] is usually only hinted at in many of the tales where the husband is too easily deceived by quite transparent stratagems, where he is momentarily blinded so that the lover can escape. [61] Cf. that monument of credulity in the story of D. Pitas Payas in Juan Ruiz' *Libro de buen amor* (coplas 474-84). [62] Henri Bergson explains this kind of laughter in terms of "l'insensibilité qui accompagne d'ordinaire le rire ... le rire n'a plus gran ennemi que l'emotion." [63] Bergson describes the comic figure: "Un personnage comique est génèralement comique dans l'exacte mésure où il s'ignore lui-même. Le comique est inconscient...." [64] Certainly the easily deceived husband is comic for this reason as is the tempted ascetic in the grip of uncontrollable forces. In these stories, the anti-feminism which calls woman the initiator of sin and the inconstant de-

---

[60] Bergsonian inversion of normal values is apparent in this story as well as the unawareness of the comic figure. The *bañador* had arranged that his wife sexually initiate the poor prince whose inadequacy is accentuated by his shape "tan grueso que non podía ver sus mienbros por do era." The wife will help the prince become "señor de sus mienbros y jazer con muger." The husband is startled, however, by his wife's evident enjoyment of her part in the charade when she refuses to leave the side of the prince, saying: "¿Cómmo yré? ca le fizo pleyto que dormiría con él toda esta noche" (*Libro de los engaños y assayamientos de las mugeres*, ed. John Esten Keller [Chapel Hill, 1959], pp. 27-28).

[61] Petrus Alphonsi in the *Disciplina Clericalis* tells of the husband who returns home with a wounded eye and whose wife covers his good eye with her mouth so that her lover can leave unobserved (ix); of the upheld sheet which serves the same purpose (x); of the lover who pretends to be running away from a group of *espadachines* to explain his presence in the lady's bedroom (xi). These stories all celebrate the woman's cleverness in deceiving her husband and demonstrate the husband's complaisance or stupidity (pp. 119 ff.). Alfonso Martínez de Toledo tells the same kind of stories (pp. 162-165), as did Cervantes much later. These tales have become a part of world folk humor, persisting into 20th-century sexual humor.

[62] Juan Ruiz, *El libro de buen amor*, ed. Joan Corominas (Madrid, 1967), pp. 221-223.

[63] Bergson, p. 4.

[64] Bergson, p. 67.

ceiver, although funny, reflects a clearly definable mistrust of women to which Fray Martín makes a forceful response. His answer, supported by examples from antiquity and the Scriptures, is that women are capable of prodigies of constancy and fidelity, even though he knows that there are many stories to the contrary. Jacob Ornstein views the preponderance of pro-feminist works in 15th-century Spain as a literary and courtly response to such works as Pere Toroellas' *Maldezir de las mujeres,* however, Fray Martín, the serious minded, scholarly cleric may well have been responding more directly to the frivolous *exempla* in the sermons of the period, and may not have been engaging in the feminist debate as such. In this respect it is well to remember Ornstein's observation that although Queen María had invited responses to the *Arcipreste de Talavera,* he could not identify any of the pro-feminist works of the period as direct responses. Clearly, Alfonso Martínez de Toledo relied on many of the traditional *exempla* presenting them with a strong humorous approach, not a consciously literary one. What comes to mind is the idea that there were, in fact, two feminist debates in 15th-century Spain —the literary competition for the favor of the mighty, rich with invective and brilliant language, and the clerical debate much of which is not visible because it took place in the pulpits of the churches, and has not been preserved.

Apart from the two principal accusations made against women — sexual temptresses and wily adulteresses — women are characterized as stingy creatures, a sin which is ancillary to avarice and greed.[65] She is accused of avarice and greed in the lofty condemnations but Alfonso Martínez de Toledo's description of her stinginess and pettiness is almost unique. Fray Martín's recommendation to Isabel that she distribute largesse gladly and that she not be avaricious (p. 237) and that she generously give of herself (p. 238) with affability are possible responses to the accusation that women are cold, with-holding creatures. In particular, Fray Martín adds the insight that liberality is related to

---

[65] Alfonso Martínez de Toledo describes woman's avaricious nature, with the tale of the avaricious queen and then includes the story of the woman distressed by the loss of the egg (pp. 121 to 129), a story which, incidentally, is found in Andreas Capellanus as well.

the freeing of the individual. Misers are "sieruos de sus riquezas" (p. 238). She is advised to treat each person with friendly words, kind works, and a pleasant expression (p. 238). Although this advice is a typical part of the "advice to princes" already discussed, it undoubtedly has some relevance to a discussion of anti-feminism. Another side of woman's personality in the general tradition is her pettiness, her addiction to gossip and her overall mean-spiritedness. Alfonso Martínez de Toledo describes woman's lack of charity to others in a devastating portrait of a woman who is "murmurante e detractadora." [66] Women are not only unloving, they are spiritually lacking in generosity. Fray Martín, on the other hand, says that women are naturally compassionate (pp. 198-202) and Isabel is counseled to be generous (p. 237). An interesting sidelight is that Fray Martín finds it necessary to admonish Isabel that she be kind and considerate of her servants (pp. 205-206). This complaint appears in the *Celestina* in Areusa's harangue against stingy, unkind mistresses. It is evident that the view of woman as ungenerous, unkind and petty in her avarice persisted through the 15th century in Spain and that Fray Martín was making a direct response to it, at the same time that he was offering to a prospective ruler the conventional advice that she be generous.

Yet another misogynistic criticism to which Fray Martín responds is that of woman's loquacity (pp. 156-57; 225-30). Strangely enough, one of Fray Martín's rare ventures into humor, is evident in his story of the two men who speak about the noise made by bones in a gourd (p. 157) in his explanation of why God chose Adam's rib as the suitable material for Eve's creation. Less certain is the humorous aspect of the selection of women as heralds of the resurrection (p. 157), because of their loquacity, although nowhere else in the *Jardín* does Fray Martín make so incongruous an observation. Alfonso Martínez de Toledo says of woman: "El callar le es muerte." [67] He also points out that "non es muger que non quisyese fablar e ser escuchada." [68] It is hard

---

[66] Alfonso Martínez de Toledo, pp. 129-132. Beside being "murmurante e detractadora," she is "cara con dos fazes" (pp. 146-150).

[67] Alfonso Martínez de Toledo, p. 129.

[68] Alfonso Martínez de Toledo, p. 168.

to believe that the *Arcipreste*'s faithful reproduction of woman's non-stop speech was not intended, in part, at least, to amuse. Fray Martín's style is usually sober and grave, but he seems to be reflecting what must have been a familiar humorous topic when he decries woman's talkativeness and when he advises Isabel that she must control her tongue. As is the case with the humorous aspect of the stories about woman as a sexual temptress and an artful deceiver of husbands, these complaints about her talkativeness do not lose their significance because they are expressed with humor. The fact remains that Fray Martín dignified these jocular complaints with an answer with the only touch of humor in the *Jardín*. It is true, however, that he does not offer a praise of woman's natural taciturnity in the same way that he opposes her natural chastity to her reputed lasciviousness. We may find confirmation in the *Jardín* of the semi-serious nature of the feminist debate in the 15th century in Spain, if we regard Fray Martín's reactions as responses to the anti-feminist content in sermons. He was, after all, writing a tract in support of the idea that a woman would rule with wisdom and justice. His pro-feminism provided the framework for his arguments.

The assumption that Fray Martín was not participating in a courtly debate, but rather in a clerical one aimed at the folk tradition of anti-feminism prevalent in the *exempla* raises a question. Why did he not refer directly to these familiar tales? In the face of ecclesiastical disapproval of the introduction of *exempla* into sermons (see n. 48 *supra*), it is no wonder that Fray Martín eschewed this type of demonstration of their sexual unreliability in the framing of his defense of women. His anecdotal proofs are limited to an episode from St. Gregory's *Dialogues*, examples from antiquity as related by Valerius Maximus, and the lives of St. Jerome's disciples. He does not refer directly to what must have been very familiar anecdotal material, but instead chooses to praise marital fidelity, womanly constancy, and the rectitude of widows just as though there were no body of stories enunciating wifely deceitfulness and womanly immorality.

Thus it can be concluded, therefore, that Fray Martín made use of existing anti-feminist attitudes, which stemmed from a variety of sources in 15th-century Spain, in the preparation of an "advice to princes" which happened to have been directed to a princess. The *Jardín* appears to have had two purposes. It was not only necessary to encourage the young princess, Isabel, to develop her talents in a useful way; it was also important to convince the populace that they could expect to be ruled well by a woman. The method chosen by Fray Martín reveals itself to have been three-fold. He refers to the faults of the previous reigns, usually indirectly; he offers his corrections of these faults; and he discusses them within the popular frame of reference of the easily recognizable feminist/anti-feminist controversy. In this sense, the persisting charges made against women, which were always to some extent pretexts for the expression of general moral wisdom, were similarly used by Fray Martín. His advice to Isabel that she be chaste, loyal, compassionate, just, and generous was a commonplace; all young rulers were thus advised (see n. 15 *supra*). The fact of Isabel's femininity gave Fray Martín the opportunity to mix these commonplaces with his observations about the nature of women, thus enabling him to write a more significant and readable book than the *Espejo de verdadera nobleza,* for instance, of Mosén Diego de Valera. All men would be more easily entertained by the introduction of the folkloric references to the wickedness of women, than they would be by a straightforward document, in which a ruler is reminded in a more abstract way of regal and human virtues. In a sense, the feminist/anti-feminist controversy provides a literary framework for the *Jardín*. As has been mentioned, much of the anti-feminist material present in the *Jardín* played a large part in folk humor. Although Fray Martín made very little conscious use of the humor inherent in the topic, he could not have been unaware of its popular appeal. If one purpose of a didactic work is to instruct and to delight, then the *Jardín de nobles donzellas* had fulfilled its purpose. It outlined a course of action or behavior for Isabel; it instructed her and the general reader as to the potential benefits of feminine rule; and at the same time it entertained with references to the popular controversy of the battle between the sexes.

# PART II
# JARDÍN DE NOBLES DONZELLAS

Enel principio desta obra pone el prólogo & la intención del autor & induze alos que han de regir que trabajen por se dar a sabiduría.

*Capítulo .j.* pone cómo fue criada la primera muger segund la Santa Escriptura & primeramente muestra de qué parte del varón fue criada.

*Capítulo .ij.* de qué fecha la primera muger & por qué dela costilla más que otra materia & allí nota buenas razones desto.

*Capítulo .iij.* en qué lugar fue la muger criada & da causas por qué en paraýso fue fecha & no el varón.

*Capítulo .iiij.* habla del tiempo quando fue criada & de qué hedad & días fue criada.

*Capítulo .v.* declara a qué fin fue la muger criada & pone tres fines a que fue criada.

*Capítulo .vj.* que Eva avn que fue hecha de Adam no se puede dezir fija suya, mas su conpañera & muger.

*Capítulo .vij.* en qué manera fue fecho el cuerpo dela muger, tan grande de tan pequeña costilla & de otros milagros que en aquella obra contescieron.

*Capítulo .viiij.* si los honbres no pecaran, en qué manera la muger seruiera ala generación humana & determina segund Sant Agustín que engendraran vírgines.

*Capítulo .jx.* habla dela generación delas mugeres naturalmente hechas de varón & muger como fueron todos excepto Eua.

La segunda parte deste libro habla delas condiciones dela muger, assí delas que han, como delas que esperan auer para ser buenas.

*Capítulo .j.* dela vna buena condición que han las mugeres que son vergonçosas & porqué son especiales razones porque las nobles donzellas han de tener vergüença.

*Capítulo .ij.* que las mugeres natural mente son piadosas & porque lo son en especial alas grandes dueñas porque han de ser piadosas.

*Capítulo .iij.* como son obsequiosas & como es esta buena propiedad enellas, ca por ésta, Jhesu Cristo & sus apóstoles las traxeron en su compañía.

*Capítulo .iiij.* delas menos buenas condiciones dela muger & de vna condición que conlas buenas es buena & conlas malas muy mala.

*Capítulo .v.* comiença delas condiciones que han de auer las nobles donzellas para que sean dignas de ser reynas & pártelas & da orden como dirá dellas & muéstrales primero temor de Dios.

*Capítulo .vj.* que deuen honrrar & amar a Dios sobre todas las cosas & más las reynas que todas las otras mugeres.

*Capítulo .vij.* en que da orden enel coraçón dela noble donzella guardándolo de amor desordenado, de riquezas, de pompas & de carnales deleytes.

*Capítulo .viij.* ordena su boca en tal manera que enlas palabras no aya demasía, ni mengua, ni discordia.

*Capítulo .jx.* ordena las manos en perfetas obras, dellas parecen de fuera, dellas quedan dentro enel ánima.

*Capítulo .x.* como se deue ordenar la señora por respeto del próximo & delos súbditos con tres virtudes, con justicia, con liberalidad, & con efabilidad.

La tercera y final parte deste tratado, enel capítulo primero dirá como se han de promouer las dueñas a bien por exenplo delas pasadas & recoje lo que fue dicho enlas dos partes del libro passadas y promueue la señora a amar sabiduría por exemplo de muchas donzellas.

*Capítulo .ij.* la prouoca a fortaleza por enxenplo de otras que fueron fuertes & de grandes coraçones.

*Capítulo .iij.* delas mugeres que ouieron constancia en buen propósito de virtudes & dela fe cathólica.

*Capítulo .iiij.* delas mugeres que se dieron ala castidad virginal que es el más excelente grado de todos.

*Capítulo .v.* delas honrradas biudas que alcançaron el segundo grado de castidad.

*Capítulo .vi.* como las dueñas han de amar & ser fieles a sus maridos, especial mente las reynas.

*Capítulo .vij.* de tres grados de castidad, conjugal, vidual, & virginal, como todos son buenos, avn que vno mejor que otro & de tres maneras de biuir los hombres.

*Capítulo .viij.* delos statutos que dieron los romanos sobre la conuersación de las dueñas con sus maridos.

*Capítulo .jx.* delo que dixo Salomón delas mugeres así buenas como comunales & desto se traherán algunas autoridades.

*Capítulo .x.* que muchos doctores diuersos dixeron delas mugeres cerca dela honestidad dellas.

# PRIMERA PARTE

Tratado que se intitula *Jardín de nobles donzellas*, copilado por Fray Martín de Córdoua dela Orden de Santo Agustín, Maestro en Sancta Theología, dirigido ala Illustríssima y muy poderosa Señora la Reyna Doña Ysabel, Señora Nuestra: hija legítima & progénita del clementíssimo & de resplandeciente memoria el Rey Don Juan, postrimero deste nombre. [1]

Comiença el prohemio

A la muy clara & sereníssima señora doña Ysabel de real simiente procreada, [2] infanta legítima heredera delos reynos de Castilla & León, el su humilde seruidor Fray Martín de Córdoua, de la Orden de Sant Agustín, Maestro en Sancta Theología, con toda reuerencia se inclina alos pies de Su Imperiosa Magestad, besando aquellas manos dignas de regir las riendas deste reyno,

---

[1] The *Titulillo* is addressed to the "muy poderosa Señora la Reyna Doña Ysabel." This would seem to indicate that the *Titulillo* was added at the time of the first printing in 1500 or at least after 1474 when Isabel became queen. In the *Prohemio*, Fray Martín calls her: "infanta legítima heredera delos reynos de Castilla y León" and refers to the necessity of mourning the death of her brother Alfonso. This places the date of the composition of the *Prohemio* in 1468. Fray Martín also refers to Isabel's "noble infancia" which he predicts will result in future glory and success. Since Fray Martín died in 1476, there is no evidence that he wrote the *Titulillo*, nor, on the other hand, is there evidence that he did not. In the Hispanic Society copy of the 1500 edition, following the last word in the *Titulillo* there is a handwritten notation in what appears to be a 15th-century hand that reads, "que fue el Rey don Juan el segundo."

[2] Isabel was born on April 22, 1451. Her mother, Isabel of Portugal, granddaughter of John I of Portugal, was Juan's second wife. His first wife, María of Aragón was the mother of Enrique *el Impotente*. This reference to Isabel's royal heredity might have been an indirect allusion to the questioned paternity of Enrique's daughter *Juana la Beltraneja*, whose appellation identifies Beltrán de la Cueva as her father.

& sobre mis ynojos cayendo con toda supplicante deuoción. Algunos, Señora, menos entendidos & por ventura no sabientes las causas naturales & morales, ni reuoluiendo las crónicas delos passados tiempos, auían a mal quando algund reyno o otra pulicía viene a regimiento de mugeres. [3] Pero yo, como abaxo diré, soy de contraria opinión, ca del comienço del mundo fasta agora vemos que Dios sienpre puso la salud en mano dela fembra, [4] porque donde nasció la muerte, de allí se leuantase la vida. Así como leemos del árbol donde vino la dapnación, que del mismo vino la salud, es assaber: del árbol de la cruz. E muchos pueblos y reynos fueron librados por muger & bien regidos, como si plaze a Dios parescerá en el processo deste tratado. Por lo qual avn que nos deuamos doler del yllustrísimo varón hermano vuestro, por quanto lo perdimos, pero de otra parte, el dolor se amansa quando vemos la noble infancia vuestra que en la hedad que es, tiene tal olor de florecientes virtudes; [5] las quales muestran que, quando el fruto será maduro, terná perfeto dulçor de graues costumbres; donde fazemos según el documento del sabio Séneca en vn libro *De remedios de fortuna* do dize: —que, quando perdemos algún bien, si nos queda otro, deuemos pensar enlo que sobra & dello gozarnos, no en lo perdido, que cobrar no se puede. [6]

---

[3] Aristotle wrote: "Sometimes however, women rule, because they are heiresses; so their rule is not in virtue of excellence, but due to wealth and power, as in oligarchies" (*Ethica Nichomachea*, trans. W. D. Ross, *The Works of Aristotle*, ed. W. D. Ross, Vol. IX [Oxford, 1925], 1161 a 1). Elsewhere he points out that men are fitter for command just as the elder are fitter than the young (*Politica*, trans. Benjamin Jowett, *The Works of Aristotle*, ed. W. D. Ross, Vol. X [Oxford, 1921], 1259 b 1-5). He also describes "the courage of a man [which] is shown in commanding, of a woman in obeying" (1260 a 24).

Could Fray Martín be referring to Muslim writers? A. J. Wensinck identifies the following: "The government of a woman does not render happy her people (*Al Bukhari* 92:18; *Al Tirmidhi* 31:75; *Al Nasa'i* 49:8)" (*A Handbook of Early Muhammadan Tradition* [Leiden, 1960], p. 255).

[4] In *Capítulo .iij. primera parte*, Fray Martín cites Solomon in Proverbs: "Que a donde la muger no es, que el enfermo gime," which continues this thought.

[5] This horticultural reference is, perhaps, an echo of earlier medieval prose in which the author would have extended the allegorical conceit of the title throughout the whole work.

[6] N. Bouillet mentions a 1492 edition published in Venice entitled *Seneca ad Gallionem de remediis fortuitorum* (L. Annaei Senecae, *Opera*

No se requiere poca sabiduría en aquéllos que tienen el gouer-
nallo delos reynos, ca vn ·hombre solo asaz es que sepa gouernar
assí mesmo donde no requiere tanta sciencia como el que ha
de governar casa, es asaber muger & fijos & otra familia; pero
el que ha de regir pueblos, conuiene que sea más sabio que todos,
que ha de gouernar así mismo como cada vno delos otros &
ha de regir su casa como los otros casados, e más ha de regir su
reyno. Donde Aristóteles en la *Política* dize: —que los hombres
que son sabios son delos otros natural mente regidores,[7] e por
esto los viejos natural mente han de regir alos moços [8] & el varón
ala muger & los hombres alas bestias & enel cuerpo humano, la

---

*Philosophica quibus Notitiam Literariam Bipontina Auctorem*, ed. N. Bouillet
[Paris, 1832], V, 726) in a section of notes concerning works falsely attributed to Seneca, relying on the classical scholarship of the experts of
Zweibrücken (Bipontium). Fray Martín does not mention the work's having
been addressed to Gallio, Seneca's brother. That the *De remediis fortuitorum*
was known in the 15th century as a Senecan work is clear from the evidence
of the 1492 ed. of Venice and two entries by Mario Schiff: A Latin edition of
Seneca, containing the *De remediis fortuitorum*, "longtemps faussement
attribué à Sénèque et dont l'auteur reste inconnu: fol. 104-105 v°," and a
Spanish translation by Alonso de Almela, *Libro de remedios contra adversa
fortuna* (*La Bibliothèque du Marquis de Santillane, Bibliothèque de l'École
des Hautes Études* Vol. 153 [Paris, 1905], pp. 102-126). The work appears
in L. Annaei Senecae, *Seneca Opera quae extant*, ed. Justi Lipsii, Vol. II
(Amsterdam, 1672); however the particular quotation does not appear. Karl
Alfred Blüher points out that Fray Martín seems to be relying on Seneca
in the *Compendio*, but is in fact quite often relying on this pseudo-Senecan
work (p. 168). See nn. 28, 29 and 30 to "Sources and Allusions" *supra*.
In Hermann Knust's edition of the *Bocados de oro*, I find: "E si tovieres
lo que quieres, seyendo errado, e perdieres lo que has, fasiendo derecho,
non torrnes por eso al yerro, nin te quites por eso de faser derecho" (p. 250).
Knust identifies the source of this aphorism as *Proverbios* by Seneca.
 As a reference to Isabel's mourning, the sentiment is a commonplace of
consolatory literature. Three examples of the admonition of not regretting
a loss are: "Consolación a Marcia, XII" where Seneca writes: "... convié-
nete no quejarte de lo que te quitó sino hacer gracias por lo que te cupo;"
"Consolación a Polibio,X": "Pues no hay nada más inconsecuente que afli-
girse por haber tenido poco tiempo a un hermano, y no alegrarse por haberle
tenido de todas maneras;" "Carta a Lucilo XCVIII": "Se nos quita el
tener, pero nunca el haber tenido" (*Obras Completas*, trans. Lorenzo Riber
[Madrid, 1966], pp. 146, 171, 698).
 [7] The 1542 ed. has *regidos*; the 1500 *regidores*. The obvious sense is
*regidores*.
 [8] Aristotle in his discussion of fitness to rule says: "... just as the elder
and full grown is superior to the younger and more immature" (*Politica*,
1259 b 5).

cabeça, do es la silla del seso, rige los otros miembros. [9] La razón desto se toma por[que] [10] regir es obra diuinal, ser regido es obra de cosas baxas como son las criaturas; [11] pues quanto la cosa es más semejante a Dios, tanto más la conuiene ser regido[r]. [12] Donde, por quanto el honbre fecho a ymagen & semejança de Dios, es más a Él semejante que las bestias, porende es natural mente señor dellas. Donde al comienço del mundo dixo Dios alos hombres: —Creced & multiplicad & henchid la tierra & sed señores delos peces del mar & delas aues del cielo & delas bestias dela tierra. [13] A do se notan dos potestades que dio alos honbres; la vna es natural quando dixo: —Creced & multiplicad. Esto se haze por natural generación & limpio matrimonio. La otra es ceuil, quando dixo: —E sed señores delas bestias. Pues hagamos tal razón: El honbre es señor delas bestias porque tiene entendimiento & razón delo qual carecen las bestias. Pues síguese que, quanto el hombre por sabiduría & virtud es más intelectual & razonal que los otros hombres, tanto es más digno de ser regidor dellos; donde el sabio se conpara alos que de sabiduría carecen, [14] como el honbre alas bestias, como los ojos alos pies,

---

[9] Aristotle uses the comparison of soul and body and ruler and ruled (*Política* 1254 a 34-36); St. Augustin relies on I Corinthians 11:3 "The head of the woman is the man" in (*Sermon on the Mount, Harmony of the Gospels, Sermons on Selected Lessons*..., trans. R. G. Mac Mullen, *A Select Library of the Nicene and Post-Nicene Fathers of the Christian Church*, ed. Philip Schaff [New York, 1888], Sermon LXXXII, 2, p. 505). In *The City of God* (trans. Gerald Walsh, *Fathers of the Church* [New York, 1952], II, 397, Bk. XIV, Ch. xxii) St. Augustin cautions: "... but it makes no sense to say that 'male' and 'female' are allegories of two qualities in a single person, for example that 'male' stands for the part that rules and 'female' for the part that is ruled."

[10] The 1542 ed. has *porque*.

[11] The divine source of a ruler's power appears most directly and succinctly in Wisdom 6:1-3: "Hear then, you kings, take this to heart; learn your lesson, lords of the wide world; lend your ears, you rulers of the multitude, whose pride is in the myriads of your people. It is the Lord who gave you your authority; your power comes from the most High."

[12] Both eds. have *regido*. The sense here seems to be *regidor*. See *supra* n. 7.

[13] See Genesis 1:28.

[14] In neither ed. is the word *sabio* capitalized so that it is not clear whether Fray Martín is referring to Solomon here or to a wise man in general. Possibly it is a reference to Proverbs 30:2-3: "Surely I am more brutish than any man and have not the understanding of a man. I neither

PRIMERA PARTE 139

como Dios alas criaturas, como el cielo ala tierra, como los latinos alos bárbaros. Dizen que bárbaros son aquellos que biuen sin ley. Los latinos son los que tienen ley. Pues derecho es delas gentes, que los honbres que biuen & se rigen por ley, sean señores delos que no tienen ley; donde sin peccado los pueden prender & hazer esclauos, porque natural mente son sieruos delos sabios & regidos por ley;[15] & de aquí podemos saber donde vino antiguamente que vn honbre fuese rey delos otros. Ca segund dize Julio Solino que los judíos solían escoger por [l]ey[16] al que veýan más sabio & de mejores costunbres & tal que alos suyos fuese clemente & piadoso; contra los enemigos, osado; por que no sola mente rigese[17] la república en tienpo de paz

---

learned wisdom, nor have the knowledge of the holy." These words are identified in Scripture as those of Agur, son of Jakeh, but since they are included in Proverbs, they could certainly have been attributed to Solomon, the traditional author of Proverbs. Also in Ecclesiastes 7:23, Solomon says: "All this have I proved by wisdom: I said, I will be wise but it was far from me."

[15] This is probably a reflection of Aristotle's views on slavery, one aspect of which is found in the *Política*: "For the slave has no deliberative faculty at all; the woman has, but it is without authority..." (1260 a 12-13).

[16] In the 1500 ed. the bottom of the letter is apparently that of an "l," but a handwritten correction has been added to change it to an "r." The 1542 ed. has *ley*. Both readings are possible, if Fray Martín considered the Talmud to be a book of law, as indeed it is.

This is a reference to C. Iulii Solini, *Collectanea Rerum Memorabilium*, ed. Th. Mommsen (Berlin, 1864), pp. 171-173. In an earlier edition, the chapter on the Jews appears: C. Iulii Solini, *Polyhistor* (Biponti: Ex Typographia Societatis, 1794), pp. 136-138. The English translation by Arthur Golding of 1587 has been reprinted (*The Excellent and Pleasant Worke, Collectanea Rerum Memorabilium*, facsimile reproduction by George Kish [Gainesville, Florida, 1955]). In none of these editions of what appears to be the only extant work of Julius Solinus is there a discussion of the Jewish method of selecting a king. The selection of a ruler on the basis of wisdom and skill does appear in *The Babylonian Talmud Seder Zera'im* (trans. I. Epstein [London: Soncino, 1948], p. 336) where the selection of Bezaleel, son of Uri is described. A test of wisdom is used, not a test of military prowess to which Fray Martín refers. In Exodus 31:2-5, the selection seems to be based on his skill as an artisan. St. Jerome refers to Bezaleel as one who was filled with wisdom, without any explanation (*Principal Works*, p. 128, Letter LX, 12) so that it might be assumed that Bezaleel had come to represent a ruler chosen for his wisdom quite early in the European tradition. Clearly, Fray Martín was aware of Solinus' chapter in praise of the Essenes, but he undoubtedly was relying on oral tradition here or on patristic sources such as St. Jerome.

[17] The 1542 ed. has *rigiese*.

con justicia, mas avn en tienpo de guerra, por armas la defensase & avn dilatase más tierras conquistando como fizieron vuestros antecesores que conquistaron las Españas & oxearon las moscas suzias de Macometo & los persiguieron con espada fasta el reyno de Granada, donde agora están por la negligencia delos modernos príncipes. [18]

Enestas presentes razones & enlas que porné después, como en jardín de donzellas, mire vuestro vivo entendimiento & tome deleyte por que, pues que la sucessión natural vos da el regimiento que no fallezca por defecto de sabiduría moral; antes la vuestra aprouada sabiduría vos haga digna de regir, como vos haze digna la real & primogénita sangre. [19] Donde, Señora, quise tomar este trabajo de hazer vna breue escriptura que hable dela generación & condición, conpusición delas nobles dueñas, en especial de aquellas que son o esperan ser reynas, esperando por

---

[18] Enrique IV's negligence in his pursuit of the reconquest of Granada was a clear political issue (see Ramón Menéndez Pidal, *Historia de España*, XVII, xii). Alonso de Palencia is cited as to his habits: "Sus aficiones, sus gustos, sus trajes son de los moros; como ellos cabalga a la jineta, se sienta en el suelo a la usanza de los moros; que así come con ellos miel, pasas, higos y manteca sin el menor recelo de veneno" (Paz y Melia, p. lxii). A petition sent by the Marqués de Santillana, D. Diego Hurtado, the Condes de Haro, Alba and Paredes, Alonso Carrillo and D. Fadrique asked that he govern according to the laws and statutes made by his ancestors and that he separate himself from the Moors in his court (Mosén Diego de Valera, *Memorial de diversas hazañas*, p. 21). This dissatisfaction culminated in the dethronement of Enrique in effigy at Ávila and the mock coronation of the young Alfonso. Luis Suárez Fernández (*Historia de España*, XV, p. 267) describes the event: "En una comedia de gusto popular, aquellos buenos vasallos leyeron a su soberano señor la larga lista de sus tremendos crímenes. Carrillo le quitó la corona, el Conde Plasencia la espada, el de Benevente el cetro y Diego López de Stuñiga derribó el espantajo a patadas acompañando el gesto con palabras soeces." Mosén Diego de Valera is the source for the following account: "Don Rodrigo Manrique [y otros] le quitaron todos los ornamentos reales, y con los pies [le] derribaron del cadalso en tierra y dixeron, 'a tierra puto'; y a todo esto gimían y lloraban la gente que lo veían" (*Memorial de diversas hazañas*, p. 33).

[19] It is hard to separate traditional flattery of a prospective monarch from reality, but here Fray Martín may be referring to a recognized intellectual interest that was to develop further in Isabel, if the testimony of her personal library is to be considered. After she ascended to the throne, Isabel studied Latin. Her teacher, Beatrix Galíndez is described by Andreas Schott (p. 341) as "salmantina non ignobilis, Isabellae Hispaniarum Reginae in Latinis Magistra."

este trabajo de sólo Dios galardón, por el qual los reyes reynan & los sieruos son dignos de ser reys. [20] Allegóse a esto la grand beniuolencia que oue a mi Señor de gloriosa memoria, el Rey Don Alfonso, [21] vuestro hermano & la grand deuoción que él en mí tenía, por su dulce & real clemencia.

---

[20] See Wisdom 6:1-3 and n. 11 *supra*. Cf. also Aristotle, *Politica* 1260 a 2-4: "It is evident therefore that both must possess virtue, but that there are differences between their virtues (as also there are differences between those who are by nature ruled").

[21] See n. 55 to "The Author and his readership" for Ramón Menéndez Pidal's opinion that Spain was at this time ruled by two kings. Alfonso's death at the age of 14 did not afford him the opportunity to display his royal clemency for very long.

Capítulo Primero

[*Capítulo .j.* pone cómo fue criada la primera muger segund la Santa Escriptura & primera mente muestra de qué parte del varón fue criada].[1]

Queriendo primera mente hablar dela generación dela muger, es aquí de notar que enlos varones ay tres maneras de ser fechos.[2] Las dos son marauillosas & la vna es natural. Las [marauillosas][3] son de Adán & de Jhesu Cristo, ca Adam fue hecho sin honbre & sin muger, mas por virtud de Dios, fecho del limo dela tierra quanto al cuerpo & inspiró enél resoplo de vida; esto es quanto al ánima. Jesucristo fue fecho tan bien por milagro, de muger sin varón, por virtud del Espíritu Sancto & avn por eso el Apóstol le llama el segundo Adán,[4] porque así como el primero fue criado de tierra virgen, así el segundo fue de carne & sangre virgen. Pues estos dos varones fueron fechos por marauilla; todos los otros fueron hechos por curso natural de varón & de muger.

Enlas mugeres no hallamos sino dos maneras de ser fechas. Es assaber, por miraglo como fue la primera muger & por curso natural com[o] son todas las otras. Pues yo, agora queriendo

---

[1] These descriptive headings appear only in the *tabla* of both eds. I will put them before each chapter as an aid to the reader.

[2] This idea is a commonplace in exegetical works. Cf. St. Jerome ("To Pammachius Against John of Jerusalem," p. 440) who writes: "Adam was created one way, Eve another, Abel another, the man Jesus Christ another."

[3] The 1500 ed. has *marouillas*.

[4] Two passages are applicable: I Corinthians 15:45: "And so it is written, The first man Adam was made a living soul; the last Adam was made a quickening spirit." I Corinthians 15:47: "The first man is of the earth, earthy: the second man is the Lord from heaven."

escreuir aquí de como la muger fue engendrada, primero diré de su fechura marauillosa & después dela natural. Quanto alo primero, digo que, por quanto la formación de la muger, primera mente es más honesta, ca Dios sin muger del varón la fizo, que la generación delas otras que se faze de varón & de muger. Por ende enla honesta, me determé más que enla otra. Porque dize Séneca enlas *Declamaciones* que, quando conlas vírgines & donzellas hablamos, que deuemos limar las palabras de toda torpedad, assí que enlas palabras ni enel seso dellas no suene cosa de que las virginales orejas se escandalizen; [5] & si esto conuiene a todo orador, mucho más a mí, que só religioso profeso de honestad. E, si a todas las vírgines assí conuiene que hablemos, quanto más a aquélla que deue ser resplandor de castidad & limpieza en todo este reyno.

Pues dela criación dela primera muger, Eua, estas cosas que se siguen diremos: ¿De qué parte del varón fue criada; de qué manera, en qué lugar; en qué tiempo & para qué fue criada; si se puede llamar hija de Adam, pues que dél fue hecha; cómo fue hecha de aquella costilla; si no peccaran, cómo seruiera la muger ala generación? Esto & todo lo que occurriere deste negocio, aquí diremos repartiendo todo esto por capítulos.

A lo primero: ¿De qué parte del varón fue criada la muger? La Escriptura dize que del costado. Donde enel segundo capítu[lo] del Génesis dize: —que como entre las criaturas no se fallase para Adán adjutorio semejante a él, es assaber para engendrar, como se hallaua entra las bestias macho & fembra, para multiplicar su linaje, Dios metió sueño en Adán & como él dormise [6] quitóle vna de sus costillas & hinchó aquel lugar de carne por ella; & el Señor Dios hedificó la costilla que tomó de Adam en muger. Aquí agora ay tres dudas: La primera ¿por qué

---

[5] Cf. L. Annaei Senecae (*Opera Declamatoria,* pars secunda, Vol. I, ed. N. Bouillet in *Bibliotheca Classica Latin sive Collectio Auctorum Classicorum* [Paris, 1831], p. 101, Controversarium Lib. 1, 2) where Seneca wrote: "Apparet quas proposui; dicendum est in puellam vehementer non sordide, nec obscoene." Fernando Rubio Álvarez locates this quotation as one from M. Annaeus Seneca, father of the "Philosopher," (*Prosistas castellanos del siglo XV, BAE* 171, p. 69, n. 3).

[6] The 1542 ed. has *dormiese.* See n. 16 to the *Prohemio* for a similar pattern of difference.

Dios crió la muger del varón, que pudiera criarlos en vno, como crió a todos los ángeles & no vno de otro? A esto asignan comúnmente los theólogos tres razones: la vna es porque Dios quiso que assí como Él hera vn principio effectiuo de todas las cosas, assí el hombre fuese principio de todos los hombres & enesto el hombre es más sublimado & más alto que el ángel; que no se halla vn ángel; que sea principio de todos los ángeles como se halla vn hombre que sea principio de todos los hombres. E así enel honbre quanto a esto reluze como la ymagen de Dios más que enel ángel: donde dize Sant Agustín que enesto la soberuia del diablo fue confundida & la humildad del hombre fue por la ymagen de Dios ensalçada, que Lucifer auía cobdiciado ser otro principio como Dios. E por que su soberuia fuese rebatida, [7] por ende, aquello recibió el honbre por don & prerogatiua lo quel diablo peruersamente robar quisiera, pero no pudo obtenerlo. Por ende la ymagen de Dios más reluzió enel hombre, por quanto, assí como Dios es principio de todas las cosas por criación, assí vn hombre fuese principio de todos los hombres por generación. [8]

---

[7] The 1542 ed. has *abatida*.

[8] Man's unique ability to procreate which makes him, in a sense, superior to the angels is frequently mentioned by St. Augustin: "When God made man according to his own image, He gave him a soul so endowed with reason and intelligence that it ranks higher than all the other creatures of the earth, the sea, the air.... Even before the nature of God is understood, it is wrong to think and say that there can be any other Creator of any nature whatsoever, however tiny and mortal it may be. Even though the angels (whom the Neo-Platonists prefer to call gods) can be ordered or permitted to aid God in producing what the earth brings forth, they can no more be called creators of animals than farmers can be called creators of crops and trees" (St. Augustin, *The City of God*, II, 290-1, Bk. XII, Ch. xxiv and xxv). Man is also superior to the angels in that once having reached heaven, he will not fall. Speaking about that human certainty, St. Augustin writes: "But if the angels have not the like certainty about themselves, we are not equal to them but more blessed than they..." (*Admonition and Grace*, trans. John Courtney Murray, *Fathers of the Church*, Vol. IV [New York, 1947], p. 278). Within the Augustinian framework, Satan's presumption was as Fray Martín said: "que cobdiciado ser otro principio como Dios," as demonstrated by St. Augustin who wrote: "And what is pride but an appetite for inordinate exaltation? Now exaltation is inordinate when the soul cuts itself off from the very source.... and somehow makes itself, and becomes an end to itself" (*The City of God*, II, 380, Bk. XIV, Ch. xiii).

La otra razón desto es: por quanto Dios quiso que entre los hombres ouiese grand paz & amor, assí como entre hermanos [9] que son nascidos de vn padre & de vna madre. Donde más ocasión han los hombres de se amar que los ángeles, que todos los honbres son de vn padre, lo que no hazen los ángeles. Otrosí más ocasión an de se amar que las bestias de vn especie, como las ouejas o los perros, entre las quales ha natural amor, como dize Salomón: —Que todo animal corre a se ayuntar con su semejante en especie. [10] Pero por las grandes malicias delos honbres, no se hallan tantas guerras ni debates entre las bestias como se hallan entre los hombres; & avn por esta razón se deue doblar el amor entre los cristianos, [11] que no sólo quanto ala carne vienen de vn padre & de vna madre como los otros hombres, mas quanto al espíritu son reengendrados por agua del Espíritu Sancto en el vientre dela madre Santa Yglesia. E por nuestra malicia, más guerras & malquerencias se hallan entre cristianos que entre moros ni judíos, ni entre otros paganos; e por esso la cristiandad es más açotada de tribulaciones & males que las otras naciones; que mayor peccado es a vn cristiano querer mal a su cristiano conel qual tiene doblada hermandad; es assaber, quanto ala carne & quanto al espíritu, que vn judío querer mal a otro judío, conel qual no tiene sino hermandad carnal. [12]

---

[9] The same idea is expressed by St. Augustin (*The City of God*, II, 289, Bk. XII, Ch. xxii) as follows: "God did not even wish to create the woman who was to be mated with man in the same way that He created man but, rather, out of him, in order that the whole human race might be derived entirely from one single individual."

[10] Ecclesiasticus 13:15-16: "Every animal loves its like, and every man his neighbor. All creatures flock together with their kind, and men form attachments with their own sort."

[11] Fray Martín is following the same sequence of ideas here as St. Augustin. The comparison between the warlike tendencies of men and beast follows St. Augustin's comments on the intention of God to create a kinship among men having created them from one single individual. See *supra* n. 8. See further St. Augustin, (*The City of God*, II, 289, Bk. XII, Ch. xxiii).

[12] St. Augustin does not develop the idea of the doubled relationship of the Christians as opposed to the single carnal one of the Jews, Moors, and pagans. In Fray Martín the unspoken comparison is made between the beasts and the non-Christian world.

La tercera razón es por quanto enesta manera de fazer la muger del varón se muestra claramente la procesión delas personas diuinales.[13] Donde así como Eua procedió de Adán, assí el hijo eternal procede del Padre por altíssima generación; e assí como de Adam & Eua procedió Abel, así del Padre & del Hijo procede eternal mente el Epíritu Sancto. Esta semejança pone Anselmo en el libro *De la procesión del Espíritu Sancto*.[14]

Así que, pues quando quistionamos por qué Dios hizo la muger del varón como la pudiera hazer de otra cosa, respondimos dando tres oportunidades por que así se fizo. La otra dubda es ¿por qué le quitó la costilla en sueño & no velando & despierto? A esto ay dos razones: La vna es ystorial, la otra figural. La ystorial dize que no sin causa fue quitada la costilla al honbre dormiendo & no despierto, dela qual la muger en adjutorio de generación fue formada. E esto se hizo por mostrar que enesto no sintió pena & porque se manifestasse el milagro dela diuinal potencia, que abrió el lado del hombre dormiente & no lo despertó de su dulce sueño;[15] como hazen los físicos

---

[13] Although exegetical literature abounds in the comparison between the creation of Adam and Eve and the coming of Christ (see nn. 2 and 4 to this chapter), Fray Martín's use of the parallel seems to be original; the image is of God, the teacher, using the sequence of creation to instruct mankind. St. Methodius uses the comparison to urge a continued generation of children of the Church applying "Be fruitful and multiply" in a spiritual sense (*The Writings of Methodius*, trans. William B. Clark and James B. H. Hawkins, *Ante-Nicene Christian Library*, ed. Alexander Roberts and James Donaldson [Edinburgh, 1880], pp. 27-29). St. Methodius does not, however, suggest that God deliberately ordained creation so as to teach a lesson; rather the lesson is to be drawn from the facts.

[14] Similarly, St. Anselm is concerned with explaining the nature of the Trinity, and does not make the same application of the relationship that Fray Martín makes. See S. Anselmi Cantuarensis Archiepiscopi, *De Processione Spiritus Sancti*, in *Opera Omnia*, ed. Franciscus Salesius Schmitt, O. S. B., 2 vols. (Edinburgh, 1946), II, 203, Ch. IX, 2; 213, Ch. XIV. See also St. Augustin, *Lectures or Tractates on the Gospel According to St. John*, trans. John Gibb and James Innes, *A Select Library of the Nicene and Post-Nicene Fathers of the Christian Church*, ed. Philip Schaff (New York, 1888), Tractate XCIX, 8, Tractate XCIX, 9, p. 384.

[15] The idea of a show of divine power in not awakening Adam is another example of Fray Martín's view of God, the teacher. Cf. n. 12 *supra*. St. Augustin comments on the miraculous nature of the act but does not gives it a specifically didactic value (*The Gospel According to St. John*, p. 67).

quando quieren hazer alguna incisión de grand dolor, dan al paciente apio & papauer que son dormideras, porque no sientan dolor enla llaga. [16] La otra razón es figural; como dize Sant Agustín en *Las cuestiones a Orozio:* en este fecho ouo gran mistión & fue figurado el sacramento de Cristo & dela Yglesia; que assí como la muger fue formada del costado del varón dormiente, assí la Yglesia fue formada delos sacramentos que manaron del costado de Cristo quando se adormió enla cruz; [17] que aquella muerte que rescibió Nuestro Señor enla cruz fue vn sueño. Bien paresce que a tres días despertó & después dela cabeça inclinada, dio el espíritu al Padre. Uno delos caualleros abrió con la lança su costado & luego de allí salió sangre & agua; la sangre para nos redimir & el agua para nos alimpiar de nuestras culpas. [18]

La otra dubda es ¿por qué la crió & formó del costado del varón más que de otra parte del cuerpo? A esto digo que fue assí hecho por mostrar que se criaua en compañía de amor y dilexión de su marido; que si Dios la criara dela cabeça del varón, paresciera que la hazía como su señora y si la criara delos pies, paresciera como que la criaua para servienta del varón. Pues por quanto [19] se hazía no por ser señora ni seruienta suya, mas para ser su compañera en matrimonio, porende fue sacada dela parte ygual, que es el costado, porquel varón ame a su muger como a socia & compañera, no la tema como a señora, nin la desdeñe como a seruienta.

---

[16] *Apio* refers to *apio de rana* of the genus *Ranunculus*, a member of which is *Aconitum napellus*, a cardiac and respiratory sedative. *Papauer* is the Latin word for poppy and the reference is clearly to an opium derivative. St. Isidore describes it as follows: "*Papaver* (adormidera), flor somnífera, de la cual dice Virgilio (Georg., 1, 78). *Lethaeo perfusa papavera somno* (La adormidera produce el sueño leteo). Hace dormir a los que la toman. Hay de dos clases: una usual y otra silvestre, de la cual fluye el jugo que se llama opio" (p. 431).

[17] The idea does not appear in the work cited, which is more properly entitled, *Ad Orosium Contra Priscillianistas et Origenistas* in Sancti Aureli Augustini, *Opera Omnia*, Vol. VIII in *Patrologiae Latinae Cursus Completus*, Series Prima XLII, ed. J. P. Migne (Paris, 1945), 666-683. It does, however, appear repeatedly in St. Augustin's *Lectures and Tractates on the Gospel According to St. John* (*Tractate*, IX, p. 66; *Tractate*, XV, 8, p. 101; *Tractate*, CXX, 2, p. 435).

[18] John 19:34.

[19] The 1542 ed. omits *por*. It reads *pues quanto*.

E por aquí podemos responder al que nos demandare de quál costado fue hecha, del derecho o del ysquierdo. Ca pues el varón auía de amar & honrrar su muger, razón hera que fuese formada del costado derecho, más que del yzquierdo. E así [20] la figura responde ala verdad, que el costado derecho de Jesucristo fue abierto con lança & de allí se formó la Yglesia. E assí hera expediente que del costado derecho fuese la muger formada, avn que no fallece quien diga que del ysquierdo fue herido Jesucristo, porque allí está más sentimiento de dolor. Pero esto contradize ala Escriptura que dize: —Vi el agua manante del templo del lado derecho. [21] E assí paresce cómo & por qué la fenbra fue formada del costado de su marido. Agora es bien que veamos de qué materia fue criada la muger.

---

[20] The 1542 ed. has *si*.
[21] I do not find the designation of the left side or the right side in the Bible. In a study of the *Lucidarios* of the 13th century, there appears a dialogue between a master and a pupil in which the pupil asks whether God used a rib from the right side or left side of Adam. The teacher explains that she was taken from the left side and therefore caused the Fall. Man's guardian angel is at his right side and his evil angel is at his left (*Los "Lucidarios" españoles*, ed. Richard P. Kinkade [Madrid: Editorial Gredos, 1968], p. 167). Fernando Rubio Álvarez identifies the quotation as part of the liturgy "en tiempo de Pascua" (*BAE*, 171, p. 77, n. 5). In the *Dictionnaire d'Archéologie Chrétienne et de Liturgie*, ed. Fernand Cabrol and Henri Leclercq (Paris, 1924), Henri Leclercq compares the right side and the left side of Christ in terms of the relative honor of being placed there in medieval art. He points out that since the sixth century, in relationship to Christ, the left side was the place of honor. However, the right side became the symbol of the sacred and the left, the profane, because of the liturgical use of the right hand to bless and the left to banish; the right hand to sign marriage contracts and the left to sign "les contrats sinistres." M. Leclercq observes a later change in which the right side becomes more important and offers as a conjecture that later the two sides were evaluated in terms of the perspective of the spectator rather than of Christ, himself. Fray Martín's assertion that the left side is more sensitive to pain might be supported by the idea that the right side is the side of life and strength; the left, the side of weakness and death according to M. Leclercq.

CAPÍTULO .ij.

[*Capítulo .ij.* de qué fue fecha la primera muger & por qué dela costilla más que de otra materia & allí nota buenas razones desto].

La formación dela muger tiene muchas excelencias sobre la del varón; la vna de las quales es que fue formada de más noble materia que el varón, porque el varón fue plasmado del limo dela tierra; la muger dela costilla del varón;[1] donde en la autoridad sobredicha dize: —que Dios ya puesto a Adam en aquel éxtasi o arrebatimiento de sueño, tiróle vna delas costillas & hedificó della la muger. Acerca desto ay aquí algunas questiones: la primera, si Dios tiró a Adam[2] vna costilla para fazer della la muger, paresce que Adam quedó amenguado en sus miembros, ca le fallece vna costilla. Como si hiziera la muger de vn dedo dela mano de Adán, quedara su mano amenguada & con quatro dedos, ca el quinto passara enel cuerpo dela muger. A esto digo que satisfaze en dos maneras: la vna es, que segund dizen algunos, que quando Dios formó el cuerpo de Adán, que le enxirió aquella costilla de más de que hiziese la muger. E

---

[1] D. Álvaro de Luna makes the same observation about Eve, that she "non ser fecha nin criada del limo de la tierra, así como Adam e todas las otras cosas que tienen ánima; mas de la más noble materia" (*Libro de las claras e virtuosas mugeres,* ed. Manuel Castillo [Madrid: Sociedad de Bibliófilos Españoles, 1908], p. 30) which seems to have been a commonplace. In spite of this idea's having been a part of the general corpus of knowledge, it must be remembered that Fray Martín had dedicated the *Compendio de la fortuna* to D. Álvaro de Luna, and that he could reasonably be expected to have a familiarity with D. Álvaro's book.

[2] The 1542 ed. has *tiró Adán*.

aquella costilla avn que fuese supérflua ensí quanto al cuerpo de Adán, pero hera necessario quanto ala multiplicación del linaje humano. E acabado que aquella costilla fue tirada de Adam, quedó él perfecto en sus miembros como si la muger Dios ouiera de fazer de vn dedo dela mano & criara enla mano de Adam seys dedos &, quitado vn dedo para hazer la muger, la mano quedara perfecta en cinco dedos. Así es aquí.

Otrosí dizen aquí que tiró a Adam vna de sus costillas & que, en lugar de aquélla como dize la Escriptura, suplió carne por ella; assí que, del lugar donde sacó la costilla, hinchólo de carne. Assí quel varón diese ala muger el huesso & Dios diese al varón, en lugar de huesso, carne. A dar a entender, que la muger es firme por el varón & el varón es flaco por la muger.

Dirá aquí alguno, si esto assí fue, quedó Adam con vna costilla menos, pues ¿por qué los hijos varones suyos no tienen menos aquella costilla? Digo que no se sigue que tengan los varones por esto vna costilla menos que las mugeres, ca enla común generación [3] vemos que, avn quel padre pierda vn mienbro, por eso no engendra hijo sin aquel mienbro, mas conél; donde si al padre cortan la mano, engendra hijos con ella; y que el padre pierda los ojos, engendra hijos que bien veen. Pues diremos segund esta [4] vía que, avn que Adam perdiese vna costilla para hazer la muger, que no quedó amenguado en sus miembros, ca Dios le suplió carne por ella. En aquella carne puso Nuestro Señor Dios virtud seminal, para que quando Adam engendrase, quel hijo touiesse tantas costillas como él tenía de antes & cada manera destas de dezir es buena & suficiente al caso,[5] pero la primera es más sotil.

---

[3] Fray Martín is possibly relying on Aristotle (*Generation of Animals*, trans. A. L. Peck [Cambridge, Massachusetts: Loeb Classical Library, 1943], 724 a 5-8): "As for mutilated parents, the cause is the same as that which makes offspring resemble their parents. And anyway, not all offspring of a mutilated parent are mutilated, any more than all offspring resemble their parents."

[4] The 1542 ed. has *según desta*.

[5] The idea of seminal virtue's presence in all parts of the body is explained by Aristotle in his discussion of dominant characteristics. The offspring resemble: "the parents from which the larger portion of the semen comes ... (this assumes that semen is drawn from each of the parts)" (*Generation of Animals*, 769 a 10-15).

Otra questión es aquí, ¿de quáles hera esta costilla, si hera delas más altas o delas más baxas, que se llaman fornecinas,⁶ o delas de medio que son mayores? A esto digo que Dios pudía fazer la muger de cada vna dellas, avn que la Escriptura no señala algo desto, pero da licencia alos doctores que piensen en cada cosa lo más conuenible. Donde podemos dezir que, como no fue expediente fazer la muger de la cabeça por que no fuese señora del marido, por esta mesma razón, no hera conueniente hazerla delas costillas más altas; & como no conuenía hazerla de los pies por que no fuese seruienta, assí ni delas más baxas, mas dela costilla que es más en medio de todas, porque fuese compañera & ygual. E esto se confirma por la lançada que tiene Jhesu Christo en medio delas costillas, la qual, como deximos, sinifica este misterio.

E si dizes: quando Dios la sacó de Adam, ¿si la sacó el huesso mondo dela carne?; digo que no, mas con carne & pellejo, porque, segund dize Job, —el cuerpo del honbre & dela muger es vestido de piel & de carne & es atado con huessos & nervios.⁷ Pues la costilla assí sacada con piel & carne auía más abilidad para formar el cuerpo dela muger, más que del hueso mondo. Donde Adán dixo después de despierto & vido la muger: —Este hueso es de mis huesos & esta carne es de mi carne; por ésta dexará el hombre al padre & ala madre & allegar se ha a su muger.⁸ Estas palabras muestran que la costilla fue arrancada con carne & piel. No digo que Dios no la pudiese hazer del hueso mondo, mas que Dios no obra absolutamente por potencia,

---

⁶ Is this related to *fornix-icis* 'arch or vault'? The etymology of the architectural term is given by St. Isidore: "*Arcos:* se dicen así porque están curvados estrechándose al final *arcta conclusione;* se llama también *fornices*" (*Etimologías,* p. 377).

⁷ Job 10:11: "Thou hast clothed me with skin and flesh and hast fenced me with bones and sinews." Fray Martín chose as support for his thesis that God created Eve out of bone and flesh this impassioned cry of Job's. This is an example of the accommodation of Biblical texts to suit new contexts.

⁸ Fray Martín's use of Genesis 2:23-24: "And Adam said, This is now bone of my bone, and flesh of my flesh; she shall be called Woman, because she was taken out of Man. Therefore shall a man cleave unto his wife and they shall be one flesh" is more appropriate than the quotation from Job. See n. 7 *supra*.

mas por obra & sapiencia & conuenencia. [9] Quiero dezir que no faze todo quanto puede, mas faze lo que conuiene; & es buen enxemplo para los poderosos que no vsen de potencia, mas de razón & justicia, poniéndose en justicia conel menor & conel mayor. Dios, pues, buen pudiere [10] hazer la muger dela costilla monda, pero no quiso, por que mientras más pasase enella dela substancia del varón, más ocasión ouiese dela amar & ella a él; & avn por eso esta costilla fue delas de en [11] medio que sciñen el coraçón & las entrañas; do dize Sant Pablo: —Varones, amad vuestras mugeres como Jesu Christo amó la Yglesia & se hizo por ella sacrificio enel ara dela cruz. [12]

Otra questión es: ¿por qué Dios hizo la muger más dela costilla que de otro miembro? A esto digo, según los philósophos, que el effecto siempre paresce & es semejante a su causa. [13] Donde por que la costilla era conuenible materia & causa material para hazer della la muger, por ende Dios la hizo de costilla. Darse pueden tres conuenencias que tiene la muger conla costilla: La vna que es flechible & significa la vertiblidad dela muger flexible. Quiere dezir que se puede hazer della vallesta, como hazen los que caçan las aues con costilla, que hazen della vallesta. E la muger es muelle & tierna, donde por eso en latín se llama *mulier*, que quiere dezir muelle. [14] Esto le viene a ella de su conplesión que es flemática & aquosa & por quanto el ánima sigue las conplesiones del cuerpo, así como la muger enel cuerpo es flaca & muelle, así enel ánima es vertible en deseos

---

[9] Although Fray Martín does not refer directly to a Biblical source here, the similarity to Jeremiah 10:12 is striking: "He hath made the earth by his power, he hath established the world by his wisdom and hath stretched out the heavens by his discretion."

[10] The 1542 ed. has *pudiera*.

[11] The 1542 ed. has *de medio*.

[12] Ephesians 5:25: "Husbands, love your wives even as Christ also loved the Church and gave himself for it."

[13] This philosophical truism can have as one of its sources: "If the cause exists, the effect exists; if the cause does not exist the effect does not exist, for the effect exists with the cause, and without cause there is nothing" (Aristotle, *The "Art" of Rhetoric* [London: Loeb Classical Library, 1939], 1400 a 36). It is curious that St. Thomas Aquinas, in the *Summa Theologiae*, II-II q. 110 a 1 § 3 should say: "The effect does not belong to the specific essence of its cause."

[14] This etymology comes directly from St. Isidore (*Etimologías*, p. 277).

& voluntades.[15] Donde según esto por que Dios sabía quel cruel caçador, Sathanás, auía de hazer armadijo conla muger para engañar al varón,[16] fizo la muger de costilla con que suelen los caçadores armar a los páxaros. E enesto auisaua a Adán que se guardase de caher enesta costilla. Do dize Sancto Ambrosio: —Que la muger es apta armadura para tomar las ánimas.[17] Ella enuistió al fuerte Sansón; ella enlazó al sancto Dauid; ella encostilló al sabio Salomón.[18] Assí que podemos dezir que Dios hizo

---

[15] Although Juan Huarte (1530-1591) wrote a century later than Fray Martín, his work is a compendium of existing attitudes towards the bodily humors. It is to be noted that women are said to have a predominance of phlegm and water, and therefore they are not as capable as men: "La razón desto es, como adelante probaremos, que la compostura natural que la muger tiene en el celebro, no es capaz de mucho ingenio, ni de mucha sabiduría.... Cuando los cuatro elementos, agua, y fuego especialmente entran en la composición del cuerpo humano en igual peso y medida, se hace el ánima prudentísima y de muy gran memoria; pero si el agua vence al fuego, queda tarde y estulta...." Huarte continues to establish that "de la flema para ninguna cosa se aprovecha el ánimo racional más que para dormir" (Juan Huarte de San Juan, *Examen de ingenios para las ciencias* [Buenos Aires: Colección Austral, 1946], pp. 42, 110, 174).

[16] St Augustin states: "The devil and his angels spread their snares as hunters do.... Let then thy way be Christ and thou shalt not fall into the snares of the devil" (*Expositions on the Book of Psalms*, ed. A. Cleveland Coxe, *A Select Library of the Nicene and Post-Nicene Fathers of the Christian Church*, ed. Philip Schaff [New York, 1888], Psalm XCI, 4, p. 446). The 1542 ed. has *maldito e cruel caçador*.

[17] St. Ambrose devotes chapter XIV in *Concerning Repentance* to the temptations of the flesh that woman represents (*Some of the Principal Works of St. Ambrose*, trans. H. Romestin and E. D. Romestin, *A Select Library...*, 2nd Series [1880; rpt. Grand Rapids, Michigan, Wm. B. Eerdmans Publishing Company, 1955], Bk. I, Ch. xiv, pp. 340-341).

[18] This is apparently a familiar catalogue of men deceived by women. Vergil and Aristotle are also often included. Domenico Comparetti (*Vergil in the Middle Ages*, trans. E. F. M. Benecke [Hamden, Connecticut, 1966]) lists a series of poetic catalogues including one by an anonymous French poet: "Par femme fut Adam déceu / Et Virgile moqué en fu, / David en fist faulx jugement / Et Salemon faulx testament: Ypocras en fu enerbé; / Sanson le fort deshonnoré; Femme chevaucha Aristote, / Il n'est rien que femme n'assote" (pp. 327-8). Comparetti also cites verses by Pau de Bellviure: "Por fembre fo Salamó enganat / lo rey Daviu e Samssó examen. / la payra Adam ne trençá'l mandament / Aristotil ne fou com ancantat, / e Virgili fou pendut en la tor, / e sent Ioan perde lo cap per llor / e Ypocras mori per llur barat" (p. 328, n. 3). Alfonso Martínez de Toledo writes: "Lee bien como fue Adam, Sansón, Davyd, Golyas, Salamón, Virgilio, Aristótiles, e otros dignos de memoria en saber e natural juycio..." (p. 55) and Calisto's query to Sempronio repeats the same theme: "Di pues, esse Adán, esse

la muger de vna vallesta de huesso & de vna costilla con que se podían enrredar los páxaros. Esta interpretación suena en mala propiedad dela muger, referiéndola a nuestra madre Eua, conla qual el [demonio] [19] encostilló a nuestro padre Adam. Pero si lo referimos ala Virgen María, será loable declaración; ca así como Eua es vituperio delas mugeres, así la Virgen es loor dellas. E assí como con Eua armó costilla el demonio al hombre, assí Dios conla Virgen María armó costilla para encepar al diablo. [20] Como dize Sant Agustín: —Que la cruz en que pendió Jhesu Cristo hera ratonera para tomar el suzio ratón Lucifer, assí la Virgen fue costilla para tomar el negro morciélago Satanás. [21] Assí que enla costilla ser flexible & apta para hazer vallesta & armadijo, podemos entender los males de Eua & delas otras mugeres que la siguen & podemos entender los bienes dela Virgen & delas otras santas fembras; ca las malas son vallesta de Cupido, ques dios de amor, & tiran saetas de furtibles ojadas & de blandas palabras para herir los coraçones delos varones & arrendarlos. Las sanctas & buenas son vallesta & arco turqués [22] para matar a Cupido & suzios amores; donde se dize dela Virgen María, que como ella fue muy hermosa, pero quando alguno la

---

Salomón, esse Dauid, esse Aristótiles, esse Virgilio, essos que dizes, ¿cómo se sometieron a ellas? (*La Celestina*, I, 50).

[19] The 1542 ed. has *demonio*.

[20] This view of woman as the weapon of the devil is strongly expressed by Luis de Lucena: "... principio de pecado, arma del diablo, expulsión de paraýso, ... puerta de la muerte, llaga de scorpión, ... diminución de las fuerzas y disformación, ... rosa que hiede" (*Repetición de amores*, p. 67). Cf. also Sempronio's statement that woman is: "Arma del diablo, cabeça de pecado, destruýción de paraýso" (*La Celestina*, I, 49-50).

[21] St. Augustin refers to the cross as a weapon: "... because the Lord was about to overcome death by dying, and by the trophy of his cross to triumph over the devil, the prince of death..." (*The Gospel According to Saint John*, Tractate LI, Ch. xii, 2, p. 283). The use of *muscipula* 'trap' instead of *laqueus* which appears in the Vulgate, is attributed to St. Jerome and to St. Cyprian in a note by W. H. Fremantle in *Principal Works of St. Jerome* (p. 6, n. 4). Elsewhere David Lenfant cites *Fragmento, Sermone in med. Tom. 10* under *crux:* "Sed venit redemptor & victus est deceptor. Et quid fecit redemptor noster captiuatori nostro? Ad pretium nostrum tetendit muscipula crucem suam; posuit ibi quasi escam sangui nem suum" (*Concordantiae Augustinianae* [Paris, 1666; Impression Anastatique, Brussels, 1965]).

[22] The *arco turqués* is not mentioned in the standard descriptions of the various kinds of bows.

miraua por corrupto & mal deseo que touiese, en mirándola luego sele apagaua el mal desseo & le venía casta & limpia voluntad. E por esso es comparada al cedro, cuyo olor mata los sapos & las sierpes. [23]

La otra propiedad dela costilla es corua & tuerta. E significa bien & mal enla muger, ca si la muger no guarda su castidad, házese corua & abaxada so la potestad del varón & pierde la derecha línea de puridad & házese tuerta & rebuelta como culebra. La muger casta es dicha como vna verga de fumo fecha de odorantes perfumes; perdiendo la castidad es retuerta & corua como costilla de asno muerto. Que la costilla sea corua [24] significa en bien, si con su castidad se acompaña la sancta humildad.

La otra propiedad es enla costilla que suena; & significa que la muger habunda enla lengua & en palabras más quel varón; donde como vno demandase a otro ¿por qué las mugeres fablan más que los varones? Respondió el otro burlando: —porquel varón fue formado & fecho de tierra, que es materia sorda & no suena nada; la muger fue fecha de huesso, donde si pones dos o tres huessos en vna calabaça y la mueues, más ruýdo y son hazen que nuezes puestas en costal. Enesto dezir dellas, no se tengan por desonrradas, ca Dios por esto sabiendo que heran parleras, primero que alos varones les reueló su resurrección [25] porque por sus lenguas fuese publicada; & avn sígueles prouecho dezirles esto, por que si son cuerdas & prudentes, el vicio a que son inclinadas & enmendarlo an, poniendo freno en sus lenguas. Do dize Valerio en el segundo: —Que hornamento & compostura graciosa dela muger es el silencio. [26] E si esto es verdad enlas

---

[23] Among the trees to which the Virgin is compared is the cedar. See Louis Réau, *Iconographie de l'Art Chrétien*, Vol. II: *Iconographie de la Bible* II, Nouveau Testament (Paris, 1957), p. 80. I have not been able to find any reference to the power of cedar to kill toads and snakes.

[24] The 1542 ed. has *corcova*.

[25] Woman's loquacity is a commonplace of misogynistic literature. See Ch. xii of the *Arcipreste de Talavera* (pp. 168-170). Is Fray Martín making a comic misapplication of Matthew 28: 1, 7, 10 here?

[26] The reference is undoubtedly to Valerius Maximus whose book about *Factorum et Dictorum Memorabilium*, Fray Martín used extensively as a source of the stories of noble women. However, in Bk. II, 3 of the *Memorable Deeds* the closest equivalent is: "Quae uno contentae matrimonio

otras dueñas, tanto más es verdad enlas grandes señoras, cuyas palabras suenan por todo su imperio & por ende deuen ser pocas & graues.

---

fuerant corona pudicitiae honorabantur..." (Valerii Maximi, *Factorum et Dictorum Memorabilium*, p. 58).

Capítulo Tercero

[*Capítulo .iij.* en qué lugar fue la muger criada & da causas por que en paraýso fue fecha & no el varón].

Visto de qué materia fue formada la muger, síguese que veamos dónde & en qué lugar fue criada; & dizen los doctores que en paraýso terrenal, donde la orden fue aquesta: Dios primero crió al hombre eneste mundo en vn campo que se llama damaceno, donde toda la tierra es colorada;[1] & de aquella tierra vermeja formó Dios al hombre quanto al cuerpo; donde por eso le llamó Adam que quiere dezir ruuio, porque fue fecho de tierra vermeja; & así es el cuerpo del hombre que es regado todo y mantenido de sangre.

Eneste campo fue después fundada la ciudad de Ebron, la principal delos filisteos, & fue primero morada delos gigantes, delos quales fue vno Golías, al que mató Dauid.[2] E desque los hijos de Ysrael ganaron la tierra de promissión, cayó en suerte

---

[1] Fray Martín is repeating here the most common of the theories as to the meaning of Adam's name. Theodor Gaster points out that "the color was probably intended to explain the redness of blood." The Hebrew word for man in general is *adam;* for ground it is *adamah* and for red is *adom* (*Myth, Legend and Custom in the Old Testament* [New York, 1969], pp. 18-19). There are various opinions about the word *damaceno:* Hebron was at one time called in Latin, *Ager Damascenus,* after Abraham's steward, Eliezer of Damascus (Zev Vilnay, *Legends of Palestine* [Philadelphia, 1932], p. 170) and St. Jerome saw the origin as the Hebrew word *Dam-Shaca,* 'irrigated with blood' because it was here that Cain killed Abel (Vilnay, p. 452). Louis Réau sees a connection with Adam's name because he was buried there (p. 72).

[2] Genesis 6:1-4.

al tribu³ de Judá & fue ciudad sacerdotal; & esta ciudad de Ebrón en lengua arábiga se llama Cariatarbe, que quiere dezir 'ciudad de quatro', por que los quatro santos patriarchas fueron allí encerrados en la cueua doble;⁴ es asaber, Adán, Abrahán, Ysach & Jacob & sus quatro mugeres, Eua, Sarra, Rebeca & Lía. Está asentada Ebrón cerca del valle delas lágrimas,⁵ assí llamado por que Adán lloró en aquel valle cient años a su hijo Abel; enel qual valle, después amonestado por el ángel a Eua su muger, & engendró a su fijo Seth,⁶ del qual, después por muchas generaciones, vino Ihesu Christo criado.

Pues Adam en aquel canpo, Dios después lo trasladó en paraýso terrenal,⁷ que allí, como dize el comienço del Génesi, formó la fembra enla manera que deximos.

---

³ The 1542 ed. has *al tributo*.
⁴ Genesis 23:2 gives the name as *Kir-jath-arba* which is translated as 'city of the four' reflecting the quadruple burial of the patriarchs (Vilnay, pp. 155-6). The place name continued as Cariath Arbe in juxtaposition with Hebron on a map of the Holy Land (*Geographiae Sacrae ex Vet.: et Novo Testamento desumptae. Tabula Secunda in qua Terra Promissa sive Iudeae in suas Tribus Partes q. distincta. Aut N. Sanson Abbavilloeo et Christianiss* [sic], Galliarum Regis Geographo [Padua, 1696]). Tradition has it that the name 'Hebron' is made up of two Hebrew words: *Haber Naeh* 'agreeable friend' referring to Abraham. The Arabs call it Al-Khalil al Rahman 'the friend of the Merciful.' Fray Martín identifies *Cariatarbe* as an Arabic place name. Was he aware of the Arabic place name *al-garia* (La Alcarria) 'la aldea, la villa'. (M. Asín Palacios, *Contribución a la toponomía árabe de España*, 2d. ed. [Madrid-Granada, 1944], pp. 52-53) which would connect the name with the Hebrew *Kiryath* 'city?' Although the Arabic name for Hebron was *Al Khalil al-Rahman*, Fray Martín might have encountered an Arabic rendering of *Kiryath arba*. As to the rendering of *arba* as 'four', E. A. Speiser mentions *Arba* for Hebron in Joshua 15:13. He translates *arba* as 'father of the giants' and suggests that 'four' was a popular adaptation of some other word that was non-Semitic as was the case with the Mesopotamian city of Arbilum (older Urbilum) which had been improperly etymologized as 'four gods' (*Anchor Bible, Genesis* [New York, 1964], p. 169, n. 2).
⁵ Contrary to expectations, the expression 'valley of tears' does not appear in the Old Testament. Zev Vilnay mentions the use of the expression to describe Hebron, by Fettelus, the Archdeacon of Antioch writing in 1130 (pp. 170-171). It was in Hebron that Adam is said to have mourned for Abel for a hundred years. D. Álvaro de Luna uses the phrase "... la más excelente, e noble criatura que Dios en lo terrenal aya fecho, e non en aqueste valle de lágrimas e mar de amargura, lleno de trabajos e tristezas, mas enel paraýso terrenal..." (p. 30).
⁶ Genesis 5:3.
⁷ Genesis 2:8.

Pero aquí hará questión, alguno: ¿por qué la muger lleua esta excelencia al varón que ella fuese criada en paraýso & el varón no, sino eneste mundo? A esto se pueden dar tres expedientes: el primero es porque Dios quiso criar el honbre del más baxo elemento de todos que es la tierra & avn dela tierra delo más baxo della. E por quanto la tierra del paraýso es más alta que la tierra deste mundo, como la tierra delos montes es más alta que la delos valles, fue expediente segund el propósito de Dios quel varón fuese criado eneste mundo, enel qual virtualmente fue criada la muger. Donde enel Génesi, enel primero capítulo, dize: —Que crió Dios al honbre ala ymagen y semejança suya, macho y fembra los crió;[8] & claro es que la fembra avn no hera fecha & ya el honbre[9] es dicho ser macho y fembra;[10] pero por quanto auía de ser fecha del costado de Adán, enél ya se contaua por sustancia del qual auía de proceder según la forma; así quel varón fue criado fuera del paraýso. E quanto ala sustancia & ala forma, la muger fue criada fuera de paraýso; quanto ala substancia fue criada en paraýso; quanto a su propia forma: enesto lleua perogatiua sobre el varón.

E para esto notas[11] vna causa muy alta & secreta, por que Dios crió al hombre compuesto de cosa vesible, que es el cuerpo, & de cosa inuesible que es el ánima; que si el honbre no fuera, pudiera ser que los ángeles que son espirituales fuesen participantes dela gloria & bien auenturança delos sanctos; pero las cosas corporales no pudieran participar aquella gloria & porende pensó Dios de hazer vna criatura compuesta de cuerpo y de ánima intelectual; & el cuerpo compuesto de quatro helementos por quel ánima leuase consigo el cuerpo ala gloria & asi los cielos & la tierra fuesen llenos dela gloria de Dios. Donde quando el hombre viene ala gloria, enél vienen todas las criaturas, ca el hombre es toda criatura; ca toda criatura o es vesible o inuisible. El hombre lo comprehende todo, para dar a entender quel hombre hera criado para poseer paraýso. El varón fue criado aquí & la henbra en paraýso.

[8] Genesis 1:27.
[9] The 1542 ed. has *y el hombre*.
[10] This passage refers to the apparent contradiction between Genesis I and Genesis 2. See *infra* n. 12.
[11] The 1542 ed. has *nota*.

El otro expediente fue por honrrar el matrimonio, que es legítima conjunción entre varón & muger, do dizen que esta dignidad tiene el sacramento del matrimonio sobre todos los otros, que los otros fueron instituýdos eneste mundo, que es valle de lágrimas, & el matrimonio en paraýso. [12] Los otros fueron instituýdos en estado de pecado; el matrimonio en estado de ynocencia. Donde por que este sacramento toma nonbre dela madre más que del padre, ca se llama matrimonio y no patrimonio, [13] fue expediente que la madre fuese honrrada, criándola en lugar honrrado, que es paraýso, ca dizen que en aquellas palabras que dixo Adam por ésta, es assaber: —Por la muger dexará el hombre al padre & ala madre & morará con su muger. Fue instituýdo el matrimonio, el qual no es otra cosa sino ayuntamiento legítimo de macho & fembra, hombres; ca entre los animales avn que sean macho & henbra ayuntados, no es matrimonio. E el ayuntamiento matrimonial retiene indeuisa costunbre deuida.

Los bienes del matrimonio son tres: es assaber, fe & casta generación & sacramento; fe que aya fieldad, la qual guarde el varón ala muger & la muger al varón; casta, quel matrimonio se haga con intención de hazer fijos, a seruicio de Dios; sacramento: que sea no partible, que no se parta vno de otro fasta la muerte, [14] donde por quel matrimonio es venerable ayuntamiento

---

[12] The statement that the sacrament of marriage was instituted before the Fall and that Adam and Eve coupled in innocence in Paradise is explained by St. Augustin: "For ourselves, we have no manner of doubt that to 'increase and multiply and fill the earth' in obedience to the blessing and command of God is the very mission which God gave to marriage as He instituted it from the beginning and, so, before the Fall. That is why He made the bodies of the two sexes male and female so manifestly different" (*The City of God*, II, 397, Bk. XIV, Ch. xxii). See *infra* n. 2 to *Capítulo octauo, primera parte* for a specific description of this innocent union (also by St. Augustin). Fray Martín's departure from Augustin is indicated by the word "honrrar." Once again, Fray Martín seems to be envisioning God, the teacher whose plan was to institute matrimony before the Fall in order to influence men's minds.

[13] It is curious that St. Isidore omits this engagingly didactic etymology.

[14] In a discussion of marriage and its irrevocability, St. Augustine (*The City of God*, II, 398, Bk. XIV, Ch. xxii) observes that Moses permitted the Israelites to dismiss their wives, but that Matthew 19:3-6 contains Jesus' answer. See in particular Matthew 19:6 "Wherefore they are no more twain, but one flesh. What therefore God hath joined together, let not

& cama limpia & lecho sin manzilla, el qual se hizo & ordenó quando la hembra fue criada, porende fue expediente que ella fuese criada en lugar sancto & limpio, que es el paraýso terrenal.

El otro expediente fue por figurar la dignidad & sanctidad dela Virgen María, donde es assaber: que por el paraýso se figura la Virgen, por siete cosas que conuienen al paraýso. [15] La primera es la interpretación del vocable, donde paraýso quiere dezir cosa que para el viso & la vista. [16] E la Virgen María, Nuestra Señora nos paró la visión de Dios, la qual Eua nos quitó, ca por su glorioso parto fue fecho visible él que primero hera inuisible. Donde dixo Sant Juan: —Nos vimos la su gloria, que es como gloria de vnigénito del padre, lleno de gracia & de verdad. [17] Abacud dixo: —Después desto fue visto enla tierra & conlos hombres conuersó. [18]

Lo segundo por la hermosura delas flores & enla Virgen fueron flores spirituales; rosas de caridad, violas de humildad, lirios de virginidad; donde enlos Cánticos: —Flores aparecieron en nuestras tierras. [19]

Lo tercero, por la compostura de muchos árboles, ca enella fueron aquellos árboles: delos quales dize el Ecclesiástico: —Como cedro só ensalçada, en el Líbano, [20] fue ella vergel de

---

man put asunder." The permission for divorce is found in Deuteronomy 24:1-5: "When a man hath taken a wife, and married her, and it come to pass that she find no favor in his eyes, because he hath found some uncleanness in her; then let him write her a bill of divorcement, and give it into her hand, and send her out of his house."

[15] Cf. the elaborate structure of the "ssiete letras de Alpha et O que muestran cada una ssiete nombres de Dios" (Alfonso el Sabio, *Setenario*, ed. Kenneth H. Vanderford [Buenos Aires, 1945], pp. 3-47). Christopher Butler cites the *De Nuptiis*, Bk. 7 of Martianus Capella who wrote in the fifth century that seven was virgin because "it is neither generated nor generating within the decad" (*Number Symbolism* [New York, 1970], p. 34).

[16] This fanciful etymology is not is St. Isidore.

[17] John 1:14: "...(and we beheld his glory, the glory as of the only begotten of the Father) full of grace and truth."

[18] This quotation does not appear in Habakkuk. See Baruch 3:38 and I Corinthians 15:6.

[19] Song of Songs 2:11: "...the flowers have begun to blossom."

[20] Ecclesiasticus 24:17: "I grew to my full stature as cedar grows in Lebanon."

Dios. Fue cedro de pudicicia que es holor de castidad; fue ciprés de puridad; fue palma de paciencia; oliva de piedad. [21]

Lo quarto, por que así como el paraýso se regaua de claras aguas, assí enla Virgen corren ríos de gracia; [22] donde enel Ecclesiástico dize Dios: —Yo regaré mi huerto de mis plantaciones; [23] enel Ecclesiastés dize: —Que todos los ríos de gracia entran enel mar; [24] es assaber, en María, donde: —*Aue gracia plena.*

Lo quinto, por que enella es la fuente que mana del lugar de deleytes, es assaber: el fijo de Dios dela eternidad del Padre.

Lo sexto, por que della, como de paraýso, salen quatro ríos: el primero es de misericordia, éste corre hazia los peccadores; el segundo es de consolación, éste corre hazia los atribulados; el tercero es de gracias, éste va hazia los justos; el quarto es de gozos, éste va hazia los beatos. [25] Pues la primera fenbra ser formada en paraýso [26] significó que la segunda auía de ser nuestro paraýso significó que la segunda es assaber, la Virgen, auía de subir

---

[21] The image of the Virgin as a garden, or more properly a grove of trees, is a familiar one, which might be considered to have its origin in the 'mixed forest' described by Ernst Curtius (pp. 194-95). Although Gonzalo de Berceo includes only fruit trees in his *locus amoenus*, in his explanation he identifies the trees as: "los santos miraclos que faz la Gloriosa" and the shade of the trees as "las oraciones que faz Santa María" (*Milagros de Nuestra Señora*, ed. Antonio G. Solalinde [Madrid: Clásicos Castellanos, 1964], p. 7, copla 23c and 25b). Of the specific trees used by Fray Martín, the medieval iconographic tradition is: "D'autres emblèmes sont empruntées aux fleurs, L'Imaculée est un *Jardin clos* (Hortus conclusus), une *Fontaine de jardin* (Fons hortorum), un *Puits d'eaux vives* (Puteus aquarum viventium). Elle est comparée au *cèdre du Liban* (Cedrus exaltata), a *l'olivier* (Oliva speciosa), au *lis qui fleurit entre les épines* (Lilium inter spinas), et a un *buisson de roses* (Plantatio rosae)" (Louis Réau, *Nouveau Testament*, p. 80). See n. 23 to *Capítulo ij, primera parte.*

[22] Genesis 2:10: "And a river went out of Eden to water the garden and from thence it was parted and became into four heads...."

[23] Ecclesiasticus 24:42-43: "I thought to refresh my well set garden, give drink to the fruits that fringe its border..."

[24] This is not found in Ecclesiastes but rather in Ecclesiasticus 40:11-12: "And all waters find their way back to the sea."

[25] Gonzalo de Berceo uses the four rivers in his idealized meadow: "Las quatro fuentes claras que del prado manavan, / Los quatro evangelios esso significavan, ..." (p. 6).

[26] It follows that, if Adam was the first man and Jesus the second, in the exegetical tradition Mary would be the second woman.

en cuerpo & en ánima a paraýso & significaua que Jhesu Christo se auía de magnifestar [27] ala muger Magdalena después dela Resurrección enel huerto en especie de ortolano. [28]

Lo séptimo, por que assí como en medio del paraýso estaua el árbol de vida, assí en medio del vientre virginal se plantó el verbo del Padre, fecho carne, para que morase con nos, donde ella es árbol de vida a todos los que la alcançan por deuoción.

La qual, avn que todos los fieles enella deuen auer, empero en especial, la señora Princesa, por que es de linaje real, como la Virgen que fue fija de reys, [29] & por que es doncella, como hera la Virgen quando concibió al fijo de Dios, & por que espera de ser reyna, como la Virgen que es Reyna delos cielos, señora delos ángeles, madre delos peccadores & manto de todos los fieles.

---

[27] This spelling common to both editions might represent a false etymology, a mixture of *'magnificare'* and *'manifestare.'*

[28] John 20:15: "...She [Mary Magdalene] supposing him to be the gardener saith unto him, Sir, if thou hast borne him hence, tell me where thou hast laid him, and I will take him away."

[29] Mary's lineage is traced to Nathan, the first son of David and Bathsheba.

Capítulo Quarto

[*Capítulo .iiij.* habla del tiempo quando fue criada & de qué hedad & días fue criada].

Por consiguiente, resta que veamos del tiempo quándo la muger fue criada & para esto saber, quiero aquí contar la creación de todas las cosas, por que veyendo quándo cada cosa fue criada, tomaremos tino dela muger quándo fue formada.

Nota, pues, aquí, que las obras que Dios al comienço fizo son departidas en tres partes:[1] es assaber, en obras de criación, en obras de distinación[2] en obras de hornato, que quiere dezir afeyte. Enesta manera se entiende, ca Dios primero crió algunas cosas, después las distinguió & después las afeytó & pintó. Las obras dela creación fueron hechas antes de todo día; es assaber, enel comienço del tiempo. Las obras dela distinción fueron repartidas por tres días primeros: estos fueron domingo, lunes, & martes. Las obras dela pintura fueron hechas enlos tres días siguientes, que son miércoles, jueues & viernes. E enel séptimo, que es el sábado, folgó Dios y cesó de más criaturas hazer.

---

[1] One of the works mentioned in the early bibliographies is a *Hexameron* by Fray Martín. Although this work has as yet not been found, it is reasonable to assume that the schematic division of the days of creation into three groups in this chapter would have been expanded in the lost book. Both Antonio Possevini whose *Apparatus sacer* was published in 1603 and 1606, and Joseph Pamphilo whose *Chronica* appeared in 1581, give the title of Fray Martín's book on Genesis as "in tria prima capita Geneseos." These scholars may be showing a familiarity with the work and may be alluding to a tripartite division of Creation as well as the first three chapters of Genesis.

[2] Both eds. have *distinación* here and later *distinción*. The sense is obviously *distinción*.

Las obras dela criación son quatro: es assaber, el cielo imperio, los ángeles, el tiempo & la materia, que hera para de que se hiziesen los quatro helementos & las cosas corporales. Donde dize el comienço del Génesi: —Enel principio crió Dios el cielo y la tierra. La tierra hera vana & vazía & las tiniebras estauan sobre la faz del abismo. E el espíritu de Dios andaua sobre las aguas.[3] Enlo que dize, enel principio, se nota el tiempo, ca quiere dezir, enel principio del tienpo. Enlo que dize, crió Dios el cielo, se nota el emperio, el qual luego como fue criado fue lleno de sanctos ángeles; donde tan bien se nota, los ángeles. Enlo que dize, que crió la tierra vana & vazía, se nota la materia de que todas las cosas corporales fueron hechas y formadas por interualo de seýs días; la qual, antes que sea formada, es grosera como tierra & vana sin operación; es vazía de ser; es tenebrosa por carecer de hermosura; es abismo por que no puede ser vista ni conoscida; es agua por que se derrama si por la forma no es contenida, assí como el agua si no es contenido enel vaso.

Assí questas quatro cosas fueron criadas en vno: el tienpo, el cielo, los ángeles & la materia primera. Donde los sanctos dizen que estas quatro cosas[son] coenas,[4] que quiere dezir de vna hedad como dos niños que nascen en vn día, coenos, que quiere dezir yguales en hedad & en tiempo.[5]

Dirá aquí alguno: ¿por qué no se haze mención dela criación delos ángeles? A esto dize Sant Agustín: —Que por que Moysé hablaua alos judíos, que hera pueblo carnal & no podía tomar nada delas cosas inuisibles & espirituales, porende no fabló dela criación delos ángeles,[6] sino so figura delas cosas corporales;

---

[3] Genesis 1:1-2: "In the beginning God created the heaven and the earth. And the earth was without form, and void; and darkness was upon the face of the deep. And the Spirit of God moved upon the face of the waters."

[4] *Coenus* in both eds. is probably a misprint for *coevos* from *co-aevus*.

[5] See St. Augustin's explanation that the angels were not co-eternal with the Creator. They must have been created simultaneously with time "for the simple reason that if there is no creature at all by whose successive movements time can be reckoned, then there can be no such thing as time at all." Further he writes: "Time is co-temporal with movement and change" (*The City of God*, II, 274, Bk. XII, Ch. xvi).

[6] The reference to Moses, here, is in his rôle as the author of the Pentateuch. A frequent feature of the iconography of Creation was: "Moïse méditant le Livre de la Génèse ou le recevant des mains de Dieu" ac-

donde los ángeles se entiende quando dize que crió el cielo, que es morada de ángeles & bien paresce que Dios no auía de criar la casa vazía de sus moradores. Pero lo que aquí dexó Moysén de hablar dellos en otros lugares dela Escriptura lo pone, donde enel Cántico delos tres niños que estauan enel fuego & no se quemauan; do llamauan todas las criaturas para bendezir a Dios, traxeron entrellas los ángeles, diziendo: —Bendezid los ángeles del Señor a El.[7]

Pues estas quatro cosas pertenescen alas obras dela criación que fueron fechos [8] en uno, antes de todo día.

Después desto síguense las obras dela distinción, que fueron hechas enlos tres primeros días. Distinción quiere dezir hazer las cosas en sus propias formas & especies, las quales antes estauan confusas en vna massa; como si vn entallador touiesse vn grand madero & de allí entallase vna figura de honbre & de muger & de cauallo & de árbol & de otras cosas. Assí Dios, dela materia que auía criado de nada, començó a formar & distinguir sus especies. Enel primero día, que fue domingo, hizo la luz, & enel segundo, que fue lunes, hizo el firmamento que es el cielo, éste que vemos sobre nos; ca el primero cielo del qual dixo enel principio, crió Dios el cielo. Otro cielo es a nos inuisibles [9] que es morada de sanctas ánimas & delos ángeles; & enel tercero día, mandó que las aguas que heran so el firmamento, que se

---

cording to Louis Réau (*Ancien Testament*, p. 68). As for the carnality or the unworthiness of the Jews to receive word of the angels from Moses, apparently the need was felt to explain why the angels were mentioned so late in the Old Testament and why they had not played a part in Genesis. The nature of the Jews is described by St. Augustin thus: "It was written, it was read; when it was recited we heard it; but we heard it as said to the Jews.... They have not joined to the society of the holy angels; they sought earthly things of the Lord; for a land of promise, victory over enemies, fruitfulness of child-bearing, increase of children, abundance of fruit, — all which things were indeed promised to them by God, the True and the Good, promised to them, however as to carnal men" (*On the Gospel According to St. John*, Tractate XXX, 7, p. 188).

[7] Undoubtedly this is a direct reference to St. Augustin, who uses the same argument with the minor difference that he does not include "The Song of the Three" in the works of Moses (*The City of God*, II, 200, Bk. XI, Ch. ix).

[8] Both eds. have *fechos* which does not refer back to *obras* or *cosas*.

[9] Both eds. have *invisibles*.

retraxesen abaxo en vn lugar & que paresciese la tierra descobierta dellas; enlo qual fueron apartados & formados los quatro elementos que deantes estauan mezclados conlas aguas. Arriba quedó el fuego & el ayre, helementos más sotiles; abaxo el agua & la tierra, elementos más gruessos. [10]

Ya, pues, enestos tres días parescieron las cosas formadas enlas mayores partes del mundo, que son: el fuego & los elementos; pero avn no tenían su apostura & pintura, la qual Dios puso enlos tres días siguientes, ca enel miércoles, que es el quarto día, pintó el cielo de sol & luna & estrellas. [11] Enel quinto día, que es el jueues, pintó dos helementos, es assaber; el ayre de aues & el agua de muchos pescados en sus linajes & especies. [12] Enel sesto día, que es el viernes, pintó la tierra de muchos animales en sus especies, ca de yerbas & árboles ya hera conpuesta quando enel tercero día fue descubierta delas aguas. E eneste mesmo día sexto crió al hombre como deximos, fuera del paraýso & luego lo trasladó & puso en paraýso. E allí puesto, hizo venir ante sí todos los animales & puso nombre a cadavno. E vido que cada animal para engendrar tenía adjutorio de fembra para engendrar semejante a sí, sino Adam. [13] E entonces le puso sueño, como deximos, & hizo dél la muger.

Assí quel varón & la muger fueron formados enel sexto día después de todos los animales & havn después de todas las cosas; pero en aquel día, primero el honbre & después la muger.

Dirás aquí: ya sé el tienpo en que fue la muger formada; querría saber el tienpo de su hedad en que fue formada. A esto digo que las cosas que Dios al comienço crió, todas las hizo perfectas para que pudiesen engendrar. Donde dizen que crió a Adán en hedad varonil, que es de treynta años. Assí podemos dezir dela fenbra que fue criada en hedad perfecta de perfectión que a ella conuenía. Esto digo por que la muger no requiere tanto tienpo para su perfectión como el varón; donde razonablemente podemos dezir que ella sería de .xxv. años; pero esto no lo digo determinando, mas conjecturando, ca no hallamos desto más

---

[10] Genesis 1:7.
[11] Genesis 1:16.
[12] Genesis 1:20.
[13] The 1542 ed. has *sino a Adán*.

enlos doctores, sino que ambos fueron criados en perfecta hedad. Pero la razón dirá: que assí como del hombre & del cauallo no es vna perfeción de hedad, ca más años requiere el hombre que el cauallo, donde vn cauallo es viejo de diez años & vn honbre de diez años es niño. Assí ay diuersidad entrel ombre & la muger & del día en que la muger fue criada & dela hedad en que fue criada asaz se he dicho.

## Capítulo Quinto

[*Capítulo .v.* declara a qué fin fue la muger criada & pone tres fines a qué fue criada].

Está de saber para qué la muger fue criada. A esto diremos breue mente que la creación dela muger ouo tres fines: es vno general en quanto es criatura razonal & enesto conuiene conlos ángeles. El otro es especial en quanto es criatura humana & enesto conuiene conel varón. El otro es más especial & este le conuiene en quanto fembra. Pues si preguntamos del fin general, ¿para qué fue criada? diremos que para aquello mismo para que fueron criados los ángeles, ca por quanto ninguna cosa no puede ser participante dela bienauenturança de Dios sino en entendimiento con que le conozca.[1] Porende, hizo Dios la criatura razonal que conosciese el bien soberano que es Dios; & conosciéndolo, lo amase; & amando, lo posseyese; & poseyendo, dél se gozasse. E departió la criatura razonal enesta guisa, que la vna parte permanesciese en puridad & no fuese vnida al cuerpo: éstos son los ángeles; e la otra parte se vniese conel cuerpo: éste es el hombre. E porende la razonal criatura departida es en espiritual & corporal. Donde el fin general para que Dios fizo la razonal

---

[1] In speaking of the creation of angels and of their relationship with God, St. Augustin writes: "... they are made participators of His eternal light, which is nothing other than the unchangeable Wisdom by which all things are made..." (*The City of God,* II, 201, Bk. XI, Ch. ix). He recognizes Adam and Eve as participators of the eternal light (*The City of God,* II, 206, Bk. XI, Ch. xii), evaluates the rational natures of men and angels so that at times "in the scale of morality good men outweigh bad angels" (*The City of God,* II, 212, Bk. XI, Ch. xvi).

criatura, assí ángel como hombre, & así varón como muger, es la bondad del Criador.[2] Donde Sant Agustín, enel libro *Dela doctrina cristiana*, dize: —Por que Dios es bueno, nos somos buenos; en quanto somos buenos, somos.[3]

E si preguntas para qué fue criada la criatura razonal, respondo: que fue criada para alabar a Dios & para servirle & para gozar dél. E esto todo haze prouecho a ella mas que no a Dios, el qual no ha menester de nuestros bienes, ca nuestros bienes no son nuestros, mas suyos. Pues que Dios criase la criatura razonal, esto se ha de referir ala bondad del Criador & al prouecho & vtilidad dela criatura.

Quando, pues, preguntan a qué fue fecha la razonal criatura, breuemente se puede responder: por que a ella le es vtile & prouechoso seruir a Dios & gozarse dél; & así es dicho quel ángel y el hombre fue hecho para Dios, no porque Dios ouiese menester el seruicio de ninguno dellos; mas por que siruiesse[4] a aquel & se alegrase dél, al qual siruiendo es reynar.

Otro fin es más especial, en quanto la hembra & el varón es de vna especie. Donde diremos que allende del fin general para que el hombre es hecho, enel qual conuiene con los ángeles, es otro fin para que especial mente el hombre es hecho, assí varón como hembra. Es assaber: para atar & ligar todas las criaturas. En vn estremo están los ángeles, que son criaturas espirituales; enel otro están las cosas visibles, que son corporales. Pues si el hombre no fuera criado, claro es quel vniuerso delas criaturas fuera desatado e porende crió Dios al hombre en medio destos cabos: tiene sobre sí a Dios, al qual ha de seruir, tiene deyuso las criaturas que le han de seruir, como dize el Apóstol, enla primera Epístola alos Chorintios: —Todas las cosas son nuestras;[5]

---

[2] St. Augustin continues: "The explanation, then of the goodness of creation is the goodness of God (*The City of God*, II, 219, Bk. XI, Ch. xxii).

[3] Fray Martín refers to the chapter dealing with "In what way God uses Man," where St. Augustin writes: "For it is because He is good we exist; and so far os we truly exist we are good" (*On Christian Doctrine*, p. 531).

[4] The 1542 ed. has *sirviessen*.

[5] I Corinthians 8:6: "But to us there is but one God, the Father, of whom are all things, and we in him: and one Lord Jesus Christ, by whom are all things, and we by him." The idea appears to be expressed more clearly in II Corinthians 5:18: "And all things are of God, who hath

es assaber: las soberanas, las yguales & las baxas. Las soberanas, para nuestra bien auenturança, como es la Sancta Trenidad, Padre & Hijo & Spíritu Sancto, vn solo Dios verdadero; las yguales son nuestras para conseruar: éstos son los ángeles, los quales avn que agora sean más altos que nos otros. Enel otro mundo, seremos a ellos yguales, ca avn agora nuestros son; ca siruen a nuestro vso y prouecho, como las cosas son del Señor, son también delos seruidores, no quanto al dominio & propiedad, mas quanto al vso & seruidumbre. Puede el seruidor caualgar enel cauallo de su maestro & señor & calçarse sus espuelas. Donde los ángeles en muchos lugares dela Escriptura se halla que ellos siruen a nos, quando por nos son embiados acá abaxo. Pues nuestras son las cosas altas & nuestras las yguales & también las cosas baxas, como son los animales & las otras cosas visibles, ca son hechas para nos seruir.

En algunos lugares dela Escriptura se halla quel honbre, así varón como hembra, fue hecho para reparar la caýda delos ángeles.[6] E segund que común mente se dize, ésta no fue total causa del hombre ser criado, avn que se ayuntan con otras causas.

Síguese ya la causa más especial, por qué la muger fue criada & para qué. Nota muchas vtilidades & prouecho de su criación. La primera es multiplicación del humanal linaje, el qual se ha tanto de multiplicar fasta que sea conplido el número delos eletos, el qual número sólo Dios sabe quánto ha de ser.[7] E para este adjutorio, dixo Dios: —Hagamos la muger. El hombre es animal perfecto, donde requiere para su generación ayuntamiento de varón & fembra por matrimonio.

La otra vtilidad fue después del pecado, por el qual la generación fue muy desordenada; & ésta ordena el matrimonio quando el marido conosce a su muger por causa de euitar fornicación.

---

reconciled us to himself by Jesus Christ." Cf. also I Corinthians 3:23: "And ye are Christ's and Christ is God's."

[6] I do not find a specific reference in Scripture to the creation of man and woman as a remedy for the Fall of the angels. Louis Ginzberg finds this view of man in Tertullian, *Adversus Marcionem*, 2,8 and in other patristic sources (*Legends of the Jews*, 6 vols. [Philadelphia, 1909-1925], V, 69, n. 12).

[7] See Revelations 14:1-2.

La otra vtilidad es reconciliación de paz, & esto es especial entre los reys. Acaesce que han contienda los grandes señores sobre partimiento de tierras & de lugares & con vna hija hazen paz & trauan parentesco. Donde no solamente los grandes señores, mas todo el humanal linaje se puede ligar por matrimonio; & avn por esto es vedado entre personas propincas en sangre, como entre hermanos, entre primos fasta el quarto grado, porque los parientes tienen razón de se amar, a lo qual abasta el parentesco, lo que no es entre los estraños. E por esso es razón que ayan entre sí matrimonio, porque tengan causa de se amar, no más quanto a esta causa.[8]

---

[8] Fray Martín is probably remembering St. Augustin's arguments which explained incest as a necessary means of increasing and multiplying among the sons and daughters of Adam and Eve (*The City of God*, II, 450, Bk. XV, Ch. xvi). St. Augustin goes on to observe that marriage outside promotes peace when men: "who both desire and ought to live in harmony, so bind themselves by the bonds of social relationships that no one man monopolizes more than one relationship,... so that a common social life of the greatest number may be fostered" (p. 451). He comments on the fact that the prohibition of incest is a moral custom and not a reflection of law in the case of marriages between first cousins (p. 453). Apparently the same extension of the prohibition of marriage between brother and sister occurred in Jewish practice, according to George Fort Moore who wrote: "The catalogue of prohibited degrees of kinship based on Leviticus 18:6-18 was extended by the rabbinical authorities by the inclusion of 'secondary relations' (*Judaism in the First Centuries of the Christian Era: The Age of the Tannaim*, 2 vols. [Cambridge, Massachusetts, 1966], II, 120-121).

Capítulo Sesto

[*Capítulo .vj.* que Eua avn que fue hecha de Adam no se puede dezir fija suya, mas su compañera & muger].

Agora es bueno que sepamos si Eua fue hija de Adam & él si fue su padre; porque paresce quando vna cosa biua nasce de otra biua & le paresce enla especie, que el que nasce es hijo de aquél de quien nasce; como vn cordero que es animal biua [1] nasce dela oueja que es biua & nasce semejante a ella enla especie de do se sigue que es su fijo & assí delas otras cosas. Pues Eua nasció de Adam & fue aél semejante, ca macho & hembra enla humana especie no varían enla semejança; yo & mi madre somos de vna especie. Entre macho & fembra de vna specie no ay diferencia de forma & especie, mas de materia, ca el cuerpo dela fembra tiene otra complesión que el del varón, pero el ánima, que es la forma, en ambos es intellectiua. A esto digo, que para que vna cosa sea fija de otra conuiene que sean biuas vna & otra; donde si son cosas inanimadas como es fuego, avn que engendre otro fuego, no es su fijo. La razón desto es, por que las cosas biuas engendran de su propia substancia que son [seminarias] [2] dela generación, como carnero & oueja engendran vn cordero mezclando sus simientes; pero las cosas sin ánimas engendran de materia agena & no de la suya; como el fuego si engendra otro fuego, engendra lo de otra materia, como es madera estopa.

---

[1] The 1542 ed. has *animal bivo*.
[2] Both eds. have *sominarias*. Is the sense *seminarias*?

E la otra condición es que lo engendrado tenga substancia propia [3] & no esté fincado en aquello de que se engendra & por esto el cabello avn que se engendra dela cabeça no es su fijo, porque está fincado enella; & los pinpollos delos árboles no son sus fijos, porque están fincados enel árbol. E si los llaman hijos es por semejança & no por verdad.

La otra condición es que lo engendrado tenga la especie de aquel que lo engendra & por esso los piojos & los gusanos que se engendran del hombre no son sus fijos. [4] La otra es que se engendre natural mente & por esto Eua no es fija de Adán porque no fue engendrada natural mente, mas por milagro. Donde si Dios criase vn hombre de mi dedo, no sería mi fijo, por quel dedo no tiene seminario de que natural mente se faga el hombre. Donde si Eua fue hecha de aquella costilla, no es hija de Adam & casándose conella no se casó con su hija, ni auía impedimiento entre ellos de parentela.

Desto ay razón. Si queremos comparar Eua a Adam & las otras fijas a sus padres, ca los otros padres engendran a sus fijas & son actores en tal generación, pero Adam no fizo nada enesta generación d'Eua, mas óuose passive [5] y Dios fue el actor d'Eua.

---

[3] The 1542 ed. has *propria*.

[4] It is probable that Fray Martín was recalling the following passage from St. Augustin: "It need not be granted then, that whatever is born of something is consequently to be called the son of that same thing. There is no need of saying that in one sense a son is born of a man, in another a hair, a louse, a stomach worm, none of these last being a son" (*Faith, Hope and Charity*, trans, Bernard M. Peebles, *Fathers of the Church* [New York, 1947], p. 404, Ch. XII, 39). In the light of Fray Martín's having written "super multos libros Aristotelis" (Santiago Vela, "Notas de interés," p. 54), he may have been aware of the following observations of Aristotle: "Why is it that, if a living creature is born of our semen, we regard it as our own offspring, but if it proceeds from any other part or excretion, we do not consider it our own? ... Speaking generally, everything which is unnatural is foreign; and many of the things which grow in the body are unnatural. If, then, a living creature originates from semen alone, that which comes from semen alone should be regarded as our offspring. If then, anything else should be born from our semen, for instance a worm from putrefying semen, or from semen which has decayed in the womb ... it must not be called our offspring" (Aristotle, *Problems*, trans. W. S. Hett [London: Loeb Classical Library, 1953], 878 a 1, 878 a 16-20).

[5] Fray Martín does not explain the use of the Latin *passive*. Felix García puts the word in quotation marks in his 1953 ed.

Los otros padres engendran sus fijos con compañía de muger; Adam sin tal compañía, donde fue hecha aquella muger de honbre sin muger. Los otros padres engendran las fijas de su natural simiente; Adán no así, salvo que le fue sacada vna costilla, como es dicho, & por esso otro respeto tenía Eua a Adán & otro alas fijas que engendró de Eua, ca a Eua tenía otro respeto de marido & compañero & ella a él de muger & compañera. Alas otras fijas tenía respeto de padre & conellas no podía casar como con Eua. En ningún tiempo fue lícito casar el padre con su fija, ni el fijo conla madre; pero al comienço dela generación delos honbres pudieron casar hermanos con hermanas, ca los fijos de Adan casaron con sus hermanas quando no auía otras mugeres avn que esto por honestad lo calla la Escriptura. Bien dize cómo los fijos de Adán engendraron, pero no dize de qué mugeres engendraron. [6] Pues claro es, que no auía otras mugeres sino sus hermanas, avn que la Biblia no nonbra sino los fijos machos de Adam; pero [Metodio] [7] en su *Crónica* dize que Adán engendró a Caýn

---

[6] St. Augustin makes the same observation as to the silence of Scripture about the identity of the wives (*The City of God*, II, 455, Bk. XV, Ch. xvii). St. Methodius uses the same arguments as St. Augustin to justify the incest among the offspring of Adam and Eve (*The Writings of Methodius*, p. 7) basing his discussion on Leviticus 20:17. A curious sidelight to the discussion is the wife-sister motif in the Bible which appears prominently in the story of Abraham and Sarah in Egypt. According to E. A. Speiser, it may have had its origin in the fratriarchal inheritance system of the Hurrians (*The Anchor Bible*: Genesis, ed. E. A. Speiser [New York, 1964], p. 92).

[7] *Mecodio* appears to be a compositorial error in both eds. Antonio Solalinde notes that the *General Estoria* of Alfonso el Sabio contained second-hand references to Methodius, not original ones (p. xvii, n. 1). The *Crónica* to which Fray Martín later refers as the *Crónica de los primeros tiempos* is not identifiable. Neither Mario Schiff's list of the Marqués de Santillana's library nor the lists of Isabel's libraries include any reference to such a work. The lost works of Methodius included *Commentaries on Genesis* (Johannes Quasten, *Patrology: The Ante Nicene Literature after Irenaeus* [Utrecht, 1953], II, 137). This might be the work alluded to by Fray Martín. Delbora, Cain's wife does not appear in the Bible, nor in Jewish legends. Luluwa is the sister, whose favors are said to have been the cause of the contention between Cain and Abel (Joseph Gaer, *The Lore of the Old Testament* [New York, 1951], p. 57). Adam's oldest daughter is identified as Azurah (Ginzberg, V, 146, n. 42). Enrique de Villena, writing in 1423, mentions the name, calling her the sister of Tubal-Cain and Jubal and crediting her with the invention of spinning (*Arte Cisoria*, ed. Felipe-Benicio Navarro [Barcelona, 1879], p. 13). Naamah is the only sister of Tubal-Cain mentioned in the Bible. Fray Martín cites

& a Délbora, conla qual casó Caýn & engendró della fijos & fijas.

Aquí es bien que digamos delos matrimonios que son entre parientes, que son llamados incestuosos, delos quales dize Sant Agustín: —Que tarde o nunca vimos salir buena generación ni permanecer antes muy cedo se amata como candela que es fecha de cera podrida. [8] En otro lugar dize: —Que la humana vergüença mira con tanta reuerencia a su sangre [9] que avn por malo que honbre sea, no sele puede quitar. [10] Quiere dezir que conlas parientas ha de ser honbre tan cortés & mesurado, que no deue querer, avn que conél dispense, tocar nigunas dellas por acto carnal. Donde los quel contrario fizieron, son enla Escriptura mucho reprouados & sofrieron muertes corporales & avn agora enel infierno padescen eternal muerte. [11] Pues si esto es dapñable a todo honbre, quanto más lo deue ser alos reys & reynas cuya generación ha de ser limpia & cuyos hijos han de aumentar la república.

---

Methodius as the unique source for the existence of Delbora. Norman Cohn mentions a work of the pseudo-Methodius, which was really written toward the end of the 7th century rather than in the 4th century which dealt with world history from the Garden of Eden to Alexander and then to the seventh century (*The Pursuit of the Millenium: Revolutionary Millenarians and Mystical Anarchists of the Middle Ages* [New York, 1970], pp. 31-32).

[8] Although St. Augustin does refer to the fruits of evil generation he does not condemn them specifically (*The Good of Marriage* in *Seventeen Short Treatises of St. Augustine*, in *A Library of Fathers of the Holy Catholic Church Anterior to the Division of the East and West* [Oxford, 1847], p. 283). I do not find the specific quotation.

[9] The 1542 ed. has *a sangre*.

[10] St. Augustin, in his discussion of suicide, condemns the shedding of human blood but offers the following exception: "The same divine law which forbids the killing of a human being allows certain exceptions, as when God authorizes killing by a general law or when He gives an explicit commission to an individual for a limited time" (*The City of God*, I, 53, Bk. I, Ch. xx).

[11] An example of harsh justice meted out to those who commit incest is the story of Amnon and Tamar (II Samuel: 13-14), although strangely enough Scripture does not speak of any retribution to be meted out to Lot's daughters, perhaps because their motives were presumably the perpetuation of the family line.

## Capítulo Séptimo

[*Capítulo .vij.* en qué manera fue fecho el cuerpo dela muger, tan grande de pequeña costilla & de otros milagros que en aquella obra contescieron].

Marauíllase el entendimiento humano, cómo de aquella costilla se pudo hazer la hembra, ca paresce cosa impossible & no pertenesciente. Lo primero, por quel cuerpo dela muger fue mucho mayor que la costilla & si Dios para hazer el cuerpo añadió alguna materia de fuera. Estonces más propiamente diríamos que la muger fue hecha dela materia añadida que hera más que dela costilla; como si vn xerope es hecho de agua & de miel & más mucho ay de miel que de agua; no desimos que este xerope es hecho de agua, mas de miel. Assí es aquí.

Si Dios hizo la muger dela costilla, añadiéndole materia de fuera que era mucho mayor que la costilla, síguese que la muger más fue hecha de aquella materia que hera más, que no dela costilla, que hera menos. E porende es determinación delos sanctos que la muger fue hecha de sola substancia dela costilla en sí misma, por virtud de Dios multiplicada sin ningún añadimiento de materia de fuera. E desto trahen [1] semejança delos cinco panes con que Nuestro Señor hartó alos cinco mile honbres. Aquellos panes fueron multiplicados por virtud de Dios, sin añadir otra niguna materia. [2] E para esto nota que Dios puede hazer tres cosas que natura no puede fazer: la vna es de nada fazer

---

[1] The 1542 ed. has *destraen*.
[2] Matthew 16:9: "Do ye not yet understand, neither remember the five loaves of the five thousand, and how many baskets ye took up?"

algo, como hizo todo el mundo de nonada.³ La otra es de algo fazer nada. La otra es multiplicar & engendrar alguna cosa, no le añadiendo alguna cosa de fuera. E assí fizo dela costilla el cuerpo dela muger.

Otras infinitas cosa puede Dios hazer, pero estas tres, mayor mente la tercera, faze a este propósito, ca así como natura no puede hazer hombre, sino de otro honbre, pero Dios puédelo fazer. Así natura no faze crecer vn niño sin comer & beuer & sin viandas que le sean ministradas de fuera; pero Dios puédelo traher a perfecta estatura sin ninguna vianda. Enxenplo desto: si los honbres quisiesen hazer que vn fuego pequeño se fiziese grand, conuernía echar leña enel & así crecería; pero si Dios lo quiere hazer grand, no ha menester echar leña, mas por su intrínsica virtud le hará crecer & súbita mente & no poco a poco como hará la leña.

Esto vale para entender cómo Helias & Moysén & Jesu Christo pudieron estar quarenta días & quarenta noches sin comer;⁴ ca diremos que lo que natura pudo hazer con viandas en aquellos quarenta días, Dios lo pudo fazer sin viandas. E mucho mejor viuían que no con vianda, ca sienpre es mejor lo que faze Dios por sí mismo, que lo que faze por causas naturales, como el vino que hizo enlas bodas fue mejor que los vinos que llevaron ni llevarán quantas viñas ay enel mundo.⁵

La razón desto es que así se conpara Dios a natura, como el maestro al discípulo & nunca la obra es tan bien fecha por el discípulo como por el maestro.⁶ Así diremos delas primeras

---

³ The 1542 ed. has *de nada*.

⁴ That God has the power to work miracles is not an uncommon observation, nevertheless, it may not be a coincidence that St. Jerome uses the same miracle to demonstrate God's power ("To Pammachius Against John of Jerusalem," in *Principal Works*, p. 442).

⁵ John 2:2-10.

⁶ See Otis H. Green, *Spain and the Western Tradition* 4 vols. (Madison, Wisconsin, 1964) II, 75-82 for a discussion of the relationship between Nature and God. Most frequently, Nature is the deputy or vicar of God, although Dr. Green cites Alanus de Insulis (Alain de Lille, d. 1202), who describes Nature as "the shaper of matter according to spiritual forms derived from God" (p. 78). This is not an explicit designation of Nature as God's pupil. As has been seen, Fray Martín tends to use the image of God, the teacher. Alfred Jacob quotes Hugh St. Victor who wrote: "Omnis natura Deum loquitur, omnis natura hominem docet, omnis natura rationem

criaturas que Dios crió. Al comienço no ouo tan perfecto honbre como Adam, ni muger como Eua antes que pecasen; ni tan perfecto cauallo como el primero, ni tan perfecta gallina como la primera & assí delas otras criaturas. Donde dize el Psalmo: —Las obras de Dios todas son perfetas.[7] Enxenplo: una muger amasa el pan conlas manos, mejor lo forma que si lo fiziese con vna paleta. Lo que haze Dios por sí conlas manos, lo faze por causas naturales con paleta.

Así mismo la manera que tuuo Dios de hazer la muger, segund los santos, fue ésta: que aquella costilla fue quitada del costado de Adán por misterio[8] delos ángeles, pero por sola virtud de Dios fue formada en muger. E por esso los ángeles no son criadores, mas administradores, por lo qual no pudieron formar la costilla en muger, ni suplir la carne en lugar della. No que no fagan algo quando Dios alguna cosa cría; mas, porende, no son criadores, mas son como los ortolanos que labran & siembran & riegan, pero ellos no hazen crecer los árboles, mas sólo Dios los faze crecer & lleuar fruto.[9] Pues, principal mente Dios fizo dela costilla el cue[r]po dela muger, avn que la costilla fue ministrada por los ángeles. El cuerpo formado dela costilla,[10] Dios infundió enél el ánima, como desque formó Dios el varón del limo dela tierra, espiró enél espiráculo de vida, que quiere dezir infundió enél ánima para que biuiese.

Algunos erraron en la animación dela muger, diziendo que como el cuerpo della fue sacado del cuerpo del varón, assí el

---

parit, et nihil in universitate infecundum est" from *Didascalion de studio legendi* (VI, 5) in his article, "The *Razón de amor* as Christian Symbolism," *HR* XX (1952), 282-301: 283.

[7] Possibly Fray Martín is referring to Psalms 19:7: The law of the Lord is perfect..." or to Deuteronomy 32:4: "He is the Rock, his work is perfect; for all his ways are judgment."

[8] In his modernization of the language of the *Jardín de nobles donzellas*, Felix García says that *misterio* is intended to be *ministerio*.

[9] Cf. St. Augustin, whose words are quoted almost directly here: "Even though the angels... can be ordered or permitted to aid God in producing what the earth brings forth, they can no more be called creators of animals than farmers can be called creators of crops and trees" (*The City of God*, II, 291, Bk. XII, Ch. xxv).

[10] Felix García punctuates this phrase, "el cuerpo formado dela costilla" followed by a period, as part of the preceding sentence. Both eds. start a new sentence with the phrase as a sort of translated ablative absolute.

ánima del ánima fue diriuada; & esto es falso, ca los hijos no toman del padre ni dela madre sino el cuerpo. Dios es aquél que cría el ánima quando el cuerpo es dispusto; ca esta dignidad tiene nuestra ánima sobre las ánimas delas bestias, que las bestias de su padre reciben cuerpo & ánima. E por esso, el cuerpo muerto, muere el ánima; por que todo salió del seno dela materia corporal & todo es mortal. Pero en nos otros, como el cuerpo salga delas simientes, es por esso mortal; pero nuestra ánima es embiada al cuerpo por imperial & diuino poder & por esso es inmortal.

## Capítulo Octauo

[*Capítulo .viij*. Si los honbres no pecaran, en qué manera la muger seruiera ala generación humana & determina, segund Sant Agustín, que engendrarán vírgines].

La muger, como deximos fue fecha para que fuese ayuda al varón, para engendrar & multiplicar los honbres, pero esta generación otra mente se hiziera sino pecaran que agora se faze; ca después del peccado, varón & muger se mezclan con ardor & suziedad & vergüença, tanto que honbres honestos dello hablar no quieren, & queda la muger corrupta e si se empreña queda pesada; desque pare queda enferma & trabajada e muchas ay que tantos dolores passan enel cuerpo que mueren.[1] Pero ante del peccado, ninguna cosa destas no fuera, ca la muger mezclada con su marido quedara entera. Tanto, que Sant Agustín dize enel capítulo .xiiij. dela *Ciudad de Dios:* —que quedará sin corrupción de su integridad, que quiere dezir virginidad.[2] Quiere dezir

---

[1] There is a possibility that Fray Martín was alluding to the confinement of Isabel's mother with Isabel on April 22, 1451, which "left her a victim of a chronic nervous depression" (William Thomas Walsh, *Isabella of Spain: The Last Crusader* [New York, 1930], p. 1). Vivid descriptions of the unattractive side of domestic life and pregnancy are found in St. Jerome (*The Perpetual Virginity of Blessed Mary* in *Principal Works,* p. 344) for example.

[2] The reference is to Bk. XIV, Ch. xxvi in the modern divisions of *The City of God*: "We have no right to reject the possibility that, at a time when there was no unruly lust to excite the organs of generation and when all that was needed was done by deliberate choice, the seminal flow could have reached the womb with as little rupture of the hymen and by the same vaginal ducts as is present the case, in reverse with the menstrual flux" (II, 406-7, Bk. XIV, Ch. xxvi). To "protect virginal ears"

que assí como las flores salen dela Virgen & no la corrompen, assí el marido conociere a su muger & no la corrompiera; antes, segund que quiere dezir, paresce que en aquel estado todas las mugeres quedarán vírgines. E por que este dicho de Sancto Agustín paresce duro de creer a algunos doctores, porné aquí primero lo que ellos dizen & después lo que a mí es visto.

Dizen, pues, algunos que lo que dize Sancto Agustín, quel varón se mezclara entonces ala muger sin ninguna corrupción de integridad o de vi[r]ginidad, no les paresce que sea cosa possible; ca si la muger quedara vírgen después dela cópula del varón, nunca ouiera mezclamiento de simientes del varón & dela muger, sin el qual mezclamiento no se puede fazer generación; por lo qual dizen que la corrupción dela virginidad dize tres cosas: abertura, pasión penal & torpe delectación.

Lo primero, según dize, es natural, ca vn cuerpo natural mente no puede salir ni entrar por las puertas cerradas. Lo segundo es de pena. Lo tercero es de vicio & corrupción.

Dizen, pues, que quando el varón conosciese a su muger enel tiempo de ynocencia que se abrieron los claustros; pero no ouiera passión penal, ni delectación fea, por que entonces la nuestra generación no fuera corronpida. Antes todos los mienbros heran subjetos ala razón, como agora obedesce la boca & las manos & la lengua; donde assí como agora abrimos la mano & la cerramos & la boca quando queremos la abrimos & cerramos, & no ay enello passión ni pena, ni delectación fea;[3] assí fiziéremos[4] en

---

this passage is left in Latin in the translation of the *Select Library of Nicene and Post-Nicene Fathers*.

[3] Fray Martín seems to be relying here on St. Augustin: "When the first man transgressed the law of God, he began to have another law in his members which was repugnant to the law of his mind, and he felt the evil of his own disobedience when he experienced in the disobedience of his flesh a most righteous retribution recoiling on himself.... Well then, how significant is the fact that the eyes, and lips, and tongue, and hands, and feet, and the bending of the back, and neck, and sides, all are placed within our power — to be applied to such operations as are suitable to them, ... but when it comes to man's great function of the procreation of children, the members which were expressly created for this purpose will not obey the direction of the will..." (*On Marriage and Concupiscence*, in *Anti-Pelagian Works*, trans. Peter Holmes and Robert Ernest Wallis, *A Select Library of the Nicene and Post-Nicene Fathers of the Christian Church*, ed. Philip Schaff [Buffalo, 1887], p. 266, Bk. I, Ch. vii).

[4] The 1542 ed. has *hiciéramos*.

aquel tiempo de ynocencia; ni fuera entonces más feo hablar delos mienbros dela generación que delas manos & delos pies, ni auían vergüença en aquel estado de verlos, ca desnudos heran antes del pecado; & luego que el pecado fue cometido, les cayó vergüença & buscaron con qué cobrir las partes vergonçosas & corrieron ala figuera, que tenía las fojas anchas & fizieron coberturas dellas. [5]

Esta es, pues, la declaración quéstos dan al dicho Sant Agustín, enel qual paresce dezir allí, que las mugeres concibieran & parieran vírgines antes del pecado. Pero hablando conel acatamiento delos questo dizen, paresce me quel dicho de Santo Agustín enesta parte se puede en tal manera entender, que sea verdad que las mugeres concibieran & parieran vírgines & para que mejor esto se entienda, porné aquí el dicho suyo enel libro de *La ciudad de Dios* al libro .xiiij. enel capítulo .xxvj. quasi en medio del capítulo. Estas son sus palabras: —En tanta facilidad de cosas & tanta felicidad de aquellos dos, es asaber de Adam & Eua, bien podían engendrar fijos sin ardor de carnalidad, mas por aquel mismo inperio de voluntad que mouían los otros mienbros, se mouieran aquellos sin ningund feo stímulo, con tranquilidad de ánima & cuerpo, & no corrupción dela integridad, el marido se ayuntara entonces con su muger. [6]

Digo, pues, quel dicho de Sant Agustín se puede entender en dos maneras: la vna, que enla concepción & el parto fuese abertura, ya por eso no se perdía la virginidad. Esto es, porque la virginidad más está enel ánima que enel cuerpo. Como dixo Santa Luzía, no se ensuzia el cuerpo si la voluntad no consiente. Donde si alguna virgen fuese por fuerça corronpida, sienpre queda virgen, [7] ni avn por esso no pierde el aureola que es doctada

---

[5] Genesis 3:7.

[6] The 1542 ed. has *libro xxiiij. cap. xxvi*. The 1500 ed. has the location *libro xiiij. cap. xxvi* (the correct location).

[7] This story is told by the *condestable*, D. Álvaro de Luna, who related that after having pledged herself to a chaste life and after having given away all her worldly goods, St. Lucia was threatened by Pasqual as follows: "Mandarte he lleuar al lugar feo, por que te sean en vno quitados el spíritu santo e la flor de la virginidad. Lucía dixo: non es dañado el cuerpo si queda el corazón non corronpido; ca si contra mi voluntad me fuere quitado el thesoro de la virginidad, ser me ha doblada la virtud de la castidad, para

alas virgines enel cielo, antes les es doblada. Así es aquí agora la corrupción dela virginidad.

Agora en tienpo de pecado, no es por la abertura dela muger, mas por que aquel acto se haze con ardor de fea delectación; & por que entonces, el acto conjugal se hiziera con horden dela razón, no saliendo los límites de justicia & honestad; & la sensualidad de la carne estaua ala razón subjecta; & todo quanto en aquel acto se fazía hera de razón, no mirando ala delectación; mas mirando ala sancta generación que hera para multiplicar el número delos escogidos que auían de ser compañeros delos ángeles, que son vírgines. Síguese que todo aquel acto hera virginal, pues que la voluntad hera regida por razón & la razón por el espíritu de Dios & la carne con sus mienbros no se mouía sino quando mandaua Dios. Donde como agora la generación humana toda es carnal, así entonces toda hera espiritual.

E desto ay semejança de vn dicho de Sancto Agustín, que dize: —que la virginidad de Sant Juan no fue más digna que el matrimonio de Abraham, ca dize que con Sarra husó templadamente & con Agar husó obedientemente, ca obedesció a Sarra enesto & con ninguna husó destemplada mente.[8] Así, diremos que las bodas en paraýso heran tan dignas como la virginidad de agora & avn más, ca la virginidad de agora passa muchas tentaciones & mouimientos carnales & pensamientos con delectaciones, los quales son pena: dellos pecado venial & avn dellos peccado mortal. E desto en aquellas bodas de paraýso no ouiera nada. E assí paresce como se entiende el dicho de Sant Agustín,

---

corona, e nunca me podrás mudar de mi propósito, para que consienta en feos deleytes..." (*Libro de las claras e virtuosas mugeres*, p. 212). Cervantes employed the same reasoning, for which there apparently was a strong theological basis, in "La fuerza de la sangre" where his violated heroine remained pure even after having given birth to a child.

[8] This is a direct reference to the following: "It remains for us to see whether at least our continent men are to be compared with the married patriarchs.... So there was not an unequal reward for continence in John who had no experience with marriage and in Abraham who begot sons. Both the celibacy of the one and the marriage of the other did service for Christ in accord with the needs of the time, but John possessed continence in practice; Abraham indeed possessed it, but only in habit" (*The Good of Marriage*, in *Treatises on Marriage and Other Subjects, Fathers of the Church*, ed. Roy J. Deferrari [New York, 1955], Ch. 19, p. 37; Ch. 21, p. 42).

quando dixo que fueran las bodas allí sin corrupción de virginidad.

La otra manera de saluar su dicho, es avn más profunda; pero es para el escuela, que no para donzellas, lo vno porque es sotil, lo otro porque no se puede explicar sin palabras vergonçosas, por que la virginidad es cosa muy limpia & sotil mente no se puede tratar sin su contrario que es corrupción; por quanto vn contrario no se conosce bien sino por otro su contrario. [9] Assí mismo aquellas bodas de paraýso fueron muy limpias & no se puede dela limpieza dellas bien explicar sino conparándolas ala suziedad destas otras. E porende ocurren en tales hablas dichos vergonçosos, donde el mismo Santo Agustín, aquí eneste allegado capítulo dize: —De cosas hablamos agora vergonçosas e porende, avn que agora pensemos [10] que tales heran antes que enellas ouiesse vergüença, donde necessario es que nuestra habla agora se refrene por la honestad. Así questa manera de saluar su dicho, agora se calle por honor delas sanctas bodas. Pues aquí abasta concluyr que, si los hombres no pecaran, la muger siruiera ala generación humana primera mente concibiendo sin corrupción & sin fealdad ninguna, lo qual agora no tienen, antes conciben con fea delectación & corrupta. Fueran preñadas sin graduedad, ca no se sintieran más pesadas ni graues quando preñadas que antes, lo que agora no tienen; antes sienten dolores, estorçones, vertígines, hastíos, ascos & peligrosas ala muerte. Parieran entonces sin dolor, lo qual el contrario agora hazen, como es aellas notorio por experiencia & alos varones por noticia.

---

[9] See *supra* n. 2 to *Capítulo octauo*. Even in the 19th century, this passage was not rendered into English, so there seems to have been a continuity in the idea of what words were shameful. Fray Martín may also be speaking generally here, indicating to the young princess that he had no intention of offending her.

[10] The 1542 ed. has *pensamos*.

CAPÍTULO .IX.

[*Capítulo .ix.* habla dela generación delas mugeres natural mente hechas de varón & muger, como fueron todas excepto Eua].

Pues que ya es dicho & largamente recontado dela creación dela primera muger, que fue marauillosa & llena de grandes misterios. Razón será segund la horden que al comienço posimos, que digamos dela generación delas otras mugeres, que es generación natural de varón & de muger.

Para lo qual es asaber que Aristótiles, enel .xix. libro *Delos animales*, busca las ca[u]sas dela generación dela muger, quiere dezir, que por qual razón se engendra alguna vez muger más que varón. E asigna desto el mismo Aristótiles muchas causas. Es asaber: tienpo & lugar, vientos, parientes.[1]

La primera causa desto, segund dize, es el tienpo, ca común mente más mugeres se engendran en verano que en enyuierno & en tiempo caliente que en tienpo frío. E digo común mente, por que las obras naturales & morales no son verdaderas siempre, mas por la mayor parte. Avn que sea verdad que la vaca empezca

---

[1]Although modern scholars use the title, *De Generatione Animalium,* evidence is found in Mario Schiff's description of the Marqués de Santillana's library that the title *Delos animales* was current in the 15th century (*La Bibliothèque du Marquis de Santillane,* p. 35). The emphasis in Aristotle is on conditions of moisture, and by inference, cold and heat (Aristotle, *De Generatione Animalium,* trans. Arthur Platt, *The Works of Aristotle,* ed. J. A. Smith, W. D. Ross, Vol. V [Oxford, 1912], 766 b 34-35). Hard waters cause infertility and cold waters the birth of females (767 a 34). The moon's influence affects the humidity and the temperature and therefore can determine the sex of a child (767 a 2). More females are produced in wet districts (*Problems,* 909 a 33). The dominance of the male or the female parent can determine the gender of the child (767 a 7-10).

alos enfermos o otra g[r]uessa vianda, acaesce que vn quartanario con deseo se harta de vaca o tocino & sana. Así auemos de entender las reglas que aquí pone. Mas donde quando dixe que más mugeres se engendran en verano que no en inuierno, por esso dize común mente, por que algunas vezes acaesce el contrario avn que pocas. Dirés: ² queremos saber la razón desto. Digo quel filósopho Aristótiles mismo la asigna, donde dize: —que para que la generación sea de hijo varón, conuiene que la virtud delos padres sea fuerte; & si por alguna causa se enflaquece, lo engendrado es hija. ³ Pues como el frío del tiempo haga ayuntar la virtud, porende, la faga más fuerte. Necessario es que el frío sea causa de engendrar fijo; & por el contrario, la calor del tiempo resuelue & haze exalar la virtud & por esso haze engendrar las hijas. Ésta es la causa por que el vino & los otros liquores, más & mucho mejor se guardan en yuierno, ques tienpo frío, que en verano, que es tienpo caliente; ca el [frío] ⁴ faze encerrar el calor natural a dentro & así lo fortifica el calor. Por el contrario, faze exalar el calor natural dela cosa & queda desierta & rala & flaca. Ésta es pues la primera causa dela feminidad.

La segunda es el lugar, ca assí como ay tienpos calientes & tienpos fríos, assí ay regiones & lugares calientes & fríos. Las regiones de leuante son más calientes; las de poniente más frías. Las regiones de África, que es en medio día, son calientes; las de Europa, que son hazia nos, son frías & avn si miráys enesta nuestra región de España, quanto las partes della van más fazia medio día, como es el Andaluzía y el reyno de Valencia, tanto son más calientes. Estas otras tierras, altas, como es Galizia, León, las tierras de Castilla, son más boreales & porende son frías; ca avn que toda España esté en ocidente, que es do se pone el sol, pero ay dos ocidentes: vno Athlántico, que es a medio día; otro boreal, que es a setentrión.

Diremos, pues, que por la misma causa que en tienpos calientes se engendran más fijas que fijos, por esa misma causa, enlos lugares calientes se engendran más ellas que no ellos; & avn más firme es la causa, la del lugar & del tiempo, por quel lugar no es

---

² Both eds. have *Dirés*.
³ See Aristotle, *De Generatione Animalium* (767 a 7-10).
⁴ The 1542 ed. has *frío* which seems to be the correct reading.

## PRIMERA PARTE

tan variable como el tienpo. Donde por esperiencia verés [5] quando [6] fuerdes en regiones calientes, que si encontráys vn honbre, verés quatro mugeres, si no se haze por ventura el contrario casual mente, o que las mugeres estén encerradas & los varones vayan por las calles. Pero común mente assí es & por contrario es en regiones frías; & es la misma causa que del tiempo. E avn por esto, como deximos del tiempo & el vino & las cosas líquidas, mejor se conseruan en tierras frías que en calientes & avn los cuerpos humanos son más sanos conel frío que no con calor.

Desto Ypocrás pone vn anforismo en que dize: —Que los estómagos más calientes son en yuierno que en estío e avn en tierras frías más que no enlas calientes. [7] Común mente hallarés que en tierras calientes los hombres tienen flacos estómagos. Pues como el fijo varón sea más fuerte que la fija, todo aquello que causa flaqueza enlas entrañas es causa de nascer fenbra; & por el contrario, lo que fortifica es causa [de] nascer fijo.

La tercera causa desto son los vientos, ca dizen que los vientos boreales son masculinos & los australes son femininos. Donde los pastores, que enestos son expertos, quando quieren que las ouejas se empreñen de corderos, esperan los vientos boreales, como es cierço & aquilo; & quando quieren que de corderas se empreñen, esperan los vientos australes, como es abrigo & sus collaterales. [8] E desto ay dos causas; la vna es como las [9] que deximos. Es assaber, calor & frialdad, ca los vientos boreales son fríos & por esso engendran machos & los australes son calientes & por esso engendran fenbras.

La otra especial, por quanto enlas generaciones delos animales mucho ayuda los vientos & estoruan, según que corren buenos

---

[5] Both eds. have *verés*.
[6] The 1542 ed. has *quanto*.
[7] Fray Martín's use of the word *anforismo* suggests that he was not showing a familiarity with the works of Hippocrates. This idea might have become a part of medical folklore. *Ypocrás* is one of the sages in the *Libro de los philosophos* where his aphorisms do not differ from those of Aristotle and Socrates. See Hermann Knust, *Mittheilungen aus dem Eskurial* (Tübingen, 1878).
[8] Aristotle in *Problems* makes the same observation using shepherds as his authority (767 a 34).
[9] The 1542 ed. has *los*.

o malos, para esto enla generación del animal no sólo se requiere calor, mas humor. Pues quando el viento es frío, haze quel humor se retenga & no espire & así causa conplexión masculina; pero quando el viento es caliente, faze espirar el humor & faze la conplexión rala & feminina; & avn desto se causa que algunos niños nascen delicados & de conplexión feminina, porque enla concepción no les corrió buen viento. Pueden ser otras causas, pero ésta es vna & desto toman los físicos juyzio para prenosticar, si la muger es preñada de fijo o de fija; toman de su leche vna gota & tráenla entre los dedos; & si se pega alos dedos, es señal que lo que nasciere será hijo; si la leche es aguanosa & rala, será fija. Otras señales ay, pero desto más saben las parteras que nos otros.

La postrera causa son los parientes, ca si el padre es de fuerte complexión & la madre delicada, común mente engendran hijos varones. E por contrario, si la madre es varonil & el marido es de simple complexión, harán hijas. E por esto los viejos común mente engendran hijas & avn los moços, si son muy moços; los viejos por que ya son flacos en virtud, los moços por que avn no alcançan su virtud. [10] A esto se allegan muchas causas particulares, como son las viandas, exercicios, los pensamientos de las [11] quales los físicos han de enformar & dela generación dela primera muger & delas otras esto abasta.

---

[10] See *supra* n. 1.
[11] The 1542 ed. has *los*.

## SEGUNDA PARTE DESTE TRACTADO

[La segunda parte deste libro habla delas condiciones dela muger, así delas que han como delas que esperan auer para ser buenas].

CAPÍTULO PRIMERO

[*Capítulo .j.* dela vna buena condición que han las mugeres que son vergonçosas & por qué son especiales razones porque las nobles donzellas an de tener vergüença].

Pues que ya hemos dicho & explanado ala Señora Princesa la generación dela muger, así diuinal como fue hecha Eua, como natural según las otras mugeres, es razón que enesta Segunda Parte desta pequeña obra digamos delas condiciones delas mugeres, así delas que tiene buenas, como de las que an de tener para ser virtuosas. Nota, pues, que según Aristótiles en su *Retórica:* —Las mugeres han algunas condiciones buenas & algunas no tales; & es bien que de todas veamos,[1] por que la Señora Princesa escoja para sí las buenas & las no tales deseche. Las condiciones buenas de las mugeres son tres, ca son las mugeres vergonçosas, son piadosas, son osequiosas.

La primera su condición buena es que son vergonçosas: aquellas mugeres son vergonçosas, especial mente las moças. Desto assina el philósopho dos razones: la vna se toma del apetito del loor & la otra se toma por que son flacas & temerosas de coraçón. Quanto alo primero, por quanto las mugeres común mente desean ser alabadas, sígueseles luego a este apetito & deseo de

---

[1] It is possible that, for the good qualities, Fray Martín was recalling the following: "Female bodily excellences are beauty and stature, their moral excellences, self-control and industrious habits, free from servility" (Aristotle, *The "Art" of Rhetoric*, trans. John Henry Freese [London, 1939], 1361 a 8). For the bad qualities see *supra* n. 22 to "The inter-relationship of 'Advices to Princes' and the feminism/anti-feminism controversy."

ser alabadas vna vergüença, que no es otra cosa sino temor de no ser aceptas o honrradas tanto como desean.

Esta diferencia dan los philósophos morales entre temor & vergüença; ca el que teme ha miedo de perder la vida o incurrir feridas o daños, enel qual temor se encoje el coraçón & trae toda la sangre así. E por esso, el que teme se torna amarillo, por que la sangre huye delos mienbros & éntrase dentro al castillo del coraçón. Pero este ome, donde enel temor contece alos humores, lo que contece alos honbres que han enemigos que, quando los vean venir, fuyen. Assí hazen los temientes; pero el que ha vergüença, ha miedo delante alguno ser desonrrado & perder su honrra & gloria & parece colorado enla cara por que allí corre la sangre do es señal de honrra & avn por esto hallarés que mejor & más noble passión es la vergüença quel temor, ca más noble cosa es pugnar por la honrra, que lo haze la vergüença, que pugnar por el prouecho & por la vida, lo que faze el themor. Por lo qual los otros animales & bestias han temor, mas no vergüença. E los villanos han más miedo que vergüença; los hidalgos han más vergüença que miedo, por lo qual los villanos más aýna huyen dela batalla que los hidalgos. Antes si buen fidalgo es & de clara sangre, se dexará morir que huyr o ser preso, por ques gran vergüença fuyr o ser preso.

Han pues, las mugeres esta buena condición, ca son vergonçosas & en tanto es vergüença ala muger natural, que no sólo enla vida, mas avn muerta guarda vergüença. Ca dizen que, quando varones & mugeres se ahogan en agua & desque muertos suben encima del agua, los varones salen la cara arriba, & las mugeres boca ayuso; casi queriendo dezir que, avn muertas, dessean cobrir sus vergüenças.

Desta primera causa se sigue por qué las mugeres son vergonçosas. Es assaber, porque dessean ser alabadas. La segunda es assaber que son vergonçosas por que son temerosas, ca por quanto ellas tanto son temerosas que casi de toda cosa han pauor, bien se sigue desto que son vergonçosas, porque como ya dixe, vergüença no es sino vn temor de recibir mengua. Ésta es, pues, vna condición natural buena delas mugeres, que son vergonçosas & avn questa condición sea loable en todas las mugeres, pero en especial enlas moças vírgines por tres razones: la vna [2] es por que refrena la hedad; la segunda, por que las viste de honestad; la tercera por que pinta la virginidad.

Quanto alo primero, es assaber, que Dios ama tanto que seamos virtuosos & que huyamos los vicios, que a cada vno dio vn freno para retenerse, que no se abalançase en peccados; e aquel mismo freno es como espuela que aguija para correr la virtud. E porende dio al varón por freno la razón, con la qual se retiene que no se despeñe enla fondura de pecados; ella misma es espuela que pune para yr alas virtudes. Donde, por que los niños & mochachos no están enla razón, ni avn tienen juyzio razonal como los grandes, púsoles Dios vergüença enla cara, que los refrenase de torpedades & aguyjase a virtudes fasta que creciessen e ya no por vergüença, mas por razón & juyzio esto fiziessen. Las mugeres, pues, moças, por dos cabos son flacas & caen, porque son mugeres & porque son moças. Pues si alos moços por falta de su hedad, con necessaria vergüença para refrenar los apetitos puerilles, mucho más es necessaria alas mugeres moças que, si vergüença no las refrena del mal & las promueue al bien, yrán como bestia desenfrenada & como cauallo sin espuelas en todo mal; & huyrán toda virtud. [3] Pues bien es verdad que la vergüença es prouechosa ala moça para refrenar la hedad, que de sí mesma es tierna para desuarar en males & no tiene para entonces otro freno sino la vergüença. Pero es aquí de notar que, si hombre haze bien & se aparta del mal, sólo por vergüença del mundo, sus virtudes son falsas & es falso ypócrita, ca no cura del testimonio de Dios & dela conciencia; mas sólo cura del testimonio del mundo & dela fama; & tales heran las cinco vírgines vanas que no traýan ólio en sus lámparas. Pues la perfecta vergüença es huyr el mal & allegar nos al bien, no sólo por vergüença delos hombres, mas principal mente por vergüença de Dios & del remordimiento de nuestra

---

[2] The 1542 ed. has *primera*.

[3] The idea of woman as an insatiable beast without control of her appetites is a commonplace of misogynist literature. Cf. *Historia de Segundo*, where we find what is almost a formulaic representation: "¿Qué es la muger? Confondimiento del omne, bestia que nunca se farta, cuydado que non fuye, guerra que non queda, peligro del omne que non ha en sí mesura" (Knust, p. 503).

conciencia. E tal vergüença ouieron las otras cinco vírgines cuerdas, por lo qual hallaron ólio en sus conciencias.[4] Do dize Séneca: —No as de auer mayor vergüença que de tí mismo, sabiendo que Dios te mira de dentro & fuera. E concluye: —¡O desauenturado de tí, menosprecias tal testigo como es Dios![5]

La otra razón por que las moças an de ser vergonçosas es por que las viste de honestad. Pertenesce segund razón ala noble donzella tener así las virtudes de dentro, que por honestad echen buen olor de fuera. Donde, si la donzella es vergonçosa, todo quanto ha de fuera es honesto. Luego los ojos hazen honestos la vergüença & los haze abaxar a tierra; cierra las orejas alas feas palabras; conpone las manos vna sobre otra; la lengua refrena, el andar viene con mesura & avn enel comer & beuer pone freno la vergüença.[6] Pues como la poca vergüença es causa de deshonestidad, así la graciosa & domicilar vergüença es más madre de honestad; ella honesta los trajes, que deshonesta la poca vergüença; ella ordenó que las mugeres se tocasen & cubriesen sus cabeças & los pechos & que traxesen faldas largas, porque niguna desonestidad enellas fuesse notada que oliese a poca vergüença. E avn por esto, quando primero casan, las velan & las lleuan la cara cubierta ala yglesia, por notar que la vergüenca haze honestad ala casada & ala virgen.

La tercera razón[7] por que la donzella ha de ser vergonçosa es por que pinta & afeyta la virginidad. Vna moça avn que sea virgen, si es desvergonçada, no la quieren por muger. Donde es

---

[4] Matthew 25: 1-13.

[5] See n. 6 *supra* to the *Prohemio* and "Sources and Allusions" for a discussion of the difficulty of isolating medieval references to Seneca. Seneca writes (*Carta* X, "De la soledad"): "¡Cuánta es la locura de los hombres de hoy día: murmuran en las orejas de los dioses deseos vergonçísimos!... Vive con los hombres como si Dios te viese; habla a Dios como si los hombres te oyeran" (*Obras completas*, p. 457).

[6] The tradition of offering advice as to deportment to women had a long history in the literature of the Christian world. St. Jerome's letters to Eustochium (XXII), to Principia (CXXVII), to Furia (LIV) are examples of the genre. For a list of later works up to the Renaissance with brief summaries, see the dissertation of Alice Adèle Hentsch (*De la littérature didactique du Moyen Age s'addressant spécialment aux femmes* [Halle, 1903]).

[7] Both eds. have *La tercera razón es, porque la donzella ha de ser vergonçosa es*...

aquí de notar, segund Sant Jherónimo, que la virginidad es como el lirio blanco; la vergüença es como vna rosa colorada.[8] Pues si queremos fazer vna guirnalda & toda es de lirios, es mucho blanca & no es tan hermosa como si le interponemos alguna rosa colorada. La virginidad es como aluayalde. La vergüença es como vn arrebol. Pues si quando la muger se pinta la cara, lo haze todo aluayalde será mucho blanca & porende es bien que mezcle el aluayalde conel arrebol para que haga vna suaue color. Assí es a nuestro propósito. Si la muger virgen quiere pintar su virginidad, conuiene que la temple con rosada vergüença.[9] E si esto es necessario a todas las donzellas, mucho más alas princesas que esperan casar con reyes & príncipes,[10] los quales lo primero que pesquisan dela esposa es, si es honesta & virtuosa & de compuesta vergüença.

---

[8] St. Jerome, Letter CXXX, p. 265.
[9] Cf. St. Jerome's indignation at the idea of cosmetics. In the letter written to Furia, St. Jerome says: "What place have rouge and white lead on the face of a Christian woman? The one simulates the natural red of the cheeks and the lips; the other the whiteness of the face and the neck" (*Principal Works*, p. 104). It is true that Fray Martín is using the idea of painting the face in a metaphorical sense, nevertheless his choice of the metaphor is unusual in a work counseling chastity and modesty. Cf. Otis H. Green's observations on the fluctuating attitudes toward the painting of the face in "'Ni es cielo ni es azul,' A Note on the Barroquism of B. L. Argensola," *RFE* XXXIV (1950), 137-50.
[10] This is one more indication that the *Jardín* was written before 1469 when Isabel married Fernando.

## Capítulo Segundo

[*Capítulo .ij.* que las mugeres natural mente son piadosas & por qué lo son en especial alas grandes dueñas por qué han de ser piadosas].

Visto como las mugeres natural mente son vergonçosas, lo qual enellas es de loable condición, veamos dela segunda buena condición dellas, que es ser piadosas. Dizen que tres son natural mente piadosas & tienen entrañable misericordia común mente. Es assaber: los moços los viejos & las mugeres; pero estos tres son piadosos por diuersas causas. Ca los moços son compassiuos por que son ynocentes & por su ynocencia miden alos otros & quando por caso veen alguno que padesce, piensan que padesce sin culpa & ynocente, & desto prouócanse a compassión & piedad. Avn podemos dar otra causa desto, por que los moços son avn muelles & tiernos &, por consiguiente, tienen el coraçón tierno como los otros mienbros, delo qual se causa la misericordia, que es blandura de coraçón.

Enlos malos ajenos los viejos son compassiuos & piadosos por otra causa; la qual es por quanto son flacos enel cuerpo & la vida les fallesce, an conpassión delos otros quando los veen mal passar como querrían que ouiessen dellos. Común dicho es delos sabios, que no sabe auer conpassión el que nunca ouo passión. Si vn hombre fue pobre & después fue rico, mejor abrá compassión delos pobres que el que nunca fue pobre. Assí haze el que en algún tiempo fue enfermo, delos enfermos; por el consiguiente, ha tan bien conpasión & assí el peregrino delos peregrinos &, por consiguiente, delas otras pasiones. Esto es, porque el viejo passa muchas pasiones que son conpañeras dela vejez. Porende es compasiuo & piadoso enlos males delos otros, como querría que lo fuessen enlos suyos.

Las mugeres son piadosas por otra razón, que dizen que han los coraçones tiernos y blandos, como deximos de los moços, por lo qual no pueden soportar ninguna dureza. Donde, quando veen que alguno padesce penas duras, luego se prouocan a lágrimas & a misericordia & conpasión. Antes, si queremos, podemos dezir que las mugeres son piadosas por todas las razones que los moços & los viejos son piadosos & subjetos a muchas pasiones. Así las mugeres son tiernas & a muchas pasiones subjetas más que los varones, como paresce quando maldixo Dios al varón & ala muger, que más maldiciones dio ala muger que no al varón.[1] Paresce, pues, cómo las mugeres son piadosas & por qué causa & de do les viene ser piadosas.

Agora, por quanto todo esto se ordena a dotrina & instrución dela princesa, quiero aplicar esto alas grandes señoras & prouar por razones que, avn que todas las mugeres sean natural mente piadosas, pero las grandes lo deuen ser más que todas. Para lo qual saber diremos que la reyna en su reyno o la princesa o otra señora en su principado o señorío tiene tres respectos por los quales & cadavno dellos deue ser a sus vasallos piadosa. Ella es madre & abogada & es escudo. Quanto alo primero hagamos tal razón: toda madre natural mente es piadosa a sus hijos. La reyna o princesa es madre de sus pueblos, pues luego síguese que deue ser aellos piadosa. Enesta razón no ay otra cosa dubdosa & de prouocar sino cómo la reyna es madre de sus pueblos, ca ella no los parió, ¿cómo pues es su madre? Pero si con paciencia oýr quisiere lo que dirá mi razón, claro le será cómo es madre de sus pueblos & más obligada aellos por piedad que a sus propios hijos que de su vientre parió.

Dize Séneca enel primero libro *De clemencia:* —que si el emperador parará mientes a su estado, hallará que es padre dela patria, que quiere dezir de su imperio.[2] E para esto entender, pónese tal enxemplo: Aquí está vn padre que me engendró, pero desque me ouo engendrado fuese & de criarme no curó. Vino

---

[1] Genesis 3:16.
[2] Lucio Anneo Séneca ("De la clemencia," in *Obras completas*, p. 248, Bk. I, Ch. xiv).

otro hombre & tomó cura de mí & crióme. Si me preguntan quál destos es más mi padre, digo quel que me crió & guardó & conseruó la vida, aquel es más mi padre. Eneste respecto está el rey con sus pueblos; que avn que a mí me engendró mi padre, pero si el rey no guardara la tierra delos enemigos, assí dela fe como del reyno [a] & de otros malfechores, que si no fuera por miedo del rey & su justicia, entraran de noche o de día a robar & matar a mi padre & a mí & a quantos héramos en casa. Pues avn que mi padre me engendró & me dio la vida, el rey me guardó & conseruó enella e porende es más continuado padre. ¿Dónde me viene que yo esté seguro en mi casa me roben o maten? Esto viene de Dios o del rey. Quando vo por un monte espesso & no hallo enel camino quién me haga mal: ¿quién lo hace esto?: El rey. E por esso, quando passo por tales passos, que he passado hartos dellos eneste mundo, & veo que vo seguro, luego fago oración a Dios por el rey o por el príncipe o señor dela tierra. Por quanto por su diligencia tuuo seguro aquel passo que no me matassen & así le deuo la vida, la qual no deuo a mi padre carnal, sino vna vez. Al rey la deuo mill vezes, antes gela deuo toda mi vida. Por lo qual el amor del rey es sobre todo parentesco o linaje. Onde si ay aquí dos batallas & enla vna está mi padre & enla otra el rey, diz que tengo de dexar la batalla de mi padre & yrme ala del rey, & poner lança en ristre contra el padre por defención de su rey.

Esto entended quando el rey es aquél que deue & no cahe en cosa por que se deua hazer el contrario. Pues como dezimos quel rey es padre, por esta misma razón dezimos que la reyna es madre, ca ella conel rey velan para nos guardar en nuestra vida & seguridad; & como yo sea obligado a amar más al rey & ala reyna que a mi padre o a mi madre, por la razón dicha, assí ellos son más obligados a mí en caso de justicia que a sus hijos. Donde leemos que los romanos príncipes muchos dellos mataron a sus hijos por mantener justicia enla república. E de Augusto Sézar se lee que, quando venía del senado, acompañáuanlo hasta a

---

[a] Cf. n. 17 to the *Prohemio*. The reference to the king's function as the protector of the realm and of the faith may be a comment on the shortcomings of Enrique IV.

palacio todos los señores cónsules & patricios; &, quando les espedía [4] ala puerta de su palacio, dezía: —Señores, aued recomendados mis hijos tanta quanto lo merecieren & no más. Assí que, segund este dezir, más amaría ala república que a sus fijos. [5]

Pues ques notorio que la princesa es madre nobilísima de sus pueblos, la razón primera está en pie. Es asaber: que desto se sigue que ha de ser a ellos piadosa & clemente como madre a hijos.

La segunda razón por que deue ser piadosa la reyna, es por quanto es no sola mente madre, mas abogada. Dizen estonces que el reyno dela tierra es bien ordenado quando es conforme al reyno del cielo, ca lo baxo se ha de conformar quanto puede alo alto & tomar dende enxemplo. Pues como enel reyno celestial el Rey, Jhesu Cristo, es juez & la Virgen Reyna es abogada, así ha de ser enel reyno terrenal, que el rey sea juez & la reyna abogada. Donde, puesto que el rey quiera tiranizar o echar demasiados tributos enel reyno, ala reyna pertenesce en tal cosa & en otros [6] semejantes abogar por el pueblo. Assí Hester conel rey Assuero, que abogó por el pueblo de Ysrael & lo libró de muerte. [7] Así cuenta Tito Liuio de Diuo Augusto, enperador, que apareaua de matar a muchos nobles mancebos que auían conjurado en su muerte e dela otra parte hauía duelo de ma[t]ar [8] tan noble juuentud & estaua ansioso entre sí. Entonces Li[v]ia, la emperatrix entró aél & rogóle que les perdonasse & assí lo hizo. No digo que esto se haga cada día, ca enesta manera perescería el themor dela justicia. Pero algunos casos ay que requieren perdón e enestos la reyna deue interponer su oficio de abogada, por que el rey más se doble a piedad & clemencia que no a

---

[4] The 1542 ed. has *despedía*.

[5] The story of Augustus Caesar and his sons may refer to the story of Augustus Caesar's rejection of the title of *dominus*. St. Isidore relates: "Y al día siguiente reprendió al pueblo con un gravísimo edicto y no permitió que se les diera este título ni aun por sus propios hijos..." (p. 225).

[6] The 1542 ed. has *otras*.

[7] See Esther 3:13; 7:3 and 7:6. See also D. Álvaro de Luna (p. 42) and St. Ambrose (*Duties of the Clergy* in *Some Principal Works*, trans. H. De Romestin, p. 187, Bk. III, Ch. xxi, 123).

[8] The 1500 ed. has *marar*.

dureza de pena.⁹ Desto podríamos traher muchos enxemplos, sino por dezir otras cosas.

Lo tercero, la señora es escudo, ca no sólo ha de ser piadosa como madre, ni como abogada cerca del rey, mas ha de ser paués & adaraga & escudo, defendiendo los menudos de las fuerças delos mayores. Ca el mundo es como la mar & los hombres como los peces, donde los mayores comen alos menores. E porende la princesa eneste mar sea como la vallena, dela qual los peces menudos hazen escudo contra los grandes. Donde, so su amparo & defendimiento, ha de recibir los humildes labradores, los deuotos horadores, los estudiosos maestros & doctores, biudas, huérfanos & pobres sin amparo. E assí será semejante ala Reyna del cielo; quando la pintan con su manto abierto, cobriente de cada parte todos los estados del mundo. Pues ya paresce cómo la señora es madre, defensora & abogada & escudo & paués delos flacos, por lo qual deue ser sobre todas piadosa. E esto es lo que eneste capítulo vos he querido declarar.

---

⁹ Although Fray Martín cites Livy here, I suspect that he was continuing to rely on Seneca (*De la clemencia*) who deals with the same episode, making the additional point that Augustus welcomed Livia's advice (*Obras completas*, p. 244, Bk. I, Ch. ix).

Capítulo Tercio

[*Capítulo .iij.* como son obsequiosas & como es esta buena propiedad enellas, ca por ésta Jhesu Cristo & sus apóstoles las traxeron en su compañia]

La tercera buena condición delas mugeres deximos de suso que heran obsequiosas, quiere dezir que son de gracioso & consolatiuo seruicio. Por lo qual dize Salamón enlos Prouerbios: —que adonde la muger no es, quel enfermo gime. [1] Este obsequio & deuoto seruicio se halla enellas en tres maneras: la vna por deuoción a Dios, la otra por compassión de próximo e la tercera por dileción a su casa.

Quanto alo primero, es de notar que común mente las mugeres son más deuotas a Dios que los varones. Por lo qual dizen que Jhesu Cristo & sus apóstoles touieron enesta compañía mugeres, las quales fueron de tanta deuoción, que, avn que los discípulos fuyeron el día dela passión & dexaron a Nuestro Señor solo, ellas no lo dexaron; mas tanto en deuoción suya presentaron, que merescieron primero saber el tiempo & la ora que Nuestro Señor resucitó & ellas lo denunciaron alos apóstoles. E si dezís que por qué son más deuotas que los varones, digo que la deuoción en Dios requiere tres cosas, alas quales son más dispuestas las mugeres que los varones. Estas son: fe, esperança & caridad. Quanto ala fe, son más aýna crédulas & muy aýna creen lo que la fe recuenta & los Evangelios & otras escripturas, dela qual fe

---

[1] I do not find this aphorism in Proverbs, Wisdom, Ecclesiastes, Ecclesiasticus nor in *The Odes and Psalms of Solomon*, ed. James Rendel Harris (Cambridge, 1909).

se sigue deuoción & afección a Dios & alas cosas diuinales; lo que no hazen los varones tan aýna, ca primero quieren inuestigar por razón lo que es de la fe, lo qual es sobre toda razón. Donde de Santo Agustín se lee, que no se bautizaua nin fazía cristiano por quanto quería con razón humana comprehender lo quel ánima deuota alcança sólo con biueza de fe.[2] Pues quando a varones & mugeres se recuenta algund misterio dela fe, más aýna lo creen las mugeres que los varones, por que menos demandan razón del propuesto que los varones.

De la grand fe se sigue luego buena esperança. Creyendo yo firme mente en Dios, creo luego que son verdaderas sus promesas & comienço a esperar enellas. E por contrario dela poca fe, se sigue flaca esperança. Quando yo sé que vn honbre es verdadero, creo lo que dize & espero bien lo que promete & de todo esto se sigue la caridad & amor de Dios, que es Señor tan verdadero & en promissiones tan largo.

Pues ved aquí la causa por que las mugeres son más deuotas a Dios que no los varones. Donde recuenta el Evangelista, que como vna vez Nuestro Señor Jhesu Christo estouiese enel templo & mírase los que echauan las ofrendas enel arca del templo, vino vna buena muger vieja & biuda & echó dos meajas. Dixo Jhesu Cristo que aquella buena muger auía echado más que todos,[3] que avn que hera poco en valor lo que auía echado, hera mucho por deuoción, que con mayor effecto dio aquello poco que los otros lo mucho.[4] Assí todas las mugeres deuen ser enesta guisa por deuoción a Dios obsequiosas, quánto más deuen ser las reynas & princesas, las quales deuen ser enxenplo a todos de honrrar & seruir a Dios & defender la Yglesia & las personas della; oýr cada día sus misas, rezar sus oras & deuociones, oýr

---

[2] St. Augustin, *Confessions*, in *Basic Writings of St. Augustine*, ed. Whitney Oates, 2 Vols. (New York, 1948), I, 11.

[3] The 1542 ed. has *todas*.

[4] Mark 12: 42-44: "And there came a certain poor widow, and threw in two mites, which make a farthing. And he called unto him his disciples and saith unto them, Verily I say unto you, that this poor widow hath cast more in, than all they which have cast into the treasury." This is an example of how a Biblical text can be taken out of context and be used to illustrate a somewhat unrelated point. Clearly, the widow in Scripture is not being singled out as a devout woman as opposed to less devout men. It is her poverty and generosity that are praised not her sex.

sermones & palabras de Dios; fazer que lean delante della, quando comen & quando están retraýdas, lecturas honestas & santas; conuersar con letrados & sabios que la pueden dotrinar de cosas diuinales; pensar sienpre enla otra vida & enla cuenta que a Dios han de dar tan estrecha; hablar & oýr fablar dela gloria de paraýso, como fazía María Magdalena asentada alos pies de Jhesu Cristo, oýa sus palabras que heran enformatiuas del Reyno de Dios. Esto es, pues, lo primero en que las sanctas dueñas & deuotas donzellas han de ser obsequiosas.

Lo segundo en que han de ser obsequiosas es por compassión al próximo. Por esto dizen que los apóstoles, después que les fue enbiado el Espíritu Santo, tenían mugeres en su conpañía por los seruicios que dellas recibían, como algunas mugeres siguieron a Jhesu Cristo para le seruir & administrar lo necessario de sus haziendas. Así quiso que algunas sanctas mugeres siguiessen alos apóstoles sus predicadores, dando a entender por todo lo que deuen los pueblos alos que predican el Sancto Evangelio. Enesta guisa Martha ministraua a Jhesu Cristo, recibiéndolo en su casa & dándolo de comer & aél & a sus discípulos.

Son obsequiosas las mugeres a enfermos, a pobres, a peregrinos & a toda otra gente desconsolada. De Sancta Moni[c]a, la madre de señor Santo Agustín se dize que por esto fue sancta; por que seguía & consolaua los pobres enfermos & vestía & amortajaua los muertos & alos huérfanos como a sus hijos guardaua; & quando veýa algunos pobres llagados, lauáuales las llagas & alimpiáualas; no mostrando asco niguno.[5] Enesto no entiendo obligar alas altas dueñas a que lo hagan por sus manos; pero que tengan limosneros que ayan[6] cargo de acorrer a semejantes necessidades & induzir mugeres otras que lo hagan quando la tal necessidad se mostrare e avn hazer quel su limosnero busque tales pobres, si los ay, por que en nombre & voz dela señora sean acorridos.

E esto primera mente en su casa a sus donzellas & otros seruidores, si cahen en enfermedad, la piedad dela señora procure que sea fecha diligencia en seruirles & darles lo que han

---

[5] St. Augustin praised his mother for the good works she performed in *Confessions* (*Basic Writings of St. Augustine*, I, 140).

[6] The 1542 ed. has *tengan*.

menester a consejo de físico. Lo contrario se haze oy enlos palacios. Síruense delos seruidores quando están sanos & desque les duele la cabeça no los quieren ver. Esto es crueldad orrible, & tal que da bozes a Dios por vengança contra su señor. No assí la nuestra noble Princesa; mas luego de su infancia crezca conella la obsequiosa piedad, nin mire alo que hazen los otros palacios, mas alo que es obligada al suyo; & abra su mano al menesteroso & sus palmas estienda alos pobres; ca sepa segund dize Santo Ambrosio: —que por pecador que sea el honbre o la muger, si husa las obras de misericordia en sus próximos, diz que será açotado por sus pecados, pero por la piedad que hizo, sepa que no parescerá. [7]

Lo tercero en que han de ser obsequiosas es en su casa. Notá que segund los philósofos, enel regimiento doméstico & casero, los oficios del varón & dela muger son repartidos, ca el marido ha de procurar lo defuera de casa & la muger lo de dentro de casa; ca natural cosa es ala muger estar sienpre en casa. E desto se sigue que la muger ha de ser obsequiosa al marido amándole, honrrándole & por sí & por otras seruiéndole. Es verdad que esto no cab[e] [8] enlas altas dueñas que tienen su estado aparte de sus maridos. Esto avn que no sea siempre, pero alo menos, quando quiera que conuenga, la dueña deue estos obsequios a su señor & marido. Alos hijos, si los touiere, es obligada deles [9] seruir, criándolos o faziéndolos criar a buenas & honestas amas & sobre todo cathólicas que, quando les dieren la teta, nonbren a Jhesu & ala Virgen María & a Sant Miguel, por que con la leche beuan deuoción deste nombre Jhesus & delos otros. Recuenta Sant Agustín, enel libro de sus *Confessiones,* que le vino en manos vn libro de Tulio Cicerón que contenía amonestación para menospreciar este mundo & dize que por esto le plugo mucho aquel libro. Pero por que no halló en todo aquel libro el nombre de Jhesus, diz que resfrióse en amar tanto aquel libro,

---

[7] St. Ambrose quotes Hosea 6:16, Matthew 9:13 and John 1:17 to show that acts of mercy redeem the sinner according to the Gospel as did sacrifice under the old Law (*Concerning Repentance,* in *Some of the Principal Works,* p. 338, Bk. I, Ch. xii).

[8] The 1500 ed. has *caba*; the 1542 *cabe*.

[9] The 1542 ed. has *de los servir*.

ca dize que este nombre auía él beuido con la tierna leche & auíale así posseýdo su coraçón que no le plazía ninguna lectura sin él.[10]

Assí que procure la cristianíssima Princesa, quando touiere hijos que sean criados por amas deuotas & católicas que les nombren a Jhesu & a Santa María & a Sant Miguel. Ha de ser obsequiosa en su casa alos seruidores & donzellas como deximos; a cadavno según que meresce & ha menester & segund el oficio que en casa tiene. E assí será semejante ala muger fuerte, dela qual fablan los Prouerbios de Salamón.[11] E henchirá la medida de sus loables condiciones que son vergüença, piedad & obsequias.

---

[10] This citation and the famous dream of St. Jerome both serve to illustrate the uneasiness of the Church Fathers with their own classical erudition. St. Augustin expresses his distrust of Cicero as a source of inspiration: "And since at that time (as Thou, O light of my heart, knowest) the words of the apostle were unknown to me, I was delighted with that exhortation ... and this alone checked me thus ardent, that the name of Christ was not in it" (*Confessions*, in *Basic Writings of St. Augustine*, I, 32).

[11] See Proverbs 12:4: "Crowned is his brow who wins a vigorous wife; sooner let thy bones rot than marry one who shames thee" and Proverbs 31:10-13: "Who can find a virtuous woman? for her price is far above rubies." The latter text goes on to specify her attentiveness to household duties, her kindness to the servants, her industry, her charity, her honor, and her piety, in fact all the qualities that Fray Martín has been praising in this chapter. In Proverbs 31:7, woman is called strong: "She girdeth her loins with strength, and strengtheneth her arms."

## Capítulo Quarto

[*Capítulo .iiij.* delas menos buenas condiciones dela muger & de vna condición que conlas buenas es buena & conlas malas muy mala].

Pues ya auemos dicho delas buenas condiciones delas mugeres, tiempo es que veamos delas otras condiciones no tan buenas por que assí haziendo, será la Princesa como el abeja que van entre las flores & coje las buenas & dexa las malas & assí haze su dulce miel.[1] Semejante pone Santo Jherónimo en vna epístola a Rústico, monje. Fue preguntado a Sant Jherónimo quál hera más sancta vida, el monje biuir solo en vn yermo o biuir en vn monasterio con otros monjes. E dize Sant Jherónimo que mejor es biuir en monesterio.[2] La razón suya es que

---

[1] Although bees and ants were common symbols of industry, Fray Martín is using the bees here as exemplars of discrimination. In the *Ars praedicandi*, Fray Martín uses the image of the bees as examples of lively and industrious activity, with the added factor that they collect nectar from many different sources as should a good preacher ("Ars praedicandi de Fray Martín de Córdoba," ed. Fernando Rubio Álvarez, *La Ciudad de Dios*, 172 [1959], pp. 329-348).

[2] W. H. Fremantle says that in Letter CXXV, *To Rusticus*, "a young monk of Toulouse ... is advised by Jerome not to become an anchorite but to continue in a community" (p. 244). St. Jerome writes as follows: "The first point to be considered is whether you ought to live by yourself or in a monastery with others. For my part, I should like you to have the society of holy men so as not to be thrown altogether upon your own resources.... In loneliness pride quickly creeps upon a man; if he has fasted for a little while and seen no one, he fancies himself a person of some note" (p. 247). St. Jerome pursues the point saying: "No art is ever learned without a master" (p. 249). The gist of this letter is not as Fray Martín says that a young man can learn even from people of limited

no ay hombre tan malo ni de tan mala condición que no tenga alguna buena propiedad. Ni le ay tan bueno que no tenga alguna mala. E porende el mejor & más cuerdo que biue entre tal gente faze como el abeja, que de cadavno coje las buenas condiciones & dexa las malas. El mal monje faze como el abispa que dexa lo bueno & toma lo podrido. Pues porende es aquí prouecho [3] dezir las buenas condiciones dela muger & las comunales por que conlas buenas, entresacadas las malas, fagamos vna guirnalda de suaues flores, que pongamos enla alta cabeça de Nuestra Señora. Grand prouecho es a cada vno saber los males a que está subjeto & aparejado, como si alguno es muy colérico & adusto de complexión, bien le es quel físico le diga cómo es dispuesto a hitericia, [4] o fiebres agudas o a frenesía & assí de otras enfermedades; por que, diziéndogelo apercibir se ha & no caerá enellas. Assí es tan bien enlo moral. Bien es que yo diga a vn moço: —Cata, que tu hedad es dispuesta a algunas buenas condiciones & a algunas malas; & dezírgelas por que sigua [5] las buenas & dexe las malas. Así es delas mugeres.

Pues es assaber que, segund los philósophos, las mugeres tienen tres menos buenas condiciones & otra tienen indiferente. Las tres menos buenas son éstas: la primera, que son intemperadas; la otra, que son parleras & porfiosas; la otra, que son variables sin constancia. La indiferente es que todo lo hazen por extremo & por cabo & ésta conlas buenas es buena & conlas malas es mala.

---

goodness. In Letter CXXXX ("To Demetrias"), St. Jerome touches upon the same subject: "Men often discuss the comparative merits of life in solitude and life in a community; and the preference is usually given to the first over the second. Still even for men there is always the risk that, being withdrawn from the society of their fellows, they may become exposed to unclean and godless imaginations..." (p. 270). He further points out that untrained persons can, without instruction, misread Scripture and cause misunderstanding in others. In this letter, St. Jerome addressing himself to Demetrias, a highborn lady of Rome, even observes that anchorites who have fasted excessively have "so impaired their faculties that they do not know what to do or where to turn, when to speak or when to be silent" (p. 270).

[3] The 1542 ed. has *prouechoso*.

[4] The 1542 ed. has *hereticia*. *Hitericia* in the 1500 ed. is undoubtedly *ictericia* (see Corominas, *DCELC*).

[5] Both eds. have *sigua*.

La primera, pues, no buena condición es que son intenperadas. Quiere dezir que siguen los apetitos carnales como es comer & dormir & folgar & otros que son peores.⁶ E estos les viene por que enellas no es tan fuerte la razón como enlos varones, que con la razón que enellos es mayor, refrenan las passiones dela carne; pero las mugeres más son carne que espíritu e porende son más inclinadas aellas que al espíritu & avn de aquí se sigue que entre los varones ay esta diferencia: que quanto el varón es más dotado de razón tanto menos sigue la inclinación dela carne. Donde los moços que avn que no tienen complimiento de razón, son dados más a golosinas y juegos y sueño que los grandes. E de vn varón a otro ay esta diferencia. E avn por esso menos preciamos alos que siguen los desseos dela carne, por que es señal que tiene[n] poco seso & no vsan de razón como honbres, mas de pasión, como bestias. Contra esta mala condición es la primera buena: que es ser vergonçosas; ca enla muger, como deximos, la vergüença es freno que no se derribe en feas & torpes passiones.

La segunda no buena es que son parleras & porfiosas. Ser parleras les viene de flaqueza, ca veyéndose flacas para poner el negocio a manos, pónenlo a palabras; por que lo que no puede el espada, que lo haga la lengua. E avn enlos varones ay esta diuersidad, que los couardes son grandes palabreros. Los osados hablan poco & luego lo ponen alos puños. Ser porfiosas les viene de falta de razón, ca no sabiendo prouar⁷ su intención con que quieren salir, porfíanlo. E avn esto viene de apetito de loor, ca les paresce que quedan menos cabadas si se dan por vencidas

---

⁶ Cf. the enthusiastic description given by the Arcipreste de Talavera of how the lover is subject to the sin of gluttony, a not wholly convincing rhapsody (pp. 106-107). We have seen before a reference to the sexual insatiability of women (see n. 3 to *Capítulo primero, segunda parte*), to which Fray Martín is undoubtedly referring as "otros que son peores." In the *Poridat de las poridades*, the pseudo-Aristotle writes to Alexander listing the qualities of a good "aguazil." Among them is "que non sea muy comedor, ni muy beuedor, nin fornaquero, et que desame los sabores deste mundo et los iuegos" (pp. 47-48). It seems that there were intemperate men, but the implication is that their intemperance was a way of sharing the faults of women.

⁷ The 1542 ed. has *ca no saben do probar*, an apparent confusion in copying.

en palabras. Y esto tiene buen remedio: que la muger ponga silencio & guarda en su lengua & quando quisiere [8] hablar que se muerda primero la lengua & los labros, por que no salga palabra que no sea limada por juyzio de razón.

La tercera no buena condición es que son mouibles & inconstantes, lo qual, por ventura, les viene dela feble complexión, ca por quanto el ánima sigue la conplexión del cuerpo, assí como las mugeres tienen el cuerpo muelle & tierno, assí sus voluntades & deseos son variables & no constantes. Pero el remedio dello es lo que hizieren, hazello con maduro consejo; & desque por razón es visto quel propósito es bueno & justo, tener por él & no lo dexar nin por amenazas ni por falagos. Así como hizo Santa Ynés, desque se vistió de propósito de sancta virginidad fundada enla fe cathólica, no huuo hombre que de allí la pudiese mouer, ni por dádiuas ni por tormentos. Assí que aquella muger hera menos variable, que el Espíritu Sancto la auía formada sobre firme piedra. [9]

Agora se sigue la otra condición, que ni es buena ni mala, sino por el adjutorio, es asaber que mucho ex[c]eden, donde quando son piadosas mucho lo son & quando son crueles mucho lo son & quando son desuergonçadas son por cabo; ca desque toman osadía, tantas fealdades cometen que no se fallaría[n] varones que tales cosas aceptasen. Esta condición, avn que enlo bueno sea loable, pero enlo malo siempre es vituperable. Ser mucho vergonçosas loable es; ser muy desuergonçadas es de vituperio segura. Verdad es que dize Terencio enla primera comedia que no ay cosa de tanto prouecho enla vida como no fazer las cosas por cabo. [10] E por el contrario, no ay enel mundo tan grand virtud como en todos los fechos tener medio, ca si bien queremos considerar todas las cosas, assí naturales como morales, quando están en su ser, son en medio. La vida del animal está en calor

---

[8] The 1542 ed. has *quiere*.

[9] D. Álvaro de Luna tells the story of St. Inés and her determination and constancy (p. 200-202).

[10] *The Lady of Andros* (also called *Andria*) in *Terence*, trans. John Sargeaunt, 2 Vols. [London: Loeb Classical Library, 1912], I, 11. St. Augustin cites what he calls the Terentian formula: "Since you can't do what you will, will what you can" (*The City of God*, II, 405, Bk. XIV, Ch. xxv), citing from *Andria* 2:15 (I, 33).

& humor templados, que si el calor es mucho, consume el humor; si es poco, ahógalo el humor; si el humor es mucho, apaga el calor; si es poco no abasta al calor. Assí es del comer, honbre no poder biuir sin comer, pero para que biua comiendo, es necessaria quel comer sea templado & tenga medio entre mucho y poco; que si es mucho, ahoga los espíritus que rompen los humores. Si es muy poco, no alcança al nudrimiento. Enxenplo desto vemos enlos molinos, que para que vn molino muela, requiérese el agua por medida &, por ende, algunas vezes no ay moliendas por muchas aguas & otras vezes dexan de moler por seca. Donde es tanto prouechoso en todo huýr los extremos, que avn enlos buenos es vituperoso tener los cabos. Como dize Salomón enel Eclesiastés: —No quieras ser mucho justo, que la mucha justicia se torna alas vezes en crueldad. [11] Callar & tener silencio loable es alas donzellas; pero tanto pudría vna donzella callar & apartarse & cerrarse, que sería tenida por menos cuerda porque avn el callar quiere mesura. [12] Es assaber: que hable quando es necessario & calle quando es oportuno & assí delas otras virtudes. Uno solo quiere extremo: esto es el amor de Dios que no lo podemos tanto amar que no seamos más obligados alo amar. Donde enlos Cánticos dize: —que las donzellas, es assaber las vírgines, te amaron Señor por cabo & muy mucho, [13] & assí paresce lo contenido eneste capítulo.

---

[11] Ecclesiastes 7:16: "Be not righteous overmuch; neither make thyself overwise: why shouldest thou destroy thyself?"

[12] Is it possible that Fray Martín is referring here to the withdrawn, depressed state of the mother of Isabel?

[13] Song of Songs 1:3.

## Capítulo Quinto

[*Capítulo .v.* comiença delas condiciones que han de auer las nobles donzellas para que sean dignas de ser reynas & pártelas & da orden cómo dirá dellas & muestra les primero el temor de Dios].

Asaz es dicho delas condiciones que han las mugeres común mente de su propiedad natural, assí buenas como menos buenas, & cómo la princesa se ha de auer conellas. Agora diré delas donzellas que han de auer & seguir la nobleza que ouieron de sus parientes, sea doblada por nobles virtudes, & así sean dignas de principiar & de regir los súditos pueblos; & esto no sólo será prouecho aellas, mas a todas las claras mugeres; que, avn que todas no puedan ser reynas ni princesas, pero todas han de trabajar de assí conponer su vida que sean dignas de ser reynas & princesas. Pues primera mente en general recontaré las ordenadas condiciones que deuen auer & dende en especial, trataré dellas.

Notá, pues,[1] que la princesa ha en tal manera de ordenar sus condiciones, que algunas sean buenas por respecto a Dios, otras por respecto de sí misma & otras por respecto del pueblo que rige. La criatura r[a]zonal[2] tiene tres respectos: vno es alo alto, que es a Dios, otro es alo igual, que es el próximo & otro es así mismo. Pues, si la princesa es bien ordenada al pueblo súbdito, no quedará nada enella desordenado. Enla orden que ha de auer a Dios, ay tres cosas. Es assaber: themor de su po-

---

[1] The 1542 ed. has *pues, la princesa.*
[2] The 1500 ed. has *rozonal.*

tencia, honor a su sapiencia & amor a su clemencia. Dios es todopoderoso & por esto deue ser temido. Dios es de todas cosas sabidor & por esto deue ser honrrado. Dios es infinita bondad por esto deue ser sobre todo amado. Assí que la señora será en buen respeto & orden a Dios su señor, si lo teme & honrra & si lo ama. Desque esta balança touiere derecha con Dios, resta que ensí mesma se ordene, lo qual fará si guarda su condición, si rige su lengua & si gouierna su obra. En nos mesmos nos desordenamos, por malos pensamientos & desseos, corrompiendo nuestros coraçones por disolutas palabras, ensuzi[a]ndo [3] nuestras bocas & por obras injustas peruertiendo nuestras manos. Pues para el contrario hazer, guardemos el coraçón de malos deseos, la lengua de malas palabras & las manos de malas obras.

Ordenada la persona real a Dios & en sí mesma, conuiene que ordene a su pueblo en tres cosas: en justicia, en franqueza & en concordia. En todas estas condiciones assí ordenadas, la primera es temor a Dios; ésta es comienço de toda sabiduría. El que tiene a Dios es sabio; el que no le tiene es loco. El temor de Dios enmienda la vida. El temor de Dios desecha los pecados. El themor de Dios haze al hombre valer & ser solícito. Donde no ay temor de Dios, allí es disolución de vida; a do temor de Dios no ay, allí es la perdición de muerte; a do temor de Dios no ay, allí es habundancia de maldades. De manera que toda criatura deue temer a Dios por tres cosas: la primera, por que es justo & nunca tuerce su justicia, ni por amor, ni por fauor, ni por presentes, ni por ruegos. No es aceptor de personas; no mira más al rico que al que poco tiene; no más al rey que al vasallo. La otra, por que es poderoso, de cuyo poder ninguno puede huyr. Los reyes terrenales tienen poder sobre el cuerpo & sobre los biuos; Dios tiene poder sobre el cuerpo & sobre el ánima. La otra, por que vee todas las cosas & las sabe antes que sean, assí que no le podemos negar nada delo que en nos otros ay, ni darle a entender lo que no es & avn que todos seamos aesto obligados, es asaber el temor de Dios; pero en especial las personas grandes, poderosas & princesas, por tres razones: la primera, por que no conoscen superior sino a Dios. Donde Dauid, que hera rey dezía:

---

[3] The 1500 ed. has *ensuziendo*.

—A tí sólo pequé,[4] como si dixese: de mi peccado atí sólo tengo de dar cuenta. No así los otros baxos, que de sus males han de dar cuenta al rey & a sus mayores. Aquí ay, pues, vna semejança: más pauor abría yo de dar cuenta de mis hechos al rey, que no al juez & más al juez mayor que no al menor. Donde quanto el juez a quien tenga de dar la cuenta es menor, tanto he menos miedo. Pues por quanto los reys & reynas no esperan de dar cuenta a otro, sino a Dios tan alto, tan poderoso, razón es que ayan más miedo dél que los otros cuya cuenta se da a sus mayores. Así quel miedo delos baxos está repartido, que dello han de sus mayores & dello han de Dios. Pero el miedo delos reys está todo cogido a Dios no temiendo otro ninguno & por esto este themor deue ser mayor. Donde dize el psalmo: —Agora los reys, entended & tomad dotrina, los que juzgáys la tierra, seruid al Señor en temor & alegrad vos a El en temor. Rescebid disciplina seyendo discípulos de los sabios & no perezcáys dela vía justa.[5] Digamos, pues, que aquellos han más de temer a Dios que no an de dar cuenta a otro sino aÉl. Los grandes reys & reynas son tales, síguese, pues, que más han de themer a Dios. Do dize Sant Pablo: —Orrible cosa es caer enlas manos de Dios biuo.[6]

La otra razón por que deuen más temer a Dios que los otros es por el terrrible juyzio que esperan más que los otros. Donde la Sabiduría dixo: —Durísimo juyzio será hecho contra los presidentes.[7] La causa es, por que no sólo han de dar cuenta de sus males, mas delos ajenos & de todos los peccados que se hazen & cometen en su reyno, por razón dela poca justicia & dela nigligencia, de no curar ni entender en regimiento ni gouernación de su reyno. Donde en otro lugar dize: —Los poderosos muy potentes

---

[4] Psalm 51:4: "Against thee only, have I sinned and done this evil in thy sight...."

[5] Psalm 2:10-12: "Be wise now therefore, O ye kings: be instructed, ye judges of the earth. Serve the Lord with fear, and rejoice with trembling. Kiss the Son, lest he be angry, and ye perish from the way, when his wrath is kindled but a little. Blessed are all they that put their trust in him."

[6] Hebrews 10:31: "It is a fearful thing to fall into the hands of the living God."

[7] Wisdom 6:6: "The small man may find pity and forgiveness, but the powerful will be called powerfully to account; for he who is all men's master is obsequious to none, and is not overawed by greatness."

tormento padescerán. ⁸ Creo que por quanto los demonios son verdugos de atormentar los dapñados, que los reys & reynas son atormentados por los más poderosos & crueles demonios, que poderosa mente & cruel los atormentan más que alos otros. E esto por sentencia de Dios. Donde enla primera tragedia de Séneca, habla Teseo, que dize auer ydo al infier[n]o con Hércoles & recuenta lo que vido & entre otras cosas dize algo que es aquí a propósito. Dize: —Vi encerrar en cárcel alos reys crueles & vi que vn tirano estaua abierto por las espaldas de açotes que le dauan los pueblos que él auía sojuzgado. Donde concluye: —El que as de ser rey, no seas cruel & derramador de sangre humana, que los peccados delos reys son tasados con penas mayores. ⁹

La otra razón es por que si a Dios la reyna no teme, tan poco será temida por sus pueblos, antes ella temerá aellas. Enxemplo desto: Si Adam temiera a Dios, guardando su mandamiento, todas las bestias lo temieran. En tanto que si dixera a vn león o a vn osso o a qualquier otra bestia: —Échate aý, que te quiero herir, luego lo fiziera. Perdió Adam el themor a Dios & perdieron las bestias el themor aél. Antes nos otros tememos aellas & tememos arañas, mosquitos, pulgas, peojos, que son las más baxas cosas del mundo. Assí hazen los grandes oy, que pierden el themor a Dios por lo qual han de temer a todos los súbditos & avn alos más viles hombres de su reyno, en especial si los reciben a sus secretos. E las princesas & grandes señoras, no temiendo a Dios, temen todas las cosas & son perdidas & subjetas a vnas viejas secretarias, que más valdría que no fuessen nascidas. ¹⁰ La primera, pues buena condición es temer a Dios, por que todas te temen & tú no a ninguno.

---

⁸ Wisdom 6:5: "Swiftly and terribly will he descend upon you, for judgment falls relentlessly upon those in high places." Wisdom 6:7: "Small and great alike are of his making, and all are under his providence equally, but it is the powerful for whom he reserves the sternest inquisition."

⁹ Lucius Annaeus Seneca, *Hercules Furens* in *Seneca's Tragedies*, trans. Frank Justus Miller, 2 Vols. (London, 1927), I, 67.

¹⁰ The exact reference is not clear here. Enríquez del Castillo refers to a conspiracy in which Doña Mencía de Padilla participated in arranging to admit the conspirators to the royal chambers (pp. 103-104). Beatriz de Bobadilla was said to have wavered in her loyalty to Isabel. Fray Martín may be speaking in general here about the atmosphere of mistrust at the court of Enrique IV.

Capítulo Sesto

[*Capítulo .vj.* que deuen honrrar & amar a Dios sobretodas las cosas & más las reynas que todas las otras mugeres].

Pues que ya es dicho cómo han de temer a Dios las nobles donzellas, queda que veamos cómo lo an de honrrar; honrrar por que es fuente de sabiduría & amar porque es piélago de todo bien. La honrra de Dios está en tres cosas: la primera, en aÉl [1] sólo adorar; la segunda, en no le blasfemar; la tercera, enlas fiestas bien guardar. La primera, pues, es no auer otro dios sino Aquel que crió el cielo & la tierra & todo quanto enello es & nos redimió por su preciosa sangre; enÉl creer, enÉl confiar, no en vanidades de sueños, ni conjuros, ni adeuinos, ni en otros maleficios. [2] Antes cumple al que manda la tierra de examinar los que tiran la honrra a Dios & la dan a ýdoles & mandrágulas. [3] Donde mandó Dios a Moysén enel Éxodo que matase los maléficos & no los dexase biuir. [4] Son maléficos los que por conjuros o hechizos empecen alos otros. Dize Dios ala princesa quando no

---

[1] The 1542 ed. has *en El*.
[2] One does not have to rely on the *Celestina* for evidence of the practice of witchcraft in 15th-century Spain. See Esteban Cirac Estopiñan, *Los procesos de hechicerías en la Inquisión de Castilla la Nueva: Tribunales de Toledo y Cuenca* (Madrid, 1942) for transcripts of some of the inquisitorial testimony of those accused of witchcraft.
[3] St. Isidore describes the mandrake root, mentioning its anthropomorphic shape and its use in the preparation of an anesthetic (p. 431). Presumably, the root was said to have a male and a female form and lent itself to use in love philtres or as part of magic rituals. It was said to have emitted human cries when pulled from the earth. Cf. also John Donne's "Song," where the root appears — "Get with child a mandrake root."
[4] Exodus 22:18: "Thou shalt not suffer a witch to live."

guarda su honor: —Si yo só Señor ¿a dónde es mi honor? E avn que todos deuemos ser zelosos dela honrra de Dios Nuestro Señor & Redemptor, pero mucho más los reyes & príncipes. La razón desto es por que son lugar tenientes de Dios. E Platón los llama medio dioses. [5] Pues como vn corregidor enbiado por el rey a vna villa o ciudad es más obligado a guardar la honrra del rey, que ninguno delos otros de aquella villa o ciudad, ca el honor del rey es suyo & su fauor. Assí enla tierra, como reynó por Dios enella, es más thenudo de honrrar a Dios que todos & de guardar & zelar su honor, ca esto es ensalçamiento de su corona; & si no lo faze, es digno de dapñación & paresce que no es lugar teniente de Dios. E avn como deximos del temor, desque veen los pueblos quel señor o la señora no honrran a Dios, tan poco se promueuen a honrrar aellos; antes dizen mal dellos & los blasfeman.

Dios se quiere honrrar con deuoción, con oración, con inclinación de espíritu & de cuerpo, con ayuno, con limosnas, con décimas, con premincias, con sacrificios. E enesto se ha de exercitar la noble princesa para honrrar a su señor Dios, no dubdando en algo de la fe, diziendo el Credo ala mañana & ala noche, creyendo ala mañana & ala noche firmemente lo que la Sancta Yglesia nuestra madre cree, refiriendo su fe alos sabios maestros & doctores dela Sancta Yglesia. Esta honrra [6] a Dios deuida se llama la cría, [7] que quiere dezir deuota seruidumbre a sólo Dios deuida. A tú Señor Dios adorarás & aÉl sólo seruirás. [8]

La otra cosa en que está la honrra de Dios es en no le blasfemar, & guardar bien que su nombre, ni de su madre, ni delos sanctos, ni sanctas no sea renegado, ni blasfemado, mas antes

---

[5] St. Augustin cites Plato's *Timaeus* in a discussion of the Supreme God and the lesser gods: "The lesser gods were responsible not for our souls but only for our bodies" (*The City of God*, II, 240, Bk. XII, Ch. xxvii). Cf. *supra Capítulo segundo, segunda parte*, where Fray Martín says that earthly kings have power only over our bodies, while God has power over our bodies and our soul. Helen Sears says that Egidio Colonna referred to kings and princes as "semidei" (p. 6, n. 18).

[6] The 1542 ed. has *E a honrra*.

[7] Both eds. have *la cria*. St. Augustin writes *latreía* (*The City of God*, II, 120, Bk. X, Ch. iii).

[8] Matthew 4:10: "Then saith Jesus unto him, Get thee hence, Satan: for it is written, Thou shalt worship the Lord, thy God, and him only shalt thou serve."

sea alabado & loado. Donde quando el contrario se haze enel reyno, Dios se querella delos príncipes por la boca de Ysaías & dize: —Los príncipes de mi tierra muy maluadamente lo hazen, ca el mi nombre cada día es blasfemado.[9] Donde los legistas tienen vna auténtica ley que dize: —Que ni el nombre de Dios sea blasfemado, ni se cometa suziedad contra natura,[10] que dize que estos dos pecados, sino son castigados, son punidos los príncipes; & toda la república & avn los padres gozan mal delos fijos, sino los castigan quando blasfeman.

Cuenta Sant Gregorio en *Los Diálogos* que vn vezino de Roma tenía vn fijo que mucho amaua &, por el tierno amor, de ninguna cosa le reprehendía. En tanto fue regalado que, si algo se hazía quél no quisiese, luego blasfemaua a Dios. Vino a ser que en vna pestilencia fue tocado de vna nascida & final mente vino ala muerte; & como su padre lo touiese en sus braços, vido venir los espíritus malignos & començó: —Arrecoje aquí, padre, arrecoje aquí. El padre preguntóle al niño qué veýa. Respondió el hijo: —Moros negros vienen aquí, que me quieren leuar. E esto diziendo, blasfemó & el ánima triste escupió. Esto hizo Dios para dar a entender por qué pecado le lleuauan los moros negros, ca por la blasfemia es dicho que le lleuó.[11]

Ponga, pues, diligencia la nuestra madre, que espera ser de todo el reyno, que Dios Padre, ni Sancta María Madre, no sea blasfemado el nombre dellos; & assí guardará la honrra de Dios, por quien ha de reynar si aÉl plaze.

Lo tercero en que está la honrra es en guardar bien fiestas de Dios & de Sancta María & delos otros sanctos, oyendo solepnes misas, buenos sermones, bísperas & [oras] canónicas, no despendiendo aquel día en vanidades, mas en deuotas oraciones. No digo que entre la yantar & las bísperas no se hagan deportes

---

[9] Isaiah 52:5: "Now therefore, what have I here, saith the Lord, that my people is taken away for nought? they that rule over them make them to howl, saith the Lord; and my name continually every day is blasphemed."

[10] The laws against blasphemy and acts against nature can be found in Leviticus 24:16 and Leviticus 18:1-30.

[11] See *The Dialogues of St. Gregory the Great,* ed. Henry James Coleridge (London, 1874), p. 235, Bk. IV, Ch. xviii, and *El espéculo de los legos: texto inédito del siglo XV,* ed. José M.ª Mohedano Hernández (Madrid, 1951), p. 52.

solepnes, que relieuen los enojos dela señora, pero esto sea honesto & seguro de sangre & de bollicio. E no sólo ella guarde las fiestas, mas que las faga guardar, dando penas alos quel contrario hizieren, si no es necesidad muy euidente.

Visto cómo & en qué cosas ha de honrrar a Dios, veamos cómo lo ha de amar, alo qual es más tenuda la noble princesa, alo quel fijo o fija es más tenida de amar a su padre, al que dexó más parte de su heredad. Pues Dios, que enel vientre dela madre dio & predestinó aésta para reyna de tan noble reyno como España, más obligada es alo amar que otra ninguna, ca los beneficios crecientes, cresce el amor. Así que todas las mugeres son tenidas de amar a Dios & mucho más las reynas & princesas, entre las quales resplandesce la nuestra, ala qual está aparejado tan bien auenturado reyno como España. Dizen quel mundo tiene dos partes principales: oriente & ocidente. En oriente puso Dios su silla, haziendo allí el paraýso eternal. E en occidente puso la silla del Rey d'España. Donde paresce que Dios partió el reyno dela tierra conel nuestro rey.[12] Es tenida delo amar por conseruar la puridad de su coraçón. No ensuzia el coraçón dela donzella sino en amar cosas viles & abáxala & fázela menos preciada; & por el contrario, amar cosa tan limpia como Dios faze el coraçón generoso & limpio & digno de toda honrra. Donde por esso dize el Sabio quel coraçón del rey es enla mano de Dios,[13] pues por que Dios no se ensuzie las manos, hablando por metáphora. Si tu coraçón ha siempre de ser enlas manos de Dios, razón es que lo guardes linpio de suzios amores, amando aÉl sobre todo & lo que amares sea amado por Él & para Él, para lo qual demanda la gracia de Dios.

---

[12] Although it is a commonplace of national pride to compare one's country with Eden, it is possible that Fray Martín is referring here to the famous praise of Spain made by Alfonso el Sabio in *La Primera Crónica General*, where Spain is said to be "tal... como el paraíso de Dios, ca riega se con cinco ríos cabdales...." This is of course, one more river than Eden had (*Antología de Alfonso X el Sabio*, ed. Antonio G. Solalinde [Madrid: Colección Austral, 1960], p. 99). Paradise is located in the east in Genesis 2:8.

[13] This is possibly a reference to Ecclesiasticus 10:4-5.

## Capítulo Séptimo

[*Capítulo .vij.* en que da orden enel coraçón dela noble donzella, guardándolo de amor desordenado de riquezas, de pompas & de carnal deleytes].

Hordenada la vida[1] dela donzella a Dios, bueno es agora la hordenemos ensí mismo según tres partes. Es assaber: coraçón, boca & manos. Para poner en orden el coraçón, conuiene purgallo de tres desordenados apetitos. Es assaber: de apetito de riquezas, de honores & deleytes; ca el apetito desordenado de honrras es soberuia; el delos deleytes es luxuria. Pues conuiene ala donzella que ame pobreza & así purgará su coraçón de auaricia, que sea humilde & así fuyrá la soberuia; que sea linpia & así oxeará los malos deseos dela carne & quedará su noble coraçón limpio & en sí mesmo bien ordenado; ca sepa quel amor de las riquezas pone enel coraçón suzia tierra & el amor delas honrras lo hinche de fumo; el deseo dela carnalidad lo ocupa con cie[n]o[2] & hedor.

Pues, quanto alo primero el real coraçón deseche amor de riquezas, las quales en sí no han verdadera suficiencia, mas son riquezas falsarias. Donde notá, según el Filósopho enel primero dela *Política:* —que dos maneras ay de riquezas: vnas llama naturales & otras artificiales. Riquezas naturales son aquellas que se produzen delas cosas naturales, como es pan & vino, olio & frutos que se cogen dela tierra, cera & miel delas abejas & assí de muchas otras cosas. Riquezas artificiales son que por

---

[1] The 1542 ed. has *La vida ordenada*.
[2] The 1542 ed. has *cieno*; the 1500, *cieuo*.

arte & induzería de honbres son halladas, como es oro & plata & toda moneda que sirue a comutar, que es comprar & vender & no suplen por sí ala necessidad corporal sino comprando conellas pan & vino & paño; & ningunas déstas son verdaderas riquezas, no primera mente las artificiales que no son riquezas sino en quanto se ordenan a auer por ellas las naturales. No son riquezas sino por ordenación delos hombres, que tanto oro o tanta plata puesta en moneda valga tanto de trigo & de vino. Esto los hombres lo ordenan. No suplen a nuestro menester, que avn que honbre touiese vn manto de oro & otro de plata, sino ouiese pan & vino para comer & beuer, moriría de hanbre. Así que, enesta razón, más son riquezas las naturales que las artificiales. [3] Donde pone el Philósopho vna hablilla de vn auariento que auía nonbre Mida, que tanto hera deseoso de oro que rogó alos dioses que todo quanto conlas manos tocase sele tornase oro & fuele otorgado. Vino ala ora del comer & assí como tocaua la carne o el pan, luego se tornaua oro & no podía comer & assí Mida moríase de hanbre con tanto oro. [4] Esta hablilla se trahe que más necesarias nos son las riquezas naturales que las artificiales, ca podemos biuir sin las artificiales & no sin las naturales.

Pero tan poco las naturales no son verdaderas riquezas, ca antes ansanchan la cobdicia que la harten; & el que más tiene dellas más ha menester para las guardar, anparar & labrar. Más ha menester el que tiene cient alançadas de viña que el que tiene vna. E por esso no ay hombre tan menesteroso enel reyno quel rey. E porende, enlas riquezas sólo auemos de buscar la necessidad en cadavno, segund su estado & desechar lo supérfluo. Donde el noble ánimo dela princesa no deue cobdiciar riquezas para atesorar, mas para dar alos suyos & hazer cosas magníficas como son templos, hospitales, puentes & cosas que hazen seruicios públicos.

Desque del coraçón sea arrancado el mal apetito de falsas riquezas, aýna desechan el vano apetito de honrras, el qual sobre

---

[3] This is not a quotation but rather a summary of a long passage in the *Politica* concerning the natural and unnatural ways of acquiring wealth (*Politics*, trans. H. Rackham [Cambridge, Massachusetts: Loeb Classical Library, 1959], pp. 33-55).

[4] See *Politica*, 1257 b 16.

todo deue aborrecer la princesa; ca otra mente seguir le han tres males. El primero, que no será buena sino de fuera & no curará ser buena dentro enla conciencia. Asi dize Aristótiles enla *Política:* —que los que curan mucho de ser honrrados son buenos enfengidos & superficiales & no son buenos dentro.[5] El segundo mal sigue alas dueñas que mucho aman honores, que son presunptuosas & no hazen nada con consejo, mas ponen así & al reyno en peligros. El tercero mal es que las tales son injustas & no yguales; ca las grandes que dan sus dones no por virtud mas por auer honrra no parte[n] los dones alos dignos & sabios, mas a aluardanes & a truhanes, que las predican & digan: —Esto me dio la señora & dexan de pagar lo que deuen a sus seruidores & den[6] lo que no deuen & adonde no deuen por conseguir honrra & vana gloria.[7]

Esto assí ordenado, por consiguiente, derraygue todo apetito de deleytes carnales. Estos son suzios deseos & bestiales, donde avn que todas las mugeres deuen ser linpias; desto, mucho más la princesa, ca tales deseos fazen la muger bestial & házenla menos preciable, disfamada & indigna de principar; que primero la hazen conpañera delas bestias, ca siguen aquellos apetitos en que nos conuenimos conlas bestias. E esto es indigno que la que ha de ser mejor que todas las mugeres, que sean en sus apetitos peor. Desto se sigue que es auida en menos precio &, por consiguiente, que es indigna de principar & regir. Muchos príncipes, assí varones como mugeres, perdieron sus principados & cayeron de sus estados, porque siguieron los apetitos carnales. Enxemplo: de Sardanáfalo, rey de Assiria, que fue muy corrupto, vn su caballero lo mató enel seno de vna moçuela, que estaua allí

---

[5] Aristotle, in describing the causes of strife mentions a group of people who are unequal but who demand equality. He names the factors over which revolutions are fought and includes honor (*Politics* 1302 a — 1302 b 3).

[6] The 1542 ed. has *dan*.

[7] The awarding of favors to the unworthy was apparently much on the minds of the authors of the day, probably in the light of their disapproval of the choice of advisors made by Juan II of D. Álvaro de Luna and the assorted favors which Enrique IV accorded to unsuitable persons such as Beltrán de la Cueva.

embeuecido. [8] Nero, él mismo se mató, que yua toda Roma tras él para lo matar, por quanto hera muy disoluto. E avn esto más se soporta enlos varones que enlas hembras, por lo qual deuen ser muy mesuradas & sojuzgar los desseos dela carne. Otra mente son perdidas, disfamadas & puestas en cánticos & trobas.

---

[8] Fray Martín may well have been remembering a similar passage in Mosén Diego de Valera who also juxtaposes the two examples of Sardanapalus and Nero (*Epístolas enbiadas,* pp. 195-6).

CAPÍTULO OCTAVO

[*Capítulo .viij.* ordena su boca en tal manera que enlas palabras no aya demasía, ni mengua, ni discordia].

No ay miembro en todo el cuerpo que tanto quiera ser ordenado, después del coraçón, como la boca en hablar. Donde Nuestro Señor dixo: —que dela habundancia del coraçón habla la boca.[1] Quales deseos, buenos o malos, honbre trae enel coraçón, tales palabras trae enla boca.[2] El filósofo dixo: —Cadavno qual es, tales cosas dize & habla.[3] Común mente verés que los que aman el vino sienpre hablan de tierras donde ay buenos vinos. Assí haze el que ama dineros o mugeres, dello fabla. Dize Aristótiles: —que las palabras son señales delos conceptos que son enel ánima.[4] E Santo Agustín dixo: —La palabra que de fuera suena, señal es dela que luze dentro.[5] E porende, los que han

---

[1] Matthew 13:34: "O generation of vipers, how can ye, being evil, speak good things for out of the abundance of the heart the mouth speaketh?" Luke 6:45: "A good man out of the good treasure of his heart bringeth forth that which is good; and an evil man out of the evil treasure of his heart bringeth forth that which is evil: for of the abundance of the heart his mouth speaketh."

[2] The 1542 ed. has *en la cabeça*.

[3] This quotation sounds like an aphorism extracted from one of the collections of Senecan wisdom so popular in the period. See n. 6 to the *Prohemio* and nn. 28, 29 and 30 for references to Seneca as "The Philosopher."

[4] Aristotle writes: "Spoken words are symbols of passions of the soul; written words are symbols of spoken words" (*Categories* and *De Interpretatione*, trans. J. L. Ackerill [Oxford, 1963], 16 a 3-4).

[5] I have not been able to find this quotation in St. Augustin.

desseos honestos & tienen sus coraçones bien ordenados, luego se parescen enlas palabras que son de Dios & de obras virtuosas.

Assí que la orden es natural, que después de ordenado el coraçón, se hordena la boca en sus palabras. Serán las palabras ordenadas si enellas no ay superfluydad, [6] si enellas no ay mengua, si enellas no ay discordia. Enel hablar yerra el hombre en tres maneras: la vna, por demasía, quando la persona es tan parlera que dize lo suyo & lo ajeno, ni dexa hablar alos otros. La otra es enel otro extremo, que habla tan poco, que no hay hombre que quiera estar conél. La otra es quando las palabras, pocas o muchas, son vistosas & derechas acusar [7] discordia entre los oyentes. Quanto alo primero, dize la Escriptura: —que enel multiloquio, que quiere dezir mucha parla no fallece peccado [8] & el que mucha habla, su ánima llaga. El que mucho habla es así como la mula que mucho anda, que común mente tropieça. [9] Assí es que de más fabla, fuerça es que yerre o que mienta. E porende, es más de loar, especial mente enlas mugeres, oýr & escuchar que no hablar. Donde Santyago dixo enla Canónica: —Sea todo honbre ligero para oýr & tardío para hablar. [10] E avn por esso dizen que Dios hizo al hombre & ala muger dos orejas & vna boca por que más larga mente se aya el hombre a oýr que a hablar.

El mucho hablar haze tres males: desuanesce la cabeça, ensuzia la conciencia & disfama la vida. Quando el hombre hable retiene el ayre enel pulmón & fázelo repercudir ala vocal arteria que es la cama del pulmón & de allí resuena enla cabeça [11] &

---

[6] The 1542 ed. has no *hay ninguna perfluidad*.

[7] Both eds. have *derechas acusar*. Is this intended to mean *dirigidas a causar*?

[8] This reference seems to be a blend of Ecclesiastes 5:2: "Be not rash with thy mouth, and let not thine heart be hasty to utter anything before God: for God is in heaven, and thou upon earth: therefore let thy words be few" and Ecclesiastes 5:7: "For in the multitude of dreams and many words there are also divers vanities: but fear thou God."

[9] Fray Martín is possibly echoing the proverb: "Quien no anda, no tropieza" (No. MK 57.831 in Luis Martínez-Kleiser, *Refranero general ideológico español* [Madrid, 1953], p. 661, col. *c*).

[10] James 1:19: "Wherefore, my beloved brethren, let every man be swift to hear, slow to speak, slow to wrath."

[11] This observation on the human voice seems to be derived from Aristotle: "We all breathe the same air, but we emit different sounds owing

casca el celebro & avn por esso los frenéticos & los que han bien beuido hablan mucho, por que tienen el celebro desuanescido & quanto más assí lo tienen, más quieren fablar. Esta pasa por experiencia alos que predican & leen en cátedra, que salen desuanescidos las cabeças de aquel acto por que hablaron mucho. E si esto enlos varones, mucho más enlas mugeres, que son más flacas.

Otro mal haze la mucha parla: que ensuzia la conciencia. La lengua es escoua dela conciencia; quando confiesa los peccados, ella mesma es esportón de vassura, quando trata vidas ajenas. Donde la Escriptura a tal lengua llama lengua coínquinada,[12] que es lengua ensuzi[a]da.[13] Aquel rico que negó las migajas a Lázaro desque fue muerto & enterrado enel infierno, dizen quel mayor tormento que passaua hera arder enla lengua; & esto hera, segund dizen [14] por que desque auía bien comido & beuido, soltaua su lengua & hablaua mal de todos; & por do pecó, por allí hera penado.[15]

El otro mal que faze el mucho parlar es disfama la vida. Grand infamia es de poco seso parlar mucho & haze al hombre desonesto & sin graueza. Donde dize Séneca en vna Epístola a Lucilo: —porque tu[s] dichos sean más graues & de más peso,

---

to the difference of the organs involved through which the breath passes to the region outside. These are the windpipe, the lung and the mouth" (800 a 16-21). In describing the difference in voices, Aristotle describes in particular a small, thick, or hard lung which "contributes to making the flow of the breath strong" (*On Things Heard*, in *Minor Works*, 800 b 5-7).

[12] We find the following warning in Colossians 3:8: "But now ye also put off all these: anger, wrath, malice, blasphemy, filthy communication out of your mouth."

[13] The 1500 ed. has *ensuzieda*.

[14] The 1542 ed. has *según que dizen*.

[15] The story is told in Luke 16:19-31. Interestingly enough, Luke does not specifically accuse the rich man of denying the crumbs from his table to Lazarus. After both men had died, the rich man called for mercy from Hell, asking Abraham to cool his tongue with water because of the torments of the flames. Abraham replied: "Son, remember that thou in thy lifetime receivedst thy good things, and likewise Lazarus evil things: but now he is comforted, and thou art tormented." Luke uses the tale to demonstrate that the poor will get their due in heaven. Fray Martín sees special significance in the mention of the tongue and the thirst the rich man suffered to show that the offending part, his tongue, was singled out for special punishment in Hell.

aconséjote que hables tard[e] & poco. ⁱ⁶ Dize Tulio: —que muchos aprenden bien fablar por rhetórica, que les valdría más que aprendiesen callar por cordura. ¹⁷ E si esto es enlos varones, ¿qué fará enlas mugeres?; delas quales desuso dezimos que toda la compostura dela muger es el silencio, que quiere dezir ser callada.

La segunda manera en que yerran algunos conla lengua es mucho callar. Siempre, como deximos, los extremos son viciosos & la virtud es enel medio, como aquí. Mucho hablar & mucho callar son dos extremos & son vicios dela lengua; & porende la virtud es hablar quando conuiene & do conuiene & como conuiene & cosas que conuienen al propósito e callar assí mismo quando conuiene. Pues como es vicio mucho hablar, assí es vicio mucho callar; mas con todo esso destos dos vicios, mayor es mucho hablar que mucho callar. E porende, quando enel hablar & callar no sabemos el medio, más seguro es hazer nos hazia el menos malo extremo que es mucho callar. Quiero dezir, que quando es necessario de hablar, que fablemos lo menos que pudiéremos. E notá que, así como el mucho hablar haze al hombre ser dissoluto, assí el mucho callar lo haze áspero & saluaje. Donde Aristótiles dixo: —que natura dio al hombre la palabra para que conlos otros conuersase & ouiesse solaz conellos. ¹⁸ Pues segund

---

[16] Lucius Annaeus Seneca, *Seneca ad Lucilium: Epistolae Morales*, trans. Richard M. Gummere (London, 1925) contains a number of references that might be appropiate here (Ep. LIX, I, 411-13; Ep. XL, I, p. 271; Ep. CV, I, 215). Seneca is quoted in the chapter on silence in the *Espéculo de los legos* (p. 410).

[17] Cicero stresses that the orator must have knowledge of his subject and notes: "If he should have to discourse even on those other subjects [of which he was ignorant] then after learning the technicalities of each from those who know the same, the orator will speak about them far better than even the men who are masters of these arts" (*De Oratore*, trans. E. W. Sutton [London: Loeb Classical Library, 1942], p. 49, Bk. I, Ch. xv).

[18] As a part of the definition of friendship, Aristotle writes: "Therefore a man ought also to share his friend's consciousness of his existence, and this is attained by their living together and by conversing and communicating their thoughts to each other; for this is the meaning of living together as applied to human beings; it does not mean merely feeding in the same place, as it does when applied to cattle" (*Nichomachean Ethics*, 1170 b 10-14). Elsewhere, Aristotle explains why man is a political animal: "For nature, as we declare, does nothing without purpose; and man alone of the animals possesses speech." He continues to explain that although animals have the power to communicate their pain and pleasure to each other,

esto, el que no habla quando conuiene de hablar & conlos que conuiene, haze se medio bestia. Donde Ysaýas dixo: —¡Guay de mí por que callé! [19] En muchos negocios no ha el hombre de callar. Primero enla confessión, quando hombre confiessa su peccado, enla oración & en loor de Dios & enla confessión dela fe. Dize el Psalmo: —Creý & porende lo hablé. [20] El que firme mente cree simple mente confiessa lo que cree. Ay otros lugares donde se requiere la fabla lo qual la prudencia enseña.

Síguese ya la postrera en que herramos conla lengua, quando nuestro hablar & callar causa discordia, como hazen los sasurrones enel pueblo, que reportan palabras de vno a otro para los enr[e]dar [21] que se quieran mal. Esto es lo que Dios mucho aborresce como dize enlos Prouerbios: —El que sienbra cizaña entre los próximos, estos son bili[n]guos, [22] los quales Aristóteles dixo a Alexandre que echase de sí, ni los touiesse en su casa. [23] Al contrario desto hazía Sancta Moni[c]a, madre de Sant Agustín, dela qual dize enel libro delas *Confessiones* que nunca reportaua de vno a otro palabra, sino tal que fuese a reconciliar entre ellos la paz, como lo habla. [24] Es causa algunas vezes de

---

"speech is designed to indicate the advantageous and the harmful, and therefore also the right and the wrong" (*Politics*, 1253 a 7-18).

[19] Isaiah 42:14: "I have a long time holden my peace; I have been still and restrained myself: now will I cry like a travailing woman; I will destroy and devour at once." This is certainly an example of one who regrets not having spoken out. Isaiah 6:5 may also be appropriate: "Then said I, Woe is me, for I am undone; because I am a man of unclean lips: for mine eyes have seen the King, the Lord of hosts."

[20] Psalms 116:10: "I believed, therefore have I spoken: I was greatly afflicted"; II Corinthians 4:13: "I believed and therefore have I spoken; we also believed and therefore speak."

[21] The 1500 ed. has *enridar*.

[22] The image of "cizaña" or 'darnel and wild oats' as a disruptive factor was a widespread one. The reference here is to Proverbs 6:14.

[23] This passage seems to come from the pseudo-Aristotle's advice to Alexander about the qualities of a good *aguazil*. The fourteenth quality which he mentions is "que non sea de mucha palabra nin iudgador nin dezidor de mal nin desdennoso" (p. 48).

[24] Both references to St. Monica in the 1500 ed. are spelled *Monia*. It does not appear to have been a compositorial error. St. Augustin writes of his mother: "She showed herself such a peacemaker between any differing and discordant spirits, that when she heard on both sides most bitter things such as swelling and indigested discord is wont to give vent to, . . . she

discordia tan bien el callar, como si yo sé vna dubda sobre que debaten otros & callo; yo do causa ala discordia callando & assí paresce cómo deuen ordenar su boca.

---

would disclose nothing about the one to the other, save what might avail to their reconcilement" (*Confessions*, in *Basic Writings*, I, 139).

## Capítulo .IX.

[*Capítulo .jx.* ordena las manos en perfetas obras, dellas parecen de fuera, dellas quedan dentro enel ánima].

No basta ala princesa, para ser en sí bien ordenada, tener limpio coraçón & honestas palabras, delo qual eneste capítulo agora fablaremos. E para esto es assaber: que vnas obras son manifiestas de fuera & otras son enel gesto [1] & enel hábito. Otras son más ocultas de dentro & éstas son enla nutritiua, que es en comer & beuer, e enla generatiua, que es enla obra conjugal. Enel gesto aya [2] modestia; enel hábito, honestad; enla nutritiua, contenencia; enla generatiua, castidad. Estas quatro cosas, en sus lugares sentadas, hazen las obras, así de fuera como de dentro, perfetas, quanto es posible a cadavno enesta vida auer perfeción de obras.

Primeramente, pues, la modestia conpone el gesto dela señora enesta guisa: que huse de cada mienbro para lo que es hecho mesurada mente. Donde, si ha de oýr o descuchar, que paren las orejas que este es el oficio dellas; no abra la boca, ca no ha de oýr por la boca, como hazen los aldeanos, que en començando el honbre a hablar conellos abren la boca. Esto es grosería & falta enel gesto. Si ha de mirar, alçe los ojos, que este es su officio & abasta le alçar los párpados, no toda la cabeça como hazen las mulas quando les dan sofrenadas. Donde el que de buen son quiere mirar, abástale alçar los ojos, sin alçar la

---
[1] The 1542 ed. omits & *enel hábito. Otras son más ocultas de dentro & éstas.* Apparently a line was skipped by the copyist.
[2] The 1542 ed. has *ay*.

cabeça, saluo si la cosa no es tan alta que sea necessario dela alçar; & estonces la necessidad haze honesto el gesto. Si ha de fablar, esto haga conla lengua, no con mouimientos grandes de cabeça & esgrimiendo las manos; & alçe la boz quanto baste a oýrla; ca otra mente hablar es falta de razón & desordena el gesto, como hazen algunos predicadores que fablan con manos & cabeça & esgrimiendo todo el cuerpo & dando bozes, como si los oyentes fuesen sordos. Donde Tulio enel libro *De Oratore* dize: —quel orador, quando razonare, que razone conla lengua no conlas manos;³ & si algunas vegadas quisiere despertar alos oyentes con gesto de manos, esto hágalo con modestia & con graue mouimiento dela mano derecha, mouiéndola honesta mente alos que habla, no arrebatada, no súbita, no expresada mente, mas tan sosegado que pueda en aquel mouimiento concluyr vna razón. Enel andar conuiene ordenar el gesto que no sea mucho apriesa, ni mucho de vagar, ni andando quebrar el passo, que es vna manera de loçanía & significa liuiandad. Así que, en todos los autos & mouimientos de fuera, conuiene auer modestia & mesura de gesto.

Lo segundo, aya enel ábito honestad, para lo qual se requieren seys condiciones: la primera, no ayan en sí nigund afeyte sofístico, ca esto es ylícito & siempre es pecado quando la muger procura parescer más hermosa delo que es, poniendo aluayalde & arrebol, açafrán & alcohol & otras posturas desonestas.⁴ La segunda, que cadavna segund su estado vaya vestida; que no es razón que la muger del oficial vaya tan bien vestida como la del cauallero, ni la del cauallero como la reyna; & esto no por vana gloria, mas por honrrar su estado. La tercera, que sean mesuradas; que cadavna sea contenta de yr vestida segund su estado, no excediendo. La quarta, que en se vestir & calçar no ponga grand estudio & diligencia, mas solamente quanto requiere su honestad. La quinta, que no ayan el otro extremo; que no sean perezosas

---

³ Cicero rejects the use of "stagy gesture reproducing the word" (*De Oratore, Book III, together with De Fato, Paradoxa Stoicorum, De Partione Oratoria,* trans. H. Rackham [Cambridge, Massachusets: Loeb Classical Library, 1960], pp. 177, 179).

⁴ See n. 9 to *Capítulo primero, segunda parte* for St. Jerome's comments on cosmetics.

& negligentes, tanto que no se vistan como su estado requiere.[5] La sesta, que no se vista ypocriticalmente, como si la princesa se vistiese de buriel, de pardo, tan bien sería desonesto, ca parescería que de tal hábito querría auer loor, diziendo que hera muy buena & santa & sería ypocrisía.[6] Dizen que Santa Cecilia, fija de rey, de fuera andaua vestida de sirgo & brocado rico & de dentro traýa cilicio áspero.[7] Enel hábito, pues, aya[8] honestad, que ni sea más delo que requiere su estado, ni tan poco que parezcan *beata mater*.

Puestos en orden los autos de fuera, que son gesto & ábito, deuemos poner orden enla nutritiua & generatiua que son autos altos.[9] E nota que Dios ha dado alos animales & por consiguiente al hombre dos potencias para se conseruar. Estas son: la nutritiua; & ésta conserua el individuo. El comer & el beuer, que son autos dela nutritiua, conseruan la persona de cadavno; pero, por que cadavno de nos otros es mortal, & avn que nos podamos conseruar a tienpo, mas no para sienpre, dio Nuestro Señor otra potencia, que es generatiua, para conseruar la specie humana que no percesciese. Donde si los honbres muriesen [y no] engendrasen otro, luego sería acabada la specie humana. Pues estas dos

---

[5] The 1542 ed. has *lo requiere*.

[6] St. Jerome gives similar advice to advice to Eustochium: "Harbour not the secret thought that having ceased to court attention in garments of gold you may begin to do so in mean attire." He particularly criticizes those women who make a show of having fasted. He describes their mien and garb colorfully: "Their dress is sombre, their girdles are of sack cloth, their hands and feet are dirty; only their stomachs — which cannot be seen — are hot with food.... Others change their garb and assume the mien of men, being ashamed of being what they were born — women. They cut off their hair and are not ashamed to look like eunuchs. Some clothe themselves in goat's hair, and, putting on hoods, think to become children again by making themselves look like so many owls" (Letter XXII, pp. 33-34).

[7] D. Álvaro de Luna describes St. Cecilia's preparations on the day she was to be married: "Ésta, seyendo desposada con Valerio, e venido el día de la boda, vestida la carne de cilicio, arreóse de sus preciosas vestiduras" (p. 239).

[8] The 1542 ed. has *hay*.

[9] The designation of the generative and nutritive factors as "autos altos" may be derived from the Platonic division of the three principles of the soul, although they both belong to the appetitive principle. See *The Republic*, trans. Benjamin Jowett (New York: Modern Library, n.d.), p. 343.

potencias ha de ordenar el virtuoso, poniendo enel comer & beuer, abstinencia & medida segund tres circunstancias que son poco & a paso & limpio. Donde la generatiua ha de ser con castidad conjugal, que fuera del matrimonio no se piense & enel matrimonio para hazer hijos a seruicio de Dios & prouecho & honrra & paz & sosiego del reyno.

CAPÍTULO .X.

[*Capítulo .x.* cómo se deue ordenar la señora por respeto del próximo & delos súbditos con tres virtudes: con justicia, con liberalidad, & con efabilidad].

Desque así la princesa fuere bien ordenada por respeto a Dios & por respeto de sí misma con las sobredichas virtudes, no le queda sino auer buena orden alos próximos & súbditos suyos; & eneste respeto ha menester tres virtudes. Éstas son: justicia, liberalidad & afabilidad.

Quanto alo primero, la justicia es tanto necesaria enlos reynos que sin ella no son sino ladronicios & compañías & simultades & vandos. Donde por esso fue dispuesto quel reyno fuesse como vn cuerpo & su cabeça fuesse el rey & la justicia es el ánima del reyno.[1] Pues como la vida desciende dela cabeça & se derrama por todo el cuerpo, assí la justicia ha de descender del príncipe & correr por todo el reyno para dar vida a todos los mienbros del reyno. Donde como el cuerpo sin cabeça es muerto, assí el reyno sin príncipe; & como el cuerpo avn que tenga cabeça, sino tiene sentido, los miembros van dissipados, assí el reyno, avn que tenga rey, sino entiende en excecución dela justicia, es muerto & enterrado. Por esto el libro dela Sabiduría de Salomón dio la primera boz, diziendo: —Amad justicia, los que juzgáis la tierra.[2]

---

[1] This simile undoubtedly belongs in the group of universal metaphors, or *topoi*. St. Augustin describes the rôle of the Head of the Church in the same terms in *De Agone Christiano* (ed. anon. members of the English Church, in *Library of the Fathers of the Holy Catholic Church* [Oxford, 1847], p. 174).

[2] Wisdom 1:1: "Love justice, you rulers of the earth..."

Porquel príncipe sin justicia es como el espantajo enla viña, como cabeça sin celebro & como ojos sin vista & como cuerpo sin vida: que los reynos sin justicia no pueden permanescer.

Ay dos razones desto: la primera es por quanto la legal justicia es toda virtud; donde auer legal justicia es conplir todo lo que manda la ley. Pues si la ley manda hazer todo bien & veda todo mal, conplir la ley es ser perfetamente virtuoso & por el contrario, no la conplir es perfecta & entera malicia. Pues como dize enel quarto libro delas *Éticas:* —El mal el mesmo se destruye & si es entero pássase insoportable.[3] Desto se sigue que aquel reyno es inportable & durar no puede enel qual niguna justicia se guarda, ca así los ciudadanos serían perfetamente malos. Donde dixo Nuestro Señor: —Todo reyno en sí deuiso será desolado & vna casa caerá sobre otra.[4] No ay cosa que tanto cause diuisión enel reyno como la poca justicia, sin la qual no puede auer paz, pues los que rigen avn por su bien & por conseruar en sus principados deuen trabajar por mantener justicia. La justicia, pues, de sí misma conserua los reynos.

La otra razón es por quel reyno es vna orden & vn principado; pues como esta orden & este principado sea entre los súditos por respecto alas leyes & al príncipe que las pone, si los súditos no participasen justicia legal, ni se reseruaría entre ellos orden, ni al rey ni alas leyes, pues luego no sería reyno, ni pulicía, como quando los miembros no han orden entre sí, ni ala cabeça no resta cuerpo.

Es aquí de notar que ay dos justicias: la vna es distributiua & ésta es enla mano del príncipe, el qual deue dar a cada vno segund sus méritos buenos o malos; es assaber: alos buenos, galardón & alos malos pena; & alos buenos segund que mejor fizieron & alos malos segund que peor. E si esta justicia el príncipe no guarda, es perdido él & el reyno; que luego nascen diuisiones & contiendas, especialmente si el galardón que meresce el bueno se da al malo. Esto es incomportable & no puede durar, como

---

[3] Aristotle points out that one person cannot possess all the excesses of anger. He explains: "This would be impossible, since evil destroys even itself, and when present in its entirety becomes unbearable" (*Nichomachean Ethics*, 1126 a 12).

[4] Mark 3:25 "And if a house be divided against itself, that house cannot stand."

dizen de Marco Antonio que hera be[u]do [5] & nunca daua sus dones sino alos que lleuauan los açores a beuer & assí de otros vicios por los qual peresció. [6]

La otra justicia es comutatiua & ésta se ha de guardar entre los vezinos & ésta yguala los contratos justamente, como es comprar & vender, prestar, alquilar. E sin esto tan poco no puede el reyno durar, ca conuiene que del reyno aya dos ygualdades: la vna es delos moradores entre sí & ésta haze la justicia comutatiua. La otra es delos moradores del príncipe & ésta haze la distributiua, como, para que el cuerpo biua, conuiene que los miembros entre sí concorden todos conla cabeça. Pertenesce, pues, ala princesa en su regimiento, guardar justicia, si quiere auer orden a sus súbditos & guardar su reyno que permanezca.

Lo segundo que deximos se requiere para auer buena orden alos súbditos es liberalidad, que quiere dezir largueza en dones; & que no sea escasa, mas tanto en dones larga que sea magnífica señora. [7] Pero esto ha de ser con tres condiciones: la primera, que no tome donde tomar no deue; la segunda, que tome con mesura donde deue; la tercera, que despienda & lo reparta como deue. Esta virtud tiene tres nombres; llámase largueza, llámase liberalidad & llámase comunicabilidad. E por estos tres nombres, esta virtud pertenece mucho alos grandes. Llámase largueza a semejança delos vasos, ca los vasos que tienen la boca estrecha no dan larga mente el liquor que tienen, como hazen los vasos delas bocas largas. Pues segund esta semejança, el que habunda en espensas & en dones se dize largo, por que es como vaso de boca larga, que largamente da lo que contiene. Pues por quanto la princesa enel reyno es como vna fuente donde todos han de sacar agua de dones, conuiene que sea larga, tanto más que los otros quanto [8] su influencia a más gentes se estiende. Esta virtud se llama liberalidad, por que los que la tienen sean a manera

---

[5] Both eds. have *bendo*. The obvious reading is *beudo* or *beodo*.

[6] Plutarch describes Marc Antony's drinking and dissipation (*Plutarch's Lives: The Translation called Dryden's*, ed. A. H. Clough, 5 Vols. [Philadelphia: The Nottingham Society, n.d.] V, 55) and his liberality with his soldiers (V, 57-58).

[7] Here Fray Martín summarizes Aristotle's comments on liberality. See *Nichomachean Ethics* (1119 b 21-1122 b 35).

[8] The 1542 ed. has *quando*.

de libres. Los auaros no son libres, antes son sieruos de sus riquezas. E por quanto no es cosa que cumple a tal señora ser sierua, sino de Dios & no de sus pecunias, conuiene que sea liberal & rescebir sus rentas, no para las retener, mas para franca mente las despender. Llámase esta virtud comunicabilidad, por quanto por ella los hombres vnos a otros se comunican sus bienes, por la qual comunicación toman entre sí amor. Donde común mente los francos & liberales son mucho amados de todos. Por lo qual, si la princesa como fue dicho deue querer ser amada de todos los de su reyno, conuiene ser liberal & dadiuosa.

La tercera virtud que hordena la señora alos suyos es afabilidad, la qual es vna virtud que haze & enseña como conuersemos conlas gentes amigablemente, rescibiendo a cadavno con buena cara & con amigables palabras & con dulces obras & suaues ofertas & cadavno segund más & menos meresce su estado & dignidad. Ay algunos que enla conuersación son ásperos, haziendo mala cara & ásperas palabras & duras obras; & éste es vicio & mala costunbre. Otrosí en otro extremo: que a todos quieren complazer. E porende, si la señora quiere ser affable, deue los buenos & virtuosos rescebir con abierto coraçon & alos malos arrugarles & torcerles la cara, porque teman la presencia de la señora. Pues ya paresce como se ha de ordenar alos súbditos con tres virtudes industriosas.

## LA TERCERA PARTE DESTE LIBRO

[La tercera & final parte deste tratado; enel capítulo primero dirá cómo se han de promouer las dueñas a bien por exenplo delas pasadas & recoje lo que fue dicho enlas dos partes del libro passadas & promueue la señora a amar sabiduría por exemplo de muchas donzellas].

[CAPITULO PRIMERO]

Conclusas & difinidas son ya las dos partes deste breue tratado, ca enla primera fue visto dela generación dela muger, assí marauillosa como natural. Enla segunda, deximos de su condición, poniendo sus buenas & menos buenas condiciones que tiene. E después asignando algunas virtuosas condiciones que ha de auer conlas quales se ha de ordenar a Dios & en sí misma & al próximo, queda agora que enesta final parte deste libro se diga de su conposición; quiero dezir, como a enxenplo delas pasadas que fueron claras dueñas, ha de conponer su vida. E quanto alo primero, digo que se deuen conponer dentro enel ánima por amor dela sabiduría la qual muchas antiguas dueñas amaron, & por el don dela sabiduría ala qual se allegaron, fueron dignas de hallar muchas industriosas artes. Dizen que la reyna de Egito, doña Iseo, falló las letras egipcianas & otras industrias prouechosas ala vida humana, por lo qual los egicianos la fizieron diosa & así la adoraron & le instituyeron tenplo & ara & diuinos sacrificios.[1] Otra muy sabia donzella, por nonbre ninfa Carmentis & otro nombre Nicostrates, dizen que falló las letras latinas.[2] Esto sin falta es de grand industria hallar cómo los ausentes pueden fablar conlos distinctos, assí en lugar como en tienpo; & las palabras

---

[1] St. Augustin describes Inachus' daughter Io, later called Isis, who was said to have been a queen who came from Ethiopia to Egypt and who engaged in the teaching of useful arts such as writing (*The City of God*, trans. Gerald G. Walsh and Daniel J. Honan in *Fathers of the Church* [New York, 1954], III, 88, Bk. XVIII, Ch. iii).

[2] St. Isidore mentions Carmentis as follows: "*Carmenta* fue la primera que llevó a Italia las letras latinas; y se le llamaba Carmenta porque decía en verso los oráculos; por lo demás propiamente se llamaba Nicostrata" (p. 8).

que buelan atarlos en escripto. Las dos sibillas, Crutea & Cumana & las otras ocho, ca segund el autor Varrón, diez fueron las sibillas,[3] las cosas por venir en metros & cánticos escriuieron. Donde la sibilla Crutea hizo metros de ambos aduenimientos de Cristo, del primero en carne & del segundo a juyzio, los quales Sant Agustín pone enel .xviij. libro de *La ciudad de Dios*.[4]

Pone Metodio en su *Crónica delos primeros tiempos* que Noema, hermana de Tubal Caýn, fijos de Lamech, con su industria halló las artes mechánicas, assí como el lanificio enel qual se husa el filar, el texer, el coser.[5] Dizen que Tubal Caýn, su hermano halló las artes fabreres que se vsan con yunque & con martillo,[6] avn que de hallar el arte de hazer paños, los libros gentiles dizen que la halló Minerua que se llama Pallas, diosa dela sabiduría. E los athenienses la adorauan & avn por eso dizen que ella puso allí su nido de estudios philosophales.[7] Dizen otros que el lanificio que es arte de hazer paños, halló

---

[3] St. Jerome refers to the number of the Sibyls thus: "What need to tell of the Sibylls of Erytrhae and Cumae, and the eight others? for Varro asserts there were ten whose ornament was virginity and divination the reward of their virginity" (*Against Jovinianus*, in *Principal Writings*, p. 379, Bk. I). It is my conjecture that Fray Martín knew Varro's *Antiquities* through his reading of *The City of God* and from allusions made by St. Jerome.

[4] St. Augustin writes: "The Sibyl of Erythrae, at any rate wrote some things that clearly concern Christ. I first read her sayings in a Latin poetic version marked by poor Latinity and poor metrical structure, but this was the fault of the blundering translator." St. Augustin goes on to tell of his encounter with Flaccianus, a man of learning who showed him a Greek manuscript containing an acrostic verse spelling out IESOUS XREITÒS THEOU UIÒS SŌTER. St. Augustin translates the verse and discusses the difficulties involved in the translation (*The City of God*, III, 114-117, Bk. XVII, Ch. xxiii).

[5] See n. 7 to *Capítulo sexto, primera parte* for a discussion of the possible identity of the *Crónica* mentioned by Fray Martín. Noema is credited with the invention of weaving by Enrique de Villena (*Arte Cisoria*, p. 13).

[6] Tubal Cain, the son of Zillah and Lamech is identified as "an instructor of every artificer in brass and iron" (Genesis 4:22).

[7] Mosén Diego de Valera describes "Mynerba, por otros llamada Palas.... Ésta perpetuamente fue virgen; por ésta fue fallado el artefício de la lana; ella buscó arte para linpiar; ésta fue la primera que la puso en rrueca e que primero pusso paño en telar; ésta el olio de oliuas ante que otra persona sacó; ésta el vsso de las carretas falló; ella fue la primera que armas deffensyuas presumió faser; ésta ordenó las primeras leyes de batalla, e la cuenta dél al guarismo ante que otra persona falló" (*Tratado en defensa de virtuosas mugeres* in *Epístolas enbiadas*, p. 149, n. 14). D. Álvaro credits

Aragnes,[8] hembra asiática & phebeya[9] & porende es llamada Aragnes, porque primera mente começo a filar como araña & a ardir sus hilos & texer su tela. E dizen que Minerua, dela que agora deximos, ella halló primero los números & los puso en orden, como fasta agora husamos dellos.[10] E della dizen los poetas que del huesso de vna çanca de vna aue halló los albogues. Otros dizen que no de hueso, más de caña fizo el primero instrumento para tañer; avn que, segund nuestra Escriptura, Jubal fue el primero que começo a tañer en cíthara & en órgano.[11]

Otras henbras ouo de grand industria, las quales aquí dexo por que paso a otros loores dellas, pero aquí ay vna quistión marauillosa; pues que enel antiguo siglo mugeres fallaron tantas industrias & artes, especialmente las letras; ¿por qué agora, eneste nuestro siglo, las henbras no se dan al estudio de artes liberales & de otras ciencias, antes paresce como le sea deuedado? A esto respondo con vna historia que puso Varrón enel *Libro delas Antigüedades,* dando la causa & razón por que aquella ciudad de Grecia, do heruió el estudio dela philosophía, se llamó después Athenas. Dize, pues, que después que la dicha ciudad fue fundada & acabada, súbito de vna parte dela ciudad appareció vn árbol de oliua & dela otra parte dela ciudad começo a manar agua. Estos agüeros diz que mouieron al rey Cíclope, que la auía fundado, & embió quien preguntase al délfico Apolo, que hera el dios delas adeuinaciones, qué auían enesto de entender & qué

---

Eusebio, *Libro de los tiempos* for his information about her spinning and weaving and "obras artificiales" (p. 153).

[8] Aragnes is undoubtedly Arachne, whose story is told by Ovid, referring to her humble station (*Metamorphoses,* trans. Horace Gregory [New York, 1958], p. 163, Bk. VIII). Ovid doesn't say that Arachne learned her art from spiders, instead he relates how after the bitter contest with Pallas (Minerva), the poor girl was turned into a spider, after having behaved like one. Fray Martín makes only one direct reference to Ovid and it is not to the *Metamorphoses.* It is somewhat unlikely that Fray Martín was an admirer of the *Metamorphoses,* since so much of what Ovid wrote was not compatible with Christian morality. See n. 41 to "Sources and Allusions" *supra.* Clearly much of Ovid had been Christianized, in works like the *Ovide moralisé.*

[9] Both eds. have *phebeya.* Could this refer to the village of Hypaepa or to the Phoebus Apollo? Félix García transcribes it as *plebeya.*

[10] See *supra,* n. 7 for Mosén Diego de Valera's inclusion of *guarismo* in the list of Minerva's accomplishments.

[11] Genesis 4:21: "And his brother's name was Jubal: he was the father of all such as handle the harp and the organ."

auían de fazer. Apolo respondió que la oliua significaua Minerua & el agua Neptuno & que hera en poder delos cibdadanos llamar la ciudad o del nombre de Minerua o de Neptuno. Auida el rey esta respuesta, hizo llamar todos los vezinos, assí varones como fembras, que estonces en aquellos lugares hera de costumbre que las hembras estuuiessen enlos públicos consejos. Consultada pues aquella muchedunbre, diz que los varones por Neptuno, las hembras por Minerua dieron sentencias; & por que se halló vna hembra más que los varones, venció Minerua & fue la ciudad nombrada della. Entonces Neptuno sañudo, como es dios delas aguas, conmouió los mares & hizo crecer el agua que despobló las tierras de Athenas. E por que la yra deste dios fuesse placada, segund dize el dicho actor Varrón, condenaron las mugeres a tres penas: la vna que dende adelante no fuesen llamadas a consejo público; la otra que nunca el hijo tomase el nonbre dela madre; la otra que ninguno no las llamase atheneas. [12] Destas tres puniciones, especial mente dela primera, paresce quel estudio les es vedado. Pues no han de entrar en consejo, no han menester ciencia para ello, ca los consejeros han de ser philósophos morales & theólogos, otra mente no podrían bien aconsejar esto. Pero entiéndese delas particulares mugeres & no delas claras, como son princesas & reynas, alas quales no es vedado estudiar en sabiduría. Como Sancta Catalina, que hera hija de rey & hera instruyda [13] en todas las artes liberales. [14] Assí que estas tres puniciones comprehendieron alas escuras & pleueyas hembras, mas no alas altas dueñas como es nuestra señora, la Princesa, por lo qual deue captar [15] algunas oras del día en que estudie & oya tales cosas que sean propias al regimiento del reyno.

---

[12] See *The City of God*, III, 94-95, Bk. XVIII, Ch. ix.
[13] The 1542 ed. has *instituida*.
[14] D. Álvaro de Luna cites Sta. Catalina's persuasive discourse with Maxencio, the emperor, when she protested the pagan sacrifices of the realm: "E fabló con él, ante la puerta del tenplo, noble mente, por muchas e diuersas conclusiones de silogismos. ... César, marauillándose de su fabla suaue, e de su doctrina grande, e de su virginal fermosura, e non podiendo yr contra sus razones, ... mandóla lleuar a su palacio real, e guardarla con diligencia." She was the daughter of the king and famed for her intellectuality, her beauty and her virtue (pp. 242-243).
[15] The 1542 ed. has *catar*.

Capítulo Segundo

[*Capítulo .ij.* la prouoca a fortaleza por enxemplo de otras que fueron fuertes & de grandes coraçones].

Las mugeres natural mente son flacas & temerosas, pero si contesce que cobran coraçón & desechen el temor, nunca gigantes osarían atender lo que ellas cometen. Ésta es regla así en naturaleza como en moralidad, que quando vna propiedad natural mente conpete a alguna cosa, si contesce que por alguna causa sale de aquella propiedad, sale della por cabo & en extremo. Desto en natura ay muchos enxenplos: la calabaça natural mente es fría & por eso la dan alos febrosos, pero aquel calor que toma quando se cueze es por cabo & más lo retiene que otras cosas calientes; así es tan bien enlas costunbres. Deximos que la muger natural mente es vergonçosa, pero si por alguna ocasión pierde la vergüença, naturalmente no ay cosa más desuergonçada. Así diremos aquí del temor & flaqueza que ala muger conpete natural mente, el qual temor & flaqueza, si por alguna cosa lo pierde, no ay cosa más osada ni más inuencible que la muger. Esto no lo quiero aquí prouar por razones, más enxenplos.

El primero reyno que fue enel comienço del mundo después del diluuio fue el reyno delos assirios, muy grande en tierra & mucho durable en tienpo. El primero rey fue Belo, fijo de Menbrot, que hedificó la torre de Babilonia.[1] Avn déste fue començado el huso de armas, que avn que los honbres peleasen entre sí

---

[1] The Temple of Belus was early identified with the Tower of Babel. It was mentioned by Herodotus and Strabo. Mosén Diego de Valera credits Nimrod with the construction (*Espejo de verdadera nobleza*, in *Epístolas enbiadas*, p. 185).

antes, pero peleauan conlos puños, donde la pelea se llamaua *pugna,* quasi hecha con puños & a puñadas. Mas este Belo halló el huso de cuchillo & enseñó pelear con hierro & dende la pelea se llamó *bello,* quasi batalla que falló Belo.[2]

Murió este Belo & suscedió Nino, su hijo. Éste fundó la ciudad de Níniue[3] & avn fue el primero que halló la ydolatría, ca hizo ymagen a su padre muerto & hízolo adorar a sus súbditos. E por esto todos los dioses delos babilonios se llamauan *bellos,* como Belzebuch, Belsigor & Belial.[4] Este Nino, rey segundo delos asirios, d[i]lató[5] el reyno después dela muger de su padre & sojuzgó toda Asia, ques la mitad dela tierra en grandeza, avn que en número es la tercera. Las otras dos son África & Europa & tanto es sola Asia como ambas. Assí que dizen sojuzgó hasta los fines de Libia, ado comiença África dela parte de oriente. Solos los dela India en todo oriente no auía sojuzgado, ca enellos halló gran resistencia.

Pero después que murió Nino, Semíramis, su muger combatió alos Indios & los sojuzgó & ganó.[6] Donde paresce la mugeril fortaleza que acabó lo que los varones no pudieron acabar. Desta

---

[2] I do not find this etymology in St. Isidore where it might be expected to appear. He mentions Ninus as the originator of war (p. 441).

[3] Genesis 10:11 credits Asshur with the building of Nineveh. However, in classical mythology Ninus and Semiramis are called the founders of Nineveh (*A Dictionary of Greek and Roman Biography and Mythology,* ed. William Smith [London, 1873], III, 776).

[4] St. Isidore identifies Bel with *"Belo, padre de Nino,"* mentioning his deification and the fact that *bal* means 'god.' He lists *Beelfegor, Belzebub* and *Belial* as evil gods. He does not make the connection between *Belo* and the subsequent gods (p. 204).

[5] Both eds. have *dolató.*

[6] Tradition has it that Semiramis did not, in fact, conquer India, a land which remained unconquerable, so that it was Alexander's dream that he surpass "the mythical exploits of Herakles, his reputed ancestor, Semiramis the fabled Assyrian queen, Cyrus, king of Persia and the divine Dionysos by effecting the subjugation of India" (Vincent A. Smith, *The Oxford History of India* [Oxford, 1923], p. 59). I have not found the source of Fray Martín's information that Semiramis had surpassed the men in her family and had conquered India, which, of course, is the reason for the inclusion of the story here. Semiramis does not usually figure in the praises of famous women in the religious didactic tradition because of her reputation for lasciviousness. Her inclusion by Fray Martín is based solely on her valor and competence in warfare.

Semíramis se lee que, como vna vez estouiese al espejo peynándose sus cabellos, & poniéndolos entreznajas, como hera costumbre & vso de aquel tiempo, ya auía hecho treznaja de vn cabo & començaua ya a componer el otro, quando le vinieron las nueuas que Babilonia, la principal ciudad de su reyno, se le hera rebellada. Ella juró que no compornía la otra parte de [sus] cabellos hasta que la ouiesse sujuzgada & caualgó & hizo caualgar la gente & assí lo hizo. Esto hecho, boluió al lugar mesmo & acabó de conponer sus cabellos. Este [7] ánimo mayor hera que de henbra. Hera ésta pagana & con su paganidad hizo triumphos muy grandes. [8]

Veamos otra a Dios del cielo deuota, que aésta sobrepujo en fortaleza, que fue la santa biuda Judic, dela qual enla Biblia, espreso libro, se pone, avn que los judíos no los reciban enel canón de su Escriptura, pero la Yglesia le pone entrellas, [9] por quanto figuró en muchas cosas la Virgen María que es archa de santas escrituras, ca ella conseruaua todas las palabras & las retenía en su coraçón. [10]

---

[7] The 1542 ed. has *Deste*.

[8] Valerius Maximus tells the story of Semiramis' interrupted toilet (p. 439, Bk. VIIII, Ch. iii).

[9] Of the canonicity of the Book of Judith, it is to be noted that it was included in the Septuagint. Clement of Rome, Clement of Alexandria, Ambrose and Augustin included it in the list of sacred books. The Council of Hippo (A. D. 397) and the Council of Carthage (A. D. 397 and 419) included it in the canon (*A Catholic Commentary*, p. 404, 308 l). D. Álvaro de Luna cites the Nicean Council's acceptance (p. 37).

[10] This idea seems to stem from the Virgin's rôle as "the temporal minister of the Word Incarnate," a designation quoted from the Venerable Bede in *A Catholic Commentary* (p. 115, 85 e). As her womb was the repository of Jesus Christ, the Word Incarnate, so she then became the repository of Holy Scripture. In medieval iconography Judith was identified as "une préfigure de la Vierge." She was associated with Jaël and Tomyris (in the *Speculum Humanae Salvationis*) "plongeant dans une vase de sang la tête du roi Cyrus," and appears as the "Vierge victorieuse du démon." In fact, St. Bonaventure compares the Virgin directly with Judith and Holofernes. Judith also appears as the Virgin of the Visitation, the symbol of sanctimony, chastity and humility who triumphs over lust and pride which Holofernes symbolizes (Louis Réau, *Ancien Testament*, p. 330).

Neither Scripture non D. Álvaro de Luna include the night long prayer vigil spent with her maid that Fray Martín describes as part of the story of Judith.

Desta, pues, sancta dueña Judic & de su fuerte osadía se lee en su libro que, como Nabugodonozor, rey delos asirios, pugnase contra Arfaxat, rey delos medos, & lo venciese, entonces diz que fue ensalçado el rey Nabugodonosor & su coraçón muy eleuado & embió a todos los que morauan en Cilicia & en Damasco & enel Líbano & alas gentes que heran enel Camelo & en Cedar & en Galilea & en Samaria & pasado el río Jordán fasta Jherusale[m] & a toda tierra de Jessén; a todos estos embió mensajeros Nabugodonozor, pero embiaron los vazíos & sin honrra. Desto Nabugodonosor fue muy sañudo & mandó a Olofernes, capitán de sus gentes, que fuese a sojuzgar aquellas tierras.[11] E quando fue cerca de Judea, los del pueblo de Ysrael començáronse a aparejar con otras gentes para resistir. E como lo sopo Olofernes, llegóse aellos & començó delos fatigar; & auido espacio de cinco días de tregua, salió Judic, biuda & santa & muy hermosa, & fuese al consejo delos judíos & díxoles que no se diessen a Olofernes, mas que esperassen en Dios. E ella hizo oración; & desque ouo acabado, despojóse las ropas de biuda & vistióse de ropas & hornamientos muy hermosos & tomó su seruienta & fuese para el real de Olofernes & díxole que venía huyendo & que le daría mañana [12] como ouiese aquella tierra. Él estaua marauillado sobre todo en su hermosura & enbeuecióse & requirióla de amores. E ella le dixo que esperase fasta la tercera noche & que en tanto se lauaría & untaría con preciosos ungüentos & él fue contento. E ella con su seruienta en lugar apartado oraua toda la noche [13] & quando vino ala tercera noche, esperó que todos fuessen ydos a dormir & ya Olofernes dormía en su alfaneque & ella entró & vido sobre su cabeça vn cuchillo colgado & muy paso lo sacó & cortóle la cabeça & púsola en vna talega que traýa; & como todos dormiesen, salióse & vínose a su ciudad & halló que las guardas la esperauan & entró & fizo poner la cabeça de Olofernes alto en vna torre. E quando los judíos vieron quel capitán hera muerto,

---

[11] D. Álvaro is more explicit about the mission of Nebuchadnezzar: "Por causa desta victoria, que él quiso ser enperador de todo el mundo; e aun no sólo esto, mas aun quiso ser adorado en dios por todas las gentes..."
[12] The 1542 ed. has *maña*.
[13] See n. 10 *supra*.

salieron contra la hueste & mataron & robaron todo quanto quisieron & siguiéronlos en alcançe mucha tierra; & assí libró Dios su pueblo por la mano de Judic del tirano & cruel Olofernes. Donde después el pueblo cantó della: —*Benedicta filia tua domine, quia per te fructum vite communicauimus.* E este canto dezimos dela Virgen María.[14]

Pues bien paresce la osadía & fortaleza dela muger. Enxemplo desto fueron las fuertes amazonas. Quedadas siempre a castidad, no consentían entrellas morar varón, mas cortáuanse las tetas derechas por que más expedita mente pudiessen husar del oficio del sagietar con arcos. Estas heran inuencibles a todo el mundo, antes heran victoriosas en toda batalla hasta el tienpo de Alexandre, el qual, quando con sus victorias se acercó aellas, rescibió dellas desafío, enlo qual respondió Alexandre que ellas heran mugeres & que no entendía delas acometer con armas sino con amores. Ellas replicaron que, avn que por naturaleza heran mugeres, pero tenían coraçones de leonas, las quales son más brauas que los leones. Estonces Alexandre con muchas gentes las acometió[15] & ante quisieron morir que ser vencidas.[16] E así es claro como las mugeres an en sí grand fortaleza, quitado el miedo.

---

[14] This is read in the Gradual of the Mass for the Feast of the Immaculate Conception. The words are used in the accommodated sense of the Virgin (*A Catholic Commentary*, p. 406, 309 m).
[15] The 1542 ed. has *cometió*.
[16] See *Quintus Curtius*, trans. John C. Rolfe, 2 Vols. (London: Loeb Classical Library, 1956), II, 24-35.

Capítulo Tercio

[*Capítulo .iij.* delas que ouieron constancia en buen propósito de virtudes & dela fe cathólica].

Dize Aristótiles que común mente las mugeres son inconstantes & se mueuen de vn propósito a otro.[1] E como deximos desuso, ésta es el arte de se hazer cadavno virtuoso que conozca sus defectos & ocurra contra ellos & pugne por seguir la virtud. Ay defectos contra la virtud, algunas vezes por la hedad, ca los moços más viuen por pasión que no por razón, algunas vezes por la conplexión; a vno son inclinados los coléricos;[2] a otro los flemáticos;[3] a otro los melencónicos;[4] & algunas vezes por la

---

[1] I do not find this observation in Aristotle, but St. Isidore cites Vergil (*Aeneid* IV, 569): "*Varium et mutabile semper / Femina.* (Varia y mudable es siempre la condición de la mujer)" (p. 450). Considering the high esteem in which both Aristotle and Vergil were held in the Middle Ages, a confusion of the two in recalling a tag of this sort is not surprising.

[2] Alfonso Martínez de Toledo characterizes *los coléricos:* "son robustos en amar, atrevidos a mal fazer, yndiscretos en la ora de la cólera, ávidos e espertos para exsecutar, non temerosos para poner por obra..." (p. 195).

[3] *Los flemáticos* are described by Martínez de Toledo as follows: "Estos tales son tibyos, nin buenos para acá, nin malos para allá, synón a manera de perezosos e ningligentes: que tanto se les da por lo que va como por lo que viene; dormidores, pesados, más floxos que madera; nin byen son para reýr, nin byen son para llorar; fríos, ynvernizos, de poco fablar, solitarios, medio mudos, fechos a machamartillo, sospechosos, non entremetidos, flacos de saber, ligeros de seso, judíos de coraçón e mucho más de fechos" (pp. 182-183).

[4] *Los melencónicos* are also descrites by Martínez de Toledo: "Estos tales son onbres muy yrados, syn tiento nin mesura. Son muy escasos en superlativo grado; son ynconportables dondequiera que usan, mucho riñosos, e con todo rifadores. Non tyenen tenprança en cosa que fagan, synón dar con la cabeça a la pared. Son muy ynicos, maldizentes, tristes, sospirantes, pensativos... porfiados, mentirosos, engañosos" (p. 183).

feminidad,[5] ca las henbras tienen otras passiones que los varones.

Pues la muger que quiere ser virtuosa ha de consentir consigo & dezir: Yo soy muger, enesto no he culpa niguna, que ser muger me dio naturaleza así como a otro ser varón, pero pues que soy muger, tengo de mirar las tachas que común mente siguen las mugeres & arredrarme dellas. Las mugeres común mente son parleras, yo quiero poner puerta a mi boca; las mugeres común mente son de poca constancia, yo quiero ser firme en mi buen propósito, que otras fueron ante mí que ouieron grand costancia & por enxenplo de aquéllas, yo quiero ser firme en virtud. E si esta conjugación an de hazer todas las mugeres, mucho más la princesa que es más que muger & en cuerpo mugeril, deue traer ánimo varonil.

Esta constancia & firmeza en buen propósito le enseñarán muchas donzellas pasadas. Dize Ambrosio que vna pitagorea entre las hablas gentiles es mucho de constancia comendado, como vn tirano la compeliese que le dixese vn secreto, el qual ella no deuía ni quería descobrir porque no touiesse llaue para abrir lo que secreto hera. Diz que conlos dientes se cortó la lengua & escupióla enla cara del tirano por que ya pues no hazía fin de preguntar que no ouiese a quien preguntase.[6] El secreto, creo que hera, si hera virgen o la virginidad hauía perdido, que si la auía perdido, ella hera fuerte de ánimo, pero flaco de vientre, donde fue enxenplo de callar, mas no de castidad, e porende castigó la lengua por negar la culpa. Así que en todo no fue inuencible.

¡Quánto son nuestras vírgines cristianas más constantes, que avn vencen las potestades que no veen, las quales no sola mente reputan victoria dela carne & sangre, mas también del Príncipe

---

[5] Fray Martín earlier described women as belonging to the group of *flemáticos* (see *supra Capítulo ii, primera parte*), but he obviously sees femininity as an extra factor above the humors which can affect the human personality.

[6] See St. Ambrose, *Concerning Virgins*, in *Some Principal Works*, p. 366, Bk. I, Ch. iv, 17-18). St. Ambrose views her resistance as heroic but praises such Christian martyrs as St. Inez more highly. For the act of biting off one's tongue in another context, see *El espéculo de los legos* (p. 62, ex. 90).

delas tinieblas! Ved Santa Ynés, menor de hedad de treze años, pero mayor en virtud, más alta en triunfo, más firmada en constancia, no se cortó por miedo la lengua, mas antes la guardó para victoria, no auía enella nada que temiesse ser magnifiesto, cuya confessión no hera criminosa, mas religiosa. Assí que la otra pitagorea enceló el secreto, solamente esta Santa Ynés prouó ser Dios, por el qual menospreció esta vida, no temía la muerte. Ved su constancia, que ni por halagos, ni por dádiuas, ni por amenazas, ni por tormentos, pudo ser vencida. [7] No fundó su casa sobre arena, mas sobre constante peña. [8] ¡O grand milagro! Que si preguntas dó hera esta circunstancia, en vna flaca muger; de qué hedad, hera de treze años. Suelen las mugeres ser flacas; suelen las niñas ser tiernas. Pero esta muger & niña, venció el fierro, sobrepujo el fuego.

Dela constancia de Santa Ynés más diría, si otras donzellas de su professión no me llamasen, que en semejante roca firmaron su constancia, por que las muchas a vna prouoquen con quien fablamos. Fue vna moçuela de noble linaje quanto a este siglo & agora es más noble quanto a Dios & como los parientes la conpeliesen a casar, fuese huyendo ala yglesia & púsose al sancto altar, por que ¿dónde mejor podía huyr la virgen, que ado se ofrece el sacrificio de virginidad? E no quedó enesto el fin de su osadía. Estaua cerca del ara de Dios la hostia limpia, el sacrificio de castidad & de allí dixo alos parientes que la seguían para casar: —¿Qué hazés vos otros, mis propincos, para qué vos trabajáys en buscarme esposo? Ya días ha que estoy proueýda. Vos otros buscáys me esposo, mucho mejor me lo hallé. Avn que el que me querés [9] dar sea rico y noble y tenga grand potencia, pero yo tengo esposo al qual no es quien se pueda conparar; rico

---

[7] In St. Ambrose's account, St. Inez precedes the virgin of Pythogorea but the comparison is the same one made by Fray Martín. Her age is given as twelve and the corroborative detail is missing. She is praised for her greater strength, since she was able to resist without having had to bite off her tongue (*Concerning Virgins*, in *Some Principal Works*, p. 366, Bk. I, Ch. iv, 19). D. Álvaro de Luna relies on St. Ambrose, adding the details of a return from school at the age of thirteen, at which time St. Inez was approached by the governor's son (p. 200).

[8] Matthew 7:26-27.

[9] The 1542 ed. has *queréis*.

en todo el mundo, poderoso en imperio, noble enel cielo. Si tal me dáys, no lo desecho, si tal no halláys, no me proués de esposo, mas auésme embidia del mío. Allí todos callaron & habló vno: —Esto no lo harías si tu padre fuese biuo. Ella respondió: —Por ventura, por esso murió, por que no diesse empacho a mi propósito. El que habló tomó esta respuesta dada del padre por sí & súbito allí murió, por que quiso empachar el propósito dela virgen. E assí los otros que allí estauan veyendo este milagro, ouieron miedo que no les contesciese a tal & començaron a fauorecer enella la virginidad que empachar querían. [10] Donde aquí an las moças premio de deuoción & los parientes dellas en enxenplo de ofensión quando tienen fija, no propongan dela casar, mas dexarla a su deuoción, otra mente aparéjanse a grand peligro dela constancia de vírgines. [11]

Santa Tecla es odorante sacrificio, la qual huyendo la cópula conjugal e por furor del esposo dapñada, mudó con veneración de su virginidad la ferocidad delas las bestias, ca aparejada alas fieras, declinaua & huýa el aspecto delos varones & ofrecíase alos leones. E assí hizo que muchos que allí traxeron los ojos impúdicos, los lleuassen de allí púdicos, ca veýan el león que lamía los pies ala virgen, echado en tierra alas plantas dela castidad, queriendo casi dezir que no podían violar el cuerpo entero por virginidad. Pues adoraua la bestia su presa & oluidando su propia naturaleza, la nuestra ánima vestid[a] la qual los hombres perdieron. [12] Allí vieras vna transfusión de natura; los hombres de fieridad vestidos mandauan crueldad ala bestia &, por el contrario, la bestia besaua los pies dela virgen & enseñaua alos hombres qué auían de hazer. Así que eneste milagro paresce cómo la

---

[10] St. Ambrose tells this horrifying story of the way the young virgin resisted the importunings of her family (*Concerning Virgins*, p. 373, Bk. I, Ch. xii, 65). There are points of similarity with St. Inez, but D. Álvaro de Luna points out that St. Inez was burned at the stake as a result of the death of the lovelorn son of the governor. Her influence was thought to have been witchcraft (p. 200).

[11] In the same passage cited in n. 10 *supra*, St. Ambrose draws the same lesson of a warning to the relatives of young virgins (p. 373).

[12] Continuing his use of *Concerning Virgins* of St. Ambrose; Fray Martín summarizes the colorful account of St. Thecla's domination of the beasts (p. 376, Bk. II, Ch. iii, 19).

constancia en propósito limpio haze mansas las fieras & faze sin lisión permanescer ala que la tiene.

Tanto, pues, más la tierna donzella deue ser en buenos deseos constante, quanto más se conosce flaca & menos a constancia dispuesta; a exenplo destas & de otras que antes se dexaron escarnificar, que negasen la fe o soltasen la virginidad.

Capítulo .iiij.

[*Capítulo .iiij*. delas mugeres que se dieron ala castidad virginal, que es más excelente grado de todos].

Todas las virtudes enla muger, avn que estouiesse vn montón dellas fasta el cielo, sin castidad no son sino como escorias & ceniza contra el viento, ca la muger que no es casta, avn que sea hermosa, se haze fea, antes fallarés que quanto es más fermosa, tanto más la suziedad la afea & deturpa. Donde la Sabiduría dixo: —¡O quánto es hermosa la casta generación con claridad![1] Si la muger no es casta, avn que sea generosa, deturpa así & a su linaje & toda su hidalguía se torna en prouerbio & escarnio. Avn que sea deuota & roya los altares & dé quanto tiene a pobres, si casta no es, todo es enella perdido. Donde Nuestro Señor dixo: —Tened los lomos ceñidos & candelas encendidas en vuestras manos,[2] sobre lo qual dize Sant Gregorio que aquí se notan dos cosas. Es asaber la castidad, enlo que dize: —Tened los lomos ceñidos; & las buenas obras, enlo que dize: —& candelas ardientes en vuestras manos. Donde concluye segund esto que ni la castidad es nada sin las buenas obras, ni buenas obras valen

---

[1] Fray Martín seems to have relied on two quotations from Wisdom. Msgr. Ronald Knox translates Wisdom 4:1: "How fair a thing is the unwedded life (Greek text: even a childless life) that is nobly lived." Wisdom 3:3 reads: "Blessed, rather her lot, that childless is yet chaste, ... offspring she will not lack." The passage is explained in *A Catholic Commentary*: "On the other hand the chaste but barren wife shall have fruit (i. e. in merit and reward) 'at the examination of souls' after death" (p. 506, 390 a).

[2] Luke 12:35: "Let your loins be girded about and your lights burning."

nada sin castidad.³ E esto, avn que sea verdad enlos varones como enlas mugeres, pero especial mente es verdad enlas mugeres, por lo qual eneste capítulo quiero recontar algunas, assí paganas como cristianas, que puñaron hasta la muerte por mantener virginidad. E primero quiero dezir delas paganas.

Enel primero lugar se presenta vna ystoria que declara donde nasció el nombre de virginidad. Recuenta Valerio, enel sexto libro enel primero capítulo, que vn varón llamado Virgineo, honbre plebeo & vulgar, pero en espíritu & ánimo fue varón patricio & consular, guardando que su casa no fuese ensuziada con fornicio, no perdonó a su propia sangre. Hera vn varón decurio, llamado Apio Claudio que deseaua dormir con vna hija virgen que tenía Virginio. El harto se defendía, pero veyendo que Apio, conla potencia que tenía, auía lo que mal deseaua de su hija, diz que Virginio sacó la moça al mercado & allí delante de todos la degolló. Donde quiso ser más verdugo de su hija virgen que no padre della corrompida.⁴ Este hecho dio ocasión que las moças enteras se llamasen vírgines, por amor de Virginio, que tanto amó la virginidad en su hija.⁵ Creo que Virginio dixo: —Hija, tú virgen nasciste & virgen hasta agora perseueraste, leuántase vn ladrón que te asecha & te quiere robar este valoroso & precioso thesoro, que vale mucho más que tu vida, pues demos tu vida porque no pierdes⁶ esta preciosa & noble margarita. E pienso que la moça fue contenta & respondía al espíritu del padre, que si él no lo fiziera, que ella misma por sus manos se matara, antes que perdiera la corona de su virginidad.

Esto hizieron las nobles cristianas vírgines. Léese que Santa Pelagia en Antiochia fue de hedad de quinze años; tenía hermanas

---

³ St. Gregory comments on Luke 12:35 in *Homilia XIII, Lectio S. Evang. Sec. Lucas,* in *Opera Omnia, Patrologiae Latinae,* LXXVI, ed. J.-P. Migne (Paris, 1865), cols. 1123-40. St. Jerome explains the symbolism of the passage citing first Job 2:3, suggesting that the term 'loin' was chosen for "decency's sake" (Letter XXII, 11, p. 26).

⁴ See Valerius Maximus, p. 271, Bk. VI, Ch. i. The imaginary dialogue appears to be Fray Martín's. D. Álvaro de Luna tells an expanded version of the story and cites "Titu Liuio enel tercero libro de la fundación de Rroma" (p. 111).

⁵ The etymology of this word is uncertain. This fanciful etymology is not reported by St. Isidore.

⁶ The 1542 ed. has *pierdas.*

vírgines & ella hera virgen; & como los persiguidores la buscassen para roballe el joyel de su castidad, ella misma antes que viniesen con sus manos se mató. E desque los malos esto vieron, fueron ala madre & alas hermanas; & ellas huyendo vinieron a vn río donde les cumplía o perder la virginidad si esperasen; o la vida si adelante fuesen, pero enesto venció el amor dela virginidad &, asidas por las manos, madre & hijas se echaron enel río, donde por la muerte escaparon de corrupción. [7]

A esto dirá aquí alguno si es lícito que la virgen se mate antes que perder la virginidad. A esto digo con Sant Agustín, enel primero dela *Ciudad de Dios*, que de ley común no es lícito que la moça, por euitar pecado ajeno, cometa en sí pecado propio, matándose. Pero de preuillejo especial, quando Dios inspira que así se haga, no sólo no es pecado, mas antes es mérito & martirio. [8] Como leemos de Sansón que él mismo se mató & es sancto. E Jepté sacrificó a su fija & ouo mérito & hizo bien; & Abraham si sacrificara a Ysaac, pues que Dios lo mandaua, grand mérito ouiera. [9] Donde Lucrecia entre las romanas es loada porque se mató, vengando en sí la castidad que perdiera. [10]

---

[7] St. Ambrose tells the story of Pelagia and her mother and sisters (*Concerning Virgins*, in *Some Principal Works*, pp. 386-387).

[8] St. Augustin answers the scorn of the pagans who apparently made much of the fact that Christian virgins in captivity had been raped, particularly consecrated virgins. The violated virgin martyrs, whose will was unyielding suffered no guilt from the acts perpetrated upon their bodies, even if these acts excited carnal pleasure (*The City of God*, I, 46, Bk. I, Ch. xvi). Cf. n. 7 to *Capítulo octauo, primera parte* of the *Jardín* for St. Lucía's comments. St. Augustin justifies their suicides in the same passage (*The City of God*, I, 46, Bk. I, Ch. xvi), pointing out that homicide is justifiable when God has authorized it (*The City of God*, I, 54, Bk. I, Ch. xxi).

[9] St. Augustin continues to justify homicide when authorized by God, using the example of Abraham's obedience to God when he consented to sacrifice Isaac and Jephte's compliance with a vow made to God in return for victory in battle (Judges 11:30-39) which forced him to sacrifice his daughter. Samson killed himself and his enemies, doing God's bidding (*The City of God*, I, 54, Bk. Il, Ch. xxi). Obviously Fray Martín was relying on the sequence of arguments in *The City of God*.

[10] Lucretia had almost become a symbolic cliché of womanly honor. Her story is told by Valerius Maximus (p. 271, Bk. VI, Ch. i). St. Jerome praises her for having used her own blood to blot out the stain on her character (*Against Jovinianus* in *Principal Works*, p. 382, Bk. I, Ch. 45). St. Augustin mentions her suicide because of her inability to bear the

Venga después Santa Soternes, virgen que por defensión dela fe & guarda de su castidad, todo el cuerpo dispuso a tormentos, en tanto que la cara, que suele ser libre delos tormentos & mirar los más que padescerlos, dio al verdugo que la firiesen tan fuerte & tan paciente, que ofreciéndole las mexillas tiernas, primero cansó el verdugo firiendo que la mártir golpes sufriendo. Nunca el vulto voluió, nunca la cara rehuyó, ni vencida por gemido, lágrimas echó. Final mente, desque ella venció todas las maneras de penas, el cuchillo que buscaua falló. [11]

Deleyte es oýr lo que pone Anbrosio enel libro *De virginidad,* de vna virgen en Antiochia, cuya tanta hera su fermosura que de todos hera deseada. E como el príncipe de aquella tierra la quisiese auer, no podía inclinarla a ello. Donde, como por grand despecho la fizo leuar al burdel ado ella estando, lloraua & oraua diciendo: —Señor, tú que heziste que las vírgines domasen los leones, da me agora, Señor, que yo pueda domar las voluntades delos honbres porque no sea ensuziado este pequeño templo tuyo. Hecha su oración, diz que entró aella vn cauallero que le dixo: —No temas, ca vine a saluar tu ánima, porende, troquemos los ábitos, porque tu saya me faga verdadero cauallero. Así que ella tomó el ábito del cauallero & él la saya della; & la virgen en tal ábito salió salua & quedó el cauallero en su lugar. Y como entrase otro, pensó fallar la virgen & falló el cauallero & salió diziéndolo alos otros; & en lugar dela virgen, el cauallero fue condepñado a muerte. E como esto oyese la virgen, vino a priesa al lugar del tormento, diziendo que aquella corona de martirio hera suya & que el cauallero no gela deuía vsurpar. El otro dezía por el contrario & la contienda piadosa de ambos se concluyó en que ambos gozassen deste triumpho. E assí fueron hechos a Dios sacrificio por martirio. [12]

---

shame of the crime inflicted upon her (*The City of God,* I, 49, Bk. I, Ch. xix).

[11] See St. Ambrose for the story of St. Sotheris (*Concerning Virgins,* in *Some Principal Works,* p. 387, Bk. III, Ch. vii).

[12] Fray Martín continues to rely on St. Ambrose for the story of the virgin rescued from the brothel by a soldier who changed places with her (*Concerning Virgins,* in *Some Principal Works,* pp. 376-379, Bk. II, Ch. iv). D. Álvaro de Luna tells the story with even more dramatic dialogue (pp. 167-168).

De Santa Brígida se lee que su padre la quería desposar con vn gentil mancebo & ella rogó a Dios que le veniesse enla cara alguna fealdad porque se estoruasse el casamiento & enla oración sele quebró vn ojo & el esposo por esto no la quiso. E ella apartóse a seruir a Dios & después le fue restituýdo su ojo.[13] E assí paresce muchos enxemplos de nobles donzellas que amaron virginidad.

---

[13] St. Brígida was the Abbess of Kildare, c. A. D. 525. Her story does not appear in the same sources as the other saints in this chapter.

## Capítulo Quinto

[*Capítulo .v.* delas honrradas biudas que alcançan el segundo grado de castidad].

El estado vidual después dela virginidad haze las mugeres honrradas & venerables matronas, pero deue ser suple modesta [1] la biuda & medio religiosa. Donde Sant Pablo: —Honrra [2] las biudas que son verdadera mente biudas, [3] como hera Ana, profetissa, hija de Samuel del tribu de Aser, que no se partía del templo, [4] mas viuía en ayunos & oraciones, seruiendo a Dios de día & de noche. [5] Donde la casada, desque pierde el marido, diz que ha de considerar que este marido o hera bueno o hera malo. Si hera bueno, diz que ha de temer que, tomando otro, no se mude la dicha & sería vna desesperación pasar del buen marido a malo. Si el que perdió fue malo, teme de hallar otro tal; & sea enesto cuerda & mire que las aues nunca tornan a caher enla red o lazo que vna vez cayeron. Antes dizen quel asno que es grosera bestia, nunca passa por do vna vez cayó. Pero eneste nuestro tienpo, vemos biudas de otras condiciones, que si perdieron marido maluado, luego buscan otro & dágelo Dios peor

---

[1] The 1542 ed. has *suplemo desta* which gives the idea of *suplemento desta* according to Félix García.

[2] Félix García assumes that *honra* is the verb of the sentence so that the reading is that St. Paul honors widows indeed instead of its being a direct quotation.

[3] I Timothy 5:3: "Honour widows that are widows indeed."

[4] D. Álvaro de Luna devotes a chapter to Ana (pp. 50-51).

[5] Fray Martín is quoting from I Timothy 5:5: "Now she that is a widow indeed, and desolate trusteth in God, and continueth in supplications and prayers night and day."

& si el que perdieron fue bueno, luego seles olvida & buscan otro. Antes vn poeta dize en latín: —*Successore novo, femina dicit ouo.* [6]

Estas deuen mirar los exenplos delas ancianas matronas. Dido, hermana de Pigmalión, desque perdió el marido en Sidonia, tomó consigo gran thesoro & vínose en África & allí fundó la ciudad de Cartago; & como Jarbas, rey de Libia, la demandase por muger, poco a poco disimuló las bodas hasta que acabase la ciudad. E después, fundó otra ciudad en memoria del marido que perdiera & más quiso quemarse que casar. [7]

Muger casta fundó Cartajena & esta misma ciudad después en loor de castidad acabó, [8] ca la muger de Astrúbal, tomada & encendida la ciudad, como viese que los romanos la querían prender, tomó de cada lado dos fijuelos que tenía & echóse de alto enel fuego que ardía en su casa & quiso más perescer que delos enemigos ser escarnecida su castidad. [9]

Después désta predican ala biuda leal, Artemisa, muger de Ma[u]soleo. Ésta dizen que fue insigne en castidad & muy loada tanto de poetas como de históricos & mayor mente porque a su marido, Desutón, assí lo amó sienpre como si fuese biuo & le hedificó sepulcro de marauillosa grandeza & fermosura, en tanto que fasta oy los sepulcros grandes & hermosos llaman ma[u]soleos tomando nonbre del marido desta reyna & otra mente se llaman monumentos por que mueuen a memoria delos que allí están enterrados, o trahen a memoria la muerte. [10]

---

[6] This tag does not appear in St. Jerome's letters to Salvina, Ageruchia, and Furia, nor does it appear in *Against Jovinianus,* the sources for almost all of the references in this chapter.

[7] D. Álvaro de Luna tells the story of Dido's widowhood citing as his source "Iustino, estoriador" (p. 154). It is, however, from St. Jerome's *Against Jovinianus* that I believe Fray Martín took this reference (p. 381).

[8] The 1542 ed. has *acabado.*

[9] D. Álvaro de Luna tells the story of Hasdrubal's wife giving as his source Valerius Maximus, Bk. III (p. 172). However, St. Jerome finishes his story of Dido with the sentence: "Carthage was built by a woman of chastity, and its end was a tribute to the excellence of the virtue." He then tells the story of Hasdrubal's wife (p. 381) making the same connection as Fray Martín.

[10] St. Jerome interposes the story of the wife of Niceratus here, and then proceeds to praise Artemisia, queen of Caria whose devotion to her dead husband was so great that she built him a great tomb (p. 381). D. Ál-

Los judíos como hazen quasi todos los bárbaros, tienen muchas mugeres & entre ellos ay ley que la muger quel marido días [11] ama que se entierre conél después de muerto el marido. [12] Las mugeres contienden del amor suyo, quál dellas lo tenía mayor; & la contienda es muy grande entre ellas, así que la que vence el pleyto pónese en ábito & aparato de bodas & asiéntase cerca del cuerpo abraçándolo & besándolo. E por loor de su castidad menosprecia la muerte, pues ésta que assí muere conel primero no entiende casar con otro. Las otras mugeres deste finado sienpre viuen con manzilla, ni ay varón que se quiera casar con ninguna dellas.

Entre las romanas fue Marcia fija de Catón, la qual como por mucho tiempo llorase al finado marido, las matronas le preguntaron hasta quando auía de llorar a su marido. Respondió ella: —No se acabará este lloro fasta que se acabe mi vida. [13] Ésta, pues, no tenía cuydado de se casar otra vez, ca no llorara tanto el perdido, si ouiera desseo de buscar otro marido. Otra fue Marcella: la madre le rogaua que se casase, pues que hera moça & quedaua biuda. Respondió: —Mi marido a vos otros es

---

varo de Luna gives as his source of the story, Valerius Maximus, Bk. IV (pp. 160-162). Mosén Diego de Valera adds the fact that Artemisia committed suicide after completing the tomb (*Tratado en defensa de virtuosas mugeres*, in *Epístolas enbiadas*, p. 153).

[11] The 1542 ed. has *más ama*. The 1500 ed. has *días*.

[12] It is my assumption that Fray Martín or the printer copying the Ms. erred here in writing "judíos" instead of "indios." Both eds. have *judíos*. However in the same portion of *Against Jovinianus* from which much of the other source material of this chapter stems, St. Jerome writes of the Indian custom of polygamy and of the rivalry of the wives for the honor of joining the departed husband on the funeral pyre (p. 381). D. Álvaro de Luna speaks of the customs of the women of India citing "Cicerón, enel libro quinto que es escripto de las cuestiones tusculanes" (p. 171), a reference to Cicero's *Tusculan Disputations* in which the custom of suttee is mentioned. Mosén Diego de Valera also describes this ritual as part of the Indian tradition (*Tratado en defensa de virtuosas mugeres*, in *Epístolas enbiadas*, p. 155). See also Yakov and María Rosa Lida de Malkiel, "The Jew and the Indian: Traces of a Confusion in the Hispanic Tradition," in *For Max Weinrich on his Seventieth Birthday* (The Hague: Mouton & Co., 1964) pp. 203-208.

[13] St. Jerome continues his list of noble widows mentioning Marcia, Cato's younger daughter who parried questions as to why she did not remarry with the comment Fray Martín quotes and also with the observation that she could not find a man who wanted her more than her money (p. 382).

muerto, pero a mí sienpre es biuo & biuirá.[14] Esta prerogatiua ouieron antigua mente las biudas que rescibieron en su casa los profetas, como paresce de aquella biuda Sareptena, que, por salud de sus hijos, soportó la hambre & no se quiso casar ni dar padrastro a sus fijos. Ésta rescibió a Helias en su posada.[15]

Cuenta San Jherónimo que en Roma ouo vn varón que auía auido veynte mugeres & vna muger que auía auido .xx. maridos; & casaron en vno & todo el pueblo romano estaua suspenso quál vencería al otro de días & fue assí que venció el marido. E quando lleuaron a enterrar ala muger, yua el marido con vna palma enla mano & dezía: —¡O muger mía, casada agora con el ataute.[16] Donde Jherónimo fabla con la biuda & dize: —Ruégote que te abaste perder el primero grado de castidad & porel .iij. veniste al segundo que es dezir que por el matrimonio veniste ala biudez. Pues guarda el segundo grado de castidad, pues que perdiste el primero.[17] Ambrosio enel *Exameron* dize: —que la tórtola si pierde su marido, nunca más toma otro.[18] Donde

---

[14] St. Jerome mentions Marcella in this part of *Against Jovinianus*, to the effect that her marriage was so satisfactory that she would never want anything more (p. 381). In a letter to Principia; Marcella is reported to have rejected Cerealis, a rich suitor for her hand after she had been widowed, because she was not seeking wealth, rather she was prepared to devote herself to perpetual chastity (Letter CXXVII). It is possible that Fray Martín confused Marcella with Valeria who is reported in *Against Jovinianus* to have rejected the idea of remarriage because her husband, Servius, was to her still alive (pp. 382-383).

[15] Luke 4:26: "But unto none of them was Elias sent, save unto Sarepta, a city of Sidon, unto a woman who was a widow." St. Ambrose tells the story of the widow of Sarepta in *Concerning Widows*, in *Some Principal Works*, p. 393, Ch. iii.

[16] St. Jerome tells this story in his letter to Ageruchia, as a true story although it appeared to be incredible. When St. Jerome served with Damasus, bishop of Rome, he met the couple in question whom he characterized as having "sprung from the very dregs of the people" (p. 233). St. Jerome does not give the victor's words as does Fray Martín and rather uses the tale to question whether they were really married because of their previous multiple experiences.

[17] St. Jerome makes several references to the second degree of chastity. One such reference is found in his letter to Eustochium (Letter XXII), where he writes about Blaesilla, Eustochium's sister (p. 27). He makes a similar comment in his letter to Ageruchia pointing out to her that, having lost the highest degree of chastity, she had already passed through the third degree of chastity as an honorable wife, she now had the opportunity to live in continence as a widow (p. 237).

[18] St. Ambrose in writing about the widowed turtle dove, quotes Vergil,

es ella regla delas biudas, enlos Cánticos dize: —Boz de tórtola fue oýda en nuestra tierra. [19] Esto es quando las honrradas matronas pierden sus maridos & no curan de buscar otros, como haze la tortolilla.

Diremos, pues, que a todas las dueñas es honesto mantenerse en estado de biuda, pero mucho más alas reynas, si les contesce perder sus maridos, no pueden casar con rey & porende es mejor así viuir en su biudez.

---

*Aeneid*, IV 17-18, concerning Dido (*Hexameron, Paradise and Cain and Abel*, trans. John J. Savage in *Fathers of the Church* [New York, 1961], Ch. xix, 62, p. 210). For more on the widowed turtle dove, see M. Bataillon, "La tortólica de *Fontefrida* y del *Cántico espiritual*," *NRFH*, VII (1953), 291-306; Eugenio Asensio, *Poética y realidad en el cancionero peninsular de la edad media* (Madrid, 1970), pp. 235-237.

[19] Song of Songs 2:2.

Capítulo vj.

[*Capítulo .vj.* cómo las dueñas han de amar & ser fieles a sus maridos, especial mente las reynas].

Como la muger es honesta & de mejor fama, si por leal amor del marido passado no toma otro, mas queda & permanesce biuda, assí es mucho más obligada de se guardar en castidad para el marido que ha de tomar. Donde podemos dezir que la donzella virgen, si quiere casar & ha intención de tomar marido, que ya antes que lo tome lo ha de amar & para él guardar su flor & castidad. Ha de ser leal desque lo ha tomado. E estas dos lealtades son necessarias so pena de pecado mortal, pero guardar lealtad al marido desque es finado esto es de honesto; ca la biuda si se casa, no peca, pero mejor haze & más honesta es si no se casa, especial mente si procede ya en días, que avn delas biudas moças el Apóstol aconseja que se casen, ca mejor es casarse que no quemarse.[1]

Leemos muchas illustres mugeres que hasta la muerte amaron sus maridos. Recuenta Valerio que Julia, fija de César, muger de Ponpeo, quando vio la vestidura de su marido toda ensangrentada, temió que le ouiesen muerto con armas & por fuerça del grand dolor mouió vn hijo de que hera preñada.[2] E las contiendas del imperio romano todas heran entre César & Pompeo, entre padre & marido; & más quisiera que venciera el

---

[1] Corinthians 7:9: "But if they cannot contain, let them marry: for it is better to marry than to burn."

[2] Valerius Maximus tells this story in a chapter dealing with conjugal love (pp. 198-199, Bk. IV, Ch. vi, 4). D. Álvaro de Luna cites both Valerius Maximus and Lucan as sources for the story (p. 141).

marido que no el padre. Ésta, avn que pagana, quería guardar, quando instituyó el matrimonio, por ésta dexará el marido a padre & a madre. Assí tan bien se ha de entender dela muger que más ha de amar a su marido que al padre ni madre.[3]

Fue otra famosa dueña romana, Porcia, hija de Catón, casada con Bruto. Ésta, como viesse a su marido a hierro muerto, demandó con grand justicia vn cuchillo para se matar; & quando vio que no gelo dauan, fuese al fuego que estaua enla sala & tomó vn puñado de carbones ardiendo & tragó selos & assí murió,[4] touo enesto el ánimo del padre, avn que más extenso, por quanto Catón se mató con hierro & la hija con fuego.

Dizen que Metridates, rey de Asia & porende enemigo delos romanos, touo vna muger que houo marauilloso amor a su marido, por el qual amor, avn que fuese muy fermosa, mudó el hábito de muger & púsose en traje de varón & tresquilóse los cabellos & husó las armas & el caballo porque pudiese mejor ayudar a su marido. E desque Metridates fue vencido de Gayo Pompeo, huyó para gentes efferadas & bárbaras, pero la muger siempre lo siguió, no sólo con ánimo mas con cuerpo. Donde esta lealtad & amor dela muger hera solaz de Metridates en todos sus trabajos, antes le parescía que, yendo conél tan fiel muger, que no hera desterrado ni vencido, mas que estaua en su casa & en su reposo.[5]

Entre tantas romanas, bien es interponer algunas macedonias & espartanas. E ocúrreme aquella fiel casada, Penélope, muger del grand cauallero Ulixes dela qual se dize que como Ulixes estouiese veynte años fuera de su casa, los diez sobre Troya & los otros diez que anduuo perdido por el mar, el padre & los parientes de Penélope, desque vieron que todos heran venidos de

---

[3] See Genesis 2:24.

[4] In the chapter on conjugal love, Valerius Maximus tells the story of the hot coals as a means of committing suicide (p. 199, Bk. IV, Ch. vi, 5). D. Álvaro tells another story about Portia who wounded herself to prevent her husband's proposed assassination attempt on the life of Caesar. He takes the story from Valerius Maximus (Bk. III, Ch. ii, 15, pp. 117-118: pp. 98-99).

[5] Valerius Maximus includes the story of Mithridates and Hypsicratea in the chapter on conjugal love (pp. 199-200, Bk. IV, Ch. vi, 5, 2). D. Álvaro de Luna quotes Valerius Maximus, Bk. IV, as his source for the story (pp. 163-164).

Troya sino Ulixes, pensaron que hera muerto & començaron de solicitar ala moça que buscase otro marido. Ella quanto pudo honestamente se escusó & quando vio que tanto la fatigauan, puso vna gentil escusa: —Yo he començado a texer vna tela, dexá mela acabar & luego haré lo que me mandáys. Ellos fueron contentos. De manera que quanto ella texía de día, tanto destexía de noche, por que nunca se acabase hasta que viniese su marido. Donde ésta es entre otras muy predicada de fieldad conjugal. Quiso Dios & vino Ulixes & assí ella fue quitada de su promessa & de su trabajo. [6]

Lacedemón es tierra de Grecia & aquí dizen que ouo mugeres muy fieles a sus maridos. Dizen que los lacedemones pugnaron con vnas gentes propincas que traýan linaje & sangre de Jasón & los lacedemones enesta pugna, que quiere dezir batalla o pelea, [7] fueron vencidos & presos & puestos en lugar donde de noche los querían sacar al tormento dela muerte. Esto sabiendo, sus mugeres, vinieron rogando & pechando alas guardas que las dexasen entrar a ver sus maridos. Entrando, pues, enla cárcel, dieron sus vestiduras alos maridos & ellas tomaron las dellos & salieron los maridos en ábitos de mugeres & quedaron ellas en ábitos de honbres; & salieron los maridos las cabeças cubiertas, mostrando dolor, por lo qual las guardas no los conoscieron. Pero quando vinieron alos justiciar, hallaron que heran las mugeres &

---

[6] D. Álvaro de Luna tells the story of Penelope and her weaving and cites "Ouidio enel su libro delas epístolas" (a reference to the *Heroides*) as his source (pp. 180-181). St. Jerome alludes to Penelope's chastity as "the theme of Homer's song" (p. 382). Although there are references to translations of the *Iliad* in 15th-century Spain, there are none to translations of the *Odyssey*. It may be assumed that Penelope had already become a household word, either through Ovid or through oral tradition. The importunities of Penelope's parents and relatives seems to be original with Fray Martín. Neither D. Álvaro de Luna nor Mosén Diego de Valera who also relates this tale (*Tratado en defensa de virtuosas mugeres* in *Epístolas enbiadas*, pp. 151-152), speak of family pressure on the chaste wife. Cf. n. 10 to *Capítulo tercio, tercera parte* and nn. 13 and 14 to *Capítulo quinto, tercera parte*, for examples of chaste young women who resisted the entreaties of their families that they marry, or in the case of widows that they remarry. Fray Martín might be including Penelope in this tradition.

[7] St. Isidore defines parts of a war as *pugnae* (p. 442).

perdonaron a tanta fieldad de matrimonio. Antes dixeron: —¡Guay de nosotros que no ouimos tales mugeres! [8]

Estos & tales enxemplos ayan las nuestras reynas para amar a sus maridos & será grand prouecho, no sola mente a ellos, mas a todo el reyno, que avrán hijos de bendición que suscedan a sus padres & mantengan el reyno en paz & justicia.

---

[8] Valerius Maximus includes the episode of the Lacedemonian women in the chapter on conjugal love (pp. 200-201, Bk. IV, Ch. vi, 5, 3).

Capítulo .vij.

[*Capítulo .vij.* de tres grados de castidad conjugal, vidual & virginal: cómo todos son buenos, avn que vno mejor que otro, & de tres maneras de biuir los hombres].

La simiente euangélica que cayó en buena tierra se hizo tres partes:[1] la vna lleuó treynta vegadas, mas la otra sesenta & la otra ciento. Estos tres grados son los escalones dela castidad. El que lleuó treynta es el estado delos casados que biuen bien, compliendo los diez mandamientos & creyendo enla Santa Trenidad. Bien paresce que tres vegadas diez hazen treynta. Los que se doblan & lleuan sesenta son las biudas, que tan bien guardan los diez mandamientos & creen enla Trenidad, pero buien en doble castidad & doblando los treynta hazen sesenta. Los que lleuan ciento son las vírgines que biuen vida angélica, no humana. La virginidad es mucho natural alas moças, más que tener dientes. Nasce la niña sin dientes pero no nasce sin virginidad. E avn por esso, Santa Apolonia más quiso perder los dientes que la virginidad.[2] Más clara fue Santa Cecilia por que

---

[1] Fray Martín is referring to the parable of the sower (Matthew 13: 18-23), but he is particularly drawing a parallel with Matthew 13:23. St. Jerome uses the same image: "If I have called virginity gold, I have spoken of marriage as silver. I have set forth that the yields an hundredfold, sixtyfold, and thirtyfold — all spring from the same sowing, although in amount they differ widely" (Letter XLVIII, p. 67).

[2] St. Apollonia was an aged deaconess, seized by the Romans in A. D. 249. Her teeth were knocked out by blows and she was threatened with burning unless she "uttered certain impious words." She begged for a delay and, once certain that she was acting freely threw herself into the flames of her own accord. Her suicide is classified by St. Augustin as one under the direction of the Holy Spirit and therefore not sinful (*Butler's Lives of the*

fue virgen que porque fue hija de rey.³ Ser hija de reyna⁴ es claridad ajena, que viene de sus parientes; ser virgen & casta es claridad propia, que le viene de su propia virtud.

Un herej[e] ouo enel tiempo de Sant Jherónimo que se llamaua Jo[u]iniano. Éste entre otros errores puso vno que las casadas & las vírgines todas heran de ygual mérito⁵ & este es extremo de otro que puso Taciano, diziendo que las bodas heran pecado.⁶ Aquél las ygualó ala virginidad; éste las ygualó ala fornicación. La verdad, pues, dela fe va por medio, diziendo que las bodas son buenas, ca si no lo fuessen, nunca Jesu Cristo & su madre & los discípulos fueran presentes aellas, donde las consagró por nueuo milagro, haziendo del agua vino.⁷ Pero no son tan buenas como la virginidad, ca bien paresce que no lleuan tanto fruto. Las bodas lleuan treynta & la virginidad ciento. Y no sólo no son tan buenas como la virginidad, mas ni avn como

---

*Saints,* ed. Herbert Thurston and Donald Attwater, 4 vols [New York, 1956], I, 286). She does not appear in D. Álvaro de Luna, nor in Mosén Diego de Valera, but she apparently was well-known, considering her early connection with dental ills. The story of the fate of an elderly deaconess whose virginity was not threatened was obviously changed by Fray Martín.

³ D. Álvaro de Luna tells of St. Cecilia and of her marriage to Valerius and of his subsequent conversion (pp. 239-242).

⁴ Is the change from "hija de rey" to "hija de reina" a significant one? This designation was reserved at the time for Juana la Beltraneja, daughter of Enrique IV, rather pointedly to underscore her doubtful paternity. Fray Martín might also be referring to Isabel I, daughter of the Queen mother, Isabel of Portugal.

⁵ St. Jerome directed his *Against Jovinianus* as an answer to the errors of Jovinianus who said that "virgins, widows, and married women, who have once been passed throught the laver of Christ, if they are on a par in other respects, are of equal merit" (p. 348).

⁶ St. Jerome criticizes Tatian for his rejection of marriage (Letter XLVIII, p. 71). Again in *Against Jovinianus,* he points out that he does not "follow the views of Marcion and Manichaeus and disparage marriage; nor deceived by the error of Tatian, the leader of the Encratites, do we think all intercourse impure" (p. 347). W. H. Fremantle in his edition of St. Jerome identifies Tatian as an Assyrian by birth, a pupil of Justin Martyr. His followers were called Encratites or Temperates because of their great austerity. They were also called Water drinkers and Renouncers (*Principal Works,* p. 347, n. 4). Later St. Jerome cites I Timothy 4:3 to show the error of Marcion and Tatian "who inculcate perpetual abstinence, to destroy, and express their hatred and contempt for the works of the Creator" (p. 400).

⁷ John 2:1-3.

las biudas. Donde assí son estos tres grados de continencia como tres metales. Es assaber: cobre, plata & oro. Bueno es el cobre, pero mejor es la plata & avn mejor es el oro. Así, buena es la continencia conjugal, pero mejor es la vidual & mucho mejor es la virginal. Donde dizen que el matrimonio es para henchir la tierra; la virginidad para henchir los cielos.[8] El que biue en matrimonio honesto, biue como hombre, pero la que biue en virginidad biue como ángel. Assí lo pone el philósopho enla *Política* que la muger o el hombre que no se casa o es mejor que honbre o es peor que bestia;[9] & dize razón, ca la moça que no quiere casar o lo haze por mucha buena intención; es assaber: por mejor seruir a Dios o por más apartarse del mundo; o lo faze por no ser sujeta al marido & biuir como quisiere & darse a quien quisiere, sin demandar gelo ninguno. Esta es mala intención & bestial.

Notá aquí quel honbre o la muger es vn medio entre los ángeles que están alto & las bestias que están baxo. Pues el hombre puede biuir en tres maneras; la vna es que biue tan perfectamente que su vida parezca angelical. Assí biuen las vírgines, delas quales dize San Jherónimo que la virginidad es parienta delos ángeles; ca sin dubda biuir enla carne & no segund la carne, no es vida terrena mas celestial. Donde enla carne hazer vida

---

[8] St. Jerome makes the explicit reference to the hundred and forty-four thousand elect in Revelations 14:3-4. He explains: "These are they who have not defiled themselves with women, for they continued virgins" (p. 378). The millenarian view was that the Lord's command to be fruitful and multiply and fill the earth had the ultimate goal of meeting the finite goal of Revelations 14:3-4, which explains Fray Martín's reference to filling heaven. It is somewhat doubtful that this apocalyptic vision continued in strength in the 15th century; the end of the world was not referred to with the same immediacy as it had been earlier. When Fray Martín alludes to the idea of filling heaven, I assume he is using the image to justify marriage.

[9] Aristotle is explaining that each individual, when separate is not self-sufficient: "He must be related to the whole state as other parts are to their whole, while a man who is incapable of entering into partnership, or who is so self-sufficient that he has no need to do so, is no part of a state, so that he must be either a lower animal or a god" (*Politica*, 1253 a 25-30). The state and the family are likened all through Bk. I and although Fray Martín's quotation is not to be found exactly, the sense of each man's having to belong to some larger entity is quite clear.

angelical mayor mérito es que de sí tener la. [10] De mayor virtud es conquistar vn reyno por sus armas que no heredarlo de su padre, ca este viénese alo ganado. El otro pone enello sus fuerças & denuedos. Así es aquí quel ángel sea virgen, esto requiere su naturaleza, pero que vna moça de carne & de huessos & de cuerpo terrenal porfíe consigo & pugne por quedar siempre virgen, esto es sobre naturaleza & es gracia & virtud.

La primera moça que en Ysrael començó esta nueva vía angélica fue nuestra Madre la Virgen María & por esso meresció ser madre de Dios. E avn por esso continua mente estauan en su cámara conella ángeles del cielo, conosciendo que la virginidad es compañera dellos & avn ésta es perrogatiua que el Apóstol Sant Juan entre los otros ouo virginidad, por la qual Nuestro Señor enla cruz colgado le encomendó ala Virgen María, su madre. [11] Assí mismo por esso le reueló el Apocalipsi por ministro delos ángeles, por que los ángeles no reuelan los secretos del cielo sino alas vírgines. [12]

Es grand milagro dela virginidad que no sola mente Dios & los ángeles & los hombres, mas avn los demonios, la aman & la temen & avn las bestias la honran. Dizen [13] que vna bestia feroz que se llama vnicornio assí la caçan: Espían el monte do anda, & pon[en] [14] vna niña virgen al cabo del monte que esté allí assentada & bien vestida & andan los monteros fatigando la bestia con canes por el monte. Dizen que, quando ya se siente

---

[10] St. Jerome writes: "For they shall neither marry, nor be given in marriage, but shall be as the angels in heaven" ("To Pammachius Against John of Jerusalem," p. 438). He goes on to ask: "Who can have any glory from a life of chastity if we have no sex which would make chastity impossible? Likeness to the angels is promised us, that is, blessedness of their angelic existence without flesh and sex will be bestowed on us in our flesh and with our sex" (p. 440).

[11] Fray Martín is referring to John 19: 26-27: "When Jesus therefore saw his mother, and the disciple standing by, whom he loved, he saith unto his mother, Woman behold thy son! Then saith he to the disciple, Behold thy mother! And from that hour that disciple took her unto his own home."

[12] After the hundred and forty-four thousand are assembled, Revelations 14:6 reads: "And I saw another angel fly in the midst of heaven, having the everlasting gospel to preach unto them that dwell on the earth, and to every nation and kindred, and tongue, and people."

[13] The 1542 ed. has *Dizien*.

[14] The 1542 ed. has *ponen*. The 1500 has *ponan*.

mucho fatigad[o], vase corriendo ala virgen & pone la cabeça en su regaço & allí espera los monteros.[15] E avn por esto enla prophecía de Balaam, el hijo de Dios se conpara al unicornio, donde dize: —Su gloria es como vnicornio[16] por que assí como éste viene alas haldas dela virgen, assí el hijo de Dios vino enel vientre virginal.

La otra manera puede biuir el hombre tan maluada mente que sea peor que bestia & enésta biuen las mundarias, rufianes, venéficos, mentirosos, lisonjeros, engañadores & otros semejantes. E ansí como los primeros son conpañeros delos ángeles buenos, assí éstos son conpañeros & miembros de Satanás. E assí como de aquéllos es el paraýso, assí, [dize][17] déstos es el infierno. Donde alos Corinthios dixe Sant Pablo: —No quiero que seáys compañeros delos demonios.[18] Los primeros por excelencia son buenos, éstos son por excelencia malos.

La tercera manera de biuir es quando el honbre biue media vida, que ni es tan perfecta como los ángeles, ni tan maluada como bestia. Pero biue como hombre casándose & conuersando conlos hombres honestamente & en su matrimonio guardando lealtad & otras cosas que deximos. La primera se llama vida angélica; la segunda se llama vida bestial; la tercera se llama vida humana. Estas tres vidas pone Aristóteles enel primero delas *Éticas* do dize que ay tres vidas. La vna es contemplatiua; la otra actiua & la otra bestial.[19] E avn por esto, después dela

---

[15] Fray Martín seems to be quoting the *Physiologus Latinus* (ed. Francis J. Carmody [Paris, 1939], p. 31). The *Physiologus* carries the simile one step further than Fray Martín, likening the crucifixion to the capture of the unicorn.

[16] In Numbers 23:22, Balaam says: "God brought them out of Egypt; he hath as it were the strength of an unicorn." The same passage is repeated in Numbers 24:8. In Deuteronomy 33:17, a reference which includes "glory" and "unicorn" is part of Moses' blessing before his death: "His glory is like the firstling of his bullock and his horns are like the horns of the unicorn." Without seeing the particular translation of Numbers and Deuteronomy, it is not possible to know if Fray Martín confused the two passages or whether his version read differently.

[17] The 1542 ed. has *dize*. The 1500 has *dezi*.

[18] I Corinthians 10:20: "And I would not that ye should have fellowship with devils."

[19] Aristotle describes the three lives: dedicated to the pursuit of pleasure, the political life and the contemplative life (*Politics*, 1095 b 17-20). He goes on to identify the political life as the Life of Action.

muerte ay tres lugares do van las ánimas, ca los contemplatiuos van luego a paraýso, los bestiales luego al infierno; los actiuos van al purgatorio. Quando Nuestro Señor estaua enla cruz, estauan estos tres: Nuestro Señor perfectíssimo luego fue a paraýso. El ladrón reprouio [20] luego fue al infierno. El buen ladrón auía de ir a purgatorio, sino que Nuestro Señor le dio absolución plenaria, que fue conél en paraýso. [21]

---

[20] Both eds. have *reprouió*. Is the sense *reprobó* or *réprobo*?

[21] In Luke 23: 39-43, one of the malefactors is described as railing at Jesus: "If thou be Christ, save thyself and us." The other one rebukes him and asks Jesus: "Lord remember me when thou comest into thy kingdom." And in Luke 23:43, Jesus promises him: "Verily I say unto thee, today thou shalt be with me in paradise."

Capítulo viij.

[*Capítulo .viij.* delos statutos que dieron los romanos sobre la conuersación delas dueñas con sus maridos].

Iusto es eneste lugar hazer memoria delos romanos estatutos que hizo antigua mente Roma cerca delas mugeres, por que la dueña cristiana, no sólo delas sanctas, mas avn delas gentiles, tome documento. Vergüença es, & juyzio duro será contra la cristiana, quando vee tantas ymágenes de virtudes enlas paganas & ella no se esfuerça a ninguna virtud, antes en todo vicio se embuelue. E porende mucho mueuen los enxemplos gentiles al cristiano para se dar a virtud, por lo qual es razón que digamos desto aquí.

Es, pues, assaber que Valerio enel segundo [libro] pone quatro estatutos que los romanos hizieron cerca de sus dueñas. El primero ha respecto a la honrra que la muger deue a su marido: donde dize que las hembras ce[n]auan[1] a sus maridos en tal guisa que ellos estauan echados; ellas no más assentadas, casi prestas para seruir al marido. Los maridos estar acostados, no se ha de entender enla cama, pero ponía vn guademecir & sus almadraquejas. Oy día lo fazen los moros & avn los cristianos enel Andaluzía: así cenan alas tardes echados de cuesta & las mugeres asentadas. Esta costumbre delos gentiles passó alos dioses, tales quales ellos selos[2] hizieron, ca enel conbite de Jupiter,

---

[1] The 1542 ed. has *ceuauan*. The 1500 ed. has confused "n" and "u" elsewhere as in *cieno/cievo* so that the reading *ceuauan* is probably a compositorial error. The Latin of Valerius Maximus reads *cenitabant*.

[2] Both eds. have *selos*. Is the sense *çelo*?

él estaua enel lecho & Juno & Minerua en sus sillas se assentauan.³ Esta cerimonia entre los hombres & entre los dioses se guardaua para mostrar la excelencia que tiene el marido sobre la muger & anotar que la muger deue ser obsequiosa al marido. En aquel tienpo, entre los romanos, las que heran contentas de vn solo matrimonio heran honrradas de corona de pudicicia⁴ & castidad, ca estimauan que los muchos matrimonios enla muger señal hera de intenperancia.⁵

El segundo estatuto miraua la vnión entre marido & muger inseparable, que mientra viuiesen no se pudiesen apartar; donde ni el marido repudiaua ala muger, ni la muger al marido. E desto dize que ninguno repudio se hizo en Roma entre la muger & el marido dende que la ciudad se fundó hasta el año centésimo & cinqu[e]nta. El primero que allí dexó su muger, por razón que hera mañera, fue Spurio Carbilio, el qual avn que paresció que lo hazía mouido por razón tollerable, es assaber, por que no podía auer hijos della, pero ya por esso no caresció de causa reprehensible, por que el deseo [de] auer hijos, no se deuía anteponer ala fe del matrimonio.⁶ No ay causa enel mundo, sino las quel derecho esplica, por quel marido pueda repudiar la muger.⁷ E si enla ley vieja se prometió libello de repudio, esto se hizo por la dureza delos judíos por que no las matasen. E permitía la ley el menor mal que hera diuorcio por refuýr el peor que hera homicidio. Donde este instituto agora se guarda entre nos, los cathólicos, avn que ¡mal peccado! hartos matrimonios distortos en Castilla se hazen.⁸

---

³ This passage is found under the heading of "De Institvtis Antiqvis" in Valerius Maximus (pp. 57-58, Bk. II, Ch. i).

⁴ The 1500 ed. has *pudicicia,* either an error or a neologism.

⁵ Although Fray Martín does not specifically mention that he continues to rely on Valerius, the observation follows directly after the discussion of dining customs (see n. 3 *supra*) (p. 58, Bk. II, 3).

⁶ Fray Martín continues to translate directly from Valerius Maximus (p. 58, Bk. II, Ch. i, 4).

⁷ Fray Martín is undoubtedly referring to Deuteronomy 24:1-3, where the reasons for divorce are "and if it come to pass that she find no favor in his eyes, because he hath found some uncleanness in her," and a more general "if the latter husband hate her...."

⁸ Fray Martín discreetly perhaps, omits the next admonition of Valerius that the Roman matron not permit anyone to touch her or her robes (pp. 58-59, Bk. II, Ch. i, 5).

El otro instituto fue sobre la modestia & temprança del vino, donde dize que en aquel tiempo el huso de beuer vino fue no conoscido alas romanas hembras, por que no cayesen en alguna suziedad & mengua. Acostumbró siempre ser muy cercano el grado desta intemperancia ala deuedada Venus. Dize Terencio que sin Ceres, ques la diosa del pan, & sin Baco, ques el dios del vino, enfríase Venus, ques la diosa de amores carnales; [9] & avn que a todos sea torpe exceder en vino, pero mucho más alas mugeres, especial mente alas grandes que tantos las miran & con tantos an de librar que no se puede encobrir. Descúbrese el vino por los ojos que luego se hazen como beços colorados, por las narizes quel huelgo les huele mal, por la boca tossiendo & echando gruesa saliua, por el andar que echan los passos inciertos, por las palabras que las dizen no conpuestas ni bien articuladas. E si esto enlos varones, mucho más enlas mugeres que son más flacas de cabeça; & ¿qué mal no hará de su cuerpo la muger que es tomada de vino? Donde Salomón dixo enel fin delos Prouerbios: —No des vino ala muger. No des vino alos reys por que no hay secreto do regna la embriagués, ca beuerán & oluidarán los juyzios & peruertirán la causa del pobre. [10] E por esta mesura que auían las romanas enel vino, los maridos las amauan & honrauan, echando sobre ellas ricas aljubas de seda & ricos collares de oro & cintas de plata & otros moniles & joyeles; & permetían que lauassen sus cabeças con lexías por que retilasen & procediesen en público con guirnaldas muy ricas & firmalles & esto todo no para ceuar los ojos delos galanes, mas para dar gozo a sus maridos.

---

[9] This linking of gluttony and lust is found in the *Eunuch* (*Terence*, trans. John Sargeaunt, 2 vols. [London: Loeb Classical Library, 1912], I, 311).

[10] Proverbs 31: 3-5: "Give not thy strength unto women, nor thy ways to that which destroyeth kings. It is not for kings, O Lemuel, it is not for kings to drink wine; nor for princes strong drink. Lest they drink and forget the law, and pervert the judgement of any of the afflicted." This passage seems to be warning against fornication and drinking. However, it offers the closest parallel that I can find to what Fray Martín is saying. There is the possibility that his version had some such phrase as *strong drink,* instead of *strength* which would have led to his interpretation of Scripture. The Arcipreste of Talavera, in his usual colorful terms warned men against women who drink (pp. 165-168).

El postrimero instituto hera para guardar la paz entre marido & muger, donde dize que, quando quier que interuenía alguna renzilla entre marido & muger, veníanse en vn chico templo dela diosa llamada Ueriplicia, que quiere dezir 'amansadora dela saña del varón'; & allí cadavno hablaua lo que quería & ala fin, echando [11] todo rancor de ánimo, concordes se tornauan a su casa. [12] Así pueden fazer agora los casados cathólicos, no enel tenplo dela ýdola, mas enla yglesia & capilla dela Virgen María, ca vna delas cosas que mucho ama Dios & la Virgen es quando dos casados entre sí son concordes en bien hazer.

---

[11] The 1542 ed. has *echado*.
[12] Fray Martín translates from Valerius Maximus (p. 59, Bk. II, Ch. i, 6).

CAPÍTULO .ix.

[*Capítulo .ix.* delo que dixo Salomón delas mugeres así buenas como comunales & desto se traherán algunas autoridades].

Salomón el sabio, mucho habló delas mugeres, [1] assí buenas como malas. Donde es bueno que de sus dichos pongamos algunos aquí a deporte & solaz delos leyentes. Primeramente, pues, dize enlos Prouerbios: —Cerco de oro enlas narizes dela puerca, la muger hermosa & vana. [2] Esto es vna comparación o semejança, ca si hincas alas narizes del puerco o dela puerca vna armella del oro, no guarda honor al[valor] [3] del oro, mas enel primero lodo o cieno que falla mete el hocico & la armella del oro todo lo deturpa. Assí la muger vana & ventosa, si por ventura contesce que tiene hermosura o enel vulto o enel ábito, pero nunca cesa de variar su cara al cieno & hedor carnal, ni cata honor a su hermosura, ni otras doradas propiedades que ella tiene; antes anda buscando cómo & en qué manera se podrá ensuziar. Dize Séneca: —Que prouecho es a toda muger mirarse al espejo, no para se pintar, mas para se castigar. [4] Enesta manera o enel espejo verá que es muger fea o que es hermosa. Si es fea, ha de dezir entre sí: —Ya que natura te hizo fea, trabaja tú con

---

[1] The 1542 ed. has *Mucho habló el sabio Salomón.*
[2] Proverbs 11:22. See also II Peter 2:22.
[3] Félix García transcribes this as *valor* which seems to make more sense than *varón* in both eds.
[4] I do not find this exact quotation in Seneca and as has been noted, many aphorisms are attributed to him in collections of proverbs. See n. 6 to the *Prohemio.* See also Ovid, *On Painting the Face,* in *The Art of Love and Other Poems,* trans. J. H. Mozley (Cambridge, Massachusetts: Loeb Classical Library, 1962), p. 5. The sentiment here is very close to Ovid's.

Dios que la fealdad dela cara sea causa dela hermosura de tu conciencia. Si es hermosa, deue trabajar por no deturpar su hermosura & que este dorado cerco no vaya por el cieno, mas la hermosura dela cara sea ocasión de guardar la del ánima. Esta consideración ouieron las santas vírgines, Ynés,[5] Catalina,[6] Ágata,[7] Cecilia,[8] delas quales cantamos:[9] —Fermosas de vulto, pero más hermosas de fe & castidad. Tres cosas son perdidas: la fortaleza enel rufián, la creencia enel honbre de mala vida & la fermosura enla muger loca.

E el otro dicho de Salomón es en fin delos Prouerbios que dize: —La muger fuerte ¿quién la hallará? De lexos & delos fines vltimos, su precio.[10] Confía enella el coraçón de su marido. Quiere dezir que la muger fuerte & virtuosa en pocos lugares se halla, pero quando se halla, su precio es inconparable, ni puede ser apreciada por quantas riquezas ay eneste mundo & el coraçón de su marido confía en tal muger como ésta. Es assaber, que la dexará todo el regimiento de su casa & todos sus secretos confía della & con ella departe sus consejos & ella es descanso de sus trabajos. Donde el prouerbio dize: —Dela muger buena, bien auenturado es el marido. Más valdría al honbre casarse con muger pobre & buena que con vna reyna & mala, ca la buena enlos trabajos consuela, la mala desconsuela. Como hizo la muger de

---

[5] See n. 10 to *Capítulo quarto, segunda parte* and n. 7 to *Capítulo tercio, tercera parte* for allusions to St. Inez.

[6] See n. 14 to *Capítulo primero, tercera parte* for references to Sta. Catalina.

[7] D. Álvaro de Luna tells of St. Agatha's resistance to the importunings of Quintinian, who, along with other torments, ordered that one of her breasts be cut off, a loss which St. Peter miraculously restored. Her persecution brought on an earthquake and, after her death, her tormentor died as a result of a horse's kicking him into a river so that his body was never found (pp. 207-210).

[8] See n. 7 to *Capítulo .ix., segunda parte* for an allusion to St. Cecilia.

[9] The 1542 ed. has *contamos*. Possibly, *cantamos* is a reference to the singing of the mass and the litanies. Cf. the *romance sagrado* in which these saintly virgins appear (*Romancero y cancionero sagrados: Colección de poesías cristianas, morales y divinas*, BAE 35, ed. Justo de Sancha [Madrid, 1855], p. 113).

[10] Proverbs 31:10: "Who can find a virtuous woman? for her price is far above rubies."

Job, que más lo afligía ella que quantos males passaua.[11] E avn assí es dela muger, por respecto del marido, que le valdría más tomar por marido vn hombre bueno avn que pobre, que vn rey malo. Pero agora no se hazen los casamientos con estos respectos, mas como dize Oracio: —La primera questión agora se haze del auer. Si es rica la esposa que tiene el esposo & assí han malas fines, como han malos principios.[12]

Después desto procede Salomón enlos Cánticos & hizo los tres libros, los Prouerbios, el Ecclesiastés & los Cánticos. Ouo Salomón tres nombres. Fue nonbrado Salomón, que quiere dezir 'pacífico'. Fue nonbrado Ídida, que fue amado del Señor. El primero por que reynó en paz; el segundo por que Dios le amó; el tercero nombre suyo fue Eclesiastés que suena cancionador & enformador de pueblos.[13] E según estos tres nonbres, así hizo tres libros, los Prouerbios en quanto pacífico, el Eclesiastés en quanto canciona- dor & los Cánticos en quanto de Dios amado. Los otros dos libros, es assaber de la Sapiencia & el Eclesiástico, no los hizo Salomón, mas otros de sus dichos los conpusieron.

Pues enestos libros, Salomón escriuió de diuersos estados & condiciones, así de honbres como de mugeres. Donde enlos Cán- ticos escriuió delos amores que son entre esposo & esposa. Donde Sant Bernardo sobre los Cánticos dize: —Enesta obra me paresce que hallo estas personas: el esposo & sus conpañeros, la esposa con sus donzellas; donde alas vezes habla el esposa, otras el esposo, otras las donzellas, otras vezes los conpañeros del espo- so.[14] Conueniente es que enlas bodas estén muchas donzellas conla esposa & muchos donzelles conel esposo. Entiende aquí que el esposo es Jesu Cristo; la esposa es la Sancta Yglesia sin man- zilla & sin ruga. Los ángeles & los sanctos son los donzelles del esposo; las donzellas dela esposa son las santas vírgines & buenas

---

[11] Job's wife was not of a consoling nature, as when, in Job 2:9, she says: "Dost thou still retain thine integrity? Curse God and die."
[12] Horace condemns greed in the selection of a wife, but not in these words (Horace, *The Satires and Epistles of Horace,* trans. Smith Palmer [Chicago, 1959], Epistle I, 2, 41-57). In the same epistle, Horace says: "Well begun is half done" (39-41).
[13] This is apparently a direct translation of St. Isidore (p. 175).
[14] I do not find this quotation in St. Bernard (*The Song of Songs: Sermones in Cantico Canticorum,* trans. by a religious of C.S.M.V. [London, 1952]).

biudas & perfectas casadas. E estos amores spirituales explícanse aquí a figura de amores carnales, por que, avn que las fieles casadas ayan de auer con sus maridos amor carnal quanto abasta ala generación de fijos, pero más deuen entre sí auer amor spiritual que es en Dios. Antes este amor es más necessario para el matrimonio quel carnal; que los adúlteros se aman carnal mente, mas por que no se aman spiritualmente no son casados.

El otro dicho es en fin del Eclesiástico do dize: —Mejor es la maldad del varón quel bien hecho dela muger.[15] Este dicho es marauilloso dezir: quel pecado de vno sea mejor que la virtud de otro & para entenderlo es de notar que aquí varón & muger se toma por misterio & semejança, que digamos que aquél es varón que es fuerte & firme en sus hechos; aquél es muger que es flaco & delicado.[16] Acaesce, pues, quel varón firme peca, pero de su pecado luego se leuanta & faze penitencia. La muger faze bien, pero desto ha vanagloria & soberuia. Pues ved aquí cómo es mejor el pecado de varón que la buena obra dela muger, que Dios más ama pecador penitente que justo soberuio. Pues la señora, avn que es henbra por naturaleza, trabaje por ser varón en virtud & assí haga bien que no se ensalce por vana gloria, mas que se abaxe por humildad.

---

[15] Ecclesiasticus 42:14.
[16] Here Fray Martín contradicts what St. Augustin wrote about the error of allegorizing "male" and "female" to stand for the ruler and the ruled (*The City of God*, II, 397, Bk. XIV, Ch. xxii).

Capítulo .x.

[*Capítulo .x.* que muchos doctores diuersos dixeron delas mugeres cerca dela honestidad dellas].

En fin, deuemos poner lo que diuersos dotores dizen delas mugeres, por que de toda parte reciban documento. Un doctor dize que Dios puso enla muger natural vergüença porque la frene de pecar & fue hecha para que siruiese al varón & no para asecharlo; pero ella, no curando dela costumbre de su estado, procura la muerte alos varones. Agora por infengidos halagos, agora por lisonjas, agora por hartibles ojadas, estudian delos traer a escándalo de vituperio. Eneste dicho ha de notar la muger moça & segund la corruptión desta carne hermosa, que de quantas ánimas de hombres es ocasión de se perder, de tantas dará razón el día del juyzio; & esto es aella importable, ca harto terná aquel día de dar razón de sí misma. Donde Jherónimo en vna epístola dize: —Aquellas mugeres escandalizan los ojos cristianos que se pintan las caras con aluayalde & arrebol & los ojos con alcohol. Hazen que las negras representan falsas blancuras; las amarillas falso color; las lagañosas encubren su mal conel alcohol; las arrugadas se mienten ser lisas. [1] Aya, pues, vergüença la cristiana sin procurar falsa hermosura, ca otras heran hermosas & se hizieron feas por huyr la concupiscencia & suziedad dela carne. ¡O fuego de mancebos! ¡O incendio de fealdad! ¡O muerte del ánima perdida! Esta pintura no es ymagen de Christo, mas de Anticristo,

---

[1] Fray Martín cites directly St. Jerome's letter to Marcella advising her about Blaesilla, daughter of Paula (Letter XXXVIII, 3, p. 48).

como dize Jherónimo enla dicha epístola.[2] Donde Guillén Pariense [sic][3] en su *Libro del Vniuerso* cuenta de vna muger, la qual, como trabajase en se peinar & pintar, otra muger ya finada le aparesció & dixo que grand tormento pasaua por que, quando eneste mundo viuió, ouo mucho cuydado de se pintar & denuncióle las penas que posseen las tales. E la biua dixo: —¡Ay qué mal tan fuerte & por tan poco pecado! Dixo la finada: —No entiendas ques poco pecado, antes muy grande & tal que pertenesce alas amargas penas del infierno que sepas que la muger que se pinta en todo es contraria al Crucifixo, el qual primera mente tiene la cabeça espinada & ésta lleua la cabeça con grandes tocas volantes & los cabellos muy rutilantes. Nuestro Señor tiene toda la cara ensangrentada; ésta la lleua bien arrebolada. Él tiene los ojos llorantes; ésta los tiene con alcohol cintillantes. Él siente hedores del lugar do estaua crucificado, que hera *Caluarie locus;*[4] ésta nin le queda almizque ni algalia, ni otros olores prouocatiuos. Él tiene la boca llena de fiel & vinagre;[5] ésta busca mil golosinas para satisfazer a su gula. Nuestro Señor tiene las manos enclauadas; ésta las lleua alheñadas & de guantes bien dotadas. Nuestro Señor tiene los pies con clauos atados; ésta, grandes chapines calçados. Él tiene saya de açotes; tú tienes cortapisas & pellotes. Así que en todo heres contraria al Crucifixo, pues es necesario que seas conforme a Satanás. Oýdo esto la biua, diz que luego quitó todo aquel aparato & puso se en ábito conueniente.[6]

---

[2] In the same letter St. Jerome makes the same allusion to the antiChrist (p. 48).

[3] It would seem that Fray Martín is citing Guillelmi Alverni, Episcopi Parisiensis, *De Universo,* (in *Opera Omnia,* 2 vols. [Paris, 1674: ex Typographiae F. Hotot, et vaneums]).

[4] This was undoubtedly a familiar etymology. It is explained as follows: "Golgotha (simplified form of Aramic *gulgotā* 'skull'; Latin 'calvaria')..." (*A Catholic Commentary,* 722c, p. 902).

[5] The reference is to Matthew 27:48, Mark 15:36, Luke 23:36, and John 19:29-30.

[6] I do not find this story in William of Auvergne's *De Universo.* In the second part, the appearance of ghosts and spirits is described, in the form of young girls or of elaborately adorned women (II, 1066). See García de Castrojeriz (II, 107), for an abbreviated version attributed to "Hugo en el tratado que fizo del mundo."

Pues eneste espejo se deuen mirar las donzellas deste tiempo & quiten de sí tan desonesta costunbre, que no es sino ábito de paganas & de mundarias. Mucho mejores composturas heran las de Santa Ynés, la qual dezía: —Con su anillo me desposó mi Señor Jesu Christo & como a su esposa me dió santa corona, mi diestra & mi cuello afeytó con inestimables margaritas & mis orejas con perlas & piedras celestiales, & mis mexillas están coloradas con su sangre de Aquel cuya madre es Virgen, cuyo padre nunca conosció fembra; con Aquel soy desposada al que siruen los ángeles; de cuya hermosura el sol & la luna se marauillan. Éstas son las arras dela sancta esposa de Jesu Christo. [7]

Dize Sant Jherónimo que los carnales amores a todos paren peligro, assí a donzelles como a donzellas, pero mucho más alas donzellas que alos mancebos; avn que conciban amor, pero tienen otras cosas en que entender, como es en monte, en caça, en domar cauallos & otros fechos humanos que les resfrían aquel amor nescio. Las donzellas, si vna vegada son ocupadas de amor, son perdidas que no tienen otro oficio sino amar. [8] Donde o se an de tornar locas o han de caher en vileza & todo es peligro. En especial a dueñas de alto estado que tienen que perder, que avn los mismos parientes suyos les son contrarios & les procuran la muerte porque ensuzia su linaje. Así contesció a vna reyna de Nápoles de nuestra memoria que se disoluió en amores & en infamia tanto que los mismos caualleros del reyno que heran sus deudos la quisieron matar. E ella huyó por la falsa puerta del castillo & fuese a Ytalia & allí murió, pobre & desauenturada. [9] Ca tal dueña no sola mente se deue guardar dela hecha, mas dela sospecha, no poniéndose con mancebos en lugares ocultos, ni en tienpos sospechosos, mas conuersando con honbres ancianos & de buena fama. [10]

---

[7] See D. Álvaro de Luna, (pp. 200-202) for an account of St. Inez' strength and constancy.

[8] I do not find this in St. Jerome.

[9] Fray Martín is probably alluding to Queen Giovanna of Naples (1343-1381) who had achieved a certain fame for her tendency to luxury, pomp and license, and who was suffocated at the command of Charles V of France.

[10] Cf. similar advice given by St. Jerome to Salvina that she choose an old man of spotless morals to supervise her domestics in order that he may guard her honor (Letter LXXXIX, p. 167).

Otra mente, avn que no lo haga, si falla ocasión de sospecha, leuántanle que rauia & dan conella al traste & niguno en tal caso no le es leal. Ouidio da buen consejo diziendo: —Que la noble donzella no dé entrada en su coraçón a ningund amor feo, mas que obste & mire alos principios. Como el huego mejor se mata antes que proceda en grand flama, quando está en centella que no desque echan llamas; [11] & todas las cosas más flacas son al principio que desque an crecido, assí haze el falso amor. Pues como dize Sant Jherónimo: —Los varones son ilustrados en Roma por ser cónsules. Otros ouieron fama eterna por eloquencia; otros por gloria militar & por triunfos de vitorias fueron muy nonbrados. La gloria & triunfo & fama eterna dela muger es castidad & pudicicia. [12] No se faze en todas las crónicas mención de muger sino es casta. [13] La castidad a Lucrecia ygualó con Bruto; [14] antes avn dizen algunos que la hizo mayor. Ésta ygualó Cornelia con Gracho; [15] ésta hizo ygual a Porcia conel otro

---

[11] In the course of advising lovers not to keep old love letters, Ovid remarks that a nearly spent cinder can be rekindled easily and that a mighty fire might ensue (*The Remedies of Love*, in *The Art of Love and Other Poems*, trans. J. H. Mozley [Cambridge, Massachusetts: Loeb Classical Library, 1962], p. 227). Quite apparently, Ovid and Fray Martín did not have the same thing in mind. L. P. Wilkinson points out that citations from Ovid were justified, because, although he wrote of "unlawful loves," his inspiration was divine. He writes: "There were even 12th-century heretics who held that 'God hath spoken in Ovid, even as in Augustine'" (*Ovid Surveyed* [Cambridge, 1962], p. 186).

[12] In a letter to Pammachius, written two years after the death of Pammachius' wife, St. Jerome praises Pammachius' decision to renounce patrician activities and consular duties in order to become a monk. In spite of this praise, St. Jerome says that he is surpassed in humility and piety by Eustochium and Paula "for considering the weakness of their sex they have done more work relatively if less absolutely" (Letter LXVI, p. 139).

[13] This bit of moral hyperbole is contradicted by Fray Martín himself. In his chapter dealing with strong women, he indulges in extensive praise of Semiramis who was hardly noted for her chastity.

[14] The story of Lucretia in D. Álvaro de Luna (pp. 79-84) bears a resemblance to the narratives which belong to the *gageure* cycle. See Gaston Paris, "Le cycle de la gageure," *Romania* XXXII (1903), 481-551, for a full description. Clearly Lucretia's suicide was equal to the vengeance of Brutus.

[15] D. Álvaro praises Cornelia for her recognition of true wealth (her sons) and her deprecation of worldly goods. In this episode Gracchus is only a shadowy figure — her husband and the father of her sons: his actions are not weighed in relation to Cornelia's (pp. 114-17).

Bruto.[16] Más hermosa es que su marido la reyna Tanoquil, ca el marido entre tantos reys que después vinieron famosos ya no paresce;[17] ella como rara entre las hembras. La virtud dela clara castidad no la dexa asconder.

Dirá alguno ¿porqué la castidad da fama immortal ala muger más que otra virtud? A esto digo que por tres razones: la primera es la dificultad de alcançar a esta virtud. Todas las virtudes son cerca de cosa difícil & trabajosa, pero en especial la castidad. E avn que sea trabajosa en varones & mugeres, pero más difícil es hallar muger casta que no varón. E porende, quando perfecta se halla enla muger, ésta es vna delas marauillas que Dios faze.

La segunda razón desto es la raridad. Dizen que toda cosa rara es preciosa, por esto el oro es más precioso que la plata & la plata más que otro metal, por que son cosas que en pocos lugares se hallan. Assí haze la muger casta que es como vn aue que se llama fénix, que en todo el mundo no se halla sino vna. Que si dezimos que los hombres son famosos por filosophía, ouo muchos filósofos; si fueron famosos por elocuencia, ouo más avn que filósofos & assí delas otras famosas artes. Pero si dezimos: —Ésta fue muger, moça fermosa. Es casta. Esto es tan raro que quando se halla, meresce infinitos loores: primero a Dios que puso tan grand fortaleza en vaso tan flaco[18] & después que se dispuso con fauor de Dios a tal aureola.

La otra razón es por que si como es difícil, no consiguiese fama, ninguna se dispornía aello. Donde no solas las cristianas, mas las paganas heran muy honrradas si heran castas. Los romanos honrraron mucho la virginidad; hizieron tenplo & monesterio

---

[16] Portia actually made an attempt to prevent her husband's attempted assassination of Caesar and later committed suicide in a spectacular fashion upon learning of Brutus' death. See n. 4 to *Capítulo vj., tercera parte.*

[17] D. Álvaro de Luna gives as his source for the story of Tanaquil, Valerius Maximus, Bk. I, and Livy "en la primera década en el primero libro del fundamentos de la çibdat de Rroma" (p. 94). Tanaquil was married to Lucomon Tarquin, whom she advised to move to Rome as a result of her divination. She continued to display great talent as a reader of auguries and, upon the death of her first husband, she secured the throne for her second husband, Servius Tullius (pp. 93-98). There is no question that she is more famous than her husbands, as Fray Martín notes.

[18] See I Peter 3:7: "Giving honor unto the wife, as unto the weaker vessel."

alas vírgines vestales & allí tenían lámparas & fuegos perpetuos a significar el resplandor dela castidad. Pues, ¿qué deuen fazer los cristianos, cuyo Dios es virgen, fijo de virgen madre & fijo de virgen padre, esposo de vírgines & amador de virginidad? Él guarda singular corona a sus esposas, dela qual nos haga participantes Jesu Cristo purísimo que, conel Padre & conel Espíritu Sancto, biue & reyna vn Dios por infinitos siglos. Amén.

Aquí pongo fin, muy preclaríssima Princesa, a este tratado intitulado *Jardín de nobles donzellas* & si en lo por mi dicho algunos herrores se hallaren, lo que no dudo, humilmente suplico sea acatada la gana de mi deseo de su seruicio tuuo & tiene, & no a mi rudeza de ingenio, quedando prostrado, sus maníficas manos besando.

Fue impresa la presente obra por Juan de Burgos en Valladolid a .xj. días del mes de nouiembre del año de quinientos años. A loor & gloria de nuestro Saluador & Redemptor Jhesu Cristo & dela gloriosa Virgen María.

DEO GRACJAS

# BIBLIOGRAPHY

Alfonso el Sabio. *Antología de Alfonso el Sabio.* Ed. Antonio G. Solalinde. Madrid: Colección Austral, 1960.
———. *General estoria.* Ed. Antonio G. Solalinde. Madrid, 1930.
Álvaro de Luna. *Libro de las claras e virtuosas mugeres.* Ed. Manuel Castillo. Madrid: Sociedad de Bibliófilos Españoles, 1908.
*The Anchor Bible: Genesis.* Ed. E.A. Speiser. New York, 1964.
*The Anchor Bible: Proverbs, Ecclesiastes.* Ed. R.B.Y. Scott. New York, 1965.
Antonio, Nicolás. *Bibliotheca Hispana Vetus sive Hispani scriptores qui ab Octaviani Augusti aevo ad annum Christi MD floruerunt.* Madrid, 1788.
S. Anselmi Cantuariensis Archiepiscopi. *Opera Omnia.* 2 vols., ed. Franciscus Salesius Schmitt. Edinburgh, 1946.
St. Ambrose. *Hexameron, Paradise, Cain and Abel.* Trans. John J. Savaje. *The Fathers of the Church.* New York, 1961.
———. *Select Works and Letters.* Trans. H. DeRomestin, E. DeRomestin, and H.H.F. Duckworth. *A Select Library of Nicene and Post-Nicene Fathers of the Christian Church.* 2nd Series. Ed. Philip Schaff. New York, 1896.
———. *Theological and Dogmatic Works.* Trans. Roy J. Deferrari. *Fathers of the Church.* Washington D.C., 1963.
Aristotle. *The "Art" of Rhetoric.* Trans. John Henry Freese. London: Loeb Classical Library, 1939.
———. *The Athenian Constitution, The Eudemian Ethics, Of Virtues and Vices.* Trans. H. Rackham. London: Loeb Classical Library, 1938.
———. *Categories and De Interpretatione.* Trans. J. L. Ackrill. Oxford: Clarendon Press, 1963.
———. *The Nichomachean Ethics.* Trans. H. Rackham. London: Loeb Classical Library, 1962.
———. *Ethica Nichomachea.* Trans. W.D. Ross. *The Works of Aristotle.* Ed. W.D. Ross. Oxford, 1912.
———. *De Generatione Animalium.* Trans. Arthur Platt. *The Works of Aristotle.* Ed. J.A. Smith and W.D. Ross. Oxford, 1912.
———. *Generation of Animals.* Trans. A.L. Peck. Cambridge: Loeb Classical Library, 1943.
———. *Metaphysica.* Trans. W.D. Ross. *Works of Aristotle.* Ed. W.D. Ross. Oxford, 1924.
———. *Minor Works.* Trans. W.S. Hett. Cambridge, Massachusetts: Loeb Classical Library, 1936.

St. Ambrose. *Politica.* Trans. Benjamin Jowett. *The Works of Aristotle.* Ed. W.D. Ross. Oxford, 1921.

─────. *Politics.* Trans. H. Rackham. London: Loeb Classical Library, 1959.

─────. *Problems* I. Trans. W.S. Hett. London: Loeb Classical Library, 1953.

Pseudo-Aristóteles. *Poridat de las poridades.* Ed. Lloyd A. Kasten. Madrid, 1957.

St. Augustin. *Admonition and Grace.* Trans. John Courtney Murray. *The Fathers of the Church.* New York, 1947.

─────. *Anti-Pelagian Works.* Trans. Peter Holmes and Robert Ernest Wallis. *A Select Library of the Nicene and Post-Nicene Fathers of the Christian Church.* Ed. Philip Schaff. New York, 1887.

─────. *Basic Writings of St. Augustine.* 2 vols. Ed. Whitney Oates. New York, 1948.

─────. *On Christian Doctrine.* Trans. J.F. Shaw, *A Select Library of the Nicene and Post-Nicene Fathers of the Christian Church.* Ed. Philip Schaff. Buffalo, 1887.

─────. *Christian Instruction.* Trans. John J. Gavigan. *The Fathers of the Church.* New York, 1947.

─────. *The City of God.* Vol. I: Bks. I-VII. Trans. Demetrius B. Zema and Gerald G. Walsh. *The Fathers of the Church.* 3 vols. New York, 1950.

─────. *The City of God.* Vol. II: Bks. VIII-XVI. Trans. Gerald G. Walsh and Grace Monahan. *The Fathers of the Church.* 3 vols. New York, 1952.

─────. *The City of God.* Vol. III: Bks. XVII-XXII. Trans. Gerald G. Walsh and Daniel Honan. *The Fathers of the Church.* 3 vols. New York, 1954.

─────. *The City of God.* Trans. Wm. M. Green. 7 vols. London: Loeb Classical Library, 1953.

─────. *Expositions on the Book of Psalms.* Trans. A. Cleveland Coxe. *A Select Library of the Nicene and Post-Nicene Fathers of the Christian Church.* Ed. Philip Schaff. New York, 1888.

─────. *Lectures or Tractates on the Gospel According to St. John.* Trans. John Gibb and James Innes. *A Select Library of the Nicene and Post-Nicene Fathers of the Christian Church,* ed. Philip Schaff. New York, 1888.

─────. *Letters.* Trans. Sister Wilfred Parsons. *The Fathers of the Church.* New York, 1951.

─────. *Opera Omnia.* Ed. J.-P. Migne. *Patriologiae Latinae Cursus Completus.* Series Prima. Paris, 1845.

─────. *The Retractations.* Trans. Sister Mary Inez Bogan. *The Fathers of the Church.* Washington, D.C., 1968.

─────. *Sermon on the Mount. Harmony of the Gospels. Homilies of the Gospels.* Trans. William Findlay, S.D.F. Salmond and R.G. MacMullen. *A Select Library of the Nicene and Post-Nicene Fathers of the Christian Church.* Ed. Philip Schaff. New York, 1888.

─────. *Seventeen Short Treatises.* Trans. Members of the English Church. *A Library of Fathers of the Holy Catholic Church Anterior to the Division of the East and West.* Oxford, 1847.

─────. *Treatises on Marriage and Other Subjects.* Ed. Roy. J. Deferrari. *The Fathers of the Church.* New York, 1955.

Ballesteros Gaibrois, Manuel. *Isabel de Castilla: Reina Católica de España*. Madrid, 1964.
Beichner, Paul F. "The Allegorical Interpretation of Medieval Literature." *Publications of the Modern Language Association*, 82 (March, 1967), pp. 33-38.
Beltrán de Heredia, Vicente. *Bolario de la Universidad de Salamanca (1219-1549)*. 3 vols. Salamanca, 1967.
Berceo, Gonzalo de. *Milagros de Nuestra Señora*. Ed. Antonio G. Solalinde. Madrid: Clásicos Castellanos, 1964.
Bergson, Henri. *Le Rire: Essai sur la significance du comique*. Paris, 1938.
St. Bernard. *Sermons for the Seasons and Principal Festivals of the Year*. Trans. a priest of Mount Melleray. 2 vols. Dublin, 1923.
———. *On the Song of Songs*. Trans. by a religious of C.S.M.V. London, 1952.
Blüher, Karl Alfred. *Seneca in Spanien: Untersuchungen zur Geschichte der Seneca-Rezeption in Spanien vom 13 bis 17 Jahrhundert*. München, 1969.
Bowers, Fredson. "Textual Criticism." *The Aims and Methods of Scholarship in Modern Languages and Literature*. Ed. James Thorpe. New York: Modern Language Association, 1963.
Briffault, Robert. *The Troubadours*. Trans. Lawrence F. Koons. Bloomington, Indiana. 1965.
Brown, Carleton. "Mulier est Hominis Confusio." *Modern Language Notes*, 35 (December, 1920), pp. 479-482.
*Butler's Lives of the Saints*. Ed. Herbert Thurston and Donald Attwater. 4 vols. New York, 1956.
Camões, Luis de. *Os Lusíadas*. Ed. Emanuel Paulo Ramos. Lisbon: Porto Editora, n.d.
Caplan, Harry. *Medieval Artes praedicandi: A Hand-list*. Ithaca, 1934.
Castro, Adolfo de. *Obras escogidas de filósofos. Biblioteca de Autores Españoles*, 65, Madrid, 1873.
Castro, Américo. *La realidad histórica de España*. México, 1954.
Charland. Th.-M. *Artes Praedicandi: Contribution a l'Histoire de la Rhétorique au Moyen Age*. Paris-Ottawa: Publications de l'Institut d'Études Médiévales d'Ottawa, 1936.
Chaytor, H. J. *From Script to Print: An Introduction to Medieval Vernacular Literature*. New York, 1967.
Cicero. *De Oratore: Together with De Fato, Paradoxa Stoicorum, De Partitione Oratoria*. Trans. H. Rackham. 2 vols. Cambridge, Massachusetts: Loeb Classical Library, 1960.
Cirac de Estopiñán, Esteban. *Los procesos de hechicerías en la Inquisición de Castilla la Nueva: Tribunales de Toledo y Cuenca*. Madrid, 1942.
Cohn, Norman. *The Pursuit of the Millenium: Revolutionary Millenarians and Mystical Anarchists of the Middle Ages*. rev. ed. New York, 1970.
Comparetti, Domenico. *Vergil in the Middle Ages*. Trans. E.F.M. Benecke. Hamden, Connecticut: Archon Books, 1966.
Conway, Daniel Moncure. *Solomon and Solomonic Literature*. Chicago, 1899.

Córdoba, Fray Martín de. *Ars praedicandi* ("Ars Praedicandi de Fray Martín de Córdoba"). Ed. Fernando Rubio Álvarez. *La Ciudad de Dios,* 172 (1959), pp. 329-348.

———.Compendio de la fortuna. Ed. Fernando Rubio Álvarez. Madrid, 1958.

———: *Jardín de nobles donzellas.* Ed. Felix García. Madrid: Joyas Bibliográficas, 1953.

———. *Jardín de nobles doncellas.* Ed. Félix García. Madrid: Clásicos Agustinos, 1956.

———. *Un tratado del siglo XV sobre la predestinación, en castellano debido al V.P. Fray Martín Alfonso de Córdoba agustiniano.* Ed. Aníbal Sánchez Fraile. Salamanca, 1956.

*Crónica de D. Álvaro de Luna.* Ed. Josef Miguel de Flores. Madrid, 1784.

*Cruden's Complete Concordance to the Old and New Testaments.* Ed. A.D. Adams, C.H. Irwin, and S.A. Waters. New York, 1949.

Curtius, Ernst Robert. *European Literature and the Latin Middle Ages.* Trans. Willard R. Trask. 1953; rpt. New York: Harper Torchbook, 1963.

Curtius, Quintus. Trans. John C. Rolfe. 2 vols. London: Loeb Classical Library, 1956.

Del Pulgar, Hernando. *Crónica de los señores Reyes Católicos Don Fernando & Doña Isabel de Castilla y de Aragón escrita por su cronista Hernando del Pulgar cotejada con antiguos manuscritos y aumentada de varias ilustraciones y enmiendas.* Ed. Josef Miguel de Flores. Madrid, 1784.

———. *Crónica de los señores Reyes Católicos Don Fernando & Doña Isabel. Biblioteca de Autores Españoles 77 (Crónicas de los reyes de Castilla desde Alfonso el Sabio hasta los Católicos Don Fernando y Doña Isabel).* Madrid, 1953.

*Dictionnaire d'Archéologie Chrétienne et de Liturgie.* Ed. Fernand Cabrol and Henri Leclerq. Paris, 1924.

Enríquez del Castillo, Diego. *Crónica del Rey D. Enrique el Quarto de este nombre por su capellán y cronista Diego Enríquez del Castillo.* Ed. Josef Miguel de Flores. Madrid, 1787.

Evans, E.P. *Animal Symbolism in Ecclesiastical Architecture.* 1896; rpt. Detroit: Gale Research Corporation, 1969.

Fraker, Charles. *Studies on the "Cancionero de Baena."* Chapel Hill, 1966.

Gaer, Joseph. *The Lore of the Old Testament.* New York, 1951.

Gallardo, Bartolomé José. *Ensayo de una biblioteca española de libros raros y curiosos.* 3 vols. Madrid, 1866.

Gaster, Theodor. *Myth, Legend and Custom in the Old Testament.* New York, 1969.

Gilbert, Allan H. *Machiavelli's "Prince" and its Forerunners: The Prince as a Typical Book de Regimie Principum.* Durham, 1938.

Ginzberg, Louis. *The Legends of the Jews.* 6 vols. Philadelphia, 1909-1925.

González de la Calle, Pedro Urbano. *Quevedo y los dos Sénecas.* México, 1965.

Green, Otis Howard. *Spain and the Western Tradition: The Castilian Mind in Literature from "El Cid" to Calderón.* 4. vols. Madison, Wisconsin, 1968.

Sancti Gregorii Papei cognomento Magna. *Opera Omnia. Patrologiae Latinae Cursus Completus.* LXXVI. Ed. J.-P. Migne. Paris, 1865.

Sancti Gregorii Papei cognomento Magna. *The Dialogues of St. Gregory the Great.* Trans. Henry James Coleridge. London, 1874.
Grunebaum, Gustave E. Von. *Medieval Islam: A Study in Cultural Orientation.* 1964; rpt. Chicago: Phoenix Press, 1962.
Guilelmi Alverni, Epsicopi Parisiensis. *Opera Omnia.* 2 vols. Paris: ex Typographiae F. Hotot el vaneums, 1674.
Haebler, Konrad. *Bibliografía ibérica del siglo XV.* The Hague, 1917.
--------. *The Early Printers of Spain and Portugal.* London, 1897.
Hafter, Monroe. *Gracián and Perfection: Spanish Moralists of the Seventeenth Century.* Cambridge, Massachusetts, 1966.
Hagendahl, Harald. *Latin Fathers and the Classics: A Study on the Apologists, Jerome and Other Christian Writers.* Göteborg, 1958.
Harris, James Rendel. *The Odes and Psalms of Solomon: Now first published from the Syriac version.* Cambridge, 1909.
Hays, H.R. *The Dangerous Sex: The Myth of Feminine Evil.* London, 1966.
Herrera, Tomás de. *Historia del convento de San Agustín de Salamanca.* Madrid, 1652.
Hentsch, Alice Adèle. *De la littérature didactique du Moyen Âge s'adressant spécialement aux femmes.* Diss. Halle, 1903.
Hoffman-Krayer, E., and H. Bächtold-Staubli. *Handwörterbuch des Deutschen Aberglaubens.* 10 vols. Berlin-Leipzig, 1927-Berlin, 1942.
Horace. *The Satires and Epistles of Horace.* Trans. Smith Palmer Bovie. Chicago, 1959.
Huizinga, Jan. *The Waning of the Middle Ages.* 1949; rpt. New York: Doubleday Anchor, 1954.
St. Isidore of Sevilla. *Etimologías.* Trans. Luis Cortés y Góngora. Madrid: Biblioteca de Autores Cristianos, 1951.
Jacob, Alfred. "The *Razón de amor* as Christian Symbolism." *Hispanic Review,* XX (1952), 282-301.
St. Jerome. *The Principal Works of St. Jerome.* Trans. W.H. Fremantle, G. Lewis, and W.G. Martley. *A Select Library of the Nicene and Post-Nicene Fathers of the Christian Church.* 2nd. Series. New York, 1893.
--------. *Opera Omnia. Patrologiae Latinae Cursus Completus.* Ed. J.-P. Migne. Paris, 1854-1890.
Keller, John Esten. "El libro de los exemplos por a.b.c." *Hispania,* XL (1957), 179-186.
--------. *Motif-Index of Medieval Spanish Exempla.* Knoxville, Tennessee, 1949.
Kelso, Ruth. *Doctrine for the Lady of the Renaissance.* Urbana, Illinois, 1956.
Kerr, Walter. *Tragedy and Comedy.* New York, 1967.
Kinkade, Richard P. *Los "Lucidarios" españoles.* Madrid: Editorial Gredos, 1968.
Knust, Hermann. *Mittheilungen aus dem Eskurial.* Tübingen, 1879.
Lea, Henry Charles. *The History of Sacerdotal Celibacy in the Christian Church.* New York, 1957.
Legman, Gerson. *Rationale of the Dirty Joke: An Analysis of Sexual Humor.* New York, 1968.
Lenfant, David. *Concordantiae Augustinianae.* Paris, 1666; rpt.; Brussels, 1965.

*El libro de los engaños y assayamientos*. Ed. John Esten Keller. Chapel Hill, 1959.
Lida de Malkiel, María Rosa. "Tres notas sobre don Juan Manuel." *Romance Philology*, IV (1950-51), 155-194.
Lovejoy, Arthur O. *The Great Chain of Being: A Study of the History of an Idea*. 1936; rpt. New York: Harper Torchbook, 1960.
Lubac, Henri du. *Exégèse Médiévale: Les Quatre Sens de l'Ecriture*. Paris, 1959.
Lucena, Luis de. *Repetición de amores*. Ed. Jacob Ornstein. Chapel Hill, 1954.
MacDonald, Donald. "Proverbs, *Sententiae* and *Exempla* in Chaucer's Comic Tales: The Function of Comic Misapplication." *Speculum*, XLI (1966), 455-460.
Manuel, D. Juan. *El libro de Patronio e por otro nombre, El Conde Lucanor*. Buenos Aires: Colección Austral, 1964.
Martínez-Kleiser, Luis *Refranero general ideológico español*. Madrid, 1953.
Martínez de Toledo, Alfonso. *Arcipreste de Talavera: Corvacho o reprobación del amor mundano*. Ed. Joaquín González Muela. Madrid, 1972.
Matulka, Barbara. *An Anti-feminist Treatise of XVth-century Spain: La repetición de amores*. New York: Institute of French Studies. *Comparative Literature Series*, 1931 (off-print).
Mena, Juan de Mena. *El laberinto de Fortuna o las trescientas*. Ed. José Manuel Blecua. Madrid: Clásicos Castellanos, 1960.
Méndez, Francisco. *Tipografía española*. Madrid, 1861.
Menéndez y Pelayo, Marcelino. *Antología de poetas líricos castellanos*. 4 vols. Santander, 1944.
St. Methodius. *The Writings of Methodius, Alexander of Lycopolis, Peter of Alexandria and several fragments. Ante-Nicene Christian Library: Translations of the Writings of the Fathers Down to A.D. 325*. Ed. Alexander Roberts and James Donaldson. Edinburgh, 1880.
Metzger, Bruce M. *An Introduction to the Apocrypha*. New York, 1963.
Mexía, Hernán. *Libro intitulado nobiliario perfetamente copylado y ordenado por el onrrado cauallero Ferrante Mexía veynte quatro de Jahen &c*. Biblioteca apostólica vaticana St. Bar BB BBB IV 22.
Moore, George Fort. *Judaism in the First Centuries of the Christian Era: The Are of the Tannaim*. 2 vols. Cambridge, Massachusetts, 1966.
Morales, Ambrosio de. *Viage de Ambrosio de Morales por orden del Rey Phelip II: A los Reynos de León y Galicia y Principado de Asturias*. Ed. Enrique Flórez. Madrid: Antonio Marín, 1765.
*The New English Bible with the Apocrypha*. Oxford, 1970.
Orchard, Bernard, Sutcliffe, Edmund, Fuller, Reginald and Russell, Ralph, eds. *A Catholic Commentary on Holy Scripture*. New York, 1953.
Ornstein, Jacob. "La misoginía y el profemenismo en la literatura castellana." *Revista de Filología Hispánica*, III (1941), 219-232.
Oñate, María del Pilar. *El feminismo en la literatura española*. Madrid, 1938.
Orozco, Alonso de. *Vergel de oración*. Ed. Fr. Tomás. Salamanca, 1895.
*Orto do Esposo: texto inédito do fim do século XIV ou começo do XV*. 3 vols. Ed. Bertil Maler. Vols. I and II, Río de Janeiro, 1956. Vol. III, Stockholm, 1964.

Ovid. *The Art of Love and Other Poems*. Trans. J.H. Mozley. Cambridge, Massachusetts: Loeb Classical Library, 1962.
———. *The Metamorphoses*. Trans. Horace Gregory. New York, 1958.
Palau y Dulcet, Antonio. *Manual del librero hispano-americano*. 7 vols. Barcelona, 1951.
Pamphilo, Joseph. *Chronica Ordinis fratrum eremitarum Sancti Augustini*. Romae: ex typographiae Georgii Ferrarii, 1581.
Paris, Gaston. "Le cycle de la gageure." *Romania*, XXXII (1903), 481-551.
Patai, Rafael. *The Hebrew Goddess*. New York, 1967.
Paz y Melia, Antonio. *El cronista Alonso de Palencia: Su vida y sus obras; sus "Décadas" y las "Crónicas" contemporáneas*. Madrid, 1914.
Pedro Alfonso. *Disciplina Clericalis*. Ed. Ángel González Palencia. Madrid, 1948.
Penzer, Norman. *Poison-Damsels and other essays in Folklore and Anthropology*. London, 1952.
Pérez de Guzmán, Fernán. *Generaciones y semblanzas*. Ed. J. Domínguez Bordona. Madrid: Clásicos Castellanos, 1924.
*Physiologus Latinus*. Ed. Francis Carmody. Paris, 1939.
Plato. *The Republic*. Trans. Benjamin Jowett. New York: Modern Library, n.d.
Plutarch. *Plutarch's Lives: The Translation called Dryden's*. Ed. A.H. Clough. 5 vols. Philadelphia, n.d.
Possevini, Antonio. *Apparatus sacer ad Scriptores veteris & noui Testamenti*. Venetis: apud Societatem Venetam, 1606.
Power, Eileen. *Medieval People*. 1924: rpt. New York: University Paperbacks, 1966.
Prescott, William H. *History of the Reign of Ferdinand and Isabela the Catholic*. 3 vols. Philadelphia, 1883.
Proctor, Robert. *An Index to the Early Printed Books in the British Museum from the Invention of Printing to the Year 1500 with Notes of those in the Bodleian Library*. London, 1960.
Quasten, Johannes. *Patrology: The Ante-Nicene Literature after Irenaeus*. Utrecht, 1953.
Réau, Louis. *Iconographie de la Bible I Ancien Testament*. Vol. II of *Iconographie de l'Art Chrétien*. 4 vols. Paris, 1956.
———. *Iconographie de la Bible II, Nouveau Testament*. Vol. III of *Iconographie de l'Art Chrétien*. 4 vols. Paris, 1957.
Reichenberger, Arnold G. "Boscán and the Classics." *Comparative Literature*, III, 1951, 97-101.
———. "The Uniqueness of the Comedia." *Hispanic Review*, XXVII (1959), 303-316.
Reik, Theodore. *The Creation of Woman: A Psychoanalytic Inquiry into the Myth of Eve*. New York, 1960.
———. *Curiosities of the Self*. New York, 1965.
Rojas, Fernando de. *La Celestina*. Ed. Julio Cejador y Frauca. 2 vols. Madrid: Clásicos Castellanos, 1966.
Romano, Egidio. *Glosa castellana al "Regimiento de Príncipes" de Egidio Romano por Juan García Castrogeriz*. Ed. Juan Beneyto Pérez. 3 vols. Madrid, 1947.

Rubio Álvarez, Fernando. "Desfavorable concepto moral de la mujer en algunas obras de origen oriental." *La Ciudad de Dios*, CLXXVII (1964), 267-287.

———. Ed. *Prosistas castellanos del siglo XV*. Biblioteca de Autores Españoles 171. Madrid, 1964.

Ruiz, Juan. *El libro de buen amor*. Ed. Julio Cejador y Frauca. 2 vols. Madrid: Clásicos Castellanos, 1963.

Salvatorelli, Luigi. *A Concise History of Italy: From Prehistoric Times to Our Own Day*. Trans. Bernard Miall. New York, 1940.

Sancha, Justo de. Ed. *Romancero y cancionero sagrados: Colección de poesías cristianas, morales y divinas*. Biblioteca de Autores Españoles 35. Madrid, 1855.

Sánchez Vercial, Clemente. *El libro de los ejemplos a.b.c.* Ed. John Esten Keller. Chapel Hill, 1961.

Santiago Vela, Gregorio. *Ensayo de una biblioteca iberoamericana de la Orden de San Agustín*. 8 vols. Madrid, 1913-1931.

———. "Notas de Interés." *Archivo histórico hispano-Augustiniano y Boletín oficial del Smo. nombre de Jesús de Filipinas*, XX (1923), 54-65.

Schott, Andreas. *Hispaniae Bibliotheca seu de Academiis ac Bibliothecis Item Elogia et Nomenclator clarorum Hispaniae Scriptorum Qui Latine disciplinas omnes illustrarunt: Philologiae, Philosophiae, Medecinae, Iurisprudentiae, ac Theologiae*. Frankfort, 1608.

Sears, Helen L. "The *Rimado de Palacio* and the 'De Regimine Principum' Tradition of the Middle Ages," *HR* XX (January, 1952).

Seneca, Lucius Annaeus. *Obras Completas*. Trans. Lorenzo Riber. Madrid, 1966.

———. *L. Annaei Senecae, pars prima sive Opera Philosophica quibus Notitiam Literariam Bipontina Auctorem*. Ed. N. Bouillet. 5 vols. Paris, 1832.

———. *Opera quae extant*. Ed. Justius Lipsius. 2 vols. Amsterdam, 1672.

———. *Seneca's Tragedies*. Trans. Frank Justus Miller. 2 vols. London: Loeb Classical Library, 1927.

Schiff, Mario. *La Bibliothèque du Marquis du Santillane*. Bibliothèque de l'Ecole des Hautes Etudes 153. Paris, 1905.

Siciliano, Italiano. *François Villonet les Thèmes Poétiques du Moyen Age*, Paris, 1933.

Simón Díaz, José. *Impresos del XVI: Religión*. Madrid, 1964.

Smalley, Beryl. *The Study of the Bible in the Middle Ages*, Oxford, 1952.

Solini, C. Iulii. *Collectanae Rerum Memorabilium*. Ed. Th. Mommsen. Berlin, 1864.

———. *The Excellent and Pleasant Worke, Collectanea Rerum Memorabilium*. Trans. Arthur Golding, 1587. Ed. in facsimile by George Kish. Gainesville, Florida, 1955.

Smith, William, ed. *A Dictionary of Greek and Roman Biography and Mythology*. 3 vols. London, 1873.

Smith, Vicent A. *The Oxford History of India: From the Earliest Times to the End of 1911*. Oxford, 1923.

Suárez Fernández, Luis, Ángel Canellas López, and Vives, Jaime Vicens. *Los Trastámaras de Castilla y Aragón en el siglo XV*. Vol. XV of *Historia de España*. Ed. Ramón Menéndez Pidal. Madrid, 1964.

*The Babylonian Talmud: Seder Zera'im.* Trans. I. Epstein. London: Socino Press, 1948.

Tate, R.B. "An apology for Monarchy: A Study of an Unpublished 15th-century Castilian Historical Pamphlet." *Romance Philology*, XV (1961-62), 111-123.

Terence. *Plays of Terence.* Trans. John Sargeaunt. 2 vols. London: Loeb Classical Library, 1912.

Thaün, Philippe de. *Le Bestiare de Philippe de Thaün.* Ed. Emmanuel Walberg. Paris, 1900.

Thomas, Henry. *Short-Title Catalogue of Spanish and Spanish American Books Printed before 1601 in the British Museum.* London, 1966.

Thompson, Stith. *Motif-Index of Folklore Literature.* 6 vols. Bloomington, Indiana, 1955-1958.

Trachtenberg, Joshua. *Jewish Magic and Superstition.* New York, 1939.

Valdés, Alfonso de. *Diálogo de Mercurio y Carón.* Ed. José F. Montesinos. Madrid: Clásicos Castellanos, 1965.

Valera, Mosén Diego de. *Epístolas y otros tratados enbiadas en diversos tiempos e a diversas personas.* Ed. José Antonio de Balenchana. Madrid: Sociedad de Bibliófilos Españoles, 1878.

——. *Memorial de diversas hazañas. Biblioteca de Autores Españoles* 70. (*Crónica de los reyes de Castilla*). Madrid, 1953.

Valerii Maximi. *Factorum et Dictorum Memorabilium Libri Novem cum Iulii Paridis et Ianvarii Nepotiani Epitomis.* Ed. Carolus Kempf. Leipzig, 1888.

Villena, Enrique de. *Arte Cisoria.* Ed. Felipe-Benicio Navarro. Madrid, 1879.

Vilnay, Zev. *Legends of Palestine.* Philadelphia, 1932.

Walsh, William Thomas. *Isabella of Spain: The Last Crusader.* New York, 1930.

Welter, J.-Th. *L'Exemplum dans la litterature réligieuse et didactique du Moyen Age.* Paris, 1927.

Wensinck, A.J. *A Handbook of Early Muhammadan Tradition.* Leiden, 1960.

White, T.H. *The Bestiary: A Book of Beasts.* 1954; rpt. New York: Capricorn Books, 1960.

Wiesen, David S. *St. Jerome as Satirist: A Study in Christian Latin Thought and Letters.* Ithaca, 1964.

Wilkinson, L.P. *Ovid Surveyed.* Cambridge, 1962.

Williams, Charles. *Witchcraft.* 1941; rpt. New York: Meridian Books, 1959.

# INDEX OF PROPER NAMES

Abraham, buried at Hebron, 159, 159, n. 4; marriage of compared to St. John's continence, 185; sacrifice of Isaac, 257

Adam, age at Creation, 168; beasts lost fear of, 216; buried at Hebron, 159; Christ is second, 143; created from less noble material, 150; Eden, created outside of, 158; name of, meaning of, 158; not Eve's father, 174; sleep of, sign of God's power, 147; sleep of compared to crucifixion, 148; sons of, married sisters, 176; valley of tears, wept in, 159, n. 7

Agatha, St., 280

*Alabanza de la virginidad,* 56

Alexander, advised by Aristotle, 96, 229; encounter with Amazons 249

Alfonso XII, affection for Fray Martín, 37; Ávila, mock crowning at, 140, n. 18; clemency of, 141; *conversos,* tolerance of, 37; death of, 136; *judaizantes,* denied privileges, 39; orthodoxy of, 39; Olmedo, led troops at, 37

Álvaro de Luna, don, author of *Libro de las claras e virtuossas mugeres,* 150, n. 1; attacked by Marqués de Santillana, 101; beheaded, 27; *Compendio de la fortuna,* dedicated to, 34; fall of mighty, exemplar of, 34; Fray Martín, relationship with, 35, 39; poisoner, possible, of Isabel of Portugal, 40; power of, 34, 34, n. 48, 50, 101; praised by Juan de Mena; Valera, Mosén Diego de, enmity with, 104

Amazons, examples of womanly strength, 249

Ambrose, St., as a source, 76, 78; cited directly, 154, 251, 258, 263

Anna, widow to be honored, 260

Anselm, St., as source, 72, 77, 78; cited directly, 147

Antolínez, Padre, praise of Fray Martín at Salamanca, 26

Apius Claudius, seducer of Virgineo's daughter, 256

Apollonia, St., loss of teeth preferable to dishonor, 269

Arachne, invented spinning and weaving, 243

Aristotle, Arabs, source of knowledge of, 81; betrayed by a woman, 81, 154, n. 18; fables, advised use of, 94; Fray Martín, wrote works about, 25, 62; major source, 81-82; cited but source is probably pseudo-Aristotle, 229; *Politics, Ethics,* roots of medieval political thought, 99; rhetorical exaggeration, described by, 92; stereotype of, 72, 81; cited directly, 137, 187, 188, 193, 221, 225, 228, 236, 250, 271, 273

*Ars praedicandi,* ed. of, 52, 60-61, style of, 89; image in, 208

Artemisa, widow of Mausolus, king of Caria, 261

Athens, naming of, 243

Augustin, St., baptized late, 204; Cicero, rejection of, by Augustin, 206, 207, n. 10; Monica, St., mother of, good works of, 205; Monica, peacemaker, 229, 230; major source, 76-77; used as classical encyclopedia, 76, Varro, cited from, 76, 241; cited directly, 145, 148, 155, 166, 171, 177, 182, 183, 184, 185, 186, 206, 225, 242, 257
Augustus Caesar, no special privilege for heirs, 200
Ávila, mock dethronement at, 140, n. 18

Babel, tower of, 245, n. 1
Barrientos, Fray Lope de, adversary of Fray Martín, 39, n. 67, supervision of education of royal children, 39-40
Beltrán de la Cueva (Conde de Ledesma), putative father of Juana la Beltraneja, 42; corrupter of Alfonso XII, 42; contests in blasphemy, organized by 107; excessive power given to, 104
Belus, first king after Flood, 245; invented war, 246, idolatry, object of, 246
Benedictines, last known possessors of Mss. of Fray Martín, 52-53
Berceo, Gonzalo, garden allegory in, 65
Bergson, humor, inversion of values, exaggeration, unawareness, 121
Bernard, St., cited, 281
Bezaleel, ruler selected for wisdom, 139, n. 16
Brigid, St., loss of eye made her undesirable, 259
Burgos, Juan de, printer of *Jardín,* 12, 68, 288

*Caballero Çifar,* similarity with, 90
Camões, Luis, advice to ruler, 99
Cariatarbe, city of four, 159, n. 4; name of Hebron, 159
Carmentis (Nicostrates) brought Latin letters to Italy, 241
Carrillo, Alfonso de (Archbishop of Toledo), burned in effigy, 43; crown, offered to Isabel, 43; Toros de Guisando, at, 42; uncle of Juan Pacheco, 42
Cartagena, founded by Dido, 261
Catalina, St., learned woman, 110, 280
Cecilia, St., daughter of king, 233, 269-270; station, dressed according to, 233; praises sung, 280
Chacón, Gonçalo de, tutor of Alfonso, 39
Cicero, Augustin rejects, 206-207; advice to princes, 98; advises four rhetorical divisions, 90; cited directly 228, 232
Cigales & Cabezón, meeting at, 42
*Claustrales,* conflict with *Observantes* in Augustinian Order, 20; in Franciscan Order, 24
*Comentarios y cuestiones sobre las Epístolas de San Pablo,* mentioned by Ambrosio de Morales in *Viage,* 21; written in Toulouse, 1461, 21; described, 55
*Comentarios sobre el Apocalipsis de San Juan,* 54
*Compendio de la fortuna,* ed. 21; France mentioned in, 21; described, 57-58; written before 1453; dedicated to D. Álvaro de Luna, 34
Córdoba, Fray Antonio de, dispute with Fray Martín, 27; Provincial, 1469, 27;
Córdoba, Fray Martín de, Alfonso, devotion to, 37-38; appointments, chronology of, 27; *bachiller,* 20, n. 9; Badajoz, bishopric, refused, 30, 31, 32; birth, place and date, 19; Chronicles, not mentioned in, 31-32;

300    JARDÍN DE NOBLES DONZELLAS

confusion with Alonso de Córdoba, 18, 29; court, importance at, 30, 51; death, date and place, 28; dedication of *Compendio* and *Jardín*, 17, discussed, 47-51; friendship with Isabel of Portugal, 41; García de Castrogeriz, parallel sentiments in; high posts, refused, 30; Salamanca, Vicar at, 22; Salamanca, first mentioned at, 18; Salamanca, held chair at, 25-28; self image as teacher, 28, 147, 179-180; *senequista*, 80; sources, misuse of, 80, 82; Toulouse, 20-21; works not in Isabel's library, 44-46; works, copies of in Valladolid, 28, 52-53; Valladolid, first there, 24; Valladolid, Vicar General, 28; Zaragoza, *Lector* at, 19
Cornelia, equal or better than Gracchus, 286

David, deceived by a woman, 154, n. 18; responsible to God alone, 214
Délbora, Cain's wife, 177, invented spinning 177
Dido, noble widow, 84, used coffers of sand, 110; 261-62

Egidio Romano (Egidio Colonna), advice to Pedro *el Cruel*, 88, 100
Elias, fasted forty days, 179; received by Widow of Sarepta, 263
Enrique IV, Ávila, mock dethronement at, 140 n. 18; befriended those who deny life after death, 107; died without naming successor, 113; discord, caused by awarding of honors, 109; effeminacy of, 39 n. 64; faith, threat to, 38; marriage of Isabel to Alfonso V of Portugal, failed, 112-13; Moors, negligent in pursuit of, 51, 140; praised by Sánchez de Arévalo, 111; recognized Isabel's claim, 43; repudiated Isabel, supported Juana, 112; witchcraft of, 38 n. 62
Erythrae, sibyl of, wrote poetry about coming of Christ, 241
*Espejo de verdadera nobleza*, compared to *Jardín*, 102-104
Espinosa, Juan de, second printer of Jardín, 12-13
Esther, advocate of people, 201
Eve, age of at creation, 169, cause of expulsion, 117
    created, from rib, 144; to be companion, not servant, 148; from more noble material, 150, 106 n. 21; in Paradise, 158; why from Adam, 147 not daughter of Adam, 175; weapon of devil, 155
Exameron (Hexameron), 54, triple structure of, 165 n. 1

Fernando, infidelities of, 113; Isabel to kiss hand of, 112; signed *Capitulaciones*, 112
Flores, Juan de, 97

Galíndez, Beatrix, Latin tutor of Isabel, 140
García de Castrogeriz, Juan, 88, 100
Gilgamesh, evil of women in, 117
Giovanna, queen of Naples, 285
Girón, Pedro de, death of, 113
Goliath, deceived by women, 154 n. 18; lived in Hebron, 159
Granada, reconquest of, advocated, 101; 140; 140 n. 18
Gregory, St., cited 219; 255
Guillelmi Alvernis, 152; 284

Hasdrubal, widow of, 261
Hebron, 158
*Hercules Furens*, 80; 216

INDEX OF PROPER NAMES   301

Hispanic Society of America, 68, 69
Horace, stereotype of, 72; cited, 281
Hypsicratea, wife of Mithridates, 266

Inés (Agnes), St., compared to Pythagorean Virgin, 251-252; constancy of, 211, 280
Isabel de Castilla, birth of, 135 n. 2; at court in 1462, 41; hasty crowning of, 112; jealousy of Fernando, 113; intellectual life of, 140; library of, 44-46; marriage of, 105; successor of Enrique, 43; strength of, 113; throne, refusal of, 37, 43;
Isabel de Portugal, Fray Martín, relationship with, 32; instability of, 39; exemplar of piety, 40; depression of, 40, 182
Iseo (Io), inventor of writing, 240
Isidore, St., etymologies from, 77, 77 n. 18; used but not cited by Alfonso el Sabio, 77 n. 20; source of natural science, 77-78

Jani, the shoemaker, story of, 21
*Jardín de nobles donzellas,* compared with *Espejo de verdadera nobleza,* 102-104; eds. modern, 11-12; 1500 ed., 63; 1542 ed. 63; 1500 ed., acquired by Hispanic Society, 68-69; mentioned by Diego de Montanches, 64; *regimiento de príncipes,* 98
Jephthah, sacrifice of daughter, 275
Jerome, St., as source, 73, 77; cited directly, 197; 208; 263; 270; 283; 284; 285; 286
Jesus, contrasted to painted woman, 284; crucified is rat-trap for Lucifer, 155; left or right side pierced, 149; fasted forty days, 179; matrimony justified by, 270; second Adam, 143
Job, wife of, 281
John, St., continence of compared to marriage of Abraham, 185
Jovinianus, heresy of, 270
Juana de Castilla, *La Beltraneja,* not called, until reign of Isabel, 42; nose broken at birth, 108; marriage to Alfonso V of Portugal, 113; supporters of, burned Alfonso de Carrillo in effigy, 43
Juana de Portugal, sexual misbehavior of, reacted against in *Jardín,* 116-117; Isabel in her care, 41-42
Juan II, advised to be strong king, 104-105; intellectual pursuits of, 110-111; studies to be restored at Convent of Salamanca, 23
Jubal, 243
Judith, book of, canonicity, 247; foreshadow of Virgin Mary, 247; Holofernes and, 248-249
Julia, Caesar's daughter, Pompey's wife, 265

Lacedemon, women of, 267
Lando, Pero Manuel de, tutor of Enrique IV, 35
Lazarus, comforted while rich man is afflicted, 227
*Libro de las claras e virtuosas mugeres,* in Isabel's library, 45; source of tales, 83; structure of, 93
*Libro de diversas historias,* 59
*Libro de los engaños,* 96, 109 n. 29
Livia, gave good advice, 201
Livy, possible incorrect attribution to, 80, cited 201

*Lógica y Filosofía,* 55-56
Lucena, Luis de, 96
Lucia, St., 184
Lucifer, presumption of, 145
Lucretia, chastity of made her equal to Brutus 286, suicide of, justified, 257-58
*Os Lusíadas,* advice to princes, 139

Marc Antony, unjust awarding of honors, 237
Marcella, unwilling to remarry, 262
Marcia, daughter of Cato, suicide of, 262
Martínez de Toledo, Alfonso, fauts of women, 109, 115; humors, bodily, 250
Mary Magdalene, learned at feet of Jesus, 204, Christ appeared to, 164
Mausolus, tomb of, 261
Mencía de Padilla, conspirator, 216
Methodius, St., Alfonso el Sabio knew of second-hand, 78 n. 24; cited, 176, 242; works lost, 176 n. 7
Mexía, Hernán, mentioned *Libro de diversas historias,* 59
Midas, story told in detail, 94; 222; symbol of greed, 72
Minerva, invented numerals, musical instruments, weaving, 243, Athens named for, 243-44
*De mística et vera teología,* 58
Mithridates, no longer common image, 72; wife of, 266
Monica, St., good works of, 205; peacemaker, 209
Montanches, Diego de, early mention of Fray Martín's works, 24-25
Morales, Ambrosio de, described library at Valladolid, 53
Moses, author of Pentateuch, 76, 166

Neptune, jealousy of, caused women to lose suffrage, 244; Nero, exemplar of cruel ruler, 72; 224
Nicholas V, restored learning to convent, 23
Nicostrates (Carmentis, Latin letter to Italy, 241
Nimrod, built tower of Babylon, 245
Ninus, conquered Asia but not India, 241; founded Nineveh, 246, invented idolatry, 246
Noema, inventor of mechanical arts, weaving, spinning, sewing, 242

*Observantes,* conflict with *claustrales,* 20, 24
Olmedo, battle of, Alfonso at, 37
Ovid, cited, 286; christianized, 80; translated widely, 83, as a source, 267 n. 6; stereotyped figure, 72

Pacheco, Juan (Marqués de Villena, royal children in his care, 42
Pandora, box of, womanly menace, 117
Paul, St. cited, 215; 260; 265; 273
Pelagia, St., voluntary drowning of, 256-57
Penelope, exemplar of faithful wife, 72, 83; 266, 267 n. 6
Petrus Alphonsi, considered to be Spanish author, 95
*Physiologus,* 77
Plato, 83, cited, 218

INDEX OF PROPER NAMES 303

Plutarch, not cited, 84
*Poridat de las poridades,* 82, 96, 99
Portia, wife of Brutus, 266; equal to Brutus, 286
Pythagoras, stereotype of, 72
Pythagorean Virgin, compared to St. Inés, 251-252

*Razón de amor,* garden allegory in, 65
Riesco Bravo, Fulgencio, firsr published *Tratado,* 60
Rojas, Fernando de, faults of women, 115
Rome, statutes dealing with women, 275-278
Rosinalda, feminine victim, 95

Samson, betrayed by a woman, 72, 154 n. 18
Sardanapalus, no longer common image, 72; 223
Sánchez de Arévalo, classical sources for added credibility, 78-79; praised Enrique, 111
Semiramis, conquered India, 111; surpassed husband, 246; toilet interrupted to put down rebellion, 247; women not to read of her, 40
Seneca, called "The Philosopher," 73; *Hercules Furens,* 80; medieval citations of difficult attributions, 136-137; 136 n. 6; stereotype of 72; cited (possibly pseudo-Seneca), 136; 144; 196; 199; 216; 227-28; 279
Socrates, antifeminism of, 96
Solinus, Julius, cited, 139
Solomon, betrayed by a woman, 154 n. 18; names of, 281; cited, 146; 203; 207; 211; 212; 279; 280
Sotheris, St., turned face to torturer, 258
Spain, earthly paradise, 220
Spurius Carbilius, divorce of, 276

Tanaquil, surpassed husbands, 286-87
Tatian, heresy of, 270
Terence, as source, 79, 79 n. 26; cited, 211; 277
Tamar, incest of, 177 n. 11
Thecla, St., thrown to beasts, 253
Thomas Aquinas, St., wrote advice to a prince, 99
Toroellas, Pere, source of courtly antifeminist debate, 96
Toros de Guisando, encounter at, 42-43
*Tratado en defensa de virtuossas mugeres,* 74 n. 9
*Tratado de la predestinación,* answer to Fray Lope de Barrientos, 39-40 n. 67; described, 60; linguistic similarity to *Jardín,* 49-50
Tubal Cain, inventor of metal working, 242

Valera, Mosén Diego de, author of the *Tratado en defensa de virtuossas mugeres,* 74; enmity with D. Álvaro de Luna, 104; dedication of *Espejo de verdadera nobleza,* 102;
Valerius Maximus, as source, 84; cited, 156; 256; 265; 275-278
Varro, known from St. Augustin, 76; cited, 241; 243
Virgin, advocate, celestial, 201 daughter of kings, 164, garden, compared to, 163; Paradise, seven reasons for association with, 162; repository of the Word, 247; sight of, changes lust into piety, 156, trees, compared with, 162-63;

Virgineo, slayer of daughter to preserve virginity, 256
Virgin of Antioch, rescued from brothel, 258
Viriplicia (Viriplaca), temple of, 278
Virgins, Vestal, 287

William of Moerbeke, translated *Politica*, 99
William of Paris, cited, 284

Ydida, Solomon's name, 281
Ypocrás, cited 181

# SUBJECT INDEX

Affability to subjects, recommended, 238
Acquired characteristics, inheritance of, 150-51
Advisors, overdependence on, ruler warned against, 104
Allegory, leap of thought, 91; Fray Martín uses garden allegory, 65-67
Angels, not co-eternal with God, 166; not creators, 146, 180; fall of caused creation of man, 172, 172 n. 6; not mentioned by Moses to Jews, 166, 166 n. 6; mentioned in "Song of the Three," 167
*Apio*, sedative, 148
Appetites, for carnal pleasure, 223, for wealth, 221, for honors, 221
Authorities, classical, 73
Authority, delegation of, 104
Astuteness, feminine, 110

Beasts, less warlike than man, 146; lost fear of Adam, 216
Bees, exemplars of discrimination, 208
*Bellum*, etymology of, 246
Bible, *sensus litteralis* and *spiritualis*, 74; texts, application of skewed, 71, 75, 205 n. 4, 227 n. 15
Blasphemy, 107; condemned by Isaiah, 219; anecdote of St. Gregory, 219; laws against, 219
Blood and water, from Christ's side, 148
Bone, makes noise, 156; flexibility of, 155

Calvary, etymology of, 284
*Capitulaciones*, signed by Isabel and Fernando, drafted by Alfonso de Carrillo; 112
Catalogues, medieval, 76
Cause and effect, 153
Cedar, kills toads and snakes, 156; Virgin compared to, 162-63
Celibacy, first enjoined, 119; purpose of, to avoid dual allegiances, 119
Chastity, praise of as response to antifeminist stereotype, 116; political importance of, 116-117; three grades of, 269; used in parable of sower, 75; virginal, most excellent, 269; widows possess second degree, 260; wifely, third degree, 265
Christians, double brotherhood of, 146
Church Fathers, use of as encyclopedia, 76; uneasy over classical erudition, 206-07, 207 n. 10

Church, sources, early ones evaluated by Santiago Vela, 29 n. 37; suffered losses because of plague, 20
Classical authority, 73; used for added credibility, 78-79
Clothes, appropriateness of, 232-33
Coffers, filled with sand, ruse of, 110 n. 32
Colostrum, determine fetal gender by means of, 190
Compassion, in women, the elderly and the young, 198-199
Conception, without sin, 182-183; 182 n. 2
Confession, tongue is broom of mind, 227
Cosmetics, as metaphor, 197; condemned, 232, 283
Cowardice, yellow complexion, sign of, 194
Creation, in three parts: creative, distinguishing, ornamental, 165
Cross, equated with trees of life, 136; weapon against devil, 155
Crucifixion, compared to sleep of Adam, 148
Cypress, Virgin compared to, 162
Cuckold, credulity of, 122

Damsel, poison, 117; Hispanic, 118
Darnel, symbol of discord, 229
Dedications, authors, postures of, 48-50; *captatio benevolentiae*, 49; to Isabel and D. Álvaro de Luna, 30; purposes of, 33; timeliness of, 33; *topoi*, 34, 47
Discord, sowed by women, 108-109
Disputes, marital, 278
Divorce, permitted to Jews to avoid murder, 276; Roman laws of, 276
Dress, appropriate to station, 232-233; elaborate, condemned, 284; elaborate allowed to Roman matrons, 277; not to give false impression of piety, 233, 233 n. 6
Drink, effects of described, 277; not to be given to women, 75, 277
Drowning, victims of, rise face up or face down, 86

Ears, virginal to be protected, 182, n. 2; 186
Earth, virginal substance, 146
Effect, similar to cause, 153
Excesses, restrained by God, 209-10
*Exempla*, comic elements in, 121; condemned in sermons, 119-20; justified, 119
*Exordia*, rules for observed, 92

Fables, recommended by Aristotle, 94
Female offspring, generation of, 187-90
Feminine rule, to be justified, 97, 105-117, 136
Fickleness, womanly, 250
Folkloric sources, not identifiable, 84

Garden, allegory of, 65, 136 n. 5; as collection 65-67
Generosity, feminine, 237
Geography, determiner of gender of offspring, 188
Gestures, moderation of, 232
Gluttony, feminine, 108

God, to be feared, 214; goodness of, 171; shared rule of world with Spanish kings, 220; the teacher, 147 nn. 13-15; 179, 179 n. 6; gives restraints to man, 195

Heresies of Jovinianus and Tatian, condemned, 277
Hermits, temptations of, 118; life of compared to monastic life, 208
Holy Spirit, relationship to Father and Son, didactic use of, 147
Homicide, when justified, 257, 257 n. 9
Homosexuality, of Enrique IV, 39 n. 4; of Beltrán de la Cueva (corruption of Alfonso XII), 42 n. 79
Honors, excessive ambition for cause of strife, 223
Humor, Bergsonian view of, 121; *exempla*, sexual humor in, 121-23
Humors, bodily, 153, 250-251, 250-51 nn. 1-5

Incest, forbidden to encourage ties with outsiders, 173, 173, n. 8; forbidden to preserve family amity and honor, 177, 177 n. 11
Intemperance, feminine, 209-10
Islam, 136 n. 3

Jews, carnal people, not told of angels, 166; divorce, permitted to, 276; Indians, confused with, 262; ruler selected according to wisdom, 139; suttee, practicers of, 262; wars, fight fewer internal, 146
Justice, impartiality of divine, 214; commutative and distributive, 236-37; rulers, suffer more extreme, at hands of God, 107

Kings, father of people more than natural fathers, 200; demigods, 218

*Latreia,* 218
Learning, dispute between Fray Martín and Fray Antonio, 27; Juan II asks for return of, 23; disdain of not part of traditional misogyny, 110; princess must love, 110, restored at Convent of Salamanca, 22-23
Liberality, recommended, 214
Lives, angelic, bestial or human, 273; active, bestial, contemplative, 273
Loquacity, feminine, 124, 156, general condemnation of, 227-228
Lust, concatenation with gluttony, 210

Maidens, advices to, 98; not to be forced to marry, 253
Male/female, ruler and ruled, 138 n. 9
Man, uniquely able to create, 146; more bellicose than beasts, 146; created because of fall of angels, 172; outside of Paradise, 160; descended from one ancestor to promote peace, 145; seeks out own kind, 146, unable to control sexuality, 183, 183 n. 3; 121-122
*Mandragora* (mandrake root), 217
Manichean heresy, 120
Matrimony, bonds of indissoluble, 276; chaste, 234; consanguineous, rules against, 173, 173 n. 8; creation, in Paradise to honor, 161; first sacrament, 120; innocence of in Eden, 120; justified by Jesus' at wedding at Cana, 270; not patrimony, 161
Men, betrayed by women, 154; to rule women, 137
Metaphors, universal, as opposed to *topoi,* 65
Misers, slaves of wealth, 238
Misogyny, serious, 96, 117

Modesty, affected, 47; feminine, 193-97
Monarchy, importance of, 109, 109 n. 31
Monastery, preferred to hermit's existence, 208
Monks, tempted by women, 118
Moors, expulsion of, 101, 140
*Mulier*, etymology of, 153

Nature, God's pupil, 179

Offspring, definition of, 175; resemble parents, 151

Pagan, virgins, not as noble as Christian martyrs, 251-54
*Papaver*, sedative, 77, 148
Parable, of sower, three grades of chastity, 75, 269, 269 n. 1
Paradise, etymology of, 162
Parents, strength of determine gender of offspring, 190
Patriarchs, buried in double cave at Hebron, 159
Peace, achieved by matrimony among adversaries, 173
Phoenix, unique creature, 287
Philosophers, identified specifically, 72-73
Plague, effects of on Church, 19-20
Poison damsel, 118
Power, divine source of, 138
Pregnancy, dangers of, 182; difficulties of 186
Princes, advice to, Biblical precedents, 98; *Jardín* and *Compendio*, 48; peninsular, 100-101; poetic, 101; desirable qualities of, 102
Profeminism, 123
*Pugna*, etymology of, 246

Quarrelsomeness, feminine, 209-10
Queens, advocate, 201; mother, 199; shield, 202; 105

Restraints, God-given, 195
Rhetoric, tripartite division, 90
Rib, choice of, persistence in folklore, 85, 85 n. 46; that she be companion, 148
    curved, twisted, 156; likened to bow, 155; upper, middle or lower, 152; with flesh, 152
Rule, women fit to, 106
Ruler, affability of, 238; head of body politic, 235; extra power brings extra responsibility, 215; wealth for public works, 222

Saints, song of, 280
Satan, pride of, 145
Samson, suicide of, 257
Scripture, as a source, 74-75
Sermon, defined by Fray Martín, 89
Sermons, not to include exempla, 119-20
Servants, mistreatment of, 205-06
Seven, virginal number, 162 n. 17
Sexuality, illicit, woman initiates, 118
Shame, fear of, noble property, 194

Sibyls, Erythraen and Cumaean, 241
Side, Jesus', left or right, 148-49
Slaves, holding of, 139, 193 n. 15
Soul, not from parents, 181; faculties of, 233
Sower, parable of, describes three grades of chastity, 269
Speech, cleanses mind in confession, 227; to be censored, 144; moderation of, 225-226; physical production of, 226-27;
Spinning, invented by Délbora, 177; invented by Arachne, 243
Statutes, Roman, marriage, 275
Suffrage, female, lost, 243-44
Suicide, justified, 257
Suttee, attributed to Jews, 262
Symbolism, relationship with allegory, 91

Tears, valley of, 159
Thieves, crucified with Jesus, 274
Throne, succession to, 106
Time, creation of, 166
Toads, odor of cedar kills, 156
Tongue, biting off of, to avoid speech, 251
Tree, of life, and cross, 136; Virgin compared to 162-63
Turkish bow, 155
Tutle dove, exemplar of faithful widow, 263, 263 n. 18
Tyranny condemned, 103

Unicorn, trapped by virgins, 272

Violation, no sin if against will, 184
Virgin, sought sanctuary at altar, 252
Virginity, first degree of chastity, 250; etymology of, 256
Virgins, five foolish, 195-96; more virtuous than angels, 272; pagan not as virtuous as Christian, 251, Romans honored, 287 wise, 196

War, defined by Isidore, 267; invented by Belus, 246; invented by Minerva, 242 n. 7; more among Chrisitians than among pagans and Jews, 146; marriages prevent, 173
Wasps, exemplars of lack of discrimination, 208
Wealth, nature of, 221-222
Weather, determines gender of offspring, 187
Weaving, invented by Noema, 242; by Minerva, 243
Widow, Dido, example of, 84, 261-262; Hasdrubal's, 261; Marcia, noble, 262; Mausolus' 261; and her mite, 71, 204-05; Sarepta, 263; possessor of second degree of chastity, 269; twenty husbands wed to widower of twenty wives 263; turtle dove symbol of chaste, 263
Wife, Brutus, 266; third degree of chastity, 269; Mithridates' (Hypsicratea), 266; Pompey's, 265; Ulysses', 72, 83, 266, 267
Winds, determine gender of offspring, 189
Wine, use of concatenation with gluttony and lust, 210; not to be given to women, 75, 277
Witchcraft, 217
Wives, Lacedemonian, 267; Roman, 275-278

Woman, bad qualities of, 115; created to reconcile warring kingdoms, 173; creation of, from rib, 85; discord, sower of, 108-09; drink, not to be given, 108; gluttony of, 108; honored by matrimony, 161; hypocrisy of, 109; liar, perjurer, 109; loquacity of, 156; man, why created from, 147; more noble material, why created from, 150; painted, contrasted to Jesus on cross, 284; paradise, created in, 160; place of creation, 158; rib, why formed from, 148; sexuality, initiator of illicit, 118; sexually, insatiable, 108; silence, 156; virtuous, hard to find, 280; weapon, 154

Women, astuteness of, 110; compassion of, 193, 198-99; generation of, wind, place, parents, season, 187-190; feminine faults to be overcome, 251; fickleness of, 209-11, 250; fit to rule, 49-50, 97, 98, 106, 136; intemperance of, 209-10; loquacity of, 124, 156; men, evil of better than good of, 282; modest, drowned, float face clown, 194; modesty of, adorns virginity, 196-97; modesty of, 183, 193; modesty of is God-given restraint, 196; not to be given drink, 277; not to read of Semiramis, 110; piety of, 193; 203-04; quarrelsomeness of, 209-10; sowers of discord, 109, n. 29; suffrage, lost because of anger of Neptune, 243-44; talkativeness of, 209-210; weakness of, 245, 194; worldly achievements, not concerned with, 285

# NORTH CAROLINA STUDIES IN THE ROMANCE LANGUAGES AND LITERATURES

I.S.B.N. Prefix 0-88438

Recent Titles

JACQUES DE LA TAILLE'S. "LA MANIERE," A CRITICAL EDITION, by Pierre Han. 1970. (No. 93). -893-X.
THE MAJOR THEMES OF EXISTENTIALISM IN THE WORK OF JOSÉ ORTEGA Y GASSET, by Janet Winecoff Díaz. 1970. (No. 94). -894-8.
CHARLES NODIER: HIS LIFE AND WORKS, by Sarah Fore Bell. 1971. (No. 95). -895-6.
RACINE AND SENECA, by Ronald W. Tobin. 1971. (No. 96). -896-4.
LOPE DE VEGA "EL PEREGRINO EN SU PATRIA," edición de Myron A. Peyton. 1971. (No. 97). -897-2.
CRITICAL REACTIONS AND THE CHRISTIAN ELEMENT IN THE POETRY OF PIERRE DE RONSARD, by Mark S. Whitney. 1971. (No. 98). -898-0.
THE REV. JOHN BOWLE. THE GENESIS OF CERVANTEAN CRITICISM, by Ralph Merritt Cox. 1971. (No. 99). -899-9.
THE FOUR INTERPOLATED STORIES IN THE "ROMAN COMIQUE": THEIR SOURCES AND UNIFYING FUNCTION, by Frederick Alfred De Armas. 1971. (No. 100). -900-6.
LE CHASTOIEMENT D'UN PERE A SON FILS, A CRITICAL EDITION, edited by Edward D. Montgomery, Jr. 1971. (No. 101). -901-4.
LE ROMMANT DE "GUY DE WARWIK" ET DE "HEROLT D'ARDENNE," edited by D. J. Conlon. 1971. (No. 102). -902-2.
THE OLD PORTUGUESE "VIDA DE SAM BERNARDO," EDITED FROM ALCOBAÇA MANUSCRIPT ccxci/200, WITH INTRODUCTION, LINGUISTIC STUDY, NOTES, TABLE OF PROPER NAMES, AND GLOSSARY, by Lawrence A. Sharpe. 1971. (No. 103). -903-0.
A CRITICAL AND ANNOTATED EDITION OF LOPE DE VEGA'S "LAS ALMENAS DE TORO," by Thomas E. Case. 1971. (No. 104). -904-9.
LOPE DE VEGA'S "LO QUE PASA EN UNA TARDE," A CRITICAL, ANNOTATED EDITION OF THE AUTOGRAPH MANUSCRIPT, by Richard Angelo Picerno. 1971. (No. 105). -905-7.
OBJECTIVE METHODS FOR TESTING AUTHENTICITY AND THE STUDY OF TEN DOUBTFUL "COMEDIAS" ATTRIBUTED TO LOPE DE VEGA, by Fred M. Clark. 1971. (No. 106). -906-5.
THE ITALIAN VERB. A MORPHOLOGICAL STUDY, by Frede Jensen. 1971. (No. 107). -907-3.
A CRITICAL EDITION OF THE OLD PROVENÇAL EPIC "DAUREL ET BETON," WITH NOTES AND PROLEGOMENA, by Arthur S. Kimmel. 1971. (No. 108). -908-1.
FRANCISCO RODRIGUES LOBO: DIALOGUE AND COURTLY LORE IN RENAISSANCE PORTUGAL, by Richard A. Preto-Rodas. 1971. (No. 109). -909-X.
RAIMOND VIDAL: POETRY AND PROSE, edited by W. H. W. Field. 1971. (No. 110). -910-3.
RELIGIOUS ELEMENTS IN THE SECULAR LYRICS OF THE TROUBADOURS, by Raymond Gay-Crosier. 1971. (No. 111). -911-1.
THE SIGNIFICANCE OF DIDEROT'S "ESSAI SUR LE MERITE ET LA VERTU," by Gordon B. Walters. 1971. (No. 112). -912-X.
PROPER NAMES IN THE LYRICS OF THE TROUBADOURS, by Frank M. Chambers. 1971. (No. 113). -913-8.
STUDIES IN HONOR OF MARIO A. PEI, edited by John Fisher and Paul A. Gaeng. 1971. (No. 114). -914-6.
DON MANUEL CAÑETE, CRONISTA LITERARIO DEL ROMANTICISMO Y DEL POSROMANTICISMO EN ESPAÑA, por Donald Allen Randolph. 1972. (No. 115). -915-4.

## Recent Titles

THE TEACHINGS OF SAINT LOUIS. A CRITICAL TEXT, by David O'Connell. 1972. (No. 116). *-916-2*.

HIGHER, HIDDEN ORDER: DESIGN AND MEANING IN THE ODES OF MALHERBE, by David Lee Rubin. 1972. (No. 117). *-917-0*.

JEAN DE LE MOTE "LE PARFAIT DU PAON," édition critique par Richard J. Carey. 1972. (No. 118). *-918-9*.

CAMUS' HELLENIC SOURCES, by Paul Archambault. 1972. (No. 119). *-919-7*.

FROM VULGAR LATIN TO OLD PROVENÇAL, by Frede Jensen. 1972. (No. 120). *-920-0*.

GOLDEN AGE DRAMA IN SPAIN: GENERAL CONSIDERATION AND UNUSUAL FEATURES, by Sturgis E. Leavitt. 1972. (No. 121). *-921-9*.

THE LEGEND OF THE "SIETE INFANTES DE LARA" (*Refundición toledana de la crónica de 1344* versión), study and edition by Thomas A. Lathrop. 1972. (No. 122). *-922-7*.

STRUCTURE AND IDEOLOGY IN BOIARDO'S "ORLANDO INNAMORATO," by Andrea di Tommaso. 1972. (No. 123). *-923-5*.

STUDIES IN HONOR OF ALFRED G. ENGSTROM, edited by Robert T. Cargo and Emanuel J. Mickel, Jr. 1972. (No. 124). *-924-3*.

A CRITICAL EDITION WITH INTRODUCTION AND NOTES OF GIL VICENTE'S "FLORESTA DE ENGANOS," by Constantine Christopher Stathatos. 1972. (No. 125). *-925-1*.

LI ROMANS DE WITASSE LE MOINE. *Roman du treizième siècle.* Édité d'après le manuscrit, fonds français 1553, de la Bibliothèque Nationale, Paris, par Denis Joseph Conlon. 1972. (No. 126). *-926-X*.

EL CRONISTA PEDRO DE ESCAVIAS. *Una vida del Siglo XV*, por Juan Bautista Avalle-Arce. 1972. (No. 127). *-927-8*.

AN EDITION OF THE FIRST ITALIAN TRANSLATION OF THE "CELESTINA," by Kathleen V. Kish. 1973. (No. 128). *-928-6*.

MOLIÈRE MOCKED. THREE CONTEMPORARY HOSTILE COMEDIES: *Zélinde, Le portrait du peintre, Élomire Hypocondre,* by Frederick Wright Vogler. 1973. (No. 129). *-929-4*.

C.-A. SAINTE-BEUVE. *Chateaubriand et son groupe littéraire sous l'empire.* Index alphabétique et analytique établi par Lorin A. Uffenbeck. 1973. (No. 130). *-930-8*.

THE ORIGINS OF THE BAROQUE CONCEPT OF "PEREGRINATIO," by Juergen Hahn. 1973. (No. 131). *-931-6*.

THE "AUTO SACRAMENTAL" AND THE PARABLE IN SPANISH GOLDEN AGE LITERATURE, by Donald Thaddeus Dietz. 1973. (No. 132). *-932-4*.

FRANCISCO DE OSUNA AND THE SPIRIT OF THE LETTER, by Laura Calvert. 1973. (No. 133). *-933-2*.

ITINERARIO DI AMORE: DIALETTICA DI AMORE E MORTE NELLA Vita Nuova, by Margherita De Bonfils Templer. 1973. (No. 134). *-934-0*.

## Symposia

LOS NARRADORES HISPANOAMERICANOS DE HOY, edited by Juan Bautista Avalle-Arce. 1973. (No. 1). *-951-0*.

When ordering please cite the *ISBN Prefix* plus the last four digits for each title.

Send orders to:
International Scholarly Book Service, Inc.
P.O. Box 4347
Portland, Oregon 97208
U.S.A.

The Department of Romance Studies Digital Arts and Collaboration Lab at the University of North Carolina at Chapel Hill is proud to support the digitization of the North Carolina Studies in the Romance Languages and Literatures series.

www.ingramcontent.com/pod-product-compliance
Lightning Source LLC
Chambersburg PA
CBHW030608230426
43661CB00053B/1894